Local Economic and Employment Development

From Immigration to Integration

LOCAL SOLUTIONS TO A GLOBAL CHALLENGE

ORGANISATION FOR ECONOMIC CO-OPERATION AND DEVELOPMENT

ORGANISATION FOR ECONOMIC CO-OPERATION AND DEVELOPMENT

The OECD is a unique forum where the governments of 30 democracies work together to address the economic, social and environmental challenges of globalisation. The OECD is also at the forefront of efforts to understand and to help governments respond to new developments and concerns, such as corporate governance, the information economy and the challenges of an ageing population. The Organisation provides a setting where governments can compare policy experiences, seek answers to common problems, identify good practice and work to co-ordinate domestic and international policies.

The OECD member countries are: Australia, Austria, Belgium, Canada, the Czech Republic, Denmark, Finland, France, Germany, Greece, Hungary, Iceland, Ireland, Italy, Japan, Korea, Luxembourg, Mexico, the Netherlands, New Zealand, Norway, Poland, Portugal, the Slovak Republic, Spain, Sweden, Switzerland, Turkey, the United Kingdom and the United States. The Commission of the European Communities takes part in the work of the OECD.

OECD Publishing disseminates widely the results of the Organisation's statistics gathering and research on economic, social and environmental issues, as well as the conventions, guidelines and standards agreed by its members.

This work is published on the responsibility of the Secretary-General of the OECD. The opinions expressed and arguments employed herein do not necessarily reflect the official views of the Organisation or of the governments of its member countries.

Also available in French under the title:
De l'immigration à l'intégration
DES SOLUTIONS LOCALES À UN DÉFI MONDIAL

© OECD 2006

No reproduction, copy, transmission or translation of this publication may be made without written permission. Applications should be sent to OECD Publishing: rights@oecd.org or by fax (33-1) 45 24 99 30. Permission to photocopy a portion of this work should be addressed to the Centre français d'exploitation du droit de copie (CFC), 20, rue des Grands-Augustins, 75006 Paris, France, fax (33-1) 46 34 67 19, contact@cfcopies.com or (for US only) to Copyright Clearance Center (CCC), 222 Rosewood Drive Danvers, MA 01923, USA, fax (978) 646 8600, info@copyright.com.

Foreword

The integration of immigrants is not only a national issue, but a local one. While a migrant's application to reside in a country may be dealt with at the national level, they will ultimately need to settle in a local community and find their place in a local labour market. Integration is also a governance issue: success is likely to occur where there is a satisfactory level of co-ordination between the actions carried out, where policy is adapted to local needs, and where business and civil society participate in shaping the measures concerned. To be sustainable and effective, integration initiatives must be embedded in broader local economic and employment development strategies, build on local competitive advantages, and receive contributions from various sectoral policies.

The integration of immigrants is one of those issues which government finds it a challenge to address. Supporting access to the labour market is typically a multifaceted issue, with both social and economic dimensions. In the case of newcomers it is no easier as it involves working with different cultures, traditions and customs, and preparing the local labour market to welcome a new source of supply. Unsurprisingly, more than one government department or agency is involved in the policy area. In fact, the stakeholders involved are many, drawn from the public service, the private sector and civil society.

It is for this reason that the LEED Directing Committee decided to contribute to the current policy debate on the integration of immigrants. LEED has developed a unique expertise on local governance and employment, specialising in the analysis of complex problems in situations of interdependence. In 1998, the Directing Committee launched a policy research agenda on local governance and employment to explore ways to take an integrated approach to social and economic problems. The decision followed the Venice high-level conference on decentralisation, which stressed the importance of improving local governance to enhance policy outcomes, as outlined by the seminal report on Local Management of Employment and Training (1998), and identified partnership and decentralisation as two principal avenues for achieving this (Decentralising Employment Policy: New Trends and Challenges, 1999). Subsequent work focused on exploring the capabilities and limits of these two instruments (Local Partnerships for Better Governance, 2001; Managing Decentralisation: A New Role for Labour Market Policy, 2003; New Forms of Governance for Economic Development, 2004). Local Governance and the Drivers of Growth released in 2005 strengthened the foundations of local governance by relating its key aspects (coordination, adaptation and participation) directly to the problem of economic growth.

There is now a breadth of policy lessons from this work that we can apply to a range of issues and contexts. A first case study of the local governance / employment nexus to be analysed was the issue of skills upgrading for the low qualified (Skills Upgrading: New Policy Perspectives, 2006). The integration of immigrants in the labour market is the second. Both explore in depth the cross-sectoral dimension of these two complex issues and propose concrete ways to improve outcomes, with proposals for action by national policy makers as well as local stakeholders.

I'm particularly glad that we are now in a position to contribute to the current debate on ways to integrate immigrants and their families in our economies and society. Immigrants are essential partners in our quest to enhance prosperity and living standards and there are mutual benefits to be gained from successfully tackling the challenge of their integration. There must be a shared acknowledgement, however, that integration is not always an easy task, and that effective solutions require more than just good policy – but also good governance.

This project would not have been possible without the contributions provided by the European Commission (DG Employment, Social Affairs and Equal Opportunity), Human Resources and Skills Development Canada, the London Development Agency, the National Employment Institute of Spain (INEM), the Federal Office for Migration of Switzerland, the Federal Reserve Bank of New York, the Autonomous Province of Trento, the Municipality of Milan, and the Region of Piemonte. I would like to thank all of them.

Sergio Arzeni
Director, Centre for Entrepreneurship, SMEs and Local Development
Head, OECD LEED Programme

Acknowledgements. This project was taken forward by Francesca Froy, Policy Analyst, under the guidance of Sylvain Giguère, Deputy Head of Local Economic and Employment Development, OECD. Ms. Froy and Mr. Giguère are the editors of this publication.

Also part of the team who implemented this project was Elena Arnal (now at Economic and Social Council of Spain). Jean-Pierre Garson and his colleagues in the Non-Member Economies and International Migration Division (NEIM) have provided invaluable advice throughout the project. Further Ditta Brickwell (Consultant), Allen Caldwell (University of California, Berkeley), August Gächter (Centre for Social Innovation, Vienna), Philip Muus (School of International Migration and Ethnic Relations at Malmö University, Sweden) have all contributed to the project thanks to the opinions they shared in study visits, seminars, meetings and written notes. Helpful assistance throughout the project was provided by Debbie Binks, Lucy Clarke, Sheelagh Delf, Damian Garnys and Kay Olbison.

The contributors to this publication are:

- Bob Birrell, Centre for Population and Urban Research, Monash University, Australia
- Jonathan Chaloff, Centre for International Policy Studies (CeSPI), Rome.
- Mary P. Corcoran, Department of Sociology, National University of Ireland, Maynooth.
- Steve Fenton, Centre for the Study of Ethnicity and Citizenship, and Institute for Public Affairs, University of Bristol.
- Francesca Froy, LEED Programme, OECD.
- Sylvain Giguère, LEED Programme, OECD.
- Anne Green, Institute for Employment Research, University of Warwick, United Kingdom.
- Elizabeth McIsaac, Maytree Foundation, Canada.

Table of contents

Executive Summary.. 11

Introduction. **Integrating Immigrants: Finding the Right Policy Mix to Tackle a Governance Problem**
    by Sylvain Giguère 21
    One of the most critical issues to be tackled by our societies today . 22
    A double governance problem 23
    Local responses... 26
    Combining the forces, developing tools 26
    Increasing the flexibility of mainstream policies 27
    Notes 29
    Bibliography 30

Chapter 1. **From Immigration to Integration: Comparing Local Practices**
    by Francesca Froy 31
    Introduction 32
    Key stakeholders working at the local level.................... 39
    The instruments used 54
    Governance issues 65
    Conclusions and policy recommendations 86
    Notes 96
    Bibliography 98

Chapter 2. **Integrating Immigrants in Canada: Addressing Skills Diversity**
    by Bob Birrell and Elisabeth McIssac 101
    The Canadian context 102
    Selected local initiatives 112
    Case study 1: Montréal, Québec............................. 112
    Case study 2: Toronto, Ontario.............................. 120
    Case study 3: Winnipeg, Manitoba 127
    Analysis 133
    Conclusions and issues for consideration 138
    Notes 142
    Bibliography 142

TABLE OF CONTENTS

Chapter 3. **Innovating in the Supply of Services to Meet the Needs of Immigrants in Italy**
by Jonathan Chaloff 145

Introduction 146
General migration trends: economic conditions and legislation 147
Local initiatives: responding to integration problems 157
Conclusions and issues for consideration 183

Notes 185

Bibliography 186

Chapter 4. **Routes into Employment for Refugees: A Review of Local Approaches in London**
by Anne E. Green 189

Introduction 190
Migrants and refugees in the UK and London labour markets 201
Local initiatives: responding to integration problems of refugees ... 209
Conclusions and issues for consideration 226

Notes 232

Bibliography 236

Chapter 5. **Local Responses to a New Issue: Integrating Immigrants in Spain**
by Mary P. Corcoran 239

The Spanish labour market and migration context 240
Governance context 247
Local initiatives: responding to integration challenges 255
Conclusions and issues for consideration 275

Notes 281

Bibliography 281

Chapter 6. **Focusing on the Young: Integration in Switzerland**
by Steve Fenton 285

The policy context 286
Local initiatives to support the integration of young people into the labour market 296
Lessons from local initiatives 309
Conclusions and issues for consideration 314

Notes 318

Bibliography 319

About the Authors 321

Boxes

1.1.	Relevant actions by local authorities	42
2.1.	Bridge Training Programmes in Québec	117
2.2.	Assistance programme for the integration of immigrants and visible minorities in employment (PRIIME)	119
2.3.	Bridging Programs funded by the Ontario Ministry of Citizenship and Immigration	121
2.4.	Employment Resource Centres (ERCs)	123
3.1.	Italian Migration Law 40/1988 as modified by law 189/2002	154
3.2.	A non-profit reception centre and dormitory in Turin: Sermig	159
3.3.	The province of Trento Information Centre for Immigration: CINFORMI	161
3.4.	Training foreign workers in their country of origin: A Trento initiative	166
3.5.	Training apprenticeships for asylum seekers and refugees	171
3.6.	The Pact for Employment in the City of Milan	173
3.7.	ACLI and its attempt to match supply and demand in domestic work in Milan	175
3.8.	Trento research action for immigrant entrepreneurs	177
3.9.	Alma Mater: intercultural centre promoting quality employment for women in Turin	179
3.10.	Casa Amica: A non-profit association for housing access	181
4.1.	Renewal	210
4.2.	RAAD Large Scale Employment and Training Project	212
4.3.	Global Grants: Eligibility criteria, outputs and exemplar projects	222
4.4.	LORECA strategic goals and activities	225
5.1.	The Forum for Social Integration of Immigrants	254
5.2.	Experimental programme to facilitate the social and labour inclusion of non EU immigrants	257
5.3.	The Elionor project	258
5.4.	Strategies to promote common citizenship and interculturalism, Mataro and Santa Coloma de Gramenet	260
5.5.	Socio-economic conditions in Santa Coloma de Gramenet and Mataro	261
5.6.	The CASI programme in Madrid	263
5.7.	The Unió de Pagesos de Catalyuna	266
5.8.	Training by Grameimpuls S.A to support labour market access by immigrants	268
6.1.	Federal Commission for Foreigners	287
6.2.	The Forum for the Integration of Migrants (FIMM Suisse)	314

Tables

1.1. Labour market participation and unemployment of foreign- and native-born populations in participating countries, 2004 35
1.2. Barriers to the labour market. 37
1.3. Types of adaptation of local initiatives to the specific needs and barriers experienced by immigrants 55
1.4. Differentiating high resource and low resource activities. 77
1.5. Targeting by length of time in the country 82
2.1. Skilled immigrant worker assessment systems: Canada and Québec government points tests compared. 104
2.2. Canada, number of permanent residents by category 106
3.1. Foreign residents in Italy holding a residence permit, 1985-2003. .. 149
3.2. Regional unemployment and migrant labour 150
3.3. New hires and expected demand of immigrants, including training needs, 2003-2004. 152
4.1. Economic position by country of birth, Greater London, 2002/03. .. 205
5.1. Employment and unemployment rates 2000-2004. 241
5.2. Immigrants with valid residency cards or permits by continent ... 242
5.3. Immigrants with valid residency cards or permits by continent, gender and age group, 31-03-2005. 243
5.4. Number of immigrants with residence authorization in autonomous communities and provinces, 31-03-2005. 244
5.5. Number of participants achieving and maintaining employment. . 268

Figures

4.1. Employment rates (working age) of Greater London residents by country of birth, 2002/03 206
4.2. Employment rates for London's larger migrant populations, 2001 . 206

Executive Summary

The integration of immigrants at the local level is a topic of significant interest for OECD countries. The growing importance of the knowledge economy means that the battle for talent is becoming as important as the battle for inward investment, and skilled migrants can offer a significant comparative advantage to local labour markets, as long as their potential is harnessed. Unskilled migrants are also in demand, particularly where rising living costs make lower paid jobs unattractive to the native population, and where demographic change and population movement combine to reduce the self-sufficiency of local labour markets. For the potential advantages of migration to be maximised however, it is crucial that immigration is accompanied by *integration*, that is, effective mechanisms for ensuring immigrants are effectively incorporated into local labour markets. Paradoxically, at the same time that migration is increasing in global importance, there is worrying evidence that integration results do not seem to be as favourable in a number of countries as they were in the past.

The integration of immigrants is a policy area where a local approach is particularly important. While immigration policy is often determined, designed and funded at national level, its impact on migrants and society are strongly felt at the local level where other policies, including labour market policy, interact. There is strong variation between local areas in terms of the number and types of migrants received. While certain agricultural areas attract large numbers of temporary migrants, migrants are more likely overall to settle in urban areas, and in certain "gateway" cities. Further, within these cities, immigrants often become concentrated in particular neighbourhoods, either through following existing family or community ties, or through minimising living costs. Local policy makers are able to take into account such variation, along with variation in labour market demand.

This publication highlights common principles and key factors which are important in supporting integration at the local level, particularly in relation to the development of effective governance approaches. A comparison of local initiatives implemented in five OECD countries: Canada, UK (London), Spain, Italy, Switzerland highlights a number of key questions facing all local policy makers working in this field. Which stakeholders should be involved and how can their contribution be maximised? How should resources best be used?

Should migrants be targeted specifically, or should policy makers develop a strategy aimed at the whole community? How can the local level support innovation, whilst also achieving a mainstreamed sustainable approach? What is the role of local partnerships in tackling this issue, and on what should partnerships focus? The publication includes case studies from each reviewed country, in addition to analysis of the principle findings and a set of policy recommendations aimed at both local and national level policy makers.

Who is involved locally?

There are a wide variety of different stakeholders involved in this policy area, reflecting the diversity of barriers to labour market integration which immigrants may face. Depending on the local area, activities to support integration can be taken forward by local and regional authorities, non-governmental organisations (NGOs), trades unions, not-for profit enterprises, and employers. Each of these organisations complement the support to immigrants which is delivered by the public employment service (PES), which in fact rarely targets immigrants specifically in its programmes. Amongst the participating countries, Canada had the most extensive and diverse set of PES programmes targeted towards immigrants, including newcomer assessment and referral projects, specialised job search and work experience programmes, mentoring schemes, and skills upgrading projects.

Despite the fact that local authorities in most cases have no specific legal competency to help people into employment, they play an important role in the local integration of immigrants in the majority of the countries covered by this study. Local policies in the field of housing, schools, social assistance and spatial planning can all have a significant impact on the ability of immigrants to access employment, and the overarching responsibility of local authorities for the social and economic well being of their local area makes them a natural lead partner in local partnerships to support integration.

Both local authorities and the PES frequently work with non-governmental organisations (NGOs) in the delivery of services to immigrants at the local level, sometimes for legal reasons (because they are able to provide support to migrants who do not have employment or resident permits) but also because NGOs provide the supportive environment and individualised "one stop shop" approaches that some migrants with multiple obstacles to employment need. Colleges and vocational schools are also particularly well placed to take forward an integration approach at the local level, in that they act as intermediaries between local people and local employers. The community college system in the United States is seen by many as acting as an "integrative social institution", for example, which actively links post-secondary education to local labour market needs, and 25% of students within this system are immigrants. Vocational schools are also central to the integration of young people in Switzerland, reflecting the central role of the Swiss apprenticeship system in the labour market.

Employers are perhaps the most important of all the stakeholders to be involved at the local level. In Canada and the United States, employers play a strong role in integration approaches in some local areas, participating in partnerships, and working together to provide employer based training opportunities for migrants. Employers are leading partners in the Toronto based Region Immigration Employment Council (TRIEC), for example, which has the mandate to improve access to the labour market for skilled immigrants in the context of demographic change and predicted skills shortages. Employers associations and chambers of commerce can also play a particularly useful role. The ability of employers associations to progressively tackle both integration and quality of work issues is illustrated in the province of Lleida, in Spain, where the local farmers association has developed an innovative model for promoting good quality employment for temporary agricultural migrants, providing accommodation, training and social support in addition to building development links with localities in countries of origin. It is important that employers associations take up this challenge; whereas unions have a natural role in helping to improve employment conditions, many of the more precarious employment sectors in which immigrants become concentrated have low unionisation, and the unions are sometimes persuaded against getting involved if it means disadvantaging their existing members. In Italy, local chambers of commerce also participate in a wide variety of initiatives, from training to accommodation and support for entrepreneurship. For example, they have been at the forefront of developing bilateral relationships with regions in countries of origin to train immigrants in skills which are in regional demand before they arrive in the country.

Not-for-profit private sector organisations such as social enterprises and community foundations can also be particularly effective in this field, not least because of the flexibility they gain from being outside of the public sector. A social enterprise in Neuchâtel in Switzerland, for example, has developed short term customised training courses for migrants which are geared to the needs of local employers. Their independence from the formal training system allows them to take a "demand led" approach, delivering modular courses all year round.

Finally, it is increasingly being recognised that immigrant associations have an important role to play in integration at the local level, in that they encourage the development of services that are culturally sensitive, and that take the demands of immigrants themselves into account. Immigrant associations already run many of the services for refugees which exist in London, for example, and are being encouraged to play more of a role in integration issues in Spain.

What are the main policy instruments used?

Many of the tools and instruments used to support the integration of migrants in the local areas studied are similar to those used within mainstream active labour market policies, including job search support, education and training, mentoring and the provision of "work experience" placements with employers. However these tools are often adapted to the specific needs and lifestyles of migrants, with specialised support being provided including help with wider social acculturation, participation and networking.

When making employment decisions about migrants, employers do not have recourse to the usual sources of information (on educational background, previous local work performance) which guide them in choosing the right employee. Local activities to ensure that employers can quickly see the potential offered by migrants are therefore crucial, including, for example, programmes that provide work experience placements, actions to support the transferability of qualifications and projects which recognise prior competencies. Language is also viewed by many local stakeholders as particularly important given the increasing relevance of communication skills within the service based and knowledge based economy. There is some concern in fact that the language courses currently on offer locally do not reach the high level of competence now required by employers, and local stakeholders in the Canadian provinces and in London are piloting higher level language and occupational specific language courses, at least on a small scale.

In Southern European countries such as Italy and Spain, much of the work carried out to support the integration of immigrants is focused on wider social integration rather than specifically on labour market integration. Building solidarity and understanding between local residents is seen as an essential element in ensuring the wider participation of migrants in society and increasing their ability to access work. In countries where much employment is advertised informally this may be an effective strategy. In Italy, the availability of affordable housing is also seen as an important determinant of labour market integration, and a number of local schemes have been developed to provide supported housing for immigrants, including a project in Bergamo which is run by a consortium of sixteen public and private bodies, including the regional and local authorities, trades unions and associations.

Finally, a number of localities focus not on supporting access to employment but on stimulating immigrant entrepreneurship. In Italy, recent national growth in the number of entrepreneurs has been identified as being entirely due to an increase in immigrant entrepreneurs, and therefore chambers of commerce have been keen to support the expansion of this area, through for example producing specialised guidance and mentoring support.

Governance issues

There a number of specific governance issues which affect the delivery of local initiatives to support the labour market integration of immigrants.

The management of change

The integration of immigrants at the local level is principally a question of the *management of change*. Effective labour market integration depends on helping migrants to manage the rapid changes which are happening in their own lives, while at the same ensuring that the local community itself evolves and responds to changes in its population and in its urban fabric. While local stakeholders need to be thinking about managing the consequences of longer term change, migrants need clear road maps to guide them between the various services which will support their transition into a new life. This means that there is a need for well coordinated and accessible local services which will meet their various needs, either through the mainstreaming of migrant-friendly approaches across all local services, or else the provision of one-stop shop approaches specifically aimed at migrants. Unfortunately the sheer number of different actors who become involved at the local level, and the fact that services have often developed on a "bottom up" basis, means that such clear route maps frequently do not exist, and provision is relatively fragmented with low levels of communication and coordination.

Such fragmentation has a number of implications. A lack of communication between the different institutions dealing with integration can reduce the ability of localities to develop a coherent strategic response. Service providers can become relatively isolated; reducing their ability to guide migrants on to other relevant support and new opportunities. Service providers can fall outside of "communities of learning" and the sharing of good practice which is essential to the development of more effective services. In addition, there is frequently a lack of communication between organisations involved in labour market supply and demand. Given the speed of local labour market change it is crucial that organisations are aware of the latest labour market demands so that they can accurately guide migrants towards realistic employment routes. While this may seem self-evident, it is apparent that supply side organisations (training institutions, NGOs) often operate without up to date information about labour market needs, providing relatively generic labour market advice. This can lead to an un-necessary focus on the perceived "deficits" of the migrant (their personal confidence and generic job search skills for example) rather than on ensuring that migrants understand and respond to local demand.

Avoiding fragmentation and supporting mainstreaming

In the face of the complexity and relative fragmentation of delivery of support to migrants in many local areas, some experts have begun to question whether mainstreaming is more effective. Encouraging mainstream local institutions to take into consideration the needs of newcomers in their wider programmes also has the benefit of being more sustainable in the longer term. In London, for example, the education and training system is relatively flexible, so rather than local initiatives developing new training courses they often provide guidance to migrants on accessing wider provision. In Italy, a major reform of the adult education system has resulted in the development of "permanent local centres for adult education" which have taken the place of third sector language courses, improving consistency in certification and reducing local level competition and duplication.

Whereas mainstreaming services can improve coordination, however, it can also reduce flexibility and innovation. Immigrant integration is a particularly diverse area of policy, and it is an area where policy makers are still learning about the most appropriate mechanisms. Because of this the local level can be particularly effective when it encourages diverse approaches and innovation. One particularly effective method of supporting innovation is the development of a seed-funding system or local "innovation grant". In Winnipeg, the flexible budget available under the Manitoba Immigrant Integration Programme has been used to fund a variety of different pilot programmes. The *Diputació de Barcelona* (provincial government of Barcelona) in Spain has also been particularly successful at accessing national and European funding to encourage innovation and to ensure that the results are circulated to other local authorities, through for example the production of methodological guides.

Mainstreaming also threatens to remove the sheltered individualised "one-stop-shop" support which can be provided by smaller organisations such as NGOs. The CASI model in Madrid has overcome this by developing a strong mainstreamed approach which also benefits from both the innovative nature of NGOs and their ability to provide individualised support. The entire region of Madrid is covered by CASI initiatives and all the local NGOs work to similar goals and methodologies, leading to a consistency in the provision. There is a degree of inbuilt flexibility in the programme, however, with block grants being allocated to each CASI which allow relative freedom in expenditure.

Local "place based" or territorial partnerships have been developed in many local areas as a mechanism for reducing the isolation of individual stakeholders, supporting innovation and encouraging mainstream organisations to adopt integration-based approaches. In London, a number of the NGOs supporting refugees are coordinated by wider partnerships bringing together a mix of social and economic partners. The Renewal partnership in West London has a £16 million budget (approx. 23 million euro) for a seven year programme, involving a wide variety of partners with a major local employer, the Ealing National Health Service Primary Care Trust as the accountable body. Renewal provides a degree of continuity within a field dominated by short-term funding programmes, and a degree of capacity building support. In Italy and Spain, the Territorial Employment Pacts (TEPs) have also provided a useful mechanism for helping local stakeholders to work together across administrative boundaries and across traditional divisions of labour.

Resources

The availability of resources is a significant issue affecting the effectiveness for local initiatives to support integration. Given that NGOs often provide the "front-line" of services to immigrants it is often within these organisations that financing issues become most apparent. The sustainability of funding for NGOs was a concern across all the participating countries, with local actors reporting not only continual efforts to access and renew funding, but also low wages and long hours, which threatened to create "burn-out" in staff.

Given the limited resources available, a key question facing local actors is where should resources best be placed? Evidence shows that a relatively focused and intensive approach is needed in order to create longer term labour market integration – cheaper interventions which are not specifically targeted at a migrant's skills level and aspirations, or linked to local labour demand, have lower long-term success. However, it is short term interventions that are the most prevalent at the local level. The performance management systems of funding programmes (with their emphasis on quick outputs) in particular encourage local initiatives to support rapid access to employment for migrants, which may ultimately produce short term labour market participation as opposed to longer term integration. Where more intensive interventions do exist they tend to be relatively small scale, leading to a relatively negligible impact on the overall integration of migrants into the labour market.

Targeting

There are, however, examples of targeted approaches at the local level which seek to maximise their impact through focusing on the specific characteristics of certain groups within the migrant population. For example, a number of initiatives target female migrants because of their poorer labour market integration rates. Other initiatives target immigrants differently according to their skills levels. Many local initiatives in Canada, for example, focus on graduates or professionals, reflecting the favourable selection of such migrants in the Canadian immigration system. Focusing on the highly skilled has the advantage of presenting a particularly positive face to employers, with migrants being seen as a "resource to be exploited" rather than a problem to be solved. However there is also the danger that imposing too many selection criteria before admission can lead to "creaming" or "screening" effects, with projects supporting those most easy to help, neglecting those that perhaps have more need of support.

Particular approaches have also been developed to reflect the amount of time that a migrant has spent in the country. A pre-apprenticeship training course in Neuchâtel Switzerland, for example, has taken the name "Jet" reflecting the fact that the new arrivals it works with are often dynamic and highly motivated to succeed, helping to create a positive profile for participants with local employers. When supporting second or third generation migrants, local initiatives often focus on providing support to children, to prevent their exclusion later in life. For example, the local development company in Santa Coloma de Gramenet in Spain has attempted to tackle immigrant underperformance in the education system through tackling issues of isolation and promoting inter-culturalism in schools.

Some initiatives focus on one particular ethnic group or community, through for example being managed by an immigrant association, thereby benefiting from greater cultural sensitivity. There are some concerns, however, that such policies can ultimately create competition between different communities rather than integration. Other localities resist the idea of targeting immigrants at all as a separate group, with a key feature of Zurich's cantonal policy on integration, for example, being to treat the problems experienced by migrants as "problems of exclusion" rather than necessarily "problems particularly experienced by migrants". Indeed some experts warn against "racialising" poverty as a social phenomenon, arguing that when poverty is associated with people from particular backgrounds and cultures, people forget that they are actually looking at a more embedded and structural issue.

Timing

Timing is particularly important in the governance of initiatives to support the integration of immigrants. Employers, in particular, stress that immigrants should not be out of the labour market for too a long period after arrival, so that they remain in touch with their relevant employment sector and their skills do not atrophy. While immigrants may need extra support to adapt to the local labour market on arrival, therefore, initiatives which allow migrants to find jobs and then "back-fill" through in-work training and up-skilling are particularly valuable, as they help avoid time-intensive periods in education and training. Where external training is necessary, modular training courses which allow migrants to build on their skills, at any point in the year, are also particularly important.

Policy recommendations

Building on local experience in participating countries, a number of policy recommendations can be made, at both the national and local levels.

At the national level

- Ensure that the national immigration system meets local labour market needs.
- Develop a consistent overarching policy framework which includes robust anti-discrimination legislation.
- Develop open and flexible mainstream programmes.
- Support the recognition of prior competences and qualifications.
- Ensure a strong culture of evaluation.

At the local level

- Ensure strong coordination and signposting between institutions at the local level.
- Bring employers on board in local partnerships.
- Support innovation and learning, through, for example local "seed" grants and flexible local budgets.
- Support adaptation to the needs of migrants within mainstream institutions, rather than the unnecessary proliferation of new actors.
- Target but with sensitivity.
- Consider the timing of interventions and ensure migrants are not out of the labour market for too long a period after arrival.

ISBN 92-64-02895-1
From Immigration to Integration
Local Solutions to a Global Challenge
© OECD 2006

Introduction

Integrating Immigrants: Finding the Right Policy Mix to Tackle a Governance Problem

by
Sylvain Giguère

The issue of integrating migrants, their families and their descendants can be assimilated to two governance issues. There is a clear mismatch between immigration and integration policies in many countries, with policies to manage immigration rarely being accompanied by strong policies to support integration. Secondly, integrating immigrants is a multifaceted issue which cuts across policy areas, creating a collective action problem and a lack of effective public sector action. While local stakeholders such as NGOs can attempt to fill the gaps in public services, this often leads to increased fragmentation at the local level. In order to better tackle the barriers facing immigrants, it may ultimately be more important to increase flexibility in the management of mainstream policies relating to the issue of labour market integration (namely training and education, labour market policy and economic development) rather than create new initiatives and partnerships locally.

INTRODUCTION

One of the most critical issues to be tackled by our societies today

Flows of migrant workers are on a steady increase. Close to three million long-term migrants enter OECD countries every year, not counting temporary and illegal migrants, who are also on the rise (OECD, 2006a). Like capital, labour is freer to move than before, as borders are abolished and restrictions reduced in many parts of the world. And like capital, which seeks profit opportunities across the globe, workers are looking for places where they can increase their standard of living. The power of attraction exerted by advanced economies is strong, enhanced by widespread access to communications technologies and media which project prospects of ease and prosperity. Stricter measures taken in some countries to prevent illegal immigration seem not to discourage many people from taking their chance of a better life.

Immigration offers a number of clear benefits to advanced economies. Given the ageing of the population resulting from low birth rates, the natural growth of the population in many OECD countries is too low to ensure the maintenance of current standards of living in the foreseeable future. In many countries, a number of sectors of the economy are already lacking the labour and the skills they need in order to meet demand. Labour is needed to ensure the direct delivery of services to the population, and these pressures are bound to increase in line with the changing demand for workers in health services and care for the elderly which will accompany demographic change. Immigration fosters the renewal of societies and of the economy, boosts innovation and brings news ideas. As a result, countries, regions and companies are competing for workers on a world scale.

However, while there are many positive drivers towards immigration, *integration* is today a source of concern. The various waves of immigrants attracted by the booming advanced economies after the Second World War and up until the 1980s were integrated relatively smoothly into the labour market in receiving societies, at least on a temporary basis. However, in many countries, the labour market situation of immigrants started to deteriorate in the 1990s, with their rates of unemployment superseding that of the native population. Immigrants are today relatively more exposed to long-term unemployment and social exclusion. Even in countries where migrants have an employment rate similar to that of the native population, immigrants are more likely to suffer from poorer working conditions and temporary employment. A lack of integration not only affects the low skilled but also increasingly the highly skilled (OECD 2006a), partly reflecting difficulties associated with the recognition of qualifications overseas.

What is more, integration problems that at first glance seemed to apply only to new waves of immigrants appear to also be experienced by second or third generations. Indeed in certain countries, it can be argued that second and third generations are less integrated in receiving societies than their parents who migrated between the 1950s and the 1970s. A recent OECD study found that many developed countries are failing to help children of immigrant families integrate into society through education, with immigrant children lagging more than two years behind their native counterparts in school performance (OECD, 2006b). This has come as a surprise to the many who believed that the offspring of immigrant families born in the host country would not face significant obstacles of integration, having received education in the host country and speaking the language of the majority of the population.

As the population facing problems integrating into the labour market widens, the problem of integration itself becomes more complex. Immigrants suffering from poverty as a result of labour market exclusion can become concentrated in areas of low housing cost, which are often isolated from employment opportunities. In more extreme cases, immigrants become "ghettoised" in areas of high deprivation, with associated high rates of worklessness, high school drop out rates and problems of disaffection. Issues associated with social and economic exclusion in this case form a set of additional barriers for immigrants seeking to access the labour market.

The problem of integration, as complex as it may have become, must be addressed now. This is an issue that concerns the social cohesion of our societies as well as the functioning of the economy. Its urgency is derived both from the recorded decline in integration outcomes, and the increasing importance being given to immigration in the context of gloomy forecasts of population decline. The population in developed countries as a whole is expected to remain unchanged until 2050, with several countries incurring a decline, while the population in many less developed countries is expected to double or triple (United Nations, 2004).

A double governance problem

The problem of the integration of migrants, their families and their descendants can be assimilated to two governance issues. The first is the mismatch between immigration and integration policies. The second is the multifaceted nature of integration.

A policy gap

There is a clear mismatch between immigration and integration policies in many countries, with policies to manage immigration rarely being accompanied by strong policies to support integration. While most countries provide specialised support to immigrants on arrival, particularly language training, after this initial period labour market integration is generally felt to be the responsibility of mainstream labour market policies.

The goal of labour market policy is to ensure the efficiency of labour markets and to increase the productivity of workers. Labour market policy usually has two components: integration into the labour market and the development of the employability of the labour force. Programmes to fulfil these purposes include placement, counselling, jobs subsidies to provide work experience, vocational training and assistance to self-employment. Migrants can access these services as anybody else if they fulfil the respective eligibility criteria.

Unfortunately mainstream labour market programmes do not always significantly help migrants to access the labour market. This is due to specific obstacles that migrants face: lack of local referees and work experience, lack of knowledge about the value of qualifications, lack of familiarity with local social networks, lack of language skills. In addition, certain migrants will have failed to see the qualifications obtained in their native country recognised, and find it difficult to make the right decisions to adapt their skills to local needs. Employment services, not well equipped to assess the value of foreign qualifications and to profile the capacities of the migrant, find it difficult to provide the right advice.

The transition from a native to a foreign labour market can be a lengthy one. During this process of trial and error, motivation can deteriorate while skills depreciate. Financial pressures may encourage migrants to take the most immediately available and accessible jobs to ensure a living, even if these jobs are not at a level commensurate with their skills and experience. Clearly skills can be lost during this process. When this happens, a loss is incurred for society as a whole: it is a loss for the receiving country as well as to the individual and the sending country. Moreover, by harming the migrant's standards of living, it may have longer term consequences for the prospects of integration for her/his family and descendants.

A coordination problem

The second governance problem relates to issues of coordination. As identified above, immigrants and their offspring often face multiple barriers to the labour market. Solutions require actions to be taken in areas as diverse as education, vocational training, economic development, social assistance, health care and security. An integrated approach is needed, involving cross-sector policy coordination and strategic planning. In particular, when new immigrants and their offspring become concentrated in areas of urban deprivation they may face social and economic problems which have become embedded over a long period of time. Only an intensive and long term coordinated action will be able to address these issues successfully.

Yet, such coordination is not an easy task for public policy. The search for competitive advantages that is a key driver of progress in our globalised economies has had a significant impact on the way public policy is designed and implemented. Like the private sector, public services are run today following strict efficiency principles. Public services are managed by objectives, which means that performance is evaluated on their attainment of predetermined targets. To achieve those targets, government agencies often contract out to private service providers and non-profit organisations. In addition, a number of policy responsibilities are devolved to regional or local authorities, which often carry out their own complementary programmes (in the area of social or employment policy for example). As a result, public policy overall is delivered through a complex set of organisations operating at various levels and linked through various bilateral mechanisms. Coordination or strategic orientation is often what is said to be lacking in this system.

The fact that responsibility for immigrant integration falls across several government departments, in addition to being reliant on bringing together services which are have been contracted out and delegated to others, raises a collective action problem. As the public departments working in the field become aware that policies fail because a complex situation demands a coordinated response, all have the possibility to initiate an action, propose a diagnosis, establish collaborative relationships, build a network and lead a process of strategic planning aimed at solving the local problem identified. However, there are costs associated with such an exercise. Clearly, it costs time to organise an effective partnership to tackle a complex issue such as the integration of immigrants. The exercise would involve establishing relationships with organisations of different administrative culture (municipalities, branches of the national public service, business organisations, civil society organisations), meaning that significant attention may need to be devoted to communication and governance issues. The agencies working in different policy areas (training, social assistance, economic development) pursue different agendas each with their own priorities. Some agencies may in addition be reluctant to be involved in tackling a politically-sensitive issue through an activity that may fail to bring positive results. At the same time, as the gains from collective action are likely to benefit all who are involved, there are limited incentives for any one department to take an active role and lead the process. Thus there are obvious disincentives to launch an action, collective or not. The outcome is often a lack of public sector activity, which is obviously suboptimal for society as a whole.

Local responses

What is common to these two governance problems undermining the integration of immigrants and their families in receiving societies is that responses have been provided at the local level. Local initiatives have been taken to fill the gap between migration and integration, complementing labour market policy in various ways; others have targeted the multifaceted barriers to the labour market encountered by immigrants and their descendants by encouraging co-ordinated action on the basis of a unified strategy. What can be learned from these initiatives? Are there mechanisms which have been piloted by local stakeholders that could also be used by government? What are the lessons learnt on how to tackle the challenges posed by the failure to integrate immigrants and their offspring?

It is in order to answer such questions, that the OECD has carried out this study on the local integration of immigrants in the labour market. The local initiatives carried out, the mechanisms, instruments and governance mechanisms they use, and their results contain information which can only benefit the current policy debate on this critical issue, as a complement to national level statistical and policy analysis.[1]

The project selected a number of local initiatives in five volunteering countries (Canada, Italy, Spain, Switzerland and the United Kingdom[2]) and carried out field examinations based on a methodological framework designed to extract lessons from local practices. The initiatives selected are as diversified as possible in order to reflect the breadth of issues faced on the ground. Actions range from facilitating the transition from school to work for young immigrants and providing vocational training, to delivering services to refugees, fighting discrimination and building social networks.

Combining the forces, developing tools

The study shows that the gap between migration and integration *can* be filled. However, for this to happen, a combination of actions at both central and local level is required. The examination of local practices reveals that there are certain mechanisms that seem to be essential in any successful policy initiatives to integrate immigrants and their families. One of them is the gathering and analysis of information on the local labour market, on the structure of the labour demand and of skills shortages in relation to the migrant population. Any effective action needs to be based on this information analysed locally. Another mechanism is intermediation between migrant groups and employers, employment services and vocational training organisations to link the demand with the supply of labour. Both these actions are determinant in explaining if a policy initiative is successful or not in delivering long term employment outcomes for immigrants at a level commensurate with their skills.

Yet, such actions have been used in too few places, and the means put at their disposal insufficient. The challenge for government is to find ways to support these relatively resource intensive mechanisms and to incorporate them into broader policy initiatives. This can be achieved not only by providing financial support to local labour market intelligence and intermediation but also by providing analytical tools that the market fails to provide and that can help local stakeholders conduct effective actions. "Job profiles" are one such tool that can help stakeholders – employers, employment services, consultants, community colleges and the immigrant themselves – make the right decisions. These profiles help to make the labour market more transparent by providing concrete information on the various skills required for particular jobs, and approximating the level of competence required for each of them. Such information is helpful in the preparation of skills assessment tests that can be used by employers, assisted by a local intermediary, to identify whether migrant workers are suited to a job. This is particularly useful where migrants do not have local references and their previous qualifications are not recognised. Where this information is made more broadly accessible, it can also help migrants to nurture the right expectations when deciding to emigrate and make appropriate qualifications decisions.

Increasing the flexibility of mainstream policies

While progress is slowly being made in combining public sector actions at national and local levels and developing effective policy mechanisms, a wide variety of other actors have undertaken to play a role in making up for the lack of effective actions by the public services. A whole range of non profit organisations, notably, provide services to immigrants and ethnic groups. Most of these services can be grouped into two categories: i) personal and skills development; and ii) access and networks. The first category of services aims to complement the services provided by government. They comprise language courses, vocational training, and courses to foster acculturation. Theses activities are sometimes tailored to ethnic groups and supported by individual mentoring and assistance. They are strengthened by the non-profit organisations' efforts to reach the groups most remote from the labour market. The second category of services aims to provide better linkages between migrant communities and other stakeholders (government agencies, employment organisations, non-government organisations) and enhance access to the programmes available. They serve as advocacy organisations and lobby for new programmes or changes to be brought to public programmes to better suit the needs of the immigrants and their offspring. They support anti-discriminatory measures and wage campaigns to encourage employers to welcome immigrants. Other activities include the stimulation of networks for hard-to-reach groups and the building of capacity for self-organisation and representation.

While both categories of initiative may help to meet the needs of the target group and influence the implementation of mainstream programmes, the sheer number of local initiatives contributes to the further fragmentation of the local policy environment. Initiatives are launched in all policy areas: social inclusion, community development, entrepreneurship assistance, education and training. These services are often relatively small scale, linked to a limited target group and delivered in a single location. Organisations often have a low critical mass and duplicate what other organisation or public services do. They have few resources to invest in their own training to enhance their capacities. Their expertise in the local labour market and their links with the employment services are especially weak. Though initiatives are sometimes organised in the form of a relatively inclusive partnerships, they are rarely genuinely able to coordinate relevant policy areas.

This is by no means a failure specific to organisations dealing with migrant-related issues. Quite on the contrary this is a shortcoming of much action taken locally, especially where community-based organisations play a strong role. In a number of local areas, area-based partnerships have been set up to attempt to tackle the challenges posed by fragmentation of employment and economic development policy, but these do not always have considerable success if not accompanied by other policy measures. As the OECD Study on Local Partnerships made clear, the establishment of area-based partnerships is not a sufficient condition for policy co-ordination. Partnerships have on average a marginal impact on the capacity for services to join forces and take an integrated approach to local problems. Problems include poor accountability relationships that limit inter-organisational commitment and strict performance management requirements that encourage individual agencies and organisaitons to take a narrow approach to policy implementation as seen above. To be in a position to have an impact on local governance – and to influence policy co-ordination, adaptation to local needs and participation of business and civil society in the shaping of measures – partnerships need to be accompanied by mechanisms to foster the convergence of policy goals at the national level, increase flexibility in the policy management framework and strengthen the accountability of partnerships in three ways : between the members, between the representatives and their organisations and to the public (OECD, 2001, 2004).

In order to tackle the barriers that immigrants and their descendants face, it may therefore be more critical to increase flexibility in the management of policies developed at the national level relating to the issue of labour market integration (namely training and education, labour market policy and economic development) rather than generating new policy initiatives and establishing new providers and new partnerships at the local level. Training and labour market policy must be tailored to the needs of the local population, including migrants. If information on the local labour market and on the skills held by migrant groups is properly gathered and analysed, this is a highly feasible task. Flexibility is required to link employment services with current business needs. It is important to articulate labour demand and to analyse the strengths and weaknesses of sectors, and to develop labour market and training actions accordingly, with the involvement of the business community as well as economic development agencies. Conversely the opportunities offered by immigration should feature directly in any strategic planning exercise on economic development issues. Mechanisms which foster skills upgrading and promote career progression opportunities for migrants already in employment (see for example OECD 2006c) are also crucial as they reduce the time migrants are forced to spend outside the labour market in re-training.

The integration of immigrants and their offspring is an issue in which all actors, at local and national levels, have an interest in tackling with success. It is a complex and challenging policy area, as integration involves a number of interrelated issues, however it is by no means impossible to achieve. The success of the exercise depends on the quality and effectiveness of the mechanisms implemented and their appropriateness to the local labour market. It requires political courage, and a willingness to address some complex administrative issues in addition to policy issues. Central government needs to trust local organisations, but at the same time give concrete guidance, build capacity and monitor policy outcomes. A good mix of local and national actions is what will make a difference.

Notes

1. The study was carried out under the supervision of the Directing Committee on Local Economic and Employment Development (LEED), in co-operation with the Employment, Labour and Social Affairs Committee (ELSAC) and its Working Party on Migration.
2. Each study involved fieldwork by OECD staff and international experts, where discussions with local, regional and national policy makers were accompanied by visits to local initiatives in case study regions. While four of the case studies analysed at least three localities, in the United Kingdom, greater focus was given to London. The initial findings of the study were debated at an international

conference organised by the OECD LEED Programme and the Federal Reserve Bank of New York on 15th December 2005, "From Immigration to Integration: Lessons Drawn from Local Responses", attended by leaders and directors of major United States workforce training programmes, community development organisations, unions, foundations, and community colleges, as well as academics, and state and local political leadership.

Bibliography

OECD (2001), *Local Partnerships for Better Governance*, OECD, Paris.

OECD (2004), *New Forms of Governance and Economic Development*, OECD, Paris.

OECD (2006a), *International Migration Outlook*, OECD, Paris.

OECD (2006b), *Where Immigrant Students Succeed – A Comparative Review of Performance and Engagement in PISA 2003*, OECD, Paris.

OECD (2006c), *Skills Upgrading: New Policy Perspectives*, OECD, Paris.

United Nations (2004), *World Population Report: The 2004 Revision*, UN, Washington.

Chapter 1

From Immigration to Integration: Comparing Local Practices

by
Francesca Froy

The integration of immigrants at the local level is principally a question of the management of change. Effective labour market integration depends on helping immigrants to manage the rapid changes which are happening in their own lives, whilst at the same ensuring that the local community itself evolves and responds to changes in its population and in its urban fabric. This has a number of implications for an effective governance response. In particular, immigrants need clear road maps to guide them between the various services which will support their transition into a new life. Local areas also need to be aware of changes in the immigrant population, and develop new techniques to maximise the opportunities brought by skilled migrants, whilst removing unnecessary barriers to the workplace. This chapter reviews the activities of local stakeholders in each of the five countries studied, highlighting innovation and good practice, while also identifying common problems, and ongoing gaps in provision.

Introduction

The integration of immigrants at the local level is a topic of significant interest for OECD countries. The growing importance of the knowledge economy means that the battle for talent is becoming as important as the battle for inward investment, and skilled migrants can offer a significant comparative advantage to local labour markets, as long as their potential is harnessed. Unskilled migrants are also in demand, as demographic change means that many localities are seeking new workers to meet labour shortages and ensure that basic services are delivered. For the potential advantages of migration to be maximised however, it is crucial that immigration is accompanied by *integration,* that is, effective mechanisms for ensuring immigrants are effectively incorporated into local labour markets.

Immigrants at all times and places have had to adapt to the host country and vice-versa. The nature of the integration process has differed from country to country and over time depending on the migration history of the country, the characteristics of arrivals, the countries overall policy towards migration, the programmes in place to assist immigrants and the host countries' general social and economic conditions. However, in light of the large numbers of immigrants who have entered OECD countries during the last decades, the question of integration seems more pressing now because: i) more countries now recognise the potential advantages that immigrants bring to their local economies and ii) integration results do not seem to be as favourable in a number of countries as they were in the past.

There is a growing body of research into the factors leading to labour market integration,[1] and among the factors under study, those pertaining to local governance are increasingly drawing the attention of policymakers. While immigration policy is often determined, designed and funded at national level, its impact on immigrants and society is strongly manifested at the local level where other policies interact. In this regard, the efficacy of the local implementation of national policies or of initiatives taken locally is a central issue for integration policy.

There are a number of reasons why the integration of immigrants into the labour market is a particularly "local" issue. Firstly, it is apparent that migration has a relatively uneven geography. Within the migrant population, different groups are likely to migrate to particular countries, following political, economic and language ties and the previous migrations of friends and relatives (immigrants to Spain are most likely to come from Latin America for example). Within countries, while certain agricultural areas attract large numbers of temporary migrants, immigrants are more likely to settle in urban areas and within those urban areas to certain "gateway" cities, particularly capital cities. This leads to local variations in both the size and the structure of the immigrant population. In the city of Toronto, for example, 49% of residents were foreign born in 2001, as compared with approximately 18% of the overall Canadian population (Canadian Census, 2001). In the Netherlands, similarly, 60% of the immigrant population live in the Western conurbation, with immigrants and their offspring constituting 47% of the population of Amsterdam in 2004 (Penninx *et al.*, 2004). Within cities, immigrants often become concentrated in certain communities, or "ethnic enclaves", either because they have chosen to move close to friends, relatives and known employment opportunities, or because they are excluded from living in other areas due to differentials in the cost of living. In the neighbourhood of North Etobicoke on the northwest side of Toronto, for example, 74.7% of residents over 15 years of age are first generation Canadians (Canadian Census 2001); partly because low accessibility means that house prices are relatively affordable in the neighbourhood. There is also local variation in the labour markets in which immigrants hope to integrate. Labour market contexts can vary to a greater extent between urban areas than they do between countries,[2] and local policy makers in capital cities, for example, often find it more useful to benchmark themselves with policy makers in other world cities, as opposed to those in smaller towns within their own country.

Local areas have a great deal to gain from the effective management of migration, and a great deal to lose if things go wrong. Sassen (1994) and Harris (2003) both emphasize that migrants are becoming essential to cities in a global economy where skills are increasingly specialised and trade relies on global interconnections. Companies are acquiring components of human capital from all over the world, with countries focusing on exporting certain kinds of education and training. This results in a decline in self sufficiency at the local level, with cities competing for foreign labour in addition to foreign based companies and their technologies. It is not just the highly skilled that are in demand. Sassen (*op. cit.*) describes how cities are also competing for unskilled and medium skilled migrants, as lower value labour and services are needed to optimise the value provided by the skilled.

Urban leaders are increasingly cognisant of the benefits that immigrants bring to their locality. The President of New York City Economic Development Cooperation recently claimed that immigrants constitute the "greatest comparative advantage" of his city. Forty-five per cent of the population of New York are immigrants (United States Census, 2000), and the city absorbs more immigrants every day than any other United States city other than Los

Angeles. The resulting diversity is reflected in the fact that the local emergency services answer the telephone in one hundred and seventy languages. The Federal Reserve Bank of New York has highlighted the key role that immigrants have played in contributing to the sustainability and productivity of the labour market of the city. Immigration has been particularly important in maintaining a constant population level during periods of relative decline, such as in the 1990s when approximately 1.3 million residents left the city. Without immigration it is estimated that New York would have lost 10% of its population.[3] The composition of the New York labour force has dramatically changed in the last 30-40 years due to the influx of immigrants, however overall employment has risen and fallen only slightly within a band of between 3.2-3.8 million. The kinds of jobs performed have also changed substantially and output has risen sharply so that NYC labour has enjoyed good gains in real income despite the lack of job growth (Bram, Haughwout, and Orr, 2002).

With the coming retirement of aging baby-boomers in many OECD countries, the potential role of migration in supporting the sustainability of local economies, and alleviating the rise in the dependency ratio, has also been the object of a certain number of studies. It is now generally recognised that increased migration inflows cannot be expected to offset fully the projected rise in old-age dependency rates in OECD member countries: the required flows would be too large. However, it is acknowledged that migration can nevertheless play a role in alleviating the adverse consequences of ageing populations, in conjunction with other policies. At the local level, the presence of a labour supply willing to provide personal and proximity services to an ageing population is also becoming increasingly important.

In the reverse case, it is clear that if immigrants are not effectively integrated into local communities this can lead to disaffection and social unrest. The unrest which took place on the outskirts of Paris and other French cities in the second half of 2005 was an effective reminder of what can happen if populations become isolated and are not effectively integrated into society. Such disturbances, as with the riots which occurred in Bradford, Burnley and Leeds in the United Kingdom in 2001, quickly become high profile media events, and as such produce an increased awareness amongst policy makers which sometimes leads to new interventions at the local level. While increased policy attention can be helpful, the fluctuation of policy response to integration issues does not encourage sustainable approaches in the longer term. Integration is a complex issue which requires a long-term strategy and a sustained investment of resources.

Obstacles faced by immigrants to the labour market

Despite growing labour demand created by economic growth and demographic change in some countries, and the relatively high success of some highly skilled immigrants,[4] many still experience obstacles to accessing good quality, sustainable employment. The recent OECD International Migration Outlook identified that in 2003-4 the participation rate of immigrants was on the whole lower than that of the native population (OECD, 2006a). In addition, in 2003, immigrants were more likely than nationals or natives to be unemployed in all OECD countries with the exception of Greece and Italy (OECD, 2005a).

Likewise, immigrants had a higher unemployment rate than nationals in all of the countries participating in the study (see Table 1.1). However Spain and Italy show relatively high employment rates for their foreign-born population, partly due to the relative importance of job-seekers in recent migration flows.

Table 1.1. **Labour market participation and unemployment of foreign- and native-born populations in participating countries, 2004**

	Participation rate (%)			Unemployment rate (%)		
	Natives	Foreign-born	Differential	Natives	Foreign-born	Differential
United Kingdom	75.7	68.4	7.3	4.3	7.3	−3
Spain	67.6	76.8	−9.2	10.8	13.8	−3
Italy	62.3	70	−7.7	7.9	9.3	−1.4
Canada	77.9*	73.5*	4.4	6.2*	8.7*	−2.5
Switzerland	81.7	78.8	2.9	3.1	8.3	−5.8

* Data only available for Canada for 2003.
Source: OECD (2006a).

OECD migration experts have recently stressed that, globally, there is increasing diversity in the economic performance of immigrants in the labour market. For example, within the overall figures above, it is noteworthy that there are different employment rates amongst immigrants from different countries and different ethnic groups. In London, for example, disaggregation of data on employment rates of working age residents by country of birth shows that while those born in high income countries outside the United Kingdom have an employment rate of 75% (exceeding the London average of 73.9%), the employment rate for those from developing countries is only 61.4%. Data from the United Kingdom 2001 Census allowing disaggregation by country also reveals that while employment rates for those from Australia and South Africa exceed 83%, for those from Somalia the employment rate is a mere 16.4%. Different legal categories of immigrant also experience different unemployment rates, with refugees being particularly vulnerable. The Department for Work and Pensions in the United Kingdom, for example, estimates that refugees have an unemployment rate of 36% – more than six times the national average (House of Commons Work and Pensions Committee, 2005). The OECD International Migration Outlook (2006a) also points out that the young, older workers and women encounter specific difficulties in the labour market.

There are a considerable number of factors which both directly and indirectly impact on the ability of an immigrant to find a job. The issues effecting immigrants who have difficulty accessing employment in many ways mirror the problems that are experienced by other unemployed groups – inappropriate skills and qualifications for the jobs on offer; a lack of skills in navigating the labour market; difficulties handling family responsibilities and other commitments, social and psychological barriers to work. However within each of these areas, immigrants are likely to face particular issues.

While unemployed people sometimes experience problems with matching their skills and competencies to the local labour market, immigrants have the added difficulty that their education and qualifications were often acquired abroad, and employers find it difficult to judge the value of these qualifications within the local labour market. While all unemployed people may have trouble obtaining a good reference, immigrants may have only previously worked abroad and it is therefore not possible for employers to refer to previous employers for any assessment of their performance. While prejudice and the ascribing of false or stereotypical characteristics can affect any job seeker, racism and the negative portrayal of immigrants in the media can increase the chances that immigrants will not access a job due to discrimination. Finally, as recent arrivals in a local area, immigrants are more susceptible to the indirect factors which can prevent people from accessing work, such as isolation from important social networks, geographical isolation in cheaper housing areas and other issues which derive from relative social exclusion.

Table 1.2 sets out in more detail the types of obstacles that unemployed people may experience to getting into work, before setting out the particular issues affecting immigrants.

The quality of employment

Unemployment is not the only issue affecting immigrants. The quality of employment accessed and the prospects for career progression are equally important. While the figures appear to suggest that immigrants are relatively well integrated into the labour market in Spain and Italy, for example, many immigrants are in fact employed in temporary jobs with low incomes and poor

Table 1.2. **Barriers to the labour market**

Areas	General issues experienced by people seeking work	Specific issues facing immigrants
Skills and competencies	Lack of generic skills (communication, self-management, professionalism)	• Language skills • Lack of socio-cultural knowledge and understanding.
	Lack of specific competencies required for job	• Competencies required may be different from those required in home country. • Lack of funding and/or subsidies to access education and training locally. • Lack of local referees and lack of local work experience to prove competencies.
	Lack of specific qualifications required for job	• Lack of knowledge about the value and relevance of qualifications and experience gained in other countries.
	Lack of skills in navigating the labour market	• Lack of knowledge of local labour markets
Accessibility issues	Geographical isolation (distance from employers, distance from transport networks)	• Concentration of some immigrants in poorer communities and in ethnic enclaves.
	Social isolation (lack of access to social capital, social networks)	• Lack of familiarity with local social networks
Availability to work	Availability of childcare and care for adult dependents	• Lack of relatives in the country may make it difficult to delegate caring responsibilities.[1]
	Social and psychological issues, motivational problems	• Immigrants who come as refugees may have particular problems with overcoming trauma. • The children of migrants may experience disaffection if their parents did not succeed in the way they had expected.
	Work in the informal economy	• Immigrants often become concentrated in the informal economy where they have entered the country illegally or their work permit has expired.
Employer attitudes	Prejudice and the ascribing of false or stereotypical characteristics (for example due to social background, residence)	• Lack of normal recourse to information on an immigrants experience and qualifications • Racism, particularly as regards visible minorities. Concentration of immigrants in poorer areas which may become stigmatised

1. In European countries for which accurate information exists on reasons for remaining outside the labour force, foreigners are more likely than nationals to cite family responsibilities as a reason for not having a job (32% as against just under 20%). See OECD (2005).

Source: OECD LIILM Project.

working conditions. The differential between the native and foreigner population in terms of the likelihood of holding a temporary job is particularly high in Spain, Portugal and Finland, all countries which themselves have high overall proportions of temporary employment (OECD, 2005a).

The underemployment of immigrants is also a significant issue, with immigrants often finding it difficult to find employment in fields and at levels which fully utilise their previous training and experience. The Longitudinal Survey of Immigrants to Canada, for example, found that the great majority of immigrants selected through the "skilled workers" programme operational in Canada had found employment within two years of their arrival. However, just over half had not found a job in their intended occupation (Statistics Canada, 2003). Where immigrants do find a job in their intended occupation it is generally less likely to be at an occupational level which corresponds to their qualifications. Unfortunately this has implications for longer term integration. Sweetman (2005) shows that the point of entry into the labour market is particularly important in determining long term career trajectories. The Conference Board of Canada (2001) estimates that underemployment costs the Canadian economy from CAD 3.5 to 5.0 billion annually.[5]

Another issue is that immigrants are often concentrated in particular sectors and industries. A number of sectors appear to favour immigrant labour, including construction, hotel and restaurant sectors, healthcare and social services (OECD, 2006a). Immigrants are also over-represented in unskilled services, and, in a number of countries, in domestic services.[6] Within the above niches, they are more likely to be concentrated in jobs that native people do not want to do, *i.e.* those that are low paid, and reflect the "three Ds": dirty, dangerous and difficult. The International Labour Organisation (ILO, 2004) has described how, despite the positive experience of many immigrants, a large proportion still face abusive and exploitative situations. These can include forced labour, low wages, poor working conditions, virtual absence of social protection, denial of freedom association and union rights, discrimination and xenophobia, as well as social exclusion.

A further factor that needs to be borne in mind is the importance of the informal economy within many countries, including two of the countries covered by the study, Spain and Italy. According to the OECD (2004a), the share of informal economic activity in Italy represents 16% of the Italian GDP. In fact, the informal economy has risen in the past few years according to ISTAT figures on the share of irregular workers (from 13.4% in 1992 to 15.1% in 2000). In Spain, equivalent data is lacking for 2004; however Schneider and Klinglmair (2004) estimate that the average size of the shadow economy (expressed as a percentage of GDP) in the years 2002-2003 in Spain was 22.3%. Though the number of illegal immigrants filling these jobs is difficult to assess, comparisons between municipal registers (which cover the entire population; irrespective of their legal status) and the residence permit system gave a figure of roughly 1 million clandestine immigrants in 2004, many of whom are likely to have taken advantage of the recent national regularisation which took place in 2005. Within the highly flexible United States labour market, Holzer (2005) has estimated that 6-7 million immigrant workers are illegal. New legislation is currently being debated in Congress to resolve this issue, at least in part through developing new forms of temporary employment permit.

Immigrants are particularly vulnerable to being exploited by the informal economy. This is a problem in both rural areas (with a high percentage of illegal work in agriculture) and in large cities, where the large numbers of people employed in unregulated jobs at least partly reflects the difficulty of legally operating low added value services at a profitable level given the high costs (land, transport) associated with such urban environments. Participation in the informal economy produces problems of legality and unprotected and unregulated employment, and in the longer term can restrict the ability of immigrants to become integrated into the formal labour market. In countries where the informal labour market is relatively entrenched, such as Spain and Italy, it is a difficult issue to tackle. While regularisation exercises obviously help, they are often relatively temporary, with some immigrants having to undergo multiple regularisations as they go in and out of employment.

Key stakeholders working at the local level

Multi level, multi-stakeholder approaches

The wide variety of different stakeholders involved at the local level in supporting the integration of immigrants into the labour market to some extent reflects the diversity of barriers which immigrants face. Depending on the local area, activities to support integration can be taken forward by local and regional authorities, non-governmental organisations (NGOs), trades unions, not-for profit enterprises, and employers. Each of these local organisations complement the support provided to immigrants in accessing the labour market by the public employment service (PES) which is delivered locally but mainly designed and developed at the national and regional levels.

The degree of involvement of different stakeholders depends very much on their traditional roles in each country, their established positions of power and their existing partnerships. Heckmann and Schnapper (2003) have pointed out that, "the way in which a country 'normally' tries to secure cohesion, conflict solution and to solve social and economic problems will also be used when integrating migrants". In the Nordic countries, for example, support is provided to immigrants by mainstream employment and social services under the relatively centralised public welfare system. In contrast, in the countries reviewed within this publication (Canada, Italy, Spain, Switzerland and the United Kingdom) the system is much more decentralised, with non-governmental organisations playing a major role in the provision of services to immigrants. In Spain, the United Kingdom and Italy, local municipal authorities take a relatively strong lead in coordinating partnership approaches, whereas they appear to have a weaker role in coordinating activities in Canada. Likewise, the trades unions play an important role in Italy, Spain and Switzerland, whereas they are largely absent from local initiatives to support integration in Canada, and the United Kingdom. The private sector produces active partners in some local regions in the United States and English speaking Canada, with employers and community foundations taking a leading role in coordinating local action in Toronto, for example, and taking responsibility for developing integration initiatives at the local level. Private sector employment is less common in Europe, although in Italy local chambers of commerce play a notable role, particularly in stimulating local immigrant entrepreneurship.

The following section briefly summarises the types of contribution made by each of these stakeholders at the local level in the countries participating in this study.

The public employment service

The public employment service (PES) is the organisation with the most obvious responsibility for supporting the integration of immigrants into the local labour market. However it is comparatively rare for the PES to specifically target immigrants in their programmes, although projects developed by other stakeholders to support immigrants at the local level are sometimes funded and supported. In Spain, for example, the regional branches of INEM part-finance projects run by regional and local authorities to generate innovation in provision for immigrants. In the United Kingdom, the Jobcentre Plus service runs ethnic minority outreach services in target areas to which refugees are eligible, and sub-contracts these to non governmental organisations. A new Jobcentre Plus refugee operational framework also supports partnership working between district offices and local refugee and community groups.

While programmes implemented by the PES are most often designed at the national level, in decentralised states regional employment services have more direct input into programmes that support immigrant integration. To help employers to recruit immigrants, INEM has developed a new catalogue of unfilled vacancies for which there is no Spanish worker available. The database is updated quarterly and if employers find that their vacancies are listed on the register they can advertise abroad without having to check locally that no other workers are available for the position. The register is run by the regional offices of the PES, and there is discretion at regional level on which jobs are placed on the register, leading to considerable variation in the type and number of jobs that are listed.

Amongst all the participating countries, Canada had the most extensive and diverse set of PES programmes targeted towards immigrants, and the regional offices of Service Canada have developed a number of specific initiatives, perhaps influenced by the fact that Canada, in common with the United States and Australia, has traditionally classified itself as a "country of immigration". In Ontario, Service Canada supports a series of targeted programmes to support immigrants including a newcomer assessment and referral project, specialised career search and work experience programmes, specialised employment centres and job finding clubs and programmes to support refugees. The Québec employment service (Emploi-Québec), in cooperation with other departments such as the Ministry of Education, Leisure and Sport and the Ministry of Health and Social Services likewise supports work experience programmes for immigrants with foreign degrees, mentoring schemes, skills upgrading projects for nurses, engineers and agriculture professionals trained abroad, and an office training project for immigrants. Government services and non-government organisations take part in recruiting and coaching those in training.

The role of local authorities

Despite the fact that in most cases they have no specific legal competency to help people into employment, local authorities play an important role in the local integration of immigrants into employment in many of the countries covered by this study. The multiple other competencies of local authorities mean that they are well placed to tackle the wide variety of issues which can indirectly prevent immigrants from accessing jobs (see Box 1.1). Whether or not they operate a specific integration policy, mainstream provision in relation to housing, schools, social assistance and spatial planning all have a significant impact on the wellbeing of immigrants and consequently on employability, particularly as these groups are less likely to be economically independent as their native counterparts and therefore more dependent on local assistance.

Ray (2003) has argued that the basic structure of a local area (its transportation, housing) is key to its ability to create social and economic cohesion, and that it is the everyday prosaic realities of a city or locality (accessibility, neighbourhood relations, access to public goods) that create both the positive successes and the barriers and sticking points in relation to integration. Through their historical development, certain localities have evolved land use patterns, housing provision and transport systems that are much better equipped to serve cultural diversity and prevent inequality through, for example, preventing the development of isolated pockets of deprivation with associated low quality housing, poor accessibility and poor quality amenities. He cites the city of Toronto in Canada as having been particularly effective in developing an integrated public transit system and tax pooling policies that did a great deal to sustain social cohesion and interaction as the city grew rapidly following World War II. However, in recent decades, low levels of investment in public transport and an absence of direct tax-sharing relationships between municipalities has contributed to increased

> **Box 1.1. Relevant actions by local authorities**
>
> **Housing:** Taking forward sensitive housing policy which avoids the concentration of immigrant and minority ethnic groups in certain areas, for example through supporting dispersed/mixed social housing development, clamping down on discriminatory landlords, avoiding the development of "back water areas" through ensuring good accessibility and tackling poor quality housing and urban decay;
>
> **Youth education:** Ensuring that the children of immigrants have equal opportunity in school, colleges and higher education: this may involve extra help when children are young to ensure that language and other barriers associated with cultural difference do not prevent learning. Ensuring mixed education, and avoiding strong concentrations of immigrants in certain schools may also be a valuable means of promoting future integration;
>
> **Adult education and skills:** Working with colleges and vocational schools to support ongoing learning of languages and vocational skills;
>
> **Entrepreneurship:** Supporting immigrants in the development of enterprises, and particularly the expansion of these enterprises beyond "home industries" that frequently involve long hours and poor working conditions;
>
> **Building social networks.** Ensuring that immigrants participate in broader social networks, which may assist in finding employment, through for example ensuring equal access to sport, cultural events and also promoting intercultural and inter-religious dialogue;
>
> **Promoting acceptable working conditions:** Working with employers and trade unions/labour to ensure that when immigrants are in employment, this is good quality employment, with acceptable working conditions, proper health and safety and acceptable hours so that immigrants do not become the "working poor". This may also involve tackling the informal labour market.
>
> **Economic development and ensuring all member of the community access the labour market:** Ensuring that immigrants and people from minority ethnic groups have equal access to economic opportunity – this may take the form of tackling basic barriers to the labour market, working with employers to prevent discrimination – whilst also ensuring that immigrants contribute as far as possible to the local economy.
>
> *Source:* OECD LIILM project.

segregation and the concentration of immigrants in poorer communities. Ray describes a growing spatial mismatch between the housing locations of less-well-off residents, many of whom are newcomers, and the distribution of employment opportunities which will have an impact on labour market integration.

The importance of in-direct factors in reducing labour market integration has been recognised by a number of local authorities. The local authority in Santa Coloma de Gramenet in Spain, for example has placed a significant emphasis on tackling local neighbourhood issues (noise control, neighbour disputes, licensing of traders) in areas of high immigrant concentration, to prevent issues between residents becoming "ethnicised", with resulting exclusion of these communities. The local development company has also focused on transport and accessibility plans as a means of helping local immigrants to access jobs in nearby labour markets, given the lack of economic development in the locality itself. Housing was a particular issue where local authorities felt able to intervene to support immigrants in Italy and Spain. Although housing may seem to have a relatively indirect relationship to the labour market, having appropriate housing close to available employment opportunities can be crucial to accessing and maintaining a job. In Italy, for example, housing plays an important role in the integration of immigrants in local labour markets because of the general housing crisis. Social housing accounts for less than 5% of the market, forcing the migrant labour force into an overcrowded rental market, and in many areas of the industrial north, housing costs are seen as the main obstacle to local labour market development. The Casa Amica project in Bergamo is a good example of a local initiative to provide housing for immigrants, involving a consortium of 16 public and private bodies, led by the regional and local authorities and comprising trades unions and associations. Casa Amica conducts research on the local housing situation and develops projects to meet needs, including the management of 132 apartments, construction of temporary housing facilities, the creation of a non-profit housing agency and the purchase and renovation of buildings for rental to single-parent families and mediation with homeowners. In Madrid, where housing costs are also particularly high, local NGOs focus on negotiating rental agreements with local landlords to help ensure that immigrants are not discriminated against or exploited.

Local authorities often become involved in immigrant integration issues through their responsibility for reception and the processing of legal papers for immigrants and through their role in emergency management situations. While decisions on the allocations of work permits to immigrants are usually made on the national level, the local level often has responsibility for administering them. For example, in Italy, foreigners are required to apply to the local police station for their residence permit. In times when large numbers of immigrants arrive this can cause long queues to form in city centres, raising public concern over the management of immigration inflows, and causing employers to lose production time. This has led the autonomous province of Trento in Italy to open a special service, CINFORMI, which has since become the principle actor in issuing permits and supporting the overall integration of immigrants locally.

Non-governmental organisations (NGOs)

Both local authorities and the PES frequently work with non-governmental organisations in the delivery of services to immigrants at the local level. This is sometimes for legal reasons: in Spain, for example, local authorities are not able to work with immigrants who do not have employment or resident permits, and therefore to some extent rely on NGOs to provide emergency support for these groups. NGOs are also favoured partners in the local integration process because they are felt to provide the supportive environment and individualised "one stop shop" approaches that immigrant with multiple obstacles to employment need.

In English speaking Canada,[7] public support to help immigrants into employment is almost entirely contracted out to NGOs at the local level, with only a small proportion of direct support being given to clients by the public employment service. NGOs frequently "mix and match" federal, provincial and municipal funding streams, in addition to private and charitable contributions, to deliver a number of different services to immigrants. In Winnipeg, Manitoba, for example, the International Centre provides both a reception service and a wide variety of other services to immigrants according to their needs, including advice on preparing CVs and navigating the local labour market, support in accessing local university training courses including advance payments on student loans, a cultural participation programme, a nutritional and wellness programme, children's recreational programme, outreach work with a social worker and translation services. Available resources to support immigrants in their job search include computers, projectors, lap tops, and a library. Despite being based in a relatively small scale facility in the community, the centre is able to help a relatively large number of immigrants: in 2004-5, 612 clients received guidance from employment facilitators, 202 participated in employment and job search workshops, and 253 gained employment directly as a result of this support.

In Madrid, the regional administration is working with non-governmental organisations at the local level to deliver a system of support to immigrants focusing on the local emergency management of extreme marginalisation and exclusion. The Social Attention Centres for Immigrants (CASI) programme provides a series of highly professionalised "one stop shop" services at the neighbourhood level, across the whole Madrid region, funded by the government but run by the voluntary sector. A team of professionals provide a range of complementary supports, with clients being offered five different services within the same location, including social work, legal, labour, inter-cultural, and social/educational services.

In Italy, the non-profit third sector has also been at the forefront of providing emergency reception facilities, and local authorities throughout the country have learned to rely heavily on shelters and services provided by associations. The most important associations and facilities have strong links to the Catholic Church. In London, a broader mix of secular and non-secular NGOs are at the forefront of provision for refugees. These NGOs (or RCOs: "Refugee and Community Organisations") provide a wide variety of services, including job search support and training in familiar local settings, funded through a variety of national, regional and European funding streams. Such RCOs are often run by immigrants associations and as such are felt to provide a community based environment for training and supporting refugees, with a strong understanding of different cultural issues affecting these groups.

Colleges and vocational schools

Colleges and vocational schools are particularly well placed to take forward an integration approach at the local level, in that they act as intermediaries between local people, local employers, and local governance structures. The community college system in the United States is seen by many as acting as an "integrative social institution" which actively links post-secondary education to local labour market needs. Over 25% of the more than 6 million students enrolled in community colleges in the United States are immigrants. La Guardia community college in New York, for example, is working with a variety of industry forums as well as immigrant entrepreneurs, concentrating on long term career path building and undertaking up-skilling programmes for immigrants in the health care industry.

Vocational schools in Switzerland have been particularly involved in providing support to immigrants because of the importance of the apprenticeship system within national vocational education. Vocational schools work with young people who have just arrived in the country to support their access to apprenticeships, which are seen as a principal route into the labour market. In particular, a number of vocational schools run pre-apprenticeship courses, which help young immigrants to address skills gaps, particularly around numeracy and literacy, before joining the mainstream programmes. The classes are small and the tutors work hard to build up links with local employers to ensure that their pupils are able to access employment placements in an increasingly competitive market. Vocational schools maintain relatively close links with federal institutions and participate in national conferences which enable them to closely follow the national policy agenda, and develop a common approach in a highly decentralised system. At the same time, their closeness to local communities enables them to carry this agenda forward with sensitivity to local conditions.

1. FROM IMMIGRATION TO INTEGRATION: COMPARING LOCAL PRACTICES

Employers

When making employment decisions about immigrants, employers do not have recourse to the usual sources of information (on educational background, previous work performance) which guide them in choosing the right employee. Local activities to ensure that employers can quickly see the potential offered by immigrants are therefore crucial, including, for example, bridging programmes that provide work experience placements for immigrants, actions to support the transferability of qualifications and projects which recognise prior competencies. In this sense employers are perhaps the most important of all the stakeholders to be involved at the local level, both because they themselves can offer opportunities to immigrants, and also because they can be involved in designing projects which are attractive to other employers.

In English-speaking Canada and the United States, this study has identified a number of examples of employers playing a relatively strong role locally, taking a lead on partnerships to develop integration approaches, and in some cases working together to provide employer based training opportunities for immigrants. Employers are leading partners in the Toronto based Region Immigration Employment Council (TRIEC), for example, which was launched in 2003 and has the mandate to improve access to the labour market for skilled immigrants. It is run by a council incorporating major employers, government representatives, trades unions and NGOs, and offers a strong example of an inclusive, but ultimately employer led approach. The employers who support TRIEC claim that local demography is a major driver: although there are no real skills shortages now in Toronto, they predict that the ageing population will produce such shortages over the next five years. They would prefer to learn the particular human resource management skills required to effectively recruit talented immigrants now, and therefore remain ahead of the game. TRIEC is seen as a "solution seeking machine" and runs a number of different programmes including "career bridging", mentoring, and the promotion of good practice in the hiring of immigrants.

In the United States, employers were also important members of the recent three year Building the New American Community initiative. This initiative was funded principally by the United States Office of Refugee Resettlement and focused on three cities: Portland, Nashville and Lowell. The aim was to develop public-private partnerships that reached across levels of government and the private sector has played a relatively strong role, particularly in Nashville, where the Nashville chamber of commerce helped to raise funding for the coalition and ensured that activities in Nashville had a strong workforce and business development orientation.

In another region of Canada, the province of Manitoba has worked with a group of local employers to provide an effective company based training system. A number of local credit unions (including Cambrian and Assiniboine) have joined forces to develop a customized training programme for immigrants seeking the position of "member service representative". The local authority has assisted the credit unions in undertaking an assessment of the various competences required by the position and using these to design a five week training course tailored specifically to the post. The training course also addresses the obstacles which immigrants can experience if they have not worked in Canada previously, including training in communication skills. The initial training period is followed by three months of paid work experience in the participating credit unions for those who successfully complete the training. The credit unions are planning to run four courses a year. The first two courses involved approximately ten participants each, selected from a pool of around 80 local immigrants who expressed an interest, with the majority going onto full time posts. The credit union industry is perhaps particularly well suited to this type of initiative, having both a community based approach, and strong pre-existing networks between its institutions. The local credit unions were particularly interested in employing immigrants in their branches in order to improve the adaptability of their services to local communities where a high concentration of immigrants are currently living. However, the local authority in Winnipeg also provided an important role in galvanizing the initiative, supporting the employers through providing a trainer, and the initial investment in the competency profiling. This "pooled training" approach for employers could be usefully copied elsewhere.

In the European countries participating in this study, local stakeholders had greater problems bringing employers into partnerships and ensuring that they participate in the design of initiatives. For example, in London, employers tend to be conspicuous by their absence from local initiatives concerned with labour market integration of refugees, despite the fact that many suffer skills shortages and skills gaps. NGOs reported difficulties in finding workplacements outside the voluntary sector, and those employers who did work with immigrants and refugees were often unwilling to publicise their work in the prevailing political and media climate surrounding immigration, since they felt that the potential adverse publicity that might follow "putting their heads above the parapet" could be damaging to their businesses. In turn, the lack of private sector involvement leads to a lack of "good practice" examples for others to follow. In Switzerland, vocational schools and other local stakeholders have experienced difficulties engaging employers, a problem which is made worse by the lack of anti-discrimination legislation existing in the country. The difficulty of involving employers in local initiatives in European countries is not peculiar to this particular policy area.

Previous LEED research has also highlighted the difficulty of encouraging employers to work towards improving the labour market integration of people who have greater difficulty in accessing the labour market, with Keane and Corman (2001) arguing that these groups are generally of lesser concern to employers. Förschner (2003b) also highlights the low level of cooperation with economic departments and entrepreneurs as being a key weakness of the European Union funded Austrian Territorial Employment pacts (TEPs).

However there are notable exceptions to the rule. For example, the potential for associations of employers to progressively tackle both integration and quality of work issues at the local level was illustrated strongly in the province of Lleida, in Spain. The Farmers Association in Catalonia (*Unió de Pagesos*, member of the Spanish network of agricultural and livestock organisations, COAG) has developed an innovative model for promoting good quality employment for temporary immigrants, bringing small-scale farmers together to co-ordinate and improve working conditions, and providing a variety of different forms of accommodation, training and social support. The advantage of the scheme from the employer's point of view is that the employees are accessible (through accommodation on site) and anti-social behaviour or absenteeism can be more easily managed. Immigrant workers benefit by being guaranteed a minimum standard of employment conditions, having their accommodation paid for, and participating in cultural programmes which support the development of positive relations with the local community. One of the progressive aspects of the programme is a transactional model that supports the creation of development projects and leadership training programmes in the immigrants' country of origin. Developing ongoing links with specific localities in sending countries has both supported a sustainable supply of workers and built a strong degree of trust, whilst supporting local development overseas. The national network provided by COAG has also provided the potential for temporary workers to extend their stay in Spain through transferring to work in different Spanish regions where the timing of the harvest is different.

In Italy, local chambers of commerce play a key role in a wide variety of initiatives, from training to accommodation and support for entrepreneurship. Italian chambers of commerce have been at the forefront of developing sector-based approaches to training and recruiting new immigrants from abroad. In order to meet demand for qualified seasonal workers in the tourism industry, for example, the Association of Commerce and Tourism in Trentino developed a bilateral project with the Romanian professional school for hotel and catering in Bucharest. The project, the first of this type in Italy, was intended to address long-term tourism sector labour needs in Trentino, and approximately fifty tourism enterprises became involved. The advantages to employers are clear. The demand for trained

Italian-language staff in the tourism sector is very high, and training costs are lower in Romania than in Trento. Trainees, on the other hand, are able to benefit from being given priority in the seasonal labour quota and a relationship with the trade association that sponsors their visa application. Eighty one students were taken on initially, and those that successfully completed a period of language training received three months professional tuition in Trento followed by additional professional training in their country of origin. Italian chambers of commerce have also been particularly active in supporting immigrant entrepreneurship at the local level. In addition, private banks have been responsible for financing local initiatives – for example the Casa Amica housing project in Bergamo outlined above.

A key challenge for all local initiatives working with employers to support integration is the issue of discrimination. While discrimination was raised as a issue in all the participating countries, and is the focus of national level policies and legislation,[8] specific local anti-discrimination initiatives were relatively lacking in the case study areas reviewed. However, in Montréal, in order to help the region's employers recruit and retain immigrants and ethnic minorities, the office of Emploi-Québec has worked with a not-for-profit organisation, "*Le Mouvement québecois de la qualité*" to prepare a guide on good human resources practices for companies that employ a multicultural workforce. In Toronto, TRIEC has also developed a marketing campaign to encourage new employers to tackle develop good practice in taking a positive approach to immigrants. The Hire Immigrants campaign recognises champions in the field, and provides training for future human resources professionals. European funded programmes at the local level such as EQUAL and in some cases the Territorial Employment Pacts (TEPs) have also supported approaches to tackling discrimination in the countries covered by the European Union. In Belgium, for example, a TEP in Brussels has developed an innovative approach to tackling discrimination on a sector basis, bringing employers together for joint training sessions on issues of discrimination in recruitment. Trade unions are also represented at the seminars, ensuring that they are challenging environments where employers are forced to examine their anti-discrimination policies in depth.

While employers are important partners, several experts have stressed the important role of the public sector in mediating between the private sector and local immigrants to ensure that the needs of the immigrant are best met. Employers may have different motivations in helping immigrants, for example, and it may not always be in their interest to support upward mobility or even sustainable employment. There is an important role for "not for profit brokers" between employers and employees.

It is also important to note that it is not only private or third sector employers that need to be brought on board in the local integration of immigrants. The public sector is also a particularly important employer at the local level, but often does not feature prominently as such in local integration initiatives.[9] The canton of Neuchâtel in Switzerland has recently been innovative in promoting public sector employment for immigrants in its legislation and planning, establishing in law that it is not necessary to have Swiss nationality to become a civil servant except in some specific services. Increasing public sector employment has also been included as one of the recommendations prepared by the canton's working group on integration for 2006-9. There are a number of good reasons for pursuing the local integration of immigrants through local public sector employment: firstly, public sector employment represents a significant sector in the labour market. Secondly, the public sector can implement equal opportunity and integration in an arena which its own agencies control, including the development of training courses aimed at disadvantaged groups within the labour market. Thirdly, non-nationals are also recipients or clients of state services, and increasing the representation of non-nationals within the public sector may increase the appropriateness of the services on offer.

The not-for-profit private sector

Not-for-profit private sector organisations such as social enterprises, local development companies, and community foundations can also be important players in the integration of immigrants into the labour market at the local level, not least due to the flexibility they gain from being outside of the public sector.

A social enterprise in Neuchâtel, Switzerland, has played an interesting role in developing customised training for immigrants which is geared to the needs of local employers. The Centre neuchâtelois (CNIP) has established itself as an important regional training centre, primarily providing training for adults to give them new skills and to assist in their reinsertion into the labour market. The centre can accommodate roughly 120 trainees at any one time, with approximately 70% being immigrants. The centre initially took out loans from the Swiss federal government in order to invest in renovating the factory, and purchasing machinery. It now relies for its income on payments per unemployed trainee from the public employment service and, to a very small degree, from the marketing of its own products. Its independence from the formal training system allows the centre to take a significant "demand led" approach, responding to employer needs by providing short and intensive training "close to the realities of industry", in day and evening classes. Because the centre does not have to conform to the annual calendar used by the vocational schools, it can offer modular courses all year round. The centre also works with particular hard to reach groups, including a number of older immigrants who have work injuries relating to previous employment. This is reflected in the centre's annual output figures: while 40% of the trainees who left the centre in 2005 went into employment, 28% had to finish training on medical grounds.

In the municipality of Santa Coloma de Gramenet, in Spain, the local authority has chosen to delegate its integration services to immigrants to a local development company Grameimpuls S.A, which is responsible for managing local economic and employment promotion policies. The company works with approximately 70-80 immigrants a year and has the advantage of being empowered to work in the relatively wide range of activities normally taken forward by local authorities whilst also retaining a relatively focused approach on economic development and integration issues. The director of the centre has been able to build up a strong local profile as a representative dealing with immigrant issues, and has build up relations of trust with local employers, community organisations and government representatives. He feels that this trust is an essential element in supporting change and helping immigrants out of situations of deprivation. The training delivered by the centre focuses on employability skills in particular, although the centre experiences some problems identifying good quality jobs for participants in a local labour market which has high rates of temporary employment: of those who left the programme in 2003, roughly a half found employment, and of those, only half again were still in employment the following year.

Community foundations are another form of semi-private organisation that play a visible role in the integration of immigrants in a number of OECD countries. In the United States, the tradition of philanthropy means that foundations are strongly involved in the development and management of integration projects. The Independence Community Foundation in New York, for example, was set up through an endowment from Independence Community Bank and focuses on community development, education, culture and the arts, poverty, housing, and economic and workforce development issues in the New York metropolitan area. It has recently funded a "Latin American Workers project" in the neighbourhood of Williamsburg, which was developed to provide a drop in centre for day labourers. In Canada, it was a private foundation, the Maytree Foundation, which played a particularly important role in stimulating the development of the TRIEC partnership to support immigrant integration in Toronto. The Foundation was responsible for developing the initial strategic vision and programme of work, and is now coordinating the partnership bodies which implement the programme. The employment council has been able to attract and maintain membership from a large number of partnerships in the region partly because the Foundation is a relatively neutral and independent coordinator.

Trade unions

Access to good quality employment is a crucial aspect of the local integration of immigrants into the labour market. Trade unions have a role to play here, although their presence in helping integration at the local level is far from uniform. The unions are more visible partners at the local level in Southern European countries, for example, such as Spain and Italy, as opposed to Canada and the United Kingdom. One factor limiting union involvement is a reluctance to get involved in supporting immigrants in temporary or undocumented employment, who may be seen to be in potential conflict with their existing members. Unions in some cases also proved negative about employer involvement in local initiatives to support access to employment, for example work experience and mentoring schemes, as this was felt to place too many extra "non-contract based" requirements on their members.

Given the right tools and motivation, however, trade unions can make a significant contribution at the local level to increasing the quality of employment on offer. In Italy, trade unions have been at the forefront of the regularisation process at the local level. In Milan, the CGIL union alone handled 30 000 applications in 2002. Equally important was the ACLI-Colf, the Catholic Worker's Association for domestic workers, which set up branches around the metropolitan area of Milan to help domestic workers with their legal procedures. This contact reinforced the role of these associations as representatives of immigrant workers, especially in a situation where institutions were unable to develop a coordinated response.

In the United States, unions are generally less involved in integration issues. However, in New York, the 32BJ Service Union has recently had important success in improving the employment conditions for their members employed in service jobs such as night-time security or cleaning commercial buildings, of which 70% are foreign born. In the last five years the union has campaigned to raise wages for 6 000 workers from USD 5 to 10 an hour, with added health care benefits. Employers pay into a training fund, to allow union members to access up to college degree courses, and there is a university scholarship programme for workers children. The union employs a number of lawyers who support union members when going through legal problems. The union also participates in a New York Civic Participation Project which is a collaboration between unions and community groups to promote low-wage immigrant worker rights. This project supports engagement by immigrant communities in civic participation at the neighbourhood and citywide level and provides community grants to support integration.

Immigrants associations

It is increasingly recognised that immigrant associations have an important role to play in integration at the local level, as they encourage the development of services that are culturally sensitive, and that take the demands of immigrants themselves into account. One of the key findings of the Building Americas New Community initiatives, for example, is that "new Americans" should be involved significantly in decision making processes. The evaluators of these initiative felt that it was particularly important that immigrants associations are not only consulted on schemes, but are also offered the possibility of active participation in design and delivery.

In Canada, immigrants associations are strongly represented at the regional level, in roundtables which comment on and feed into employment policy. At the local level, they also help to deliver employment programmes. For example in Montréal , an association which represents Jewish residents, Jewish Employment Montréal (JEM) works as a matching agency for immigrants, drawing upon a database of approximately 2500 employers, mainly from the local Jewish business community. It aims to offer a professional approach with strong awareness of the needs and interests of business, whilst also offering the benefits of a supportive community group to their clients. Immigrants associations are also responsible for running many of the refugee and community organisations operational in London. The London case study, for example, highlights projects that are working specifically with refugees from the Somali, Iranian, Arab, Filipino, African, Asian, Latin American, Cameroonian or Hindu communities. There is also a strong recent history of immigrants associations being involved in local regeneration partnerships, such as the Renewal partnership in West London, enabling them to take an active role in the design and management of partnership projects at the local level.

The high profile given to immigrants associations in work to support integration and social cohesion in the United Kingdom is not without its critics however. Kenan Malik has recently argued[10] that funding targeted at particular immigrants associations has been divisive, encouraging competition between different communities for resources and power. He feels that focusing on ethnicity sidelines issues of poverty and equality, and creates a politics of difference. A reluctance to single out particular communities for attention may also at least partly explain the relatively low involvement of immigrant associations in Spain and Switzerland at the local level. In Switzerland, immigrants associations played a strong role in supporting integration up until relatively recently, in the absence of public sector support. However, now that both the federal level and the cantons are taking a more active role, policy makers are reluctant to work with immigrants associations locally as they do not want to be seen to favour particular groups in society. This standpoint is also reflected in France, where the republican national model means that ethnic communities are not directly taken into consideration in policy making and implementation. Despite this, Moore (2004) has recently demonstrated that this is sometimes subverted at the local level, where crisis situations in areas of high immigrant concentration in Marseille and Toulouse have led to the unofficial appointment of North African mediators to serve as links between policy makers and immigrants. Immigrants associations have also played a relatively limited role in supporting integration issues in Spain, which has been blamed on a historic lack of "associationalism"; however the national government is now trying to build capacity in these groups to ensure that they play a role in the new integration agenda which has been taken forward by the new government in Spain since 2004.

The instruments used

Many of the tools and instruments used to support the integration of immigrants in the local areas studied are similar to those used within mainstream active labour market policies. For example, the majority of local activities focused on job search support, education and training, mentoring and the provision of work experience placements, although they adapted this support so that it responded to the specific needs and lifestyles of the local immigrant population. In addition, local initiatives also provided specialised support to immigrants including language tuition, the recognition of qualifications and skills gained overseas, and help with wider social acculturation, participation and networking. Table 1.3 summarises the types of adaptation developed by initiatives to meet the specific needs and barriers experienced by immigrants.

Job search and self-presentation

Many of the local initiatives reviewed as part of this study focused at least in part on improving the ability of immigrants to "navigate" the local labour market. On arriving in a new country it can be difficult to understand the methods which local people use to find jobs, particularly where the majority of jobs are not formally advertised (such as is the case in Canada and Italy). For example, in London, the Refugee Education and Training Advisory Service (RETAS) offers a series of two week job search and orientation courses which were run throughout the year, including an overview of the United Kingdom job market, and individual careers assessments. Many local initiatives provided access to the internet and newspapers and advice on making prospective calls to employers. In addition, support is given on self-presentation techniques – how to write CVs and covering letters, and how to

Table 1.3. **Types of adaptation of local initiatives to the specific needs and barriers experienced by immigrants**

Issue	Barrier	Adaptation
Skills and competencies	• Language skills, socio-cultural knowledge and understanding, lack of funding and/or subsidies to access education and training locally, qualifications gained overseas, lack of local referees and lack of local work experience to prove competencies	• Language courses • High staff to participant ratios on other training courses to give additional language assistance and help with interpreting and navigating local cultural norms • Support with acculturation to the local community • Provision of information on local institutions and governance frameworks, including the local education system • Recognition of qualifications • Education and training courses • Organisation of work experience placements with local employers
Accessibility issues	• Lack of knowledge of local labour markets, concentration of some immigrants in poorer communities and in ethnic enclaves • Lack of local social networks	• Courses in navigating the local labour market • Support with accessing neighbouring labour markets • Support with social networking
Availability	• Lack of relatives in the country may make it difficult to delegate caring responsibilities • Problems with overcoming socio-psychological issues trauma, disaffection and low motivation (particularly second or third generations) • Migration status (rules around whether asylum seekers are able to work for example) • Availability of work permits for particular jobs • Immigrants often become concentrated in the informal economy where they have entered the country illegally or their work permit has expired.	• Provision of evening classes • Provision of childcare along side training courses • Social and psychological support, confidence building and re-motivation courses • Work with children to ensure that they succeed in the education system • Support with navigating the legal permit system • Local projects to encourage the better regulation of employment
Employer attitudes	• Lack of normal recourse to information on immigrants experience and qualifications • Lack of knowledge about the value and relevance of qualifications and experience gained in other countries. • Racism, particularly as regards visible minorities. Concentration of immigrants in poorer areas which may become stigmatised	• Initiatives to bring employers into contact with immigrants and build trust, including mentoring and work experience • Initiatives to reduce prejudice and discrimination amongst employers

Source: OECD LIILM Project.

succeed in an interview. In some cases, advice was given at least initially on navigating the wider social environment – the role and functions of local institutions, where to seek support and advice, as this was felt to be a necessary first step before improving access to employment opportunities.

A number of local initiatives studied had also developed targeted approaches to helping different types of immigrant navigate the labour market. While some initiatives chose to target a particular labour market sector, others focused on particular groups within the immigrant community. In London, for example, Education Action International have published an "Employment resource handbook for refugee engineers" which aims to provide essential information on the job hunting culture in the United Kingdom in addition to an overview of the engineering profession (Rogic and Feldman, 2004). The Rexdale Employment Resource Centre (ERC), operated by Humber College in North Etobicoke, Toronto runs a job-search course which targets a number of different sectors, but focuses on a particular type of immigrant – the highly skilled. The centre provides four week courses for "Foreign Trained Professionals and Tradespeople" which are explicitly designed to help professional migrants gain professional-level employment. The courses are relatively resource intensive, each course involving roughly 20 participants and costing around CAD 2 000 (EUR 1 400)[11] per participant but outcomes appeared to be positive, with the majority of participants finding professional-level work after finishing the course.

Education and training

Many local initiatives provide education and training courses for immigrants in basic skills such as IT and numeracy in order to build up their employability. Such courses are frequently adapted to the specific needs of migrants, for example through the provision of additional language support and help with understanding cultural norms specific to the host country. A number of local initiatives also ensure that courses are accessible to immigrants who have constraints on their availability (due to having taken "survival employment" or due to responsibilities to dependents), providing evening classes, and associated childcare, although such support is less common. Training is often delivered within a broader set of activities and support. For example, the RAAD Large Scale Employment and Training project for refugees and asylum seekers in London includes a raft of different forms of support including training, advice in job search and job creation initiatives – since 2002, in addition to awarding 329 qualifications (many in short courses such as forklift truck driving and IT) the initiative has created 111 jobs in medicine, industry, the voluntary sector, customer services and the retail sector.

While many local initiatives offer training in basic and generic skills, some choose to focus on specific skills required for certain professions. Again in London, a project run by the Arab Group focuses on the provision of dressmaking skills in order to increase the opportunities available to local Arab women and Arab refugees. Between 2002 and 2005, 42 candidates were trained by the project, of whom 18 have gained a formal vocational qualification in fashion and dressmaking, eight have directly accessed jobs in linen and upholstery factories and two have opened their own tailoring businesses. In some cases, education and training is used to help re-direct immigrants who are already employed in low quality and low paid jobs into occupations with more chance of career progression. For example the Alma Mater project in Italy has developed a number of small scale intensive re-training programmes for women in low skilled-low paid jobs. One such project re-trained women in the domestic services sector in skills required to develop a career in banking. Following the course, twelve women left domestic employment and began long-term contracts in Italian banks as bank-clerks.

Languages

Language was viewed by many local stakeholders as crucial to the local integration of immigrants, and language tuition was a common element in almost all of the local initiatives visited in the participating countries. Language and communication skills are becoming increasingly important as a requirement for employment in the service based and knowledge based economy, and increasingly it is these jobs which immigrants are hoping to access. Whereas traditionally, activities of the secondary sector accounted for a large portion of foreign employment in most OECD countries, recent years have seen a gradual spread of foreign employment into the tertiary sector. In 2002-03, that sector accounted for more than three-quarters of foreign jobs in the United Kingdom (83.3%), in Sweden (76.1%) and in Finland (75.6%). More than 70% of foreigners also work in services in Australia, Canada, the United States, Ireland, Luxembourg, Norway and the Netherlands (OECD, 2005a).

Languages are often taught as part of wider training courses – for example language is a key element in the pre-apprenticeship courses provided in Swiss vocational schools. In other initiatives languages were taught as part of a package of job search support, sometimes in conjunction with basic numeracy training. Despite the emphasis on language teaching, many local stakeholders complained that freely available language courses were oversubscribed. In London, for example, expenditure on English as a Second Language (ESOL) has risen significantly in the United Kingdom over the last few years, but the Strategy Unit (2004) suggested that the volume of demand for ESOL still far outstripped supply. A further issue for London, and for the other countries covered by the study is how and whether provision matches the needs of learners and the demands of the economy – in terms of level (introductory/intermediate/specialist), and content (specifically in relation to fulfilling workplace needs).

The *level* of language provision was a particular issue raised in countries recruiting relatively high skilled immigrants. In most countries language tuition was offered at a relatively basic level, however it was evident that many employers were seeking relatively high levels of language competency.

Canada, for example, employs a language competency benchmarking system, with a scale ranging from 1 to 12; with most employers requiring a language level of 8 or above. Only the province of Manitoba currently provides widely available language training up to that level. In most cases generally available language training stops at the level of 5 or 6.

It was also found that generalised language courses are not always enough to meet the specific occupational requirements of different labour market sectors. In both London and the Canadian provinces local stakeholders have placed growing emphasis on occupational language courses which are targeted to particular professions. Occupational language tuition is an important element of the training schemes being operated in Canada to provide top up training for immigrants wishing to enter a profession. The Enhanced Language Training (ELT) initiative funded by Citizenship and Immigration Canada also provides job-specific language training to enable immigrants to gain the language skills they need to flourish in the workplace across a number of different sectors including teaching, nursing, engineering and medicine, while separate communication skills courses have also been developed for accountants and call centre staff. In London, the Renewal partnership has also developed occupational language courses, in combination with adaptation programmes and workplacements as part of specialist packages aimed at particular employment sectors. Likewise, bilingual vocational courses with an emphasis on English in specific workplace contexts have recently been established in the London Borough of Croydon.

In the light of the demands of the knowledge and service based economy it is likely that language tuition will be given increased importance at the local level in the future. A number of national governments are giving new priority to language training in their integration and immigration strategies. In the United Kingdom, language tuition is an important element in a recent joint statement by the Home Office, the TUC and the Confederation of British Industry to support managed migration in the interests of the United Kingdom economy. The Home Office have also introduced a language standard as one of their requirements for United Kingdom citizenship. In Canada, a key element of a new agreement on immigration which has recently been negotiated between Canada and Ontario is a commitment to improve the availability of language services, through for example expanding language training, assessment and referral services and ensuring that they are delivered through appropriate partnerships, including those with employers, regulatory bodies, and professional and trade associations.[12] Language tuition was also identified as a key issue for future investment by the evaluation of the three Building New American Communities pilots in the United States.

Recognition of skills and qualifications

Another instrument which has been given particular support in Canada, the United States and the United Kingdom, is the recognition of qualifications gained overseas. Credential and educational attainment recognition was seen as one of the main issues for investment emerging from the evaluation of the Building New American Communities initiative as it is a key component in the process of ensuring that employers can take maximum advantage of the previous knowledge, training, skills and experience brought by immigrants.

Recognition of qualifications is particularly challenging in Canada because its ten provinces and three territories have jurisdictional responsibility for the regulation of skilled trades and some professions, which in many cases has been delegated to regulatory bodies through legislation. There are over 400 such bodies responsible for regulating approximately 20% of the Canadian workforce. In Québec, the Québec Ministry for Immigration and Cultural Communities (MICC) runs a Centre for the Recognition of Skills and Competences for immigrants with prior qualifications. The centre carried out approximately 14 104 comparative assessments of diplomas in 2005-6, mainly for people outside the professions. In addition, the Regulated Profession Information Office (SIPR) informs immigrants established in Québec of how to gain access to occupations regulated by professional corporations as well as certain other trades and occupations whose entry or eligibility conditions are subject to regulatory requirements.

The recognition of qualifications is also taken seriously in the United Kingdom. According to a conservative Refugee Council estimate there were nearly 1 000 refugee medical doctors in Britain in 2003[13] unable to work because of qualification difficulties, despite substantial experience in their native countries. The National Academic Recognition Information Centre (NARIC) provides a benchmarking service for international qualifications, operating as a private organisation funded partly by the Department for Employment and Skills and partly by corporate membership. Part of a wider European network of national centres of recognition, the NARIC services form an essential component of a number of local projects delivered in London to assist refugees, such as the pan-London Migrants and Refugees Qualifications project.

Supporting the recognition of qualifications is often just one stage of a skilled person's route into employment. The assessment of qualifications and competences can act as a baseline for a further investment in skills and work experience and in many cases migrants only need a short amount of extra training, or indeed the recognition of their existing competencies which do not fall within formal qualifications. Emploi-Québec, for example, provides modular "bridging" courses for up-skilling immigrants so that their skills will be recognised by local employers, running a number of different skills upgrading programmes for nurses, agronomists and different categories of engineers. The training in nursing and engineering, in particular, facilitates admission to the corresponding professional corporations. The Early Childhood Educator (ECE) Qualifications Recognition Programme in Winnipeg is another example of the work being done in Canada to better assess prior levels of competence, as a way of enabling immigrants to avoid long period of re-training. Up until recently, it was necessary to do a 2 year community college training course to qualify for early childhood education in the province. A representative of the Manitoba Child Care Programme has sought to adapt this to the specific needs of migrants, and recently launched a new 14 week pilot training project involving work based assessment and training, based on a "competency assessment framework" which was designed with a local college. In addition to recognising previous competencies, the course also focuses on skills that immigrants may currently lack such as awareness of cultural and occupational norms in Canada. This type of training is particularly effective in that it allows immigrants to quickly enter the labour market whilst still building relevant skills.

It has been argued that outside the professions, having a qualification is a proxy used by employers for general competency, and as such is a mechanism for establishing whether a person has the professionalism and commitment to learn to carry out a job. Often, what employers are particularly interested in, for example, are the generic attributes of a person (their time management, commitment and professional manner) which are proved indirectly by their ability to compete a degree or training course. The Neuchâtel social enterprise CNIP in Switzerland has placed considerable emphasis on providing certification of relatively basic skills through their training modules as an important mechanism for building trust amongst employers. After each module trainees are given an evaluation dossier containing a very precise description of the modules taken, and the quality of work carried out. CNIP places strong emphasis in the certification of the professional competences exhibited by trainees during their training modules. The evaluation of a trainee covers the learning of practical skills *e.g.* manual skills, as well as intellectual qualities such as the ability to concentrate, memorise materials and use abstractions. Behaviour, personal style, team work and motivation are also validated. The certification of these elements provides an important point of reference for potential employers.

Skills audits are another useful tool for recognising the wider skills and competencies which immigrants may have that fall outside of recognised qualifications. In the city of Leicester in the United Kingdom, NIACE (the National Organisation for Adult Learning) has worked with Leicester City Council and the East Midlands Consortium for Asylum Seekers Support to develop a skills audit initiative to explore the skills and qualifications of asylum seekers, to find ways of presenting these skills in a positive way to employers, and to consider how they might be used for the benefit of the local and regional economy. The project sent a survey to the 440 registered asylum seekers in Leicester in 2001 and then conducted follow up interviews with 70 respondents to identify their skills and experience (Aldridge and Waddington, 2001). The project also focused on encouraging people working in the field of accommodation for refugees and asylum seekers to record the qualifications, skills and previous work experience of individuals as essential information for forward planning. In London, similarly, the Mayor has launched a skills audit of refugee women in London from the teaching, nursing and medical professions entitled, "Missed Opportunities" (Dumper, 2002).

In the Southern European countries of Italy and Spain there is less emphasis on the recognition of skills and qualifications at the local level. This partly reflects the fact that these countries do not have a national policy to attract skilled immigrants, and are in many cases trying to attract immigrants to fill their lowest skilled positions. There is a tendency for local initiatives in Spain, for example, to concentrate on supporting immigrants into low skilled positions rather than actively recognizing skills and supporting career progression. Though this may be an appropriate recognition of the jobs available in the local labour market, this has several consequences: on the one hand many low-skilled positions are relatively temporary meaning that immigrants come in and out of employment support programmes. Further, in many cases immigrants are over-qualified for the positions they take, which could store up problems of frustration for the future.

Work placements

The interest of employers in generic skills is also apparent in the emphasis that many employers place on the need for applicants with local work experience. The absence of Canadian work experience is a key obstacle cited by Canadian companies to employing immigrants, for example. While some local stakeholders see this as an example of unnecessary discrimination by employers, others have reacted more pragmatically by ensuring that such experience is quickly accessible to immigrants at the local level. Work experience placements were one of the key instruments used by TRIEC. Local immigrants are selected to join the TRIEC Career Bridge Scheme on the basis of their qualifications, employability and language level. To access this pool of pre-selected graduates, employers pay an upfront fee of CAD 10 000 (approx EUR 7 180) and are able to hire a immigrant for a paid work experience with the company for up to twelve months. The scheme is managed through a website, and is so popular that the site can only be opened for applications three hours every month. A network of NGOs also sources potential participants. By April 2006, three hundred internships had already taken place with 85% receiving offers of full employment, although not always in the same company.

In the Career Bridge scheme, the emphasis was on finding work experience placements with relatively large employers, and TRIEC had experienced some difficulties engaging SMEs in the programme. In Montréal, Emploi-Quebec has supported a programme (developed by the Industrial Adjustment Service Committee for Immigrants, IASCI) known as "Professional immersion activities for immigrants with foreign degrees" which has been successful at involving small to medium enterprises in addition to other sizes of company, and local community organisations. This programme is administered by Emploi-Québec with the help of local NGOs, who both process applications and identify placements within the local community. The scheme has a particularly impressive success rate, a longitudinal study revealed a 72% job placement rate immediately after the immersion activity. The level of satisfaction with the programme is also high, with participants being particularly positive about the strong interrelationship between the professional immersion activity and the respondents' main field of expertise: placements are only organised when there is an explicit relationship between a job and a candidate's previous training.

In Switzerland, identifying workplacements is a crucial part of the apprenticeship system, and one of the difficulties experienced by pre-apprenticeship courses in Geneva and Neuchâtel was finding an appropriate placement for immigrants. In Geneva, a private organisation, known as Interface Enterprises, has developed a useful linking role between vocational schools and local employers, setting up a large scale database of potential placements which staff can then use to place trainees. They have also launched a project to encourage local ethnic entrepreneurs to offer placements to new immigrants seeking work experience and apprenticeships.

Soft inputs: social capital, network building and acculturation

Field work in both Spain and London points to the important amount of work that is done by NGOs to help immigrants that are at some distance from the labour market due to social and psychological difficulties. Many of the CASI clients in Madrid have multiple social and psychological problems and they require an important amount of support before employability can even be considered. In London, refugee and community organisations often make a considerable investment in building the personal confidence and social skills of refugees as a prerequisite to then developing specific employability skills and finding an appropriate job.

Other types of "soft input" notable within the case studies include support with social network building and acculturation. In Southern European countries such as Italy and Spain, much of the work carried out to support the integration of immigrants is focused on wider social integration rather than specifically on labour market integration. Building solidarity and understanding between local residents is seen as an essential element in ensuring the wider participation of immigrants in society and as such their ability to access work. In countries where much employment is advertised informally this may be an effective strategy. For example, in Italy, the PES can only provide a limited role in matching immigrants to employment demand in contexts where most jobs are advertised informally. In fact, studies involving employers in Italy have found that the majority of employers seek employees not through temporary work agencies or public employment centres but through informal channels. In the province of Turin, a 2003 study found that 57% of businesses hired new employees through contacts with friends and family; 14% were acquaintances of current employees (Ricerche e Progetti, 2003). In Canada, a similar situation exists, with approximately 80% of vacancies being advertised informally. This places newcomers to the labour market, and especially immigrants, who are less likely to have an extended social network, at a disadvantage when seeking employment opportunities.

Many of the local initiatives reviewed within the case study countries helped immigrants to establish social networks which might help them to acquire a job. Interface Enterprises in Geneva explicitly set out to encourage young immigrants to exploit their local social networks in the search of job opportunities, approaching key figures in their community, such as their "concierge", about local jobs. Informal job search mechanisms are also favoured by JEM in Montréal, word of mouth being their main basis for drawing up their 2500 strong database of local employers. JEM engages with employers in its work both to canvass the availability of job placements and to persuade employers to accept some responsibility for taking on new members of their community. One strategy is to hold meetings with "employer clusters" – that is employers in particular fields and sectors – in order to review the curriculum vita of prospective employees. JEM receives some 400 to 500 applications per year for its placement services. Around 25 % succeed in getting jobs; while another 50 % are referred to various education options.

Networking as a route to employment is one of the principal aims of mentoring projects, although confidence building and advice on "route planning" towards a particular job or career are also important components of this type of support. Mentoring was highlighted as a particularly popular means of helping immigrants to access the labour market in London, and in Switzerland and Canada. TRIEC in Toronto, for example, has developed a large scale mentoring programme. Since February 2005 over 1 000 matches have been made with mentors working in both the public and private sector in Toronto. Responsibility for organising the mentoring scheme is franchised out to eight different NGOs, while TRIEC itself recruits workplaces and mentors. The scheme is partly sponsored by private companies, and large companies such as Deloitte Touche and TD are active members – for example 10% of Deloitte's senior managers currently act as mentors – and this helps considerably in encouraging other companies to join.

Mentoring has also proved successful in London, with mentee health professionals reporting that mentors had facilitated their access to, and initial progress within the National Health Service. The goals of mentoring sessions in the Mentoring Programme for Refugee Doctors, for example, are to provide refugee doctors with advice on the United Kingdom health system, medical career paths, professional registration, recruitment processes, specialist training, and employment opportunities; to facilitate access of refugee doctors to clinical attachments, employment opportunities and further training; and to support refugee doctors in search for appropriate employment.

The Italian experience also shows that networking is useful not only in terms of accessing a first job, but also in supporting ongoing career progression. The Alma Mater permanent centre in Turin, in addition to providing vocational training and qualifications, also has the unintentional effect of establishing close relationships between immigrant and native women leading to better employment outcomes. Alma Mater serves as a meeting place for foreign and Italian women, providing social activities and common cultural and social projects. Women working together in this context establish friendship bonds which have often led to upward movement in the labour market.

One problem with "soft approaches" to integration is that they are inherently difficult to evaluate. For example, Alma Mater do not consider the longer term opportunities they indirectly create for women as a noteworthy outcome of their activities, since it is not within the framework of a single project and is neither extendable nor fundable. RCOs in London also reported difficulty in evaluating the "softer" elements of their work such as confidence building. Despite this difficulty, such approaches can be crucial to supporting longer term labour market integration and cannot be neglected.

Support to entrepreneurship

Finally, not all local initiatives in the participating countries focused on supporting immigrants into existing employment. A number of localities also focused on stimulating immigrant entrepreneurship. In Italy, entrepreneurship amongst migrants has been identified as an important economic driver, with recent national growth in the number of entrepreneurs being entirely due to an increase in immigrant entrepreneurs. Chambers of commerce have therefore been keen to support the expansion of this area.

In Milan the local chamber of commerce has been active in supporting immigrant entrepreneurs through its agency Formaper. Partly funded by the European Social Fund, it has worked to address the special requirements of self-employed immigrants, promoting mentoring by immigrants of the same community and attempting to mediate with banks to facilitate access to credit, one of the most serious obstacles to growth. In addition, in Turin, the chamber of commerce has published a guide in the nine principal foreign languages spoken in the region, providing information on the local legal context for entrepreneurs and services that would be useful for immigrants wishing to start a business. Sector based employers confederations have also taken an active role in promoting entrepreneurship. The National Artisan Confederation (CAN) has actively recruited immigrant entrepreneurs for a number of years and in Bologna, has opened a special office providing a wide range of consulting, orientation and mediation services for more than 500 local immigrant entrepreneurs. The service supports the development of business plans and runs training courses.

In London, ethnic entrepreneurship is seen as a major growth area, and is the target of a number of London Development Agency initiatives. The refugee support agency, RETAS, also runs specific Business Start-Up courses for refugees in London, focusing on issues and information related to the small business environment in the United Kingdom.

Governance issues

The number of stakeholders active in the field of supporting the local integration of immigrants, and the number of instruments used, leads to a significant governance challenge at the local level. A number of the issues are familiar ones. The factors which prevent effective support being given to immigrants also undermine wider policies to produce economic development and social cohesion: poor communication and coordination between stakeholders, a lack of integration between supply and demand, a poor prioritisation of resources, an emphasis on short-term impacts rather than long term change and a grants based culture of provision which does not encourage either mainstreaming or sustainability. The following section discusses each of these issues in turn, highlighting the specific policy issues and policy dilemmas affecting activities to support the integration of immigrants.

Policy fragmentation

Given the number of actors involved in supporting integration, regular communication between local organisations is vital to ensuring that immigrants are guided or "signposted" to appropriate forms of support at the local level. Unfortunately communication is often hampered by the relative fragmentation of this policy area, heavy work-loads and lack of resources held by the organisations involved.

At the national level, responsibility for the integration of immigrants often falls across a number of different government departments, each of which may produce relevant funding programmes. In the United Kingdom, for example, the Home Office, Department for Work and Pensions, Department for Education and Skills and Department of Communities and Local Government all implement programmes targeted towards immigrants and ethnic minorities. In English speaking Canada, likewise, immigration is the focus of both Citizenship and Immigration Canada and Human Resources and Skills Development Canada among others.[14] In effect, local service providers such as NGOs often provide a point of "integration" for different national government programmes of support to help immigrants at the local level, combining a number of different approaches in a one-stop shop environment. This may be of benefit to end users, and to some extent NGOs value the spread of financial risk between a number of different funding organisations. However they also bear the burden of an important degree of resulting bureaucracy. The International Centre in Winnipeg, Canada, for example is an established NGO which has been providing one stop shop settlement services to immigrants for 57 years and currently has a 2 million dollar budget. However this budget is made up of seven different grants, six of which are renewable on an annual basis.

Fragmentation between the different institutions dealing with integration also exists at the local level. Although service providers such as NGOs may effectively coordinate national or regional funding streams, their communication and coordination with other local actors is often less developed – indeed the way that national and regional funding streams are structured often means that they are in competition. In Winnipeg for example, it was apparent that many of the local stakeholders were not aware of the other services for immigrants operating in their area, despite the fact that many of these organisations had existed for many years.[15] Likewise, local initiatives in London have grown up organically in a piecemeal manner, and over time, this has led to a particularly complex system.

Fragmentation has a number of repercussions at the local level. In Italy, the sheer number of organisations involved in supporting the integration of immigrants into the labour market may have reduced the ability of local actors to develop a strategic local approach. Local authorities have difficulty assuming control and determining local strategies to support integration in view of the myriad of stakeholders and subcontracted service providers involved in integration issues, and the dominance of the social partners in determining the direction of local economic policy.

Fragmentation of delivery can also lead to service providers being particularly isolated, which does not help in their mission to help immigrants become better integrated into wider society. A key strength of NGOs is that they are able to engage immigrants, at least in the first instance, in a localised environment where they feel comfortable. However, in order to combat any possibility of ghettoisation, there is ultimately a need to encourage immigrants to extend their horizons and move beyond the "comfort zone" of their immediate local area and community to mix more widely and encounter new challenges. The London case study has identified this as being analogous to the need to supplement "bonding" social capital with "bridging" social capital, so as to link unemployed immigrants onto both future support and employment opportunities. Considine (2003) has pointed to the issue of "network closure", describing how "what makes a group strong in social capital terms may be the same thing that makes it exclusive and restrictive". He also points out that while some organisations may maintain good links this does not necessarily lead to general information sharing, as "some classes of insiders are restricted to limited roles and information flows are confined to one or two well-worn pathways". This was also reported as an issue in some of the local areas studied, with certain prominent NGOs in local areas maintaining good linkages, while others "fell between the gaps".

A further problem caused by the potential for isolation is that service providers fall outside of "communities of learning" and the sharing of good practice which is essential to the development of more effective services. Taking advantage of their independence from the mainstream employment system, many NGOs innovate and develop their own methodologies for working with clients, which can in some cases be a major advantage: NGOs offer a personalised service flexible enough to be adapted to the needs of the people they are working with. However their lack of connection to mainstream services can also have its dangers. Not all NGOs are aware of good practice methodologies, for example, which results in them either appearing to "reinvent the wheel" or repeating problems which have been identified elsewhere. Where they do not form part of a wider delivery structure, NGOs can also be dominated by certain individuals who develop a strong leadership style. Such individuals can develop a strong local profile, and indeed Eberts (2003) has highlighted the important role that such dynamic leaders are able to play within local development through motivating staff, inspiring the recipients of services and building informal partnerships based on a shared vision. However, such leaders can also make projects vulnerable in the long-term, and lead to service provision becoming potentially paternalistic in character.

The gap between labour market supply and demand

A further problem arising from the relative fragmentation of provision at the local level is the lack of communication between organisations involved in supply and demand. Rath has stressed that it is vital that the labour market context, and in particular the local "opportunity structure" is taken into account when developing local initiatives – otherwise immigrants risk being prepared for jobs which do not exist.[16] Given the speed of local labour market change it is crucial that organisations are aware of the latest labour market demands so they can accurately guide immigrants towards employment routes that are most in demand. While this may seem self-evident, it is apparent that supply side organisations (training institutions, NGOs) often operate without up to date information about labour market needs, providing relatively generic labour market advice, without adequate information or understanding of the longer term needs of the local labour market. This can lead to an un-necessary focus on the perceived "deficits" of the immigrant (their personal confidence and generic job search skills for example) rather than on ensuring that immigrants understand and can respond to local demand. NGOs in Spain often focus on "employability" and ensuring that immigrants are work ready, rather than directly accessing jobs and workplacements. While this may be because immigrants are not yet ready for work, it may also be due to organisational deficiencies which prevent NGOs from effectively linking with local employers. Likewise Italian training organisations often seem to be driven more by institutional priorities than by local needs.

Remaining in close contact with the local labour market is not only important to providing specific training to meet skills gaps, but also to monitoring the ongoing relevance of tools and instruments in times of labour market change. Some question whether apprenticeships, which are at the heart of post-compulsory vocational training for immigrants in Switzerland, are less suited to the work environment than they were once were. It is suggested, for example, that apprenticeships are perhaps more appropriate to employment in manufacturing and trades, and less suited to an economy based on information technology and both high and low-skill services. This may be adding an additional barrier to the labour market for immigrants whose education is concentrated in the dual apprenticeship based system.

It is clear that bringing on board employers (both private and public) at the local level is crucial to improving labour market knowledge in the longer term. The advantages of such a demand led approach are clearly demonstrated in a number of the local areas reviewed by the study. However, in many countries, this may take some time. It is therefore important that local stakeholders also find alternative ways to fill their knowledge gap through communicating with local organisations that are most aware of economic and labour market trends. The case studies reveal that intermediary organisations such as colleges can play an important role in linking employers with other stakeholders. In both London, and in Canada, local colleges are central players in the provision of bridging courses that support access by immigrants to sectors where skills shortages exist. In the United States, efforts in this area have gone one step further, taking into account forecasting of future economic growth areas. As part of the federal level High Growth Strategy, one stop shops have been developed at the local level which guide immigrants into a set of high growth occupational areas.

Regional authorities have also in some cases started to look at immigration as a way of contributing to wider regional economic development objectives. In addition to the bilateral arrangements established between Trentino and Bucharest outlined above, the Region of Lombardia also promotes training programmes in countries of origin, aimed at providing specific skills to meet regional needs. Various small scale courses have been organised by the region in Tunisia, Slovakia and Moldavia, with eighteen Tunisians and fourteen Slovaks being trained in construction skills in 2005, for example. The CVs of the participants have been catalogued on special on-line databases allowing employers in Lombardia to examine and call candidates as needed.

Working towards better coordination

In the face of the complexity and relative fragmentation of delivery for support to immigrants in many local areas, some experts have begun to question whether mainstreaming is a more effective means of service delivery. Mainstreaming can allow local areas to avoid a grants based culture (with its associated short-termism and bureaucracy) and unnecessary proliferation of actors in the same field, by encouraging core local institutions to take into consideration the needs of newcomers in their wider programmes. The relative benefits of mainstreaming language training are evident in the Italian context. In 1997 a major reform of the adult education system resulted in the development of "permanent local centres for adult education" with the assignment of elementary and middle school teachers to adult education. The local authorities covered by the study (excluding Trento which operates its own system) rapidly responded to the new national programme, ceasing to sponsor third sector language classes for immigrants and starting to work with the new centres to coordinate language, literacy and middle school certification for all. The courses offered by the third sector were slowly eliminated through better coordination and competition from the official educational structures. Reliance on a national public system has solved the problems of a lack of consistent certification and the uncoordinated supply of language courses which often resulted in duplication.

In London, the education and training system is relatively flexible, so rather than local initiatives developing new training courses they often refer immigrants to mainstream services. Access to education and training, is facilitated by a relatively open system offering a wide range of opportunities for lifelong learning. However it is recognised that refugees may face difficulties in comprehending and navigating the complex system and RETAS provides a range of guides aimed at refugees, including a "Handbook on Education for Refugees in the United Kingdom" (2004), providing an overview and introduction to the system, and including sources for further information. Similarly, in Trento in Italy, CINFORMI sees its role as facilitating access to existing services rather than supplying a specially targeted version of the same service to an exclusively immigrant population. It is in this spirit that the centre does not offer, for example, support for immigrant entrepreneurs, but rather orients immigrants towards existing services.

In some cases local areas have gone further in the direction of mainstreaming to target all local residents in their strategy to promote integration. The municipality of Mataro in the province of Barcelona in Spain, for example, has developed a broad "citizenship plan" based on a shared notion of citizenship for the whole community: the plan has been developed under the auspices of a special council made up of 35 representatives of municipal groups, citizen groups, and immigrant associations, and explicitly states that all mainstream programmes must welcome new arrivals. To achieve the objectives of the new plan, the town council has proposed fourteen action programmes including the provision of information to vocational guidance (facilitation access to information and services); and a programme for aiding job integration (with professional training and integration of those with particular difficulties). The benefit of such a strategy is that it involves the whole community in creating a positive and welcoming local environment for immigrants and a shared notion of citizenship.

Whereas mainstreaming services can improve coordination, however, it can also reduce flexibility and innovation. Immigrant integration is a particularly diverse area of policy, and it is an area where policy makers are still learning about the most appropriate mechanisms. Because of this the local level can be particularly effective when it encourages diverse approaches and innovation. One particularly effective solution to support innovation at the local level is the development of a seed-funding system or local "innovation grant". In Winnipeg, Canada, the Manitoba Immigrant Integration Programme has been used to fund a variety of different pilot programmes, including the Winnipeg-based Credit Union scheme and the Early Childhood Educator Qualifications Recognition Programme identified above.

The *Diputació de Barcelona* (provincial government of Barcelona) in Spain has also been particularly successful at accessing national and European funding to encourage innovation. Approximately two hundred of its municipalities are currently carrying out some work with immigrant groups, although the most activities are occurring in municipalities where there is a high concentration of immigrants. The *Diputació* supports the sharing of the results of innovative projects, and encourages other municipalities to adapt successful programmes to their own localities, using tools such as methodological guides.

Mainstreaming also threatens to remove the sheltered individualised "one-stop-shop" support which can be provided by smaller organisations such as NGOs. The CASI model in Madrid has overcome this by developing a strong mainstreamed approach which also benefits from both the innovative nature of NGOs and their ability to provide individualised support. The entire region of Madrid is covered by CASI initiatives and all the local NGOs work to similar goals and methodologies, leading to a consistency in provision. There is a degree of inbuilt flexibility in the programme, however, with block grants being allocated to each CASI. Within certain constraints, this grant can be used as the CASI sees fit, and the two CASIs in Fuenlabrada and Ciudad Lineal had developed a number of innovative projects, including a guidance project for immigrant parents on the education system, and a project to tackle gang culture through developing alternative activities for young immigrants, including dance programmes.

Outreach projects are another way of combining the professionalism of mainstream services, with the more innovative and individualised approaches provided by local service providers such as NGOs. In London, for example, the Somali Women's Group ICT Training Project in Hillingdon works in partnership with Uxbridge College, to provide training at a local community centre. Staff from the college provide tutorage at the community centre which is in close proximity to an estate where many refugees live and many project participants are refugees. In this way the women can learn in an environment which is comfortable to them whilst also obtaining more specialised help. It is felt that refugee and community organisations in London could perhaps do more to ensure that qualifications gained in the community setting are followed up by courses in more mainstream environments, however, to support the bridging of refugees into the wider community.

Partnerships

Local "place based" or territorial partnerships have been developed in many local areas as a mechanism for reducing the isolation of individual stakeholders, supporting innovation and encouraging mainstream organisations to adopt integration-based approaches. In Canada, the Toronto Regional Immigrant Employment Council is an obvious example of the benefits of bringing a number of different stakeholders to tackle the common issue of integration, bringing NGOs, employers, unions, policy makers around the same table to produce both innovative programmes, and to stimulate the emergence of more permanent mainstream institutional change. As the cities in Canada differ significantly, both in terms of the local labour market and the local immigrant population, a "place-based" integration programme was considered to be especially important. The partnership grew initially out of the Toronto Summit which involved high level stakeholders in developing a city based vision and predicting key issues that would affect the city in the years to come. In Québec, likewise, each sub-region has a council of labour market partners, unions, employers and community groups who work together on local integration issues.

In London, a number of the community organisations supporting refugees are coordinated by wider partnerships bringing together a mix of social and economic partners. The Renewal partnership in West London was set up under the United Kingdom's Single Regeneration Budget using a grant of GBP 6 million (approx. EUR 8.9 million), and levering in a further GBP 10 million (approx EUR 14.8 million). It covers six different boroughs in West London, involves a number of partners including refugee groups, local authorities, local career guidance services (Connexions), the West London Learning and Skills Council and the Association of London Government. It also has a major public sector employer (the Ealing National Health Service Primary Care Trust) as its accountable body. The aim is to support refugees in West London through funding projects, linking labour demand and supply, building the capacity of refugee community organisations, and conducting research and mapping exercises. The Renewal partnership stresses that an integrated, partnership approach is crucial for tackling refugee integration, as it involves tackling a series of long-term problems that are interlinked and cannot be dealt with in isolation. The partnership considers that, in particular, it is vital that social integration factors are viewed alongside economic integration and are addressed in genuine partnership with refugees. Renewal provides a degree of continuity for RCOs within a field dominated by short-term funding programmes, and a degree of capacity building support, which can be time intensive and require assistance over a number of years. The ultimate aim of the partnership, however, is to create a step change in the way all public services respond to the needs of refugees.

Partnerships at higher governance levels are also important. The region of Madrid has used a partnership approach to draw up multi-annual strategies for integration across the Madrid community, involving a wide variety of local partners such as experts in immigration from Madrid's universities (who form a technical support team), representatives from all programmes oriented toward immigrants, and representatives from different ministries. The aim is to use the partnership approach to bring together theory and practice. A strong element of reflexivity is built into the approach through feedback from the various partners, and the creation of awareness in the different departments of the regional administration is an important part of the planning process.

In London, in order to facilitate the development of a strategic co-ordinated approach to refugees, the London Development Agency and the Regional Skills Partnership has established LORECA (London Refugee Economic Action) as the lead body on employment, enterprise and training for refugee and asylum seekers. The agency, funded by the London Development Agency, the Learning and Skills Council and the European Social Fund, has already developed a complex guide to services in London, aimed to support the development of "route maps" for refugees to guide them through the relatively fragmented local services. The partnership is also able to speak authoritatively with government, employer bodies, funding organisations, training providers and professional bodies about the needs of this target group. The guiding principle of LORECA is "strategy not delivery".

Partnerships can be particularly useful in supporting greater coordination *between* governance levels. In Canada, there are a number of provincial and territorial agreements in place, and the provinces and territories are consulted on federal programmes. Despite this, it is still felt that there is room for increased communication between the federal, provincial and local levels of government to improve coordination and joint planning and all the provinces are currently working on this. In addition, TRIEC has established an "Intergovernmental Relations Committee" in Toronto to bring policy makers together to discuss integration issues. It is the first time the departments have sat down together to develop a common research tool on integration, analysing gaps in services, and looking at over supported, and under supported areas in the locality. The meetings allow people from different jurisdictions to have regular frank exchanges in a "safe environment". In Quebec, the establishment of regional action plans and the development of regional conferences involving mayors and municipalities as part of the provincial integration strategy "Shared values, common interests" is also a clear step towards developing a multi-level governance approach to this issue.

Inter-service agreements are a further way of ensuring cooperation on the issue of integration. Also in Québec, the Ministry of Immigration and

Cultural Communities and the Ministry of Employment and Social Solidarity signed a three-year agreement in 2004 to promote the job market integration of immigrants and visible minorities. Through this agreement, the departments seek to combine their efforts to optimise their respective activities in order to promote the social and economic integration of newcomers and to harmonise their activities to ensure a continuum of services, measures and programmes between the two departments. In the Montréal area, two service harmonisation agreements have also been signed between local employment centres and Immigration-Québec services for the north and south parts of the Island of Montréal to improve immigrant services. The main purpose of these harmonisation measures is to enhance the quality and speed of services to immigrants in order to accelerate the job integration and retention process.

Developing complementary services between different regional and local governance institutions is particularly important in view of the different competences often held by these institutions. While the municipality of Milan is tackling complex integration issues through its responsibility for governing the heart of an industrialised province, for example, it does not have responsibility for labour policy, which is held by the province. This issue has been addressed via the evolution of a comprehensive Pact for Employment involving eighteen different stakeholders. The municipality, which is normally excluded from an active role in employment services, thus became the coordinator for a wide range of initiatives including attracting and managing European Social Fund resources. In Barcelona, territorial employment pacts have also proved effective in enabling local authorities to work together over administrative boundaries to tackle labour market issues affecting immigrants. The relatively independent status granted to the territorial employment pacts as also allowed these partnerships to work on helping undocumented immigrants who are otherwise excluded from public sector support.

Coalitions or partnerships were the main vehicles used as part of the three year pilot Building the New American Community initiative. Each area developed a public-private partnership that reached across levels of government and included a broad array of non-governmental organisations, as well as institutions and individuals from many different segments of society including refugee- and immigrant-serving organisations, business associations, faith-based organisations, and neighbourhood and social service providers. In each case the coalition was assisted by a national team of policy analysts, advocates and researchers from the National Conference of State Legislatures, the National Immigration Forum, the Southeast Asia Resource Action Centre, The Urban Institute, and the Migration Policy Institute.

A Migration Policy Unit review of the lessons of the BNAC initiative (2005) found that it was crucial that partnerships extend beyond the "usual suspects" to engage mainstream policy makers and institutions, acting as "coalitions of change". They found that engaging such institutions allowed them to "slowly effect changes in laws, rules, practices and norms of organisations and official institutions, which may have been formulated decades before a new wave of immigrants arrives in a city". Part of this process involved a need to "deepen the expertise of the public servants who administer the myriad programmes that will drive the pace of integration" (Fix, Papademetriou and Cooper 2005).

Thematic partnerships, which look at the issue of immigration but are not necessarily territorially based, are also useful tools, particularly in view of the fact that they can stimulate activities at the local level. The role of partnerships in "catalysing" action at lower governance levels was apparent in a number of the local initiatives reviewed in Winnipeg, for example. Both the Winnipeg-based credit union scheme and Early Childhood Educator Qualifications Recognition Programme developed because their lead actor had participated in partnerships focused on issues facing immigrants, which galvanised them into action.

Prioritising limited resources

Another important issue effecting actors at the local level is the resources available to support integration. There is significant variation in the resources available to local areas to integrate immigrants, both between and within the countries participating in the study. Canada, for example, allocates a relatively high amount of resources to integration through its provincial programmes, however this varies between the provinces and their specific agreements with the federal government. In 2005-06 the per capita allocations for Ontario and Manitoba were approximately CAD 850 (EUR 590) and CAD 1 200 (EUR 835) respectively, whereas in 2004-5 Québec received CAD 3 800 (EUR 2 646) per immigrant. These differences mainly result from independent negotiation procedures between each province and the federal level and are subject to change.[17] Spain similarly allocates different resources to integration depending on the locality and region, with regions such as Madrid, Catalonia and Andalusia allocating greater resources because of the higher concentration of immigrants in these areas.

The general resources available to a local authority can also have a significant effect on the iniatives taken forward, with localities which have strong economic development and more significant local budgets evidently possessing the means to develop more ambitious projects than poorer localities. The types of initiative being taken forward by the two municipalities of Mataro and Santa Coloma de Gramenet in Barcelona, Spain, for example, reflected differences in their resource base, with Mataro benefiting from a higher degree of economic development and therefore higher business rates. Indeed, Zapata-Barrero (2003) reports that in fact many local institutions in Spain lack the necessary financing and infrastructure to enable effective policy implementation. The central administration has recently taken action to address this situation by developing a new cooperation framework for the management of a "Support fund for refugees and the integration of immigrants, as well as for their educational reinforcement". The fund was created in 2005 as a tool to establish a cooperation model between the general administration of the state, the autonomous communities and local councils, with the purpose of promoting and strengthening public policies in these fields and, consequently, reinforcing social cohesion. As part of the framework, 50% of the overall funding allocation to the autonomous communities was required to go to projects that had been devised and delivered locally in 2005, falling to 40% in 2006. In Italy, some local authorities are also hampered in their attempts to promote integration through a general scarcity of resources, with the municipality of Milan, for example, being forced to compete with neighbouring local authorities for a limited amount of resources to provide services for employers. Projects such as the Milan territorial employment pact are important in drawing down funding in this respect.

Given that NGOs often provide the "front-line" of services to immigrants it is within these organisations that financing issues become most apparent. The sustainability of funding for NGOs was a concern across all the participating countries, with local actors reporting not only continual efforts to access and renew funding, but also low wages and long hours, which threatened to create "burn-out" in staff. In Spain, much of the work done by NGOs at the local level is reliant on volunteerism, private donations and European Union grants in addition to funding from the central administration. European funding in particular is less likely to be available in the future given the new financial priorities of the EU following enlargement. In London, many RCOs are competing for similar sources (*e.g.* from the European Social Fund, from a fragmented public sector, from lottery sources) for limited and unstable funding. In view of the important role of philanthropy in the United States and Canada, there is perhaps scope for greater effort by large employers and employers' organisations to fund training and work-experience initiatives in Europe, especially since they stand to benefit from the outcome. However, the very instability associated with current activities is often felt to undermine the clarity and consistency that the private sector needs to see before committing resources.

Deciding on the timing and intensity of interventions

Given the limited resources available at the local level, a key question facing local actors is where should resources best be placed? Should funding be distributed widely so that support is available for every immigrant? Or should funding be channelled into relative intensive schemes that produce greater long term integration for certain groups?

Evidence from the case studies shows that in order to create longer term labour market integration a relatively focused and intensive approach is needed – cheaper interventions which are not specifically targeted at an immigrant's skills level and aspirations have lower long-term success. In Canada, for example, TRIEC have analysed the use of resources in the Ontario region and found that the majority of funding goes into low intensity support (see Table 1.4) which is relatively unsuccessful in terms of supporting immigrants into appropriate employment. The most effective programmes (such as "career bridge" and subsidised employment placements) produce more effective results, with over 80% effectiveness in placing people into jobs, however they are relatively resource intensive and so not widely accessible. Within the Career Bridge scheme, for example, only 10% of the over 1 200 candidates who have registered their interest in the database have so far been allocated an internship.

Table 1.4. **Differentiating high resource and low resource activities**

Low resource activities	High resource activities
• Job search • Confidence building, help with social networking • CV preparation • Short-term training • Basic language training • Mentoring	• Work experience programmes • Medium to longer term "bridging" training in medium-high skills areas • Recognition of qualifications gained abroad • Projects to tackle discrimination in recruitment procedures • Training in home countries to meet local skills gaps • Higher levels of language training, including occupationally specific language use

Source: OECD LIILM Project.

In the main, the emphasis on short-term support found in Ontario is reflected across the other case study countries. Both the performance management systems of funding programmes (with their emphasis on quick outputs), and in some cases employment service regulations themselves encourage local initiatives to support rapid access to employment for immigrants, which may ultimately produce short term labour market participation as opposed to longer term integration. While local initiatives in Italy have some success in placing immigrants into work, for example, success stories in integrating immigrants into quality employment with the same conditions for immigrant workers as for Italians, are rare. Similarly, London experiences problems of a grants based culture where local projects respond to the requests of funders to produce short term outputs, as opposed to working towards longer term gains. Where more intensive interventions do exist they tend to be relatively small scale, leading to a relatively negligible impact on the overall integration of immigrants into the labour market.

An additional factor which encourages local organisations to provide relatively short term programmes is their wish to prevent immigrants from being outside of the labour market for too long. Local stakeholders in Canada warn against investing in support which will take immigrants out of the labour market for lengthy periods. In the Canadian context timing is particularly important as the likely period of re-training necessary to meet professional skills requirements can be significant. The employers represented on the TRIEC partnership in Toronto emphasized that the sooner that a immigrant comes into professional employment after arrival, the better, and similarly stakeholders in Winnipeg pointed out that if a immigrant has not found employment in their own field within two years, then it becomes more difficult to re-enter their sector. Awareness of such attitudes has led some local providers to respond pragmatically when developing programmes of immigrant support. In Montréal, for example, JEM advises immigrants to retrain for lower skilled but available positions in the short term, rather than sticking to their profession and undergoing several more years of studies outside of the labour force. A different approach is taken in the regional programming developed by Emploi-Québec where one of the stipulations for financial assistance is that training courses are related to the individual's previous field of studies.

Local stakeholders in other countries also argue that it is best to get immigrants into employment quickly and then "back-fill", avoiding time-intensive periods in education and training. In London, for example, despite the recent policy emphasis on language acquisition, there is a commonly held view that the stress should be on ensuring individuals have sufficient language ability to function in a specific workplace environment as soon as possible, rather than ensuring maximum language competence if this delays entry to the labour market. In this context, initiatives which blend employment placements and training are particularly valuable, as are training schemes devised by employers as part of workforce skills upgrading strategies (see for example OECD, 2006b). In Montréal, for example, the regional labour market training programme has recently included a commitment to work with Emploi-Québec on the delivery of language training to employed persons. Where external training is necessary, modular training courses which allow immigrants to quickly build on their existing skills are also particularly important.

Targeting

One mechanism for influencing the intensity and effectiveness of interventions without necessarily increasing the length of the intervention is to ensure that actions are accurately targeted to a migrants needs. It is evident that in many local areas integration policy is becoming increasingly sophisticated in recognising differences within groups of immigrants and actively responding to such differences. For example, despite the overall reluctance of Spanish policy makers to single out particular groups in the population to receive support, the *Diputació de Barcelona* has developed an interesting project to identify particular "incidence groups" within the population, reflecting the different barriers which are faced by specific types of individual to the labour market. Participants in the programme underwent an occupational analysis of strengths, weaknesses, potentials and barriers before identifying appropriate actions to support their labour market integration. At the CASI project in Fuenlabrada, Madrid staff have also identified a model for identifying people at different stages of work readiness, developing a three-fold approach that has proved useful in directing resources toward those most in need. For immigrants with the highest employability (people with work permits and professional skills) the emphasis was on immediately finding a job or appropriate occupational training. For those with lower employability – generally women with children who have no Spanish and who are socially isolated – the focus is on social and personal development training, instruction in how to read maps and manage public space, and language and literacy classes.

All the CASI projects in Madrid worked with a high percentage of women as a group particularly vulnerable to exclusion. This focus on women was also common elsewhere in the case study countries in reflection of their lower employment and higher unemployment rates. The particular issues women face include relative isolation from support due to arrival through family reunification programmes (where immigrants often do not receive the same sort of support to enter the labour market), lack of qualifications and experience due to discrimination in the country of origin, and concentration in certain sectors vulnerable to the informal economy and high temporary employment, such as the domestic economy.

Other initiatives targeted the immigrants who had the highest skills levels and employability. The initiatives reviewed in Canada, for example, in many cases focused on the highly skilled due to the specific recruitment of this group to Canada through the national selection system. Targeting immigrants with particularly high employability can have the advantage of allowing local initiatives to present a particularly positive face to employers, promoting immigrants as a potential "resource to be exploited" rather than a problem to be solved. However there is also the danger that imposing too many selection criteria before admission can lead to "creaming" or "screening" effects, with projects helping those most easy to help, neglecting those that perhaps have more need of support. In Switzerland, one question facing the vocational schools working with young immigrants is how much they can invest in the education of students whose lack of previous education means that they need intensive help. The dilemma is that if vocational schools carry out direct intensive integration with the most intractable cases it is on the one hand costly and on the other hand uncertain of success. Output based performance management systems can in particular encourage screening effects, by encouraging service providers to work with the people for whom they are most likely to achieve a positive output.[18] This situation is at least partly mitigated in Canada by the fact that NGOs are able to access more general funding (for example from charitable organisations such as the United Way) which is not tied to outputs, and can therefore be used flexibly to support immigrants needing longer term support. However NGOs in other countries do not always have recourse to such a flexible funding base.

Some initiatives target immigrants differently depending on whether they were newcomers or are already second or third generation immigrants, reflecting the different barriers experienced by these groups. Definitions are important here – in the United Kingdom the fact that the majority of children of immigrants born in the United Kingdom are British citizens[19] means that they are automatically targeted differently in local programmes. In Switzerland, even the third and fourth generations of immigrants are still classified as foreigners if they do not have access to Swiss passport (which is not uncommon) and this has resulted in a certain blurring of target groups at the local level. While the vocational school in Neuchâtel focused on recent young immigrants and identified that they were often highly motivated to succeed (reflected in their naming the pre-apprenticeship course "JET"), another project helping both first and second generation immigrants categorised both generations as having motivational problems. Such differences in approach may be subtle but are reflected in both the way that immigrants are treated, and the messages given out to others. Indeed, the recognition of the high motivation of the young immigrants participating in the JET programme meant that they have now developed a reputation as a particularly dynamic and successful group, increasing their positive reception in the vocational school itself and within local companies.

When supporting second or third generation immigrants, local initiatives often focus on providing support at a young age, to prevent exclusion later in life. In Spain, the local development company in Santa Coloma de Gramenet saw the relative isolation of immigrants as a key factor leading to the underperformance of their children in the education system: there is a 40%

school failure rate in the municipality. They have therefore supported the promotion of inter-culturalism in schools, encouraging children to learn about the different languages, cultural and ethnic practices in the community. They also foster exchanges between sports clubs and families to increase mutual understanding. Similarly, despite the fact that the children of immigrants tend to perform relatively well educationally compared with their native counterparts in the United States and Canada (see Reitz, 2003), Norwalk Community College is particularly concerned about the performance of the children of first generation immigrants and has developed the "ACTS for children programme" which gives priority to tackling early childhood education and youth gang membership. The project uses a partnership approach involving the mayor, school superintendent, teachers union, head of city housing authority, and local chamber of commerce among others, to addresses concern about an achievement gap amongst local students in the Norwalk Public Schools and to cultivate successful learners from birth.

Table 1.5 below provides a summary of different types of support given based on the length of time which immigrants have been in the country (from newcomers to second or third generation offspring).

Finally, a number of local initiatives target their activities by focusing on particular ethnic groups. As noted above, it is felt by some that working with individual communities can allow an understanding of the specific types of issue likely to affect these communities in accessing employment (e.g. the nature and structure of the labour market in the country of origin, particular cultural and religious practices, and particular issues of racism and discrimination). There are some concerns, however, that such policies can ultimately create competition between different communities and therefore be divisive.

In France, Spain and Switzerland, local policy makers have attempted to get around such problems by targeting particular local neighbourhoods (where immigrant communities may be concentrated) rather than specific ethnic groups, and indeed some localities avoid directly targeting immigrants at all in their policies. A key feature of Zurich's cantonal policy on integration, for example, was to treat the problems experienced by immigrants as "problems of exclusion" rather than necessarily "problems particularly experienced by immigrants". Indeed some experts warn against "racialising" or "culturalising" exclusion as a social phenomenon, arguing that when people associate poverty with people from particular backgrounds and cultures, they forget that they are actually looking at poverty as an issue. In Europe, for example, migration has to be seen in the context of the high rate of unemployment in some European countries, and the existence of "urban poverty sinks" in which both native born people and immigrants become concentrated. A key issue in relation to such "urban sinks" is visibility, and one of the factors identified as

Table 1.5. **Targeting by length of time in the country**

Length of time in country	
Newcomers	2nd/3rd generation
Language training	Outreach training projects in local communities
Job search support and general orientation guidance	Projects which seek to reintegrate demoralised and disenfranchised groups
CV preparation	
Providing advice and information on good practice to employers on employing newcomers	Projects to improve employment rights and conditions, and tackle the informal economy
Occupational language training	Projects to tackle racism
Skills audits and prior learning assessments	Initiatives to reduce isolation in certain communities
Recognition and validation of qualifications gained abroad.	Projects aimed at the children of immigrants to support educational attainment.
Mentoring projects	
Supported workplacements and career bridging programmes	Positive action projects
	Mentoring projects and support/guidance with career progression

Source: OECD LIILM Project.

leading to the recent disturbances in the suburbs in France has been the housing of poorer groups on the outskirts of cities, out of sight of wider society. This lack of exposure and the "racialisation" of the issue combine to prevent the wider population from looking for effective solutions.

The role of national actors: creating a supportive policy environment

It was apparent in all the countries under study that the national policy context had a significant impact on the ability for regional and local actors to support the integration of immigrants. Not all local stakeholders felt that they had the required support from the national level to take forward the integration agenda locally. Indeed, local actors often appear to develop effective integration approaches despite, rather than because of, national policies and programmes.

A strong national policy environment is important in a number of different areas. Horizontal communication at the local level is not the only tool to ensure greater matching between supply and demand: vertical communication is also important. It is difficult, for example, for local actors to have a significant impact in supporting integration if the overall intake of immigrants coming to the country does not have the appropriate profile and skills to meet labour market demand. In Canada for example, a number of local stakeholders expressed concern regarding the national "human capital" model which recruits highly skilled graduates, when their local labour markets feature lower skilled and vocational job vacancies. They point to high levels of frustration amongst highly qualified immigrants who had been recruited to Canada on the basis of their professional skills, but have ultimately been forced to accept a lower skilled job. While not necessarily recommending that the model itself should be changed, it is evident that the emphasis on "adaptability" which is at the heart of the human capital model needs to be better communicated to future immigrants.

Strong communication between local/regional and national policy makers is particularly important because of the variation which exists in labour demand. Harris (2003), for example, has argued that cities have particular skills needs which are not always reflected in national immigration policy, and he finds it hypocritical that governments restrict the integration of low skilled workers needed to perform basic services, which leads to a large proportion of this immigration occurring on a clandestine basis. In order to reduce such mismatches and optimise the contribution of immigrants to the labour market, it is important that the legal framework and selection programmes for immigration take account of local variation in demand.

Canada has attempted to better match immigrants to their host regions by introducing accords and "provincial nominee agreements" which allow the provinces to have some control over the selection of immigrants coming to their region. The Québec Accord provides the province with a strong determining role in immigration selection, and the ability to search for certain skills amongst new migrants, particularly the ability to speak the French language. Québec is responsible for determining the number of immigrants it wishes to receive, selecting most immigrants (excluding refugee claimants and family class immigrants), and designing and implementing its own immigrant welcome and integration programs. Québec's selection process is currently being updated to take better account of the needs of the Québec labour market, particularly for technical workers. Manitoba has more recently developed its own very active provincial nominee programme; however the province has downplayed their emphasis on skill requirements, partly because the labour market is changing too fast to allow effective forecasting, and partly because their highest priority is now generating loyalty to the region, in the context of a loss of immigrants to neighbouring provinces. Skills requirements have been superseded by ties to friends and family already living in the province.

The new register for unfilled jobs in Spain represents a way of ensuring that all regions have their say in identifying skills in demand and directly recruiting immigrants to these positions, due to the strong role given to the regional authorities in updating the register. However, the register only records current unfilled vacancies, rather than forecasting those which will have high future demand, and the competitive job market means that they are largely at the low skilled end of the spectrum. In Italy there is some freedom for regions to influence the number of immigrants they receive through the national quota system and it is clear that some local areas are better at having a voice on this issue than others: Trento, for example, has been particularly effective at arguing for increased numbers of immigrants, helped by the fact that the province has been able to prove that it can effectively manage immigration at the local level, effectively matching supply and demand and ensuring that temporary workers did not stay in the region at the end of their contracts.

A further particularly important area for national policy support is anti-discrimination legislation. Local actors need recourse to strong and easily understandable anti-discrimination legislation when tackling negative attitudes amongst employers. In the United Kingdom for example equal opportunities legislation has been important in preventing discrimination against visible minorities amongst immigrants and their offspring. Spain is currently following in the United Kingdom's footsteps, having recently set up a "Council for the Promotion of Equal Opportunities and the Non-Discrimination of Persons due to their Racial or Ethnic Origin", along the lines of the United Kingdom's Commission for Racial Equality. In contrast, Switzerland's legislation against racial discrimination is relatively weak and this has undermined the ability of local actors to encourage employers to take recent immigrants into employment. A number of the local vocational schools reported discriminatory attitudes towards their students for example but given the lack of a federal anti-discrimination law, the only tool open to them was persuasion, often on an individual basis.

National policy makers can also support local and regional actors through developing an overarching strategy and consistent policy message on the value of immigrants to society. Such policy messages are crucial for building positive attitudes towards immigrants, in the context of the increasing scale and importance of migration and, in some cases, negative media coverage. In Canada, for example, particular care has been taken to ensure that positive messages are sent regarding new migrants, deliberating separating the services provided to immigrants from generalised welfare provision in order to dissociate immigration from issues of welfare dependency. The widespread use of the term "newcomer" rather than immigrant can be seen to be synonymous with this approach, given that the term immigrant can in some cases be seen to have negative connotations. The new integration strategies in Spain and Switzerland, whilst still being fully introduced, also bode well in terms of creating a common positive commitment towards integration.

It is particularly important that the national level avoids contradictions in their policy messages, in order to avoid confusion amongst both the relevant actors and local employers. While both the United Kingdom government and the Mayor of London promote a pro-diversity message, in which immigration and diversity is hailed as an opportunity, national policy makers have recently restricted access to employment and training for asylum seekers in order to prevent asylum from being seen as an effective economic route into the country. While this may be laudable, it has sent a negative message to both NGOs (who are frustrated because asylum seekers lose skills and credibility with employers during the asylum process) and employers who are left confused about the legality of employing different types of immigrant. Transparency is of key importance for employers as the legislation involved in employing immigrants can seem like a potential minefield, with complications regarding permit regulations being seen to increase the perceived "risk" involved with taking on recent immigrants.

Decentralisation can produce a particular confusing picture about the value given to immigrants in the economy and wider society. In Switzerland, differences between cantonal policies on integration have led to a patchwork of policies, and seemingly arbitrary differences in the reception conditions for migrants. The federal level is currently attempting to rectify this through the development of a strong decentralised framework for its integration policy that ensures that each canton has an "integration delegate", that is a cantonal official whose job it is to maintain links with federal policies and agencies and to act as a focal point for the development of integration policies. In Neuchâtel, for example, the integration delegate has taken on a wide range of responsibilities, supporting training programmes for young immigrants and working with local housing authorities to attempt to avoid concentrations of specific groups in certain buildings and housing areas. The policy of introducing integration delegates is relatively new and it is therefore difficult to evaluate how it is working in all cantons; however the value of sharing approaches at cantonal level can already be seen to be working to some extent in the education sector, with vocational school heads participating regularly in inter-cantonal discussions on integration.

In the context of decentralisation, it is also important that the national level supports the transfer of innovation and good practice from one region to another, particularly in the case of the emergence of new regions which have not dealt with immigration issues before. In the United States, demonstration grants have a useful role in "seeding" the development of experimentation and good practice and encouraging other areas to learn from the results of such pilots. The Building the New American Community initiative, for example, was implemented in three cities which have not experienced immigration until recently. This has allowed both the piloting of new approaches in areas which has a relatively "blank slate" in terms of policy development, and at the same time the import of good practice from elsewhere.

Conclusions and policy recommendations

Drawing on the analysis of the practices reviewed and of the gaps identified in current provision, a number of policy recommendations emerge for local, regional and national policy makers working in the field.

At the local and regional levels

Ensure strong coordination and signposting between institutions

It is vital that strong linkages are maintained between organisations working at the local level to support the labour market integration of immigrants, so as to ensure that immigrants are adequately signposted towards new sources of help in their transition from immigration to employment.

Such coordination may require the establishment of partnerships and networks where stakeholders can regularly meet and share experiences. Such governance mechanisms should be managed in a way which allows local actors to share good practice and information about potentially complimentary services, and to develop common involvement in policies and programmes, while also discussing ways of better adapting mainstream programmes to the needs of immigrants.[20] Partnerships need to be set up with relatively long term goals in mind, as integration is often only a gradual process. The Renewal partnership in London is one example of a partnership which has enabled local actors to overcome the short-termism inherent in grant funded programmes, through taking a longer term strategic view.

Given the number of stakeholders active in this area it is obviously important that partnerships are inclusive. However, perhaps the most important partners to bring on board are employers. Allowing employers to have an active role in designing policies and programmes will ensure that these policies and programmes meet demand needs, and are attractive to other local employers, as demonstrated by the TRIEC partnership in Toronto. Employers can therefore play a crucial role in reducing the gap between labour market supply and labour market demand at the local level. Acquiring the involvement of such stakeholders, and maintaining this involvement, can be hard work, and partnerships need to be well managed, and in many cases be directed by a specific partnership coordinator with responsibility for attracting and maintaining a broad membership. The BNAC coalition in Nashville, for example, started off with a strong representation of private sector actors due to the leading role played by the local chamber of commerce. However when the chamber representative left the coalition the partnership had problems maintaining the involvement of demand side stakeholders, which undermined its overall success (Migration Policy Institute, 2004). Where it is not possible for employers to be involved, it is essential that local stakeholders at least make reference to local labour market information in planning and reviewing their activities, including current and forecasted skills needs and gaps.

It is likely that the priority given to the linking of local labour market supply and demand within immigration/integration policy may increase as regions experience greater skills gaps and local labour markets become less self sufficient in the context of demographic change. Regional and local bodies are already beginning to consider immigration as a potential opportunity within their economic development strategies in Canada, Italy, and some United States cities. In Canada, the desire to attract new immigrants is an essential part of Winnipeg's development strategy, and the basis for their provincial nominee programme. Québec has also been actively trying to attract immigrants over a long period, and other Canadian provinces are following suit: in 2005, mayors from Nova Scotia, New Brunswick, Prince Edward Island, Newfoundland and Labrador participated in a conference to find new ways of making their region more attractive to immigrants, who are becoming essential to local economies undergoing ageing and negative demographic change.[21] Cleveland Ohio is one example of a city in the United States where there is an explicit strategic goal to attract skilled, foreign-born nationals.[22] In Italy, local stakeholders have gone further by developing particular bilateral relationships with local areas in sending countries to ensure that future migrants are trained in skills that will be helpful to the local Italian economy, such as in tourism. Such bilateral arrangements could usefully be adopted elsewhere, particularly as they can assist regional planning in both sending and receiving countries (see also OECD, 2004c).

Support innovation, in addition to the mainstreaming of good practice

The promotion of innovation and flexibility is crucial in a policy area which is relatively new to many localities. The case studies highlight a number of tools for supporting innovative approaches, including territorial and thematic partnerships, and the provision of flexible budgets (as in the case of the Madrid CASI programme) and local grants for innovation (such as the Manitoba Immigrant Integration Programme Fund). However it is also crucial that innovations are mainstreamed so that, ultimately, all local services are better adapted to the needs of immigrants. A key finding of the Building the New American Community initiative was that integration is a process that involves an entire community, not just its most recent members. While immigrants need to change and adapt to their new society, it is also important for society to respond and to bring about systemic change to adapt to the needs of immigrants. Ultimately real improvement in the integration of immigrants may come not from specific local initiatives but from mainstream developments such as improvement in employment conditions and the regularisation of the informal labour market, reduction in obstacles to entering professions, the availability of modular courses which are available throughout the year and which assess and take account of prior competences and skills, better childcare, affordable housing and the elimination of pockets of deprivation, and job centres which seriously take into account peoples skills and qualifications (whether gained locally or abroad). Giguère (2004), for example, has found that although partnerships and projects fill policy gaps and bring benefits to the local community, new services may be more effectively delivered by public institutions. Discussing the role of new services developed by partnerships in particular, he argues that "delivery of services in parallel with the public sector reduces the scope for the latter to learn new techniques of working and improving its methods. The impact on governance is greatest when the partnership helps the partners, including the public services, to do a better job". As such, partnerships in the field of immigrant integration may be most effective when they focus not on the delivery of new services, but on becoming "agents of change". In order to support such mainstream developments it is imperative that local stakeholders establish processes for mutual learning, and for the transfer of good practice from other local areas and regions, and that lessons are transferred to the national offices of more centralised services and institutions.

Target resources effectively

It is important that local actors consider the appropriate balance between providing support for all new immigrants, and developing more targeted and intensive approaches that enable more sustainable labour market integration for certain groups. Targeting immigrants according to skills levels, employability and other factors would seem to be a valuable approach to maximising the effectiveness of limited funds for at least some elements of the immigrant population. Indeed, Siemon (2003) has described the benefits of "turning away from the watering can principle" in order to focus on key areas of local opportunity. However targeting can also generate problems of "screening" (i.e. helping those who are more likely to find employment) and, at the other extreme, stigmatisation.

The timing of interventions is particularly important. It is crucial that local actors provide support which does not keep immigrants outside of the labour market for too long a period. Modular training courses, which allow immigrants to quickly build on their skills to meet local labour market needs, are vital, and should be available at all times of the year, so that immigrant are not penalised by their date of arrival. Stakeholders in the Canadian provinces and in London have developed strong modular "bridging" schemes to retrain immigrants who had qualified overseas, although these are necessarily small scale due to the cost of implementation. The Neuchâtel social enterprise in

Switzerland also offers a strong model for providing short modular courses for low skilled immigrants in competences that are in demand in the local economy.

Initiatives which involve training in combination with employer placements would also seem to be particularly successful, at least in reference to the paid work experience or "immersion" schemes that have been developed in Canada. The Swiss apprenticeship model is another, and in this case long established, mechanism for supporting the training of young people whilst they are in employment which immigrants can take advantage of. However in developing such schemes it is crucial that immigrants are guided towards employment placements that reflect their previous skills and career aspirations. To achieve real success, such interventions also require the strong cooperation of local employers. Ensuring such involvement may require that local actors build up trust and good communication over a period of time, as can be seen with the Toronto based Career bridge scheme and the Québec "Immersion" programme in Canada. The development of initiatives to highlight good practice amongst employers is also a useful mechanism for speeding up employer participation. Finally, evening classes are also helpful in that they allow immigrants to undertake training while working or engaged in job search.

Support the recognition and development of skills

It is important that local areas support the recognition and development of skills, even if they are relatively low level, through skills audits, and the recognition of competencies and qualifications gained overseas. This may involve subsidising access to national or regional mechanisms for the recognition of qualifications. Local initiatives in Canada and in London have built on the work of national and provincial recognition bodies to develop innovative schemes to help those trained aboard to re-qualify. The Swiss social enterprise in Neuchâtel also provides a strong example of the development of certificated courses for more discrete technical skills that are relevant to local employers, whilst also recording information about generic skills and competences which help to build up employer trust.

In knowledge based and service based economies language is particularly important, and local areas should ensure that high level language courses are available that meet the needs of employers. In many cases such language needs will be generic, and may include training in the overall communication skills essential to knowledge or service based economies. However, language courses that are occupationally specific should also be readily available to allow immigrants to develop a vocabulary that prepares them for specific workplaces. Such occupational language courses have been successfully piloted in London and also in the Canadian provinces.

Tackle the informal labour market

In Spain and Italy, the involvement of immigrants in the informal labour market is a major barrier to supporting effective labour market integration. While the local branches of centralised institutions often have difficulty working in this area, it is apparent that local NGOs can make some in-roads into helping illegal immigrants into regularity, even if they cannot tackle the wider informal economy per se. In addition, it is clear that employers associations and unions can prove effective in improving conditions for immigrants within employment sectors which fall victim to informal practices and poor employment conditions, as demonstrated by the local farmers association in Lleida, Spain and the 32BJ Services Union in New York. Local actors should attempt to engage such organisations in this process where possible, while recognising that in many cases unions will be a reluctant partner in activities which appear to disadvantage their existing members.

Support wider networking

In countries where much employment is advertised informally, such as Italy and Canada, projects to support wider social networking are crucial to enabling immigrants to access work. A number of the case studies, especially in Spain and Italy, showed the value of "softer" support activities which allowed immigrants to build contacts as a means of establishing routes into employment. Mentoring in particular received support across many of the participating countries. Again this requires strong involvement for private sector employers and the identification of mentors in a immigrant's chosen field and specialism. Local actors should be prepared to support such "soft" initiatives, even if the outcomes of such work can be relatively long term, and therefore difficult to monitor.

Promote employment within the public sector

The local level should pursue opportunities for the integration of immigrants through public sector employment, taking advantage of the fact that the public sector frequently represents a significant sector in the local labour market. The public sector can implement equal opportunity and integration within areas which its own agencies control, acting at the same time as a demonstration to others. At the same time, given that non-nationals are also recipients or clients of state services, increasing the representation of non-nationals within the public sector may increase the appropriateness of the services on offer.

Think in the longer term

It is important that local integration policy is developed with a long term view. Particularly in countries that are newly experiencing immigration, it is important that local policy makers think beyond helping newcomers and also take into account the needs of their offspring. Ensuring that all local children have equal access to good quality education, and that extra assistance is provided to the children of immigrants where needed (in the form of extra language teaching, for example) will prove crucial to preventing their future exclusion from the labour market. Local projects to promote inter-culturalism amongst the young, as developed in Santa Coloma de Gramenet for example, will also be an important means of producing future social cohesion.

At the national level

While the local level provides significant added value in supporting the integration of immigrants, it is apparent that there are a number of areas where local activity will result in inconsistency and duplication. In view of this, national policy makers need to:

Ensure that the national immigration system meets local labour market needs

It is likely that improving forecasting of local skills requirements and the clear communication of these needs to national policy makers will be crucial to better planning the integration of immigrants in the future. In order to develop effective immigration selection policies, national policy makers need to be aware of current and likely future skills demands, and how these vary between different localities, according to both sector and types of position. To be effective, this process will require consultation and planning with local and regional stakeholders involved in economic development, training and labour market policy.

It is also essential that local actors are able to communicate a clear picture of the extent of the informal economy in their locality and the types of sector and position that this involves. Supporting managed migration into these sectors at the national level may be the most important mechanism for reducing the informal employment of immigrants in the longer term, an issue which local actors felt was crucial, but over which they had little control. The recent regularisation in Spain and the introduction of the INEM employment register to communicate regional skills needs are examples of a proactive approach to dealing with this issue.

Develop a consistent overarching policy framework which includes robust anti-discrimination legislation

It is important that national policy makers establish a positive framework for integrating immigrants, and that employers are sent clear and coherent messages about the value of employing immigrants. This includes highlighting the economic value of immigration and developing strong anti-discrimination legislation to support work with employers at the local level. In order to be effective anti-discrimination strategies will need to be built through collaboration and consultation with employer organisations, with a role identified for such organisations in coordinating and disseminating information at an early stage. National policy makers should also be particularly careful to ensure that immigration legislation is transparent and not confusing to employers.

Develop open and flexible mainstream programmes

It is important that the national level takes responsibility for developing mainstream employment and training systems that are flexible and open to immigrants. The particular mechanisms adopted by local service providers such as NGOs in order to adapt to immigrant needs (flexible opening hours and evening appointments, job search support targeted towards particular groups according to gender or skills levels) could usefully be adopted by the mainstream public employment service. The studies also show the value of adult education systems which are flexible enough to respond to training needs on a modular basis throughout the year and which provide the opportunity for immigrants to quickly take stock of their skills and build on them to meet local labour market needs. The need to provide more flexibility in the management of key policies (labour market, training, education) so that they are better adapted to local conditions and better coordinated to respond to multifaceted problems has already been documented in previous work (Giguère, 2005).

National policy makers and employers are increasingly recognising the need for consistent and broadly accessible systems of language provision which meet the higher levels demanded by employers, and offer training in the specific language requirements of occupations and sectors. Establishing such provision may involve discussing language requirements with employers on a sector by sector basis, and establishing a minimum threshold below which language training should be publicly available. The language benchmark system in Canada, for example, has been a useful instrument in raising the game in the provinces, with Manitoba, Québec and Ontario working towards widely available language training at a standard which is in line with the needs of employers.

Ensure that the local level is adequately resourced to support integration

In view of the importance of relatively intensive and targeted approaches at the local level it is important that adequate resources are available to local actors taking forward this increasingly important policy area. Funding needs to be long term, to avoid the current situation where many local stakeholders are competing for, and managing short term funding programmes. Local stakeholders are also hampered by the frequent fragmentation of responsibility for integration policies and programmes between different national government institutions, which results in their having to manage a number of different funding streams on the ground. Greater coordination between national ministries to produce joint funding programmes would help alleviate unnecessary bureaucracy at the local level.

Aside from resourcing issues, it is also vital that local organisations have the skills and capacities to deliver programmes to support immigrants given that they are the "front-line" in supporting immigrant integration. Training and capacity building should be provided to local stakeholders where possible in effective tools and instruments, particularly in areas where immigration is relatively new, or which are experiencing particularly high rates of immigration. Again mechanisms for sharing good practice between local stakeholders, and between regions and countries are crucial.

Support the recognition of prior competences and qualifications

While important work is being carried out in a number of countries at the provincial and local levels on the recognition of qualifications and prior competences, it is clear that in order to avoid duplication and provide consistency, national or federal systems of skills recognition will be crucial in the longer term. In the Canada and the United States, World Education Services, a private sector organisation, are already providing certification services to a variety of different states and provinces, and the NARIQ network performs a similar role in Europe. However these organisations are limited to the valorisation of qualifications gained overseas, rather than attempting to assess broader skills and competences. National systems for the valorisation of non-formal learning and prior competency testing (of which an inventory is currently being gathered at the European Commission[23]) are likely to play a key role in supporting integration by allowing immigrants to demonstrate their skills in a systematic way to employers without recourse to extra training or work experience. In developing such national systems, it is important that provinces and regions, territories, professional organisations and unions are given a strong role at an early stage to ensure that they result in qualifications that are as widely recognised as possible.

1. FROM IMMIGRATION TO INTEGRATION: COMPARING LOCAL PRACTICES

Ensure a strong culture of evaluation

A further area where national stimulus is needed is in creating a strong culture of evaluation. A key problem arising out of all the case studies was the lack of strong evaluation data available for the initiatives visited. In order to understand the effectiveness of local initiatives and their longer term impact on immigrants it is vital that policy makers create and maintain a strong culture of accountability and evaluation. This is particularly important in what is a relatively new policy area in many countries, where innovative approaches are being tried and tested. Canada stands out as being the most successful of the participating countries in ensuring the collection of evaluation data, making it possible for organisations such as TRIEC to assess the relative value and cost of different integration approaches in supporting labour market success. At the same time it needs to be recognised that evaluation and monitoring can be more difficult when local initiatives are delivering "soft" interventions. Outputs should be broad and long-term enough to avoid encouraging local policy makers to deliver short-term responses to integration issues without investing in longer career progression for immigrants or encouraging more systemic change. Mechanisms for negotiating the dilemma faced by local policy makers in ensuring accountability whilst also ensuring flexibility are discussed in more detail in the OECD publication, *Managing Decentralisation; A New Role for Labour Market Policy* (OECD, 2003b).

Evaluation should be complimented by the greater monitoring and collection of data on the performance of immigrants in the labour market as a whole, preferably using a longitudinal approach, and providing data by country of birth, country of birth of parent, ethnicity, gender and postcode. In Canada, the Longitudinal Immigration Database (IMDB) has been crucial to supporting the recent recognition in Canada that immigrants are no longer closing the gap with the native population in terms of labour market performance as rapidly as was previously the case.[24] Such information can be extremely important in stimulating research into changing barriers and needs that will ultimately lead to revised approaches to supporting immigrants at the local level.

In conclusion

A key finding across the country studies carried out within the framework of this study is that the integration of immigrants at the local level is principally a question of the *management of change*. Effective labour market integration depends on helping immigrants to manage the rapid changes which are happening in their own lives, whilst at the same ensuring that the local community itself evolves and responds to changes in its population and in its urban fabric. This has a number of implications for an effective governance response. Immigrants need clear road maps to guide them between the various services which will support their transition into a new life. This means that there is a need for well coordinated and accessible local services which will meet their various needs, either through the mainstreaming of migrant-friendly approaches across all local services, or else the provision of one-stop shop approaches specifically aimed at immigrants. In either case, some immigrants need a wide variety of support mechanisms to establish themselves in local society, requiring a multi-stakeholder approach. Strong ongoing communication is needed between the different partners involved to ensure the development of complementary and connected services, and to ensure the sharing of good practice.

While the mainstreaming of services to immigrants can support a clear and consistent approach to the problems experienced by immigrants, the changing nature of both the migrant population and local labour markets also means that local governance systems have to support innovation and be flexible enough to accommodate change. In the case of immigration this means changes in the migrant population, in national and regional migration policies, and in the labour market itself. The speed of this change in many countries has meant that local authorities are still learning about the most appropriate mechanisms to assist immigrants. Because of this the local level can be particularly effective when it is given a flexible budget that supports diverse approaches and encourages innovation. Effective mechanisms then need to be put into place to harness and circulate good practice so that in can be incorporated into mainstream practices. It is evident that the best examples of local practice combine both mainstreaming and innovative approaches which are responsive to dynamic local conditions.

Another factor which calls for the management of change is the changing experience of immigrants across generations. Immigrant integration is a multi-generational process, with "upward mobility" for the first generation often largely being the move to a different country itself, where this results in an associated increase in quality of life. Normally, there is a tendency for the second generation to progress further in the labour market and become fully integrated at a degree commensurate with their competences and skills. However different countries, and within them, different local areas, perform very differently in relation to this progression. Education systems and school to work transitions are particularly important in this process, as the children of immigrants can become concentrated in the lowest educational strands and within the worst schools, where their parents suffer from relative poverty and exclusion. The second generation also confronts a series of other obstacles, including discrimination (particularly in the case of visible minorities) and in some cases de-motivation and disaffection. The fact that different barriers are faced by different generations means that different approaches need to be adapted for different target groups, and it is crucial that policy makers develop strong approaches which go across the generations.

Immigrants do not have the opportunity to become professionals at immigration; they are in every sense "amateurs", particularly as people often only migrate once in their lifetimes. However local actors do have the opportunity to build their professionalism in receiving and integrating immigrants, developing what Gächter (2005) calls "reception competence". It is clear from this study that we are only beginning to understand the issue of integration can best managed and governed at the local level, particularly as it relates to ensuring access to the labour market. The participating countries have developed a variety of promising initiatives, but barriers and challenges remain which prevent the effective linking of immigrants to sustainable opportunities that match their skills and aspirations in the labour market, and which offer appropriate career progression. Programmes of exchange and mutual learning between local areas on mechanisms for overcoming such challenges can only be beneficial in the future to help improve overall integration outcomes, and maximise the benefits of immigration for local economies.

Notes

1. See for example the work by the OECD's Employment, Labour and Social Affairs Committee and its Working Party on Migration on labour market integration in Germany and Sweden (OECD 2006c and 2006d forthcoming).

2. See Reitz (1998) who argued that interurban differences in the performance of immigrants on the labour market are relatively significant in the United States, although less so in Canada and Australia.

3. Federal Reserve Bank of New York estimate based on the United States Census 2000.

4. Skilled immigrants have employment rates which are systematically higher than immigrants whose studies have been of shorter duration, implying that education facilitates entry into the labour market. However the difference in their participation rate with the native population remains negative in almost all countries where graduates of higher education are concerned. See OECD (2006a).

5. The Conference Board of Canada makes the assumption of equivalence between the education and work experience of foreign-born individuals with that of native-born residents.

6. Domestic services account for 12% of immigrant employment in Spain and 13% in Greece (OECD, 2006a).

7. In Quebec government services deal directly with immigrants while delegating certain more specialised services to NGOs through partnership agreements.

8. Canada and the United Kingdom in particular have a strong history of anti-discrimination policies and legislation, with Spain and Italy, as countries which

are newly experiencing significant immigration, also beginning to increase their focus on this area. Spain, for example, has recently developed a new "Council for the Promotion of Equal Opportunities and the Non Discrimination of Persons due to their Racial or Ethnic origin", based at least partly on the model of the Commission for Racial Equality in the United Kingdom.

9. Indeed immigrants have been found to be under-represented in the public sector more generally in OECD countries, although immigrant women have relatively high participation levels in the sectors of education and health in some countries (OECD, 2006a).

10. See for example Kenan Malik's ongoing debate with Sir Bernard Crick, JCWI Quarterly Bulletin, Winter 2004-5.

11. Funded by the public employment service, Service Canada.

12. The Canada-Ontario Immigration Agreement (21st November, 2005). See www.cic.gc.ca/english/policy/fed-prov/ont-2005-agree.html.

13. *British Medical Journal Career Focus* (2003), 327:28.

14. In Quebec the provincial government has responsibility for integration and labour market policy.

15. Manitoba has in fact recently received federal funding from HRSDC (Human Resources and Skills Development Canada) to address this issue.

16. See for example Kloosterman and Rath (2001) and Rath (2002).

17. Source: Citizenship and Immigration Canada (CIC). CIC points out that comparisons of per capita allocations between Canadian provinces can be potentially misleading as figures may not accurately reflect the needs of the immigrant population (based on factors such as mix) and the capacity of immigrant serving organisations in different provinces.

18. See OECD (2003b) which describes how performance management systems can have the effect of privileging short-term unemployed individuals over individuals with less skills and work experience.

19. Children born in the United Kingdom are automatically British citizens as long as their parents are legally settled in the country. If only the father is legally settled then the parents need to be married prior to the birth.

20. For further information about good practice in relation to local forms of governance and partnership see OECD publications, *Local Partnerships for Better Governance* (2001) and *New Forms of Governance for Economic Development* (2004b) and *Local Governance and Drivers of Growth* (2005b).

21. The Atlantic Immigration Conference (May 15th-17th 2005) hosted by The Atlantic Mayors' Congress, Halifax.

22. See, for example, www.city.cleveland.oh.us/government/departments/econdev/CIC_Task_force.html.

23. See the website of the European Inventory for the Validation of Non-Formal and Informal Learning: www.ecotec.com/europeaninventory/.

24. Immigrants used to catch up with their native counterparts in terms of labour market position (salary and level of post) in their life time, while this is no longer the case. Reitz (2003) also makes the point that in 1980, a male immigrant who had been in Canada for 10 years earned an average CAD 1.04 for every dollar earned by

his Canadian-born counterpart. By 1990 the parallel figure had dropped to CAD 0.90 and by 2000 to CAD 0.80.

Bibliography

Aldridge, F. and S. Waddington (2001), "Research findings and recommendations: NIACE Asylum Seekers' Skills and Qualifications Audit Pilot Project", East Midlands Development Agency's Skills Development Fund (47/00).

Bloom, M. and M. Grant (2001), "Brain Gain: The Economic Benefits of Recognizing Learning and Learning Credentials in Canada", Conference Board of Canada, Detailed Findings.

Bram, J., A. Haughwout and J. Orr (2002), "Has September 11 Effected New York City's Economic Growth Potential?" The Economic and Policy Review, Federal Reserve Bank of New York www.newyorkfed.org/research/epr/02v08n2/0211bram.pdf.

Considine, M. (2003), "Local Partnerships: Different Histories, Common Challenges – A Synthesis" pages 253-272 in OECD, *Managing Decentralisation: A New Role for Labour Market Policy*, OECD, Paris.

Dumper, H. (2002), "Missed Opportunities: A Skills Audit of Refugee Women in London from the Teaching, Nursing and Medical Professions", The Mayor of London in Association with the Refugee Women's Association.

Easton, G. (2003), *British Medical Journal Career Focus* 2003, 327:28.

Eberts, R. (2003), "The US: Leveraging Government Capacity through New Forms of Governance", pages 301-311 in OECD, *Managing Decentralisation: A New Role for Labour Market Policy*, OECD, Paris.

Fix M, D. Papademetriou and B. Cooper (2005), "Leaving Too Much to Chance: a Roundtable on Immigrant Integration Policy", Migration Policy Institute.

Forschner, M. (2003), "Austria: Bridging Economic Development and Labour Market Policy" p 325-332 in OECD, *Managing Decentralisation: A New Role for Labour Market Policy*, OECD, Paris.

Gächter, A. (2005), "Migration Challenge – Austria as a Country of Immigration: Considerations on the Active Reception of Migrants in a Society with Increasing Diversity"; p. 23-34 in: Heraus Forderung Migration, "Beiträge zur Aktions- und Informationswoche der Universität Wien anlässlich des 'UN International Migrant's Day'", Abhandlungen zur Geographie und Regionalforschung Nr. 7, ed. Susanne Binder, Gabriele Rasuly-Paleczek und Maria Six-Hohenbalken, Vienna.

Giguère, S. (2004), "Building New Forms of Governance for Economic and Employment Development" in OECD, *New Forms of Governance for Economic Development*, OECD, Paris.

Giguère, S. (2005), "The Drivers of Growth: Why Governance Matters" in OECD, *Local Governance and Drivers of Growth*, OECD, Paris.

Harris, N. (2003), *The Return of Cosmopolitan Capital – Globalization, the State and War*, IB Tauris.

Heckmann, F. and D. Schnapper (2003), *The Integration of Immigrants in European Societies. National Differences and Trends of Convergence*, Stuttgart, Lucius and Lucius.

Holzer, H.J. (2005), "Economic Impacts of Immigration Testimony to the Committee on Education and the Workforce", US House of Representatives, 16 November 2005.

House of Commons Work and Pensions Committee (2005), "Department for Work and Pensions: Delivery of Services to Ethnic Minority Clients", HMSO, London.

International Labour Organisation (2004), "Towards a Fair Deal for Migrant Workers in the Global Economy", 92nd Session.

Keane, M.J. and M. Corman (2001), "Tripartism, Partnership and regional integration of policies in Denmark" in OECD, *Local Partnerships for Better Governance*, OECD, Paris.

Kloosterman, R. and J. Rath (2001), "Immigrant Entrepreneurs in Advanced Economies: Mixed Embeddedness Further Explored", for *Journal of Ethnic and Migration Studies, Special issue on Immigrant Entrepreneurship*, Vol. 27, No. 2, April 2001, pp. 189-202.

Malik, K. and Crick, Sir B. (2004-5), "Letters", *Joint Council for the Welfare of Immigrants Quarterly Bulletin*, Winter.

Migration Policy Institute (2004), "Final Report on the Building the New American Community Newcomer Integration and Inclusion Experiences in Non-Traditional Gateway Cities".

Moore, D. (2004), "Migrants as Mediators in a Comparative Perspective" Chapter 7 in Penninx, R, Kraal, K, Martiniello, M and Vertovec, S eds. *Citizenship in European Cities Immigrants, Local Politics and Integration Policies*, Ashgate, Aldershot.

OECD (1998), *Immigrants, Integration and Cities: Exploring the Links*, OECD, Paris.

OECD (2001), *Local Partnerships for Better Governance*, OECD, Paris.

OECD (2003a), Department of Employment, Labour and Social Affairs "Background Note 2003(9)", OECD, Paris.

OECD (2003b), *Managing Decentralisation: A New Role for Labour Market Policy*, OECD, Paris.

OECD (2004a), *Employment Outlook*, OECD, Paris.

OECD (2004b), *New Forms of Governance for Economic Development*, OECD, Paris.

OECD (2004c), *Migration for Employment: Bilateral Agreements at a Crossroads*, OECD, Paris.

OECD (2005a), *Trends in International Migration*, OECD, Paris.

OECD (2005b), *Local Governance and Drivers of Growth*, OECD, Paris.

OECD (2006a), *OECD International Migration Outlook*, OECD, Paris.

OECD (2006b), *Skills Upgrading: New Policy Perspectives*, OECD, Paris.

OECD (2006c forthcoming), *The Integration of Immigrants into the Labour Market: the Case of Sweden*, OECD, Paris.

OECD (2006d forthcoming), *The Labour Market Integration of Immigrants in Germany*, OECD, Paris.

OECD (2006e forthcoming), *Level of Education of Immigrants and the Labour Market: Estimating the Prevalence of Over-education*, OECD, Paris.

Penninx, R., K. Kraal, M. Martiniello and S. Vertovec (eds.) (2004), *Citizenship in European Cities Immigrants, Local Politics and Integration Policies*, Ashgate, Aldershot.

Ricerche e Progetti (2003), "Ricerca di mercato e analisi dei Servizi per il Lavoro rivolti alle imprese esistenti nella Provincia di Torino" , in *NotizieR&P – Ricerche e Progetti* 10, 2.

Rath, J. (2002), *Unravelling the Rag Trade: Immigrant Entrepreneurship in Seven World Cities*, Berg Publishers, Oxford.

Ray, B. (2003), "The Role of Cities in Immigrant Integration", Migration Policy Institute.

Reitz, J.G. (1998), *Warmth of the Welcome: The Social Causes of Economic Success for Immigrants in Different Nations and Cities*. Westview Press, Boulder, CO.

Reitz, J.G. (2003), "Educational Expansion and the Employment Success of Immigrants in the United States and Canada, 1970-1990", in J.G. Reitz (ed.) *Host Societies and the Reception of Immigrants*, Centre for Comparative Immigration Studies, University of California San Diego.

Reitz, J.G. and Y. Zhang (2005), "National and Urban Contexts for the Integration of the Immigrant Second Generation in the United States and Canada", University of Toronto.

Rogic, J and P. Feldman (2004), *Employment Resource Handbook for Refugee Engineers*, Education Action International, London.

Schneider, F and R. Klinglmair (2004), "Shadow Economies Around the World: What Do We Know?", Cesifo Working Paper No. 1167.

Siemon, H. (2003), "Germany: the Challenge of Taking an Integrated Approach in a Centralised Framework", p. 87-95 in OECD, *Managing decentralisation: A new role for labour market policy*, OECD, Paris.

Sassen, S. (2006), *Cities in a World Economy*, Pine Forge Press, Thousand Oaks, Calif.

Statistics Canada (2003), *Longitudinal Survey of Immigrants to Canada, Progress and Challenges of New Immigrants in the Workforce*.

Strategy Unit (2004), "London Project Report", Strategy Unit, Cabinet Office, London.

Sweetman, A. (2005), "Immigration as a Labour Market Strategy – European and North American Perspectives".

Zapata-Barrero, R. (2003), "EU and US Approaches to the Management of Immigration: Spain", Migration Policy Group, Brussels.

Chapter 2

Integrating Immigrants in Canada: Addressing Skills Diversity

by
Bob Birrell and Elizabeth McIsaac

> *Canada takes pride in being a "country of immigration"; however the rates of labour market integration for immigrants are less impressive today than they have been in the past. The decentralised employment service means that NGOs play an important role in labour market integration but they are hampered by bureaucracy associated with their reliance on a number of different funding streams. While the three Canadian cities of Montreal, Toronto and Winnipeg offer strong examples of innovative local practices, often based on partnerships with the private sector, there are concerns that current local interventions are too small scale to address the persisting reluctance by employers and trades organisations to accept qualifications and experience gained overseas.*

The Canadian context

Canada is a nation built on immigrants, and immigration is seen as closely intertwined with Canada's image of itself as a diverse, tolerant and multicultural nation. The result is a favourable setting for the public acceptance of a large immigration programme, and a generally welcoming environment for immigrants. However recent longitudinal surveys show worrying evidence that integration outcomes are not as positive now as they have been in the past. This chapter looks at the role of local initiatives aimed at the integration of immigrants in Canada, examining how such initiatives are linked to local governance structures, the broader context and policies for economic and employment development. It focuses on a number of case studies from Montréal, Winnipeg and Toronto in order to develop an insight into the mechanisms that are in existence to support the labour market integration of immigrants, setting these in the context of provincial and federal policies and governance arrangements. Given the emphasis within Canada's selection procedures on recruiting immigrants who are highly skilled, many immigrants come to the country with degrees and professional qualifications gained overseas, creating a particular context for local initiatives working in this area.

The Canadian social and political setting

The Canadian government and people are well accustomed to high flows of immigration. Since 1967 there has been rapid growth in the diversity of Canada's cultural communities when explicit discriminatory barriers to the selection of immigrants from non-European source countries were removed from Canada's immigration regulations. These communities include a large, non-white "visible minority". Canada has also been a pioneer in multicultural policies, which seek to assure immigrants that their cultures and contributions are welcomed and respected. Such policies were developed in response to the Royal Commission on Bilingualism and Biculturalism, which, while outlining the distinctive role of francophone culture within the Canadian landscape, left a void on the role and protection for non-British/non-French communities. The first multicultural policy, introduced in 1971, outlined federal multiculturalism, which would not involve an official culture, but would support a context of official bilingualism. Canada's position on multiculturalism was further entrenched in 1988 when it became the first country to introduce national legislation on multiculturalism.

Canada's business and public policy leaders are also supportive of immigration on economic grounds. There is widespread belief that if Canada is to compete in the global marketplace it must increase the size of its population. Immigration is considered to be crucial to resolving Canada's demographic imbalances. As a consequence of Canada's low fertility level and ageing population, labour force growth is expected to contract sharply. By 2011, it is expected that 100 % of net labour force growth will be derived from immigration (Canadian Labour and Business Centre, 2005).

The Canadian Immigration Programme

The Canadian system is highly decentralised,[1] and constitutional responsibility for immigration is shared between the federal government and the provinces. In practice, the federal government is the main player as regards policy and the administration of immigrant selection. Most provinces have agreements with the Canadian government, which, among other policy and resource issues negotiated, allow them to participate in the selection of immigrants to their province within the ambit of the federal programme. In the case of Québec, the Canada-Québec Accord Relating to Immigration and Temporary Admission of Aliens, more simply known as the Canada-Québec Accord, provides the province with a unique role in immigration selection (and the exclusive responsibility of welcoming and integrating immigrants who settle in the province). Under the terms of the Canada-Québec Accord, the government of Canada defines immigration categories, establishes selection criteria for family, and makes determinations regarding eligibility for family class and refugee status. Québec, on the other hand, directly selects refugees and independent immigrants from abroad.

Canadian selection priorities

Canada selects immigrants under three broad classes: economic (including skilled immigrants), family, and refugees. In 1993 the federal government initiated a public consultation process which was the prelude to new approaches in the immigrant selection process. The outcome was a recommendation that the priority in selection should be with education, experience, language skills, age and employability. It was argued that the previous system placed too much emphasis on intended occupation (CIC, 1994). The underlying rationale was that at a time of rapid structural change in the Canadian economy it was better to focus on generic skills. Those well endowed with "human capital" were thought to be best able to adapt flexibly to changes in the labour market. This priority has shaped the selection system since the second half of the 1990s and was reaffirmed in 2002 with the introduction of the Immigration and Refugee Protection Act and a revised point system.

Table 2.1 lists the factors currently utilised for assessing immigrants applying as skilled workers in the skill selection systems of the federal government and the Québec provincial government. The federal selection process now gives priority to applicants with high levels of education, language skills, job experience, age, arranged employment and adaptability. In the case of the education factor, 25 points is allocated to those with Masters Degree or PhD and 20-22 points to those with trade qualifications. Persons with a bachelor degree receive 20 points, those with a one-year diploma, 15 points, and those who have completed high school, 5 points.

Table 2.1. **Skilled immigrant worker assessment systems: Canada and Québec government points tests compared**

Canada	Maximum points	Québec	Maximum points
Education (high school – PhD)	25	Training	11
		Training – second speciality	4
		Training – preferred education	4
Language (English and/or French)	24	Language – French	18
		Language – English	6
Experience (1-4 years work experience)	21	Professional experience (6 mths-5yrs)	10
Age (21-49 years)	10	Age (20-45years)	10
Arranged employment (confirmed)	10	Employment – Have to pass Employability and Occupation Mobility (EMP) Grid to gain 8 points, 12 if Profession in demand, 15 if assured employment	15
Adaptability (spouse's education, previous study in Canada, previous work in Canada, arranged employment, relatives in Canada)	10	Spouse (Max 5 for training, 1 for professional experience, 2 for age, 8 for French language)	16
		Children (2 per child aged < 13, 1 per child aged 13-17)	8
		Financial autonomy	1
		Suitability	10
Maximum possible score	100	Maximum without a spouse (excludes suitability points)	96
		Maximum with a spouse (excludes suitability)	113
		Maximum without a spouse	106
		Maximum with a spouse	123
		Passing score (without Factor 4 – Suitability)	
		Unmarried applicant = 50 points	
		Married applicant = 58 points	
		If unmarried applicant obtains a score of 60 or a married obtains a score of 68, they may be exempted from personal interview	

In order to obtain points for language skills, applicants do not have to pass a professionally administered language test. The assessment of language skills is determined through internationally available language assessment tools: the International English Language Testing System (IELTS), Canadian English Language Proficiency Index Programme (CELPIP), or the *Test d'évaluation de français* (TEF, evaluation test for the French language), and points are awarded based on the level scored within these assessments.

Because of the emphasis on education and language skills, the federal system favours applicants with tertiary education. However, the federal selection system does not include an assessment factor that rewards those with skills in demand in Canada. The only priority given on these grounds is the points allocated to those who obtain a job offer before making their immigration application. The Québec government's selection policy, also outlined in Table 2.1, is similar except that it does include additional points to applicants whose skills are in demand. In addition, it gives priority to French speakers, and includes a demographic factor; that is, extra points for those with children, especially younger children.

Regarding other provinces, their role in selection is limited to the nomination of immigrants under the Provincial Nominee Programme (PNP), within the economic class. The province of Manitoba has been very active in implementing and developing the PNP, and has focused on immigrants with skills identified as in short supply, which are mainly technical and trade level skills. However those with existing links to the province (*e.g.* through family already living in Manitoba) are now being given increased priority. As Table 2.2 indicates, the Canadian immigration programme includes a family reunification programme that extends beyond spouses to include parents and grandparents, and a humanitarian programme, neither of which applies any skill or language assessment criteria.

Profile of immigrants

Over the past two decades, an increasing share of the immigration intake has come from Asian source countries, particularly China, India, Pakistan, the Philippines and South-East Asia. On the other hand, the number of economic immigrants arriving from Europe has fallen to comparatively low levels. There has also been a decline in the numbers from the more affluent Asian countries of Hong Kong, South Korea and Taiwan. In the case of Québec, there is a substantial flow from North Africa, owing to the priority given to French language skills.

A high proportion of those selected to enter Canada hold university credentials in engineering, IT and business (e.g. accounting, administration and marketing). Immigrants to Canada possess more years of tertiary

Table 2.2. **Canada, number of permanent residents by category**

Category	1995	1996	1997	1998	1999	2000	2001	2002	2003	2004
Spouses and partners	30 151	31 562	29 774	28 064	32 789	35 294	37 761	32 767	38 748	43 985
Parents and grandparents	32 998	24 545	20 153	14 165	14 481	17 768	21 340	22 228	19 384	12 732
Other family[2]	13 306	11 617	9 611	8 370	7 957	7 550	7 691	7 304	6 993	5 529
Total family	76 455	67 724	59 538	50 599	55 227	60 612	66 792	62 299	65 125	62 246
Skilled workers[1]	80 823	97 125	104 924	80 814	92 382	118 567	137 197	122 705	105 220	113 442
Other economic	24 831	27 403	22 689	16 644	16 755	17 700	18 489	15 133	15 822	20 304
Total economic	105 654	124 528	127 613	97 458	109 137	136 267	155 686	137 838	121 042	133 746
Total refugees	27 193	28 097	23 865	22 506	24 357	30 078	27 914	25 109	25 981	32 685
Others	3 567	5 724	5 022	3 637	1 245	508	246	3 794	9 207	7 147
Total permanent residents	212 869	226 073	216 038	174 200	189 966	227 465	250 638	229 040	221 355	235 824

1. Includes children.
2. Includes independents and assisted relatives.
Source: Citizenship and Immigration Canada, available at www.cic.gc.ca/english/pub/facts2004/overview/1.html.

education on average than do Canadian residents. In 2005, 50 % of immigrants over the age of 15 years who landed in Canada possessed a tertiary diploma or degree (CIC, 2006). The proportion of those with degrees coming under the skilled programme is even higher. According to the 2001 Canadian Census data, persons born overseas who had arrived in Canada over the preceding five years constituted 20 % of the degree-qualified Canadian resident workforce.

Immigrants to Canada have a high propensity to settle in cities, and three metropolitan areas in particular. In the years 2002 and 2003 almost half were locating in the Toronto region, with Montréal and Vancouver each receiving 13-15% (CIC, 2003). The only other major destination was Alberta, particularly Calgary, with around 7% moving to this province. However, the proportion locating in Alberta was higher in previous years. This trend is significant because it indicates that the level of labour demand is not the only factor shaping settlement location. The most important factor identified by recent immigrants is the presence of family and friends, and established immigrant communities (Statistics Canada, 2005). These may not coincide with locations where skill shortages are most severe.

Another key fact in determining where immigrants will locate within cities is affordability. Within larger metropolitan areas where housing prices are high, this has led to a high concentration of new immigrants in more affordable outlying suburban areas. In some instances this has led to the aggregation of migrants who are also coping with problems of high unemployment, with associated issues of social cohesion and the need for strategic service delivery planning. This type of localised poverty is relatively new in Canada, and was fully explored in the Toronto context following a review of the 2001 census (United Way of Greater Toronto and the Canadian Council on Social Development, 2004).

Employment outcomes

There is a consensus amongst Canadian scholars that immigrants arriving in Canada over the past couple of decades are not doing as well in gaining employment in their fields of qualification, or in the level of their earnings, as did their counterparts who arrived after the 1967 reforms. The main reason for this outcome is thought to be the situation in the labour market in the 1970s. At that time, demand for tertiary-trained persons was high, and the supply of locally trained persons was insufficient to satisfy this demand (Reitz, 2003). A striking summary of the situation is provided by a comparison of immigrant earnings with Canadian-born earnings. In 1980, a male immigrant who had been in Canada for 10 years earned an average of CAD 1.04 (Canadian Dollar) for every dollar earned by his Canadian-born counterpart. By 1990, the parallel figure had dropped to CAD 0.90 and by 2000 to CAD 0.80. For women, the equivalent figures were CAD 1.03, CAD 0.93 and CAD 0.87 (Statistics Canada, 2003a).

Canada's labour market is relatively buoyant[2] and for persons anxious for work, as is usually the case with recently arrived immigrants, a job can normally be found. The problem immigrants face is finding employment appropriate to their education and experience, and avoiding an increasingly pervasive situation of underemployment. These concerns are confirmed by the Longitudinal Survey of Immigrants to Canada, which examined the situation of immigrants in 2003, approximately two years after their arrival in Canada. The survey indicated that the great majority of immigrants selected through the skilled programme had found employment. However, almost 60% had not found a job in their intended occupation and were effectively underemployed (Statistics Canada, 2003b).

Barriers to immigrant labour force integration in Canada

The challenges that immigrants face in finding appropriate employment are sometimes complex and interrelated. The main barriers that immigrants themselves note, and that government and private sector echo, are explored below.

Canadian work experience

A frequent barrier cited in relation to the employment of immigrants is that employers are reluctant to take on professionals from countries where they have little knowledge of the experience and credentials immigrants bring with them. Employers themselves have identified immigrant professionals without Canadian experience, which serves as a proxy for credential and/or skills assessment, as a risk factor in hiring (Public Policy Forum, 2004). In fact, many employers prefer to hire local graduates rather than persons trained overseas because they are familiar with the standards of local university qualifications and are experienced in incorporating local graduates into their workforce.

One might imagine that, in a situation of labour shortage, employers would have to make the required adjustment to accessing a wider labour pool. There are reports of severe skill shortages in Canada. According to a study on long-term vacancies in small businesses, the Canadian Federation of Independent Business (CFIB) has found that the persistent shortage of qualified labour has challenged small business owners and threatens their potential to grow. When polled at the end of 2005, one-in-two small business owners in Canada (52%) mentioned employee shortages as an issue of concern for their business (Canadian Federation of Independent Business, 2006). Skill shortages are particularly evident within the booming oil industry in Alberta, where predicted shortfalls of skilled labour are expected to reach 100 000 workers over the next ten years. However, outside such employment hotspots, the current labour market for professionals in Canada is relatively balanced. Although demographic factors are increasingly being felt, for the most part, employers can currently fill skilled vacancies from Canadian-trained sources. A contributing factor is that enrolment levels in Canadian universities grew rapidly during the 1980s and again in the late 1990s (Association of Universities and Colleges of Canada, 2002). They are expected to grow strongly during this decade, fuelled by a surge in the population aged 18-24 and increases in higher education participation rates.

Credential recognition

Recently arrived immigrants holding professional and trade qualifications often face the hurdle of stringent credential assessment rules within their profession or trade. There is a wide range of such professions and trades where employment is not permitted until the assessment authority has approved the credentials and the individual has met all the requirements of licensure or certification. In Canada, regulation of trades and professions is under provincial jurisdiction, which means that each province/territory has its own series of occupational regulatory bodies setting standards and requirements for certification and licensure. In some cases there may be fast tracked recognition where mutual recognition agreements exist between professional bodies.

Certification and licensure is not generally a simple matter of submitting transcripts to credentialing authorities. Although processes vary by profession and trade, oftentimes candidates are required to sit examinations, and may be required to fulfil Canadian work experience requirements as well as language assessment requirements. The Canadian work experience requirement is a significant barrier as there are few examples of standardised programmes or opportunities for obtaining this experience. Many recently arrived skilled immigrants have to find employment in order to meet their living expenses. Because they are usually not eligible to work in their field immediately, they often have to take sub-professional or "survival" jobs. Thus, many find it difficult to undertake the training necessary for accreditation in their field or to find the kind of employment needed for full registration. This situation is further exacerbated the longer an individual is out of their field, as their chances of re-integrating into their profession becomes less likely over time.

The outcome is that many immigrant professionals struggle to gain employment appropriate to their education and training. Further, this may have longer term consequences, as Sweetman (2005) shows that the point of entry into the labour market is particularly important in determining long term career trajectories. There is a high degree of awareness about the problem in government and community circles within Canada. The Director of a community agency in Winnipeg, the Success Skills Centre, which serves about 300 professional immigrants a year has stated in evidence given to a 2003 Federal immigration inquiry that:

> Clients are not told abroad how long it really takes to settle in Canada and how long it will take to get their credentials recognised. Many an independent immigrant has told us that had they known it would take anywhere from four to seven years to re-write what they already know in order to work in their field, they would not have come. Maybe that's why we're not telling them abroad? (Feist, 2003).

Indeed, the situation is widely regarded as a crisis, and is regarded as a gross waste of talent from the point of view of Canada's potential economic productivity.

In 2006 the government of Canada budget announced CAD18 million over two years (approx. € 12.7 million) for a national agency for foreign credential recognition. The goal of the agency is to assist those with international qualifications to determine whether their credentials meet Canadian standards, ideally beginning the process overseas, while getting those who are trained and ready to work in their fields of expertise into the workforce more quickly.

Communication skills

Another significant barrier impacting labour market integration of immigrants is communication skills. Though English or French language skills are a requirement for selection as a skilled immigrant, the effective capacity of individuals is often well below what is expected by employers seeking professional or managerial level staff. The Federal Department of Citizenship and Immigration does accept responsibility for providing English/French language training (as does the Québec government, for French language training only) as part of the initial settlement services offered to immigrants. But these language programmes have in the main only focused on functional language levels, not labour market oriented, professional level skills. The province of Manitoba currently offers language skills up to level 8, using the Canadian Language Benchmark system which runs from 1-12. Québec offers instruction to level 9, although the majority of training is at the intermediate level. While the level of education of skilled immigrants has increased and the profile of immigrants has changed significantly over the past 20 years, language programmes have not kept pace. In response to this gap, new language programmes are now being developed at both the federal and provincial levels to raise the level of training to meet labour market requirements.

Discrimination and racism

Given the increasing representation of visible minorities among new immigrants to Canada, the issue of racism and discrimination has to be considered in their labour market experiences. NGOs that provide employment services to new immigrants consistently reference racism and discrimination as barriers to effective labour market inclusion of their immigrant clients. This may be expressed through recognition of credentials from some countries over others, accent discrimination, or preference for limited expressions of cultural difference. This may have longer term impacts. While there is a clear legislative framework that supports official multiculturalism in Canada, and public opinion is generally favourable to it, analysis of census data has shown that there is a disproportionate experience of poverty in Canada among racialised communities.[3]

Policy and programme delivery

Settlement policy

As noted above, the federal government sets the framework in relation to immigration policy (including target numbers), devises the selection criteria and procedures and undertakes the selection of immigrants for all of Canada except Québec, where the Québec government performs these functions for the province. With respect to settlement and integration policy and programming, the division of responsibilities is more complex. The federal government, through the Department of Citizenship and Immigration, provides for initial settlement services, and does so through the context of various agreements signed with individual provinces. In the case of Québec for example, the province is given full autonomy in the management and disbursement of the funds. Most other agreements allow for the federal department to have greater influence on the direction and management of the programmes.

The main focus of these settlement services is English and French language instruction. The objective is to ensure immigrants attain a functional level of English or French. As well, settlement services and limited programming for initial labour market entry support is provided through the Department of Citizenship and Immigration. With the exception of government-sponsored refugees, the federal government does not provide income support, or support for other settlement needs such as housing. The expectation is that immigrants will provide for themselves.

Labour market integration

With respect to Canadian labour market programming, most of the responsibility rests with the Federal Department of Human Resources and Social Development and with provincial ministries with responsibilities for training and employment. As with settlement services, the provision of programmes and services is determined by individual federal-provincial labour market agreements. Except for Québec, most labour market programming is made available through employment insurance funds, which require that an individual is entitled to benefits under the federal plan; that is to say, they have been employed in Canada and have paid into the fund. Consequently, most programmes and benefits under this plan are not generally available to newly arrived immigrants who do not have employment history in Canada.

The provision of programmes and services for labour market integration of immigrants is complicated in Canada because of the silo effect of policy and programme development. The discrete and clearly demarcated areas of responsibility and accountability between departments and ministries at both levels of government, federal and provincial, produce challenges in coordination vertically and horizontally. The government departments at each level are developing mechanisms to address this barrier and work is ongoing. However, currently the result for immigrants seeking to enter the labour market is that the services and supports they may require are not connected in a clearly identifiable system. The lack of coordination in the planning, development and delivery of immigrant integration and labour market services and programmes impacts directly on the experience of the immigrant.

Service delivery

The administrative arrangement for the delivery of migrant services varies among Canadian provinces. For example, programmes for language training or programmes to facilitate work experience with employers, are delivered by an extensive network of NGOs and other institutions, including colleges or universities in Ontario and Manitoba, while in Québec the province has a more significant role in service delivery. Many NGOs are the key players not only in providing basic language and job placement services but also as advocates for additional services. In each of the three provinces, NGOs are well positioned for such advocacy because of their local organisation, first-hand experience with the problems immigrants encounter and often their links with ethno-specific communities.

Selected local initiatives

The following section outlines and assesses local responses, initiatives and programmes designed to address barriers to the labour market integration of immigrants in Montréal, Toronto and Winnipeg, setting these in the context of the different provincial governance frameworks in Québec, Ontario and Manitoba respectively. The effectiveness of these local initiatives in addressing some of the key barriers experienced by immigrants to the labour market is then analysed in more detail.

Case study 1: Montréal, Québec

Around one fifth of the immigrants attracted to Canada are settling in Québec, the great majority of whom locate in Montréal. Nearly 60% of the immigrants settling in Québec are selected by the Québec government's Ministry for Immigration and Cultural Communities (MICC) through its skilled worker programme. Another 22% enter under the family reunion category and 18% as refugees. There are similar proportions by class settling in Montréal.

Table 2.1 above details the selection grid used by MICC to select skilled immigrants. Preference is given to French speakers and, as with the federal selection system, to those with university education. This approach is consistent with the human capital model employed in the federal system. However, unlike the federal system, the Québec system allocates points to those with labour market skills in demand in Québec.

The characteristics of the immigrants arriving in Québec differ from those settling elsewhere in Canada, in that a significant share (26.1 % over the four years 2000 to 2004) were born in Africa – primarily North Africa. Most of these immigrants are French speakers. Another 33.1% were born in Asia and 23.8% in Europe (MICC, 2005). As to their linguistic background, of those arriving in 2000 to 2004, 49.8% (55% in 2004) were French speakers (including about half of whom were both French and English speakers), another 16.9% spoke English only and the rest (33.3%) spoke neither French nor English.

Employment outcomes

Despite the relatively high proportions of immigrants settling in Montréal who hold university qualifications, the employment outcomes have been relatively poor. At the time of the 2001 Census, some 13% of persons born overseas were unemployed compared with 9.2% of the entire Montréal workforce. The situation is worse for recently arrived immigrants in Montréal. According to the Longitudinal Survey of Immigrants to Canada, of the immigrants arriving in Montréal in 2001, only 65% of those aged 25-44 had worked in any job by 2003, compared with 84% of those arriving in Toronto over the same period. The employment rate of these immigrants after two years in Montréal (that is, at the time of the survey in 2003) was 45% compared with 69% in Toronto. Of those who were selected as skilled immigrants in this 25-44 age group, the employment rate was 51%. Only 53% of the recently arrived skilled immigrants living in Montréal who had worked had found employment in their intended area of work (Statistics Canada, 2006).

The problems that immigrants in Québec face in finding employment mirror those identified in the federal context, and include difficulties in gaining recognition of overseas credentials. In the case of regulated professions, there are some forty-five professional corporations in Québec that manage entry into their respective fields. The requirements for licensure are sometimes complex, creating barriers for immigrant applicants. One unique aspect of the Québec context in Canada however, is the fact that the Office for the Professions in Québec (*Office des professions du Québec* – OPQ) makes sure that each of these professional regulatory bodies fulfils its function of protecting the public and exercises a function of control and supervision. The fact that the OPQ advises the government on improvements to be made to the professional recognition system provides an opportunity for addressing systemic barriers that exist for immigrant professionals.

Communications is also a problem for many immigrants, and this barrier is experienced uniquely in the Montréal context. Employers often require their staff to be bilingual in French and English because they usually have to deal with French- and English-speaking clients and customers.

Policy framework and programme responses

As outlined by the Canada-Québec Accord, as well as through a federal-provincial labour market development agreement,[4] all immigrant settlement services and all employment services are delivered by the province of Québec. The province is funded at a rate of over CAD 3 000 (Citizenship and Immigration Canada, 2004) per immigrant, by the federal government. The funds are directed to the central revenue of the province, not directly to specific programme allocations and are redistributed among the various departments that deliver immigrant integration services.

The publication of an action plan entitled "Shared Values, Common Interests" in May 2004 has highlighted the priority which the Québec government now gives to immigration and restates the Québec government's commitment to a sustained high immigration programme. Like the rest of Canada, the Québec government is keen to promote immigration as it is concerned about the long-term demographic implications of the province's low birth rate and about the impending retirement of a very large cohort of baby boomers. It acknowledges that concerted action – particularly between the various departments and organisations participating in immigrant integration – is needed to make its immigration programme work successfully, both for the immigrants themselves and the Québec community. To this end, the document lays out a programme of action around two goals: one being rapid and successful integration of newcomers into the labour market and the other to encourage harmonious intercultural relations.

In relation to the first goal, two pillars for action were recommended. The first concerned the establishment of an immigration policy "true to Québec's needs and values" (government of Québec, 2004). This is significant because it indicates a move away from the human capital approach to immigrant selection, which dominates federal immigration policy. The document calls for the establishment of guidelines "for selecting skilled workers based on Québec's present and future needs" and a directive to "match vacant positions in Québec with foreign candidates whose professional profiles meet the needs expressed". The second pillar concerned "Reception and lasting job integration." The actions proposed to deal with these issues included working with professional orders and education institutions in order to find solutions to the credential issue, the provision of personalised guidance for immigrants entering the labour market and advocacy programmes directed at persuading employers to be more open and accommodating in employing skilled immigrants. The plan has been accompanied by regional conferences involving mayors and municipalities and the development of regional action plans, and so embodies a multi-level governance approach. In addition, Québec has also taken action to counter job discrimination. For example, in order to help the region's employers recruit and retain immigrants and visible minorities, the Montréal office of Emploi-Québec (the provincial employment service) has worked together with a not-for-profit organisation *Mouvement québécois de la qualité*, to prepare a guide on good human resource management practices for companies that wish to or already hire multicultural employees.

The MICC is responsible for the delivery of language training and settlement services. French language training for newcomers in Québec is delivered through a programme for the linguistic integration of immigrants (*Programme d'intégration linguistique pour les immigrants – PILI*). It provides basic language training for new immigrants (in Canada less than five years) who do not have a sufficient level of French for living and working. In addition to basic French, there are also some occupation-specific courses available. This programme is delivered through colleges, universities and community agencies, though instructors are employees of MICC. Participants in PILI may apply for financial aid if they are taking full-time training and funding is provided for transportation and childcare costs. As a result, immigrants located in Montréal have excellent access to free language programmes but these usually take the immigrant only as far as an intermediate level. Customized courses and written French courses are available following the regular programme. In addition, francisation activities may take place in the workplace. The Ministry of Education, Leisure and Sport (*Ministère de l'Éducation, du Loisir et du Sport – MELS*) through its network of school boards, also provides adults, immigrants and anglophones, regardless of date of arrival with a French as a second language option. In Québec, government funded programmes are available only for French language training, although, as noted above, the labour market often requires English language skills as well.

Settlement services are delivered through a programme of accompaniment for new arrivals (*Programme d'accompagnement des nouveaux arrivants – PANA*), to facilitate the social and economic integration of new immigrants into Québec society. For 2005-06, MICC indicates that some 68 organisations in Québec (37 in Montréal) are to be allocated CAD 7.1 million for the provision of labour-market reception and integration services (MICC, 2005). There is a similar arrangement regarding language services.

The Ministry of Employment and Social Solidarity (*Ministère de l'Emploi et de la Solidarité sociale – MESS*) has responsibility for employment programmes for the general population of the province. Government employment services (Emploi-Québec) are for all local people and businesses, and access to public employment services is not solely determined by Employment Insurance eligibility. Immigrants and visible minorities – as people at risk of underemployment, chronic unemployment, exclusion and poverty – are a priority for Emploi-Québec. Individuals born outside Canada accounted for nearly 15% of new beneficiaries of Emploi-Québec measures according to preliminary data for 2004-2005 (in Montréal, people born outside Canada represent nearly 40% of those who take part in active measures). Certain programmes have been adapted to better meet immigrants' needs in order to facilitate their employment integration. An example of this is the on-the-job immersion activities between 1998 and 2005, an initiative of the Industrial Adjustment Service Committee for Immigrants (IASCI) and later Emploi-Québec through its salary subsidy measures. On-the-job immersion activities are designed for immigrant graduates who are having a hard time breaking into the labour market in their field of expertise, in order to facilitate their employment while helping reduce employer perceptions that hiring them is a risk. Internships, which last a maximum of six months, provide a wage subsidy to the employer, covering 50% of the employment cost and are primarily designed to give participants the opportunity to gain their first work experience in their field of expertise. The programme has had a very high success rate with close to 72% of participants being retained by the employer after the subsidy period. The level of satisfaction with the programme is also high, with participants being particularly positive about the strong interrelationship between the professional immersion activity and the respondents' main field of expertise: placements are only organised when there is an explicit relationship between a job and a candidate's previous training.

In order to counter any silo effects of having both departments involved in immigrant settlement MICC and MESS signed an agreement in 2004 to promote immigrant and visible minority job integration. In the Montréal area, two local service harmonisation agreements were signed between local employment centres and Immigration Québec services in recent years. These agreements are designed to enhance the quality and speed of immigrant services at both organisations in order to accelerate the job integration and retention process. Moreover, the Montréal branches of MELS, Emploi-Québec and MICC have agreed on a regional action plan that takes into account the unique difficulties immigrants and newcomers face in the Montréal area.

While there is not a broad based system or programme of retraining or bridging courses to help the large number of immigrants already in Montréal meet the assessment standards required by accrediting authorities, the Québec government has supported new initiatives of this sort. Emploi-Québec, MICC, MELS and the Ministry of Health have worked together to establish college based bridging programmes for nurses, doctors and engineers. The numbers of immigrants involved is limited to about 1 000 per year in Montréal, which is well short of what is needed. More action on this front is likely, following a report from a new task force on access to regulated trades and professions. A work team on the recognition of diplomas and competencies of overseas trained professionals was set up, with one of its objectives being to enhance recognition of training and experience. This includes establishment of workshops, retraining and study groups to facilitate preparation of nurses and engineers for accreditation tests (see the Box 2.1). In addition, the MICC has set up a Centre of Recognition of Skills and Competences which has carried out 14 104 comparative assessments of diplomas in 2005-2006. It focuses mainly on qualifications gained outside the professions, however the centre also advises local immigrants on the procedures necessary to register with professional associations.

Box 2.1. **Bridge Training Programmes in Québec**

- Skills upgrading project of nurses with foreign degrees – 2004-05 budget CAD 330 000 (€ 233 485.46). This project provides financial help for foreign nurses while preparing for the nursing accreditation tests (retraining and reference documents to prepare candidates for the professional corporation's exam).

- Quick Access Project for engineers – 2004-05 budget CAD 180 000 (€ 127 345). Helps foreign trained engineers prepare for the professional order of engineers in Québec (*Ordre des ingénieurs du Québec*) membership entrance exam.

- École Polytechnique programmes to facilitate access to *Ordre des ingénieurs du Québec*. Funded by the Québec government. Some 100 people have been helped in ten fields of engineering.

- Auxiliary nurses – skills upgrading project for nurses with foreign degrees – 2004-05 budget: CAD 211 376 (€ 149 582).

Local initiatives

At the local level there are a large number of community based organisations which provide services to immigrants in Montréal. The Montréal branch of Emploi-Québec works closely with external specialised resources to help develop immigrant job readiness and has agreements with over 25 organisations to provide immigrants and visible minorities with employment assistance services. However, the range of services offered by agencies varies from organisation to organisation. Some agencies, such as Promis and Hirondelle, receive government funding to provide services to the general immigrant population, as well as to the broader community, while others, such as JEM receive community and business support to focus a least part of their services on a specific immigrant community. The value of having this option, from the vantage point of the immigrant, is the additional language or culturally sensitive services that are available.

Promis

Promis (*PROMotion-Intégration Société nouvelle*) is a community-based organisation with a long record of social services. Founded in 1988, PROMIS seeks to help immigrants integrate into society; foster a sense of mutual support among them; and develop services that promote independence. PROMIS provides a variety of services and activities designed to meet the community's needs through a comprehensive integration approach. The services and activities are available to newcomers across the Island of Montréal. Of note among these services are MICC's newcomer help and assistance programme (PANA), family assistance, francisation, employment integration, regionalisation, Saturday school, group kitchens and nursery school. PROMIS is involved in the implementation of the professional immersion programme, running a component of the immigrant and visible minority employment integration assistance programme (PRIIME) administered by Emploi-Québec (see Box 2.2). Promis monitors the experience of clients placed in the programme with follow up visits one month and three months after the initial placement. Through Promis, 48 people were placed in 2005. Their programme has a 90% success rate, resulting in permanent employment. The overall immersion programme in Montréal places approximately 360 people per year.

Hirondelle

Hirondelle is a community-based organisation in Montréal involved in job placement, mainly for university-qualified immigrants. They see approximately 1 000 clients a year, offering free service in a supportive environment. Hirondelle staff see their role as advocates for their immigrant clientele. Funding for services comes from government, community and business supporters. Hirondelle participates (via recruitment and coaching) in a bridging initiative for immigrant nurses. The Québec government provides financial support for these nurses while they are engaged in bridging courses provided by separate educational providers. The bridging courses prepare nurses for the professional nursing examinations. Nurses have three chances to pass this examination and only 50% are successful on their first attempt.

Jewish Employment Montréal (JEM)

While both Promis and Hirondelle offer their services to immigrants from many different backgrounds, JEM gives special emphasis to Jewish immigrants as a specific group within the immigrant population. JEM has some 2 500 employers on its data base through which they seek placement for their

> Box 2.2. **Assistance programme for the integration of immigrants and visible minorities in employment (PRIIME)**
>
> This joint programme by MICC and *Investissement Québec* is run by Emploi-Québec and implemented through its network of local employment centres (CLE). It was first established in 2004.
>
> PRIIME (*Programme d'aide à l'intégration des immigrants et des minorités visibles en emploi*) is designed to support employers in hiring immigrants and visible minorities to fill regular positions that become vacant. This incentive measure encourages small and medium-sized businesses (SMEs) to foster the integration of immigrants and visible minorities into the job market.
>
> More specifically, PRIIME is designed to encourage Québec SMEs to hire immigrant workers and visible minorities to meet their human resource requirements and to help SMEs orient and integrate these people into the workplace. The programme helps newcomers acquire their first work experience in North America, facilitates their socioeconomic and linguistic integration into the workplace, and fosters job retention.
>
> Assistance under PRIIME is in the form of salary subsidies for candidates and their coaches within the company, and also includes financial assistance for candidate training and cultural diversity management activities. In its first year of operation, 769 people took advantage of the programme across Québec, including 439 in the Montréal area. Data on job retention is not yet available.
>
> However, to participate, immigrants need professional level French or English skills, which can be a challenge because of the lack of subsidised language courses available at this level. There must be a potential permanent job on offer when the client takes on the placement, and the resulting employment must be in a field relevant to the immigrant's training.

clients. They engage these employers in their work both to canvass the availability of job placements and to persuade employers to accept some responsibility for hiring new immigrants in their community. One strategy is to hold meetings with "employer clusters" – that is employers in particular fields – where those assembled review the curriculum vita of prospective clients and provide employment to qualified individuals. JEM receives some 400 to 500 applications per year for its placement services. Around 25% succeed in getting jobs; while another 50 % are referred to various education options. The rest, according to the director, struggle to find work, and this outcome was attributed to the linguistic and credential recognition difficulties which many immigrants face. Those lacking English face particular problems because there are relatively few free English courses available in Montréal and because, as noted above, employers often require English as well as French.

JEM seeks to fill this gap through the provision of a variety of English courses. Because of the time that it can take to gain credential recognition, JEM encourages migrants to be pragmatic when they are searching for employment, in many cases encouraging those with qualifications gained abroad to search for alternative professions rather than undertaking long periods of training to requalify in Canada.

Case study 2: Toronto, Ontario

The context of immigration in Toronto is unique. While the breakdown of categories of immigrants locating in Toronto and the profile of source countries roughly approximates the national average, what makes Toronto a special case is the sheer scale of immigrant settlement in the region. Each year the Greater Toronto Area welcomes almost half of all immigrants who arrive in Canada.

Immigrants residing in the province of Ontario have higher levels of education than those residing in other provinces. Among prime working-age immigrants in Canada (24-44 years), 68% had university education. In Ontario, education levels were highest for principal applicants in the skilled worker category (88%). This compares to the total prime working-age population in Ontario, where 25% had university education (Statistics Canada, 2006). The influx of this highly educated and skilled cohort of immigrants implies a significant human capital asset for the city region. However, immigrants have not performed in the labour market as would be expected by their education and skills.

Employment outcomes

The Longitudinal Survey of Immigrants to Canada reported on the situation in 2003 of immigrants who had arrived in Canada between April 2001 and May 2002. The survey reports that most of the skilled immigrants settling in Toronto possessed university level qualifications but that, after two years in Toronto, 45% of these skilled immigrants had yet to find employment in their intended field. The majority had encountered some difficulties in seeking employment. The most serious of these difficulties, according to the Toronto respondents surveyed, were lack of Canadian job experience and non-acceptance of their qualifications or work experience. This outcome mirrors the national picture.

Policy framework and programme responses

The province of Ontario and the federal government are set to implement two agreements that may have significant impact on coherence and coordination between settlement and labour market policy in Ontario: the

Canada-Ontario Agreement on Settlement and a Labour Market Development Agreement. Funding has been committed in the 2006/7 federal budget.

Until these agreements are implemented, the existing framework for service delivery includes two broad streams of services. First, settlement and language training, which is provided through local NGOs, as well as an increasing array of service providers that include community colleges and schools. The largest part of these services is funded by the federal government through Citizenship and Immigration Canada, but there is also provincially funded language training and settlement services programme funded through the Ontario Ministry of Citizenship and Immigration (MCI). The second area of service delivery is directed toward labour market entry, where services and programmes are again delivered through a broad network of NGOs, and are developed and funded federally through Service Canada, and provincially through the Ministry of Training, Colleges and Universities. In addition, MCI houses the Labour Market Integration Unit (established as the Access to Professions and Trades Unit in 1995) which funds a number of programmes dealing explicitly with labour market access issues for immigrants. These include bridging programmes which are mostly occupation specific; for example within health care there are specific programmes for nursing, pharmacy, medical lab technicians, etc. (see Box 2.3). In 2005 there were approximately 5 000 immigrants participating in these courses.

Box 2.3. **Bridging Programs funded by the Ontario Ministry of Citizenship and Immigration**

Accounting	Hospital Administration
Agricultural Industry	Massage Therapy
Architecture	Midwifery
Carpentry	Nursing
Construction Trades	Optometry
Dieticians	Physiotherapy
Early Childhood Educators	Social Work
Employment Counsellors	Teaching
Engineers	Tourism Sector
Engineering Technology	University Professors
Environmental Planners and Geoscientists	Veterinarians

One example of a bridging programme is a new initiative being piloted by the Centre for Language Training and Assessment and the Ontario Association of Certified Engineering Technicians and Technologists (OACETT). Depending on an initial assessment of the applicant's skills and credentials, participants can be directed to three different streams within the project. One is referral to appropriate academic qualification courses, including preparation for the OACETT examination. Another is a language and communication stream, which provides occupation-specific language training. The third is an employment readiness stream, which includes sector-specific workforce preparation advice and mentoring opportunities through OACETT chapter meetings and tours.

Local initiatives

NGOs figure prominently in the provision of services to immigrants in Toronto. There are more than 80 NGOs in the Toronto Region that provide services to immigrants. The extent and direction of their activities is shaped by federal and provincial government programmes since, with the exception of some charitable support, government bodies are the primary funders of immigrant services. As Toronto has long been a reception centre for new immigrants to Canada, there is a well developed infrastructure of community agencies that provide settlement services and employment programmes (of which the COSTI initiative below is an example), and a strong network of ethno-specific organisations that provide varying supports to newly arrived immigrants. As immigration flows change and the cost of housing rises in the centre of Toronto, there is some concern that the current distribution of services within local communities has not kept pace with the increasing settlement of new immigrants towards the outskirts of the city. Humber College's Rexdale Employment Resource Centre, also outlined below, is one organisation addressing this concern. It provides support to immigrants who are facing problems of geographical accessibility to employment opportunities.

COSTI Immigrant Services

COSTI is the largest NGO providing services to immigrants in Toronto, with an annual budget of CAD 20 million, a staff of 150 and a number of branches and outreach centres throughout the Toronto region. It has three divisions, one for settlement counselling (particularly for refugees), another for education and language training, and a third which focuses on employment programmes for immigrants. The organisation has to bid in a competitive market for contracts from the federal and provincial governments in order to finance these services.

With respect to employment services, COSTI staff provide advice about credential recognition and licensing requirements, job search support (resume preparation, interviewing and networking) and employment placement. In this latter task, COSTI networks with prospective employers to build relationships for placing its clients. As with other Canadian government funded NGOs that provide employment services, there is no commercial relationship between COSTI and the immigrant or employer; that is there are no fee-for-service charges. COSTI's costs are covered by its contract with the government agency which commissioned the service agreement. Nevertheless, COSTI's performance in achieving good employment outcomes is taken into account when it seeks renewal of its contracts with the government agency in question.

COSTI is innovative in developing employment services. It has established a variety of four to five week courses for immigrant professionals. For example one course provided information on building codes and other related information needed by skilled immigrants wishing to get started as tradespersons in the Toronto building industry. Another involved the provision of work experience placements for people wishing to work in Biotech companies. COSTI also provides training in childcare.

Rexdale Employment Resource Centre

The Rexdale Employment Resource Centre (ERC) (see Box 2.4), operated by Humber College, is located in an outer suburban region of Toronto with a high immigrant concentration, primarily South Asians. The area is notable for high levels of unemployment amongst immigrants. According to the 2001 Canadian Census, immigrants made up 60.4% of the 62 735 people in the community where the centre is located.

Box 2.4. Employment Resource Centres (ERCs)

Employment Resource Centres (ERCs) are funded by Service Canada (federal) as a generally available service where people can access job information on a free, self-service basis, with access to computer terminals with limited Internet access, as well as faxes, phones and photocopiers. They can also attend regular workshops on the employment market and on how to access vacancies.

The Rexdale ERC directs its activities toward the provision of employment services, with particular emphasis on the needs of skilled immigrants. It has produced guides to the credential and licensing situation within particular professions. The ERC averages some 200 visitors per day.

Co-located with the Rexdale ERC and also operated by Humber College is the Centre for Foreign Trained Professionals and Tradespeople. The centre provides four-week courses explicitly designed to assist professional immigrants in finding professional-level employment. The intake is limited to immigrants who have been in Canada less than three years, who are unable to find work in their field and who have moderate English language skills. Nearly half the participants hold engineering and computing qualifications. The four-week courses, offered to groups of 20 or so participants, cost around CAD 2 000 (approx € 1 400) per capita to run and are entirely federally funded by Service Canada. Participants undergo a skills profile and personality assessment, which are used as a basis for recommending job search strategies. The course provides information on and orientation to the Canadian labour market context, including information on credential assessments, job search strategies and interview skills. Outcomes of the programme are positive, with most participants finding professional-level work in areas like IT programming or as project engineers after finishing the course. Some participants also need actual bridging programmes to bring their skills up to the level required by credentialing authorities and employers and are referred on where possible. No financial support is available to support the living expenses of participants while they are in the programme.

Toronto Region Immigrant Employment Council (TRIEC)

In addition to the community based services identified above, the sheer scale of immigration into Toronto has prompted a high level of civic awareness of the issue of immigration, resulting in an innovative partnership based model for supporting the integration of immigrants, the Toronto Region Immigrant Employment Council (TRIEC). TRIEC emerged from a summit of Toronto community and business leaders in 2003. These leaders identified the flow of immigration to Toronto as a vital asset for the region, but one which was not being effectively leveraged as the emerging evidence showed that immigrants were not performing in the labour market as might be expected given their skills and education. Since its formation, TRIEC has involved business leaders, post-secondary institutions, assessment service providers, occupational regulatory bodies, NGOs, academics, and immigrant organisations in its leadership core. In fact, the corporate sector has very deliberately been positioned in the leadership of this initiative in order to focus attention on bringing the private sector more directly into the development of solutions. The chair of TRIEC is the president and chief executive officer of Manulife Financial, one of Canada's largest insurance companies. The decision to be involved and to provide leadership on this issue was driven by their assessment of their own business imperative to be better able to include immigrants in their company, and an interest in ensuring a healthy city region.

TRIEC is not a direct provider of immigrant services. Where it is engaged in piloting initiatives it outsources the operational role to other organisations, with the belief that there is a vibrant infrastructure of service delivery agents. It sees its own role as convening the various stakeholders, identifying and developing solutions, and actioning them. It has received funding from three federal departments (Citizenship and Immigration Canada, Canadian Heritage, and Human Resources and Skills Development Canada) as well as provincial funding (Ontario Ministry of Citizenship and Immigration). Another major donor is the Maytree Foundation, a private charitable foundation which also provides organisational support as well as leadership on the immigrant issue. TRIEC has also received significant funding from the private sector, with contributions from TD Bank Financial Group, a major financial institution in Canada, and Manulife Financial. TRIEC has deliberately set itself the role of influencing public policy on this issue. Its aim is also to convince Toronto employers that they need to better appreciate the value of immigrant workers, especially since 100% of the region's labour force growth is already derived from immigration.

TRIEC recognises that there are gaps in government policy and practice as regards the integration of immigrants into the labour market and has set itself the task of identifying these gaps and of articulating solutions. It has established an Intergovernmental Relations committee, which seeks to engage all three levels of government – federal, provincial and municipal – in information sharing, shared priority setting, and policy coordination. As part of this process it has initiated a mapping exercise to identify gaps and overlaps in the current funding landscape. TRIEC has tapped into academic and other expertise to help identify policy issues and their solutions.

TRIEC also has a practical agenda. This mainly focuses on two goals; increasing access to value added services to move immigrants more effectively into appropriate employment, and working with employers to build their capacity to better recruit, retain and promoted skilled immigrants in their workplaces. To this end TRIEC has initiated the following projects:

- **Hireimmigrants.ca**. This initiative promotes the potential value of immigrant expertise to employers, particularly the human resources officers within major corporations. The website *www.hireimmigrants.ca* is a platform from which a learning community of human resources professionals and other employers is being cultivated. The site contains case studies with "promising practices" from actual employers, and organises the examples according to human resources practice.

- **Career Bridge**. An internship programme offered through the Career Edge Organisation (a Canada wide private sector not-for-profit organisation founded by Canadian employers) that provides skilled immigrants

"Canadian work experience". The programme involves a pool of skilled immigrants who have been screened for language skills and qualifications. Over 1 200 candidates are on the programme's web based database. Employers post positions on the website and candidates apply online. Employers interview and select candidates, and the internships can last four to twelve months, during which time the immigrant receives a CAD 1 500 stipend per month. The employer pays the cost of the stipend as well as a programme fee, which may potentially be prohibitive for certain companies (such as small to medium enterprises) wanting to join the scheme. However, in April 2006, approximately 300 internships had been initiated with 85% of those participating working full time by the end of the internship (not necessarily with the same employer). The project has been attractive to immigrants and far more have applied than can be accommodated within the programme: only 10% of the over 1 200 candidates who have registered their interest in a database have been allocated an internship. The core challenge of the programme is to expand its capacity and the number of internships available. Its value is that it enables immigrants to "get a foot in the door".

- **The mentoring partnership**. This programme brings together professional immigrants who are not yet employed in their field with mentors established within their respective occupation in a mentoring relationship. Mentors and mentees meet for an average of an hour and a half per week over a four-month period. Mentors are volunteers who share advice, ranging from information about the professional field to instruction on how best to present a CV and to conduct an employment interview, and share professional networks. Since initiated in February 2005, over 1 000 matches have been made. Of the mentoring relationships completed, 72% have found employment, with 68% finding employment in their own field or a related one. There has been a positive response from corporate partners that include the City of Toronto as well as several private sector employers. In particular, one of Canada's largest financial institutions is funding part of the programme, as well as having provided over 100 mentors. The value of the relationship to the immigrant professional is the social capital gap that it fills. When immigrants arrive they lack these informal and formal connections that can often be critical in establishing meaningful links to the labour market.

TRIEC has had considerable success in involving local stakeholders in their initiatives, however the local trade unions have been less easy to bring on board, despite the fact that they are represented on the partnership. Projects such as mentoring and internships are not easily incorporated within the structures of collective agreements, and because of this, TRIEC has in many cases had to find placements and mentors within the non-unionised elements of the local workforce, restricting the opportunities available.

Case study 3: Winnipeg, Manitoba

Winnipeg provides a very different context to Toronto for newly arriving immigrants. While Toronto is a fast growing city, between 1996 and 2001, Winnipeg grew only 0.6% – one of the lowest growth rates of the large city centres in Canada. At the same time the national population grew at a rate of 4%. Overall, the province of Manitoba had a net outflow of migration to other provinces. In this context therefore, immigration is viewed very much as a population growth policy for the region, as a well as a tool for regional economic development.

The desire amongst policy makers to increase immigration in Manitoba has resulted in the negotiation of a provincial nominee programme which allows the province considerable control over the selection of new immigrants. As a result of the programme, the numbers of immigrants locating in Manitoba (around 80% of whom settle in Winnipeg) has increased sharply in recent years. In 2004, there were 7 427 immigrants, up from 4 621 in 2002. The provincial government has a target outcome of 10 000 immigrants per year. Provincial nominees make up 54% of migrants with another 13% through federal economic streams, 15% as family class and 17% refugees.

Employment outcomes

One of the reasons for the exodus of Manitoba residents to other Canadian locations is the relatively subdued nature of the region's economy. It might therefore be expected that immigrants would experience more difficulties finding work in Manitoba in their intended fields than has been reported for the other two destinations examined. The most recent longitudinal survey of immigrants to Canada brackets immigrants locating in Manitoba and Saskatchewan together – thus it is not possible to isolate those living in Manitoba. However, the record of new immigrants gaining employment between 2001 and 2003 is better than for immigrants locating elsewhere in Canada,[5] though the proportion who found a job in the same occupational group as their intended occupation, at 43%, was about the same as for other newcomers in Canada (42%) (Statistics Canada, 2006).

This positive outcome may be linked to the fact that Manitoba's provincial nominee programme selects immigrants with an eye to the skills needed in Manitoba. Most of those nominated are tradespersons or semi-skilled workers. The largest individual occupational group of these nominees in 2004 was welders, followed by farmers and farm managers, carpenters, mechanics and truck drivers (Manitoba Labour and Immigration, 2005). However factors relating to skills and labour market need have more recently been downplayed in the province following difficulties in maintaining an up to date picture of the labour market. In addition, Manitoba feels that their most important priority is attracting people who will be loyal to the region, to minimise the risk that people will move on to other provinces and cities after arrival. Strong emphasis is now placed on building up social capital, and on prioritising family and other ties to existing Manitoban residents within the selection process.

Despite the relatively positive employment outcomes, service providers report concern about pockets of poverty which exist in the city, where disproportionate numbers of migrants have become concentrated. This has resulted in an effort by NGOs to support not just first generation immigrants but also the second and third generations, who in some cases are still experiencing barriers to education and employment combined with high secondary school drop out rates. The Alicia Rae Careers Centre in Winnipeg, for example, has developed a specific project to create training and work experience opportunities to support high school completion.

Policy framework and programme responses

The Canada-Manitoba Immigration Agreement is a federal-provincial agreement signed in 1998 and renewed in 2003 that outlines both governments' shared interest in providing effective services for the social, cultural and economic integration of immigrants, and effecting regional dispersion of immigrants.

In terms of service provision and integration of immigrants, the new agreement delineates roles and responsibilities for the two parties, and the financial supports to be provided by the federal government. Other stakeholders with whom work on the issue may be undertaken are also identified, and include; municipal governments, education, health and human service sectors, settlement and immigrant serving agencies, religious and ethnic organisations, labour and business groups, as well as individuals.

The agreement recognises all streams of immigration to Manitoba and introduces new objectives related to regional immigration, qualifications recognition and official language minority development. It will allow for greater provincial flexibility in planning for immigration levels and responding creatively to meeting emerging needs. New provisions strengthen provincial nominee processing to meet targets and affirm primary provincial settlement and integration responsibilities in cooperation with enduring federal roles. Information sharing is expanded through a new annex on the provision of data. Two key elements which have been expanded include:

- Provincial nominee programme – Manitoba has increased capacity to request temporary work permits and make linkages to the provincial nominee programme and temporary movements including international students.
- Settlement of immigrants and refugees – Under the agreement, Manitoba is fully responsible for the delivery of settlement services for immigrants in the province.

Arrangements for the delivery of immigrant services in Manitoba are similar to those in Ontario. Most of these services are provided by non-profit community-based organisations (NOGs), which focus on English language training and settlement services. There is also a strong commitment on the part of agencies to provide employment placement options and training programmes for professional and trade immigrants in Manitoba.

There are currently a variety of bridge training programmes available. Funding from the Ministry of Labour and Immigration, under its Manitoba Immigration Integration Programme (MIIP), with financial assistance from Citizenship and Immigration Canada, supports labour-market placement services, including various pilot projects involving training initiatives. These include provisions in certain circumstances for training allowances. For example, the University of Manitoba provides a bridging programme for engineers designed to assist them in meeting the academic qualifications specified by the Association of Professional Engineers and Geoscientists of Manitoba, as well as a bridging programme for teachers. The Winnipeg Technical College also conducts bridging programmes, including hairdressing and accounting. The MIIP is an effective funding tool for bridging the immigrant and labour market service delivery framework, and has sufficient flexibility to fund such pilot initiatives.

However, the consensus among service providers in Winnipeg is that overall the range of available courses for immigrants who need to study to meet credential assessments, or need systematic retraining, could be increased. To the extent that bridge training is available, there is also limited financial support to immigrants while taking these courses, which may act as a barrier to uptake.

Local initiatives

As in Montréal and Toronto, there are many different community organisations delivering settlement services for immigrants in Winnipeg, dependent on various funding grants from the government and local charitable funds. Such initiatives also depend in part on volunteers to provide their services and local NGOs report some funding difficulties, in part because the pot of federal money currently available to the province of Manitoba is capped and does not take account of recent growth in the number of immigrants, a situation which is currently under review.

The International Centre, and Employment Projects of Winnipeg (described below) are two community based organisations in Winnipeg which deliver a variety of different services to support integration of immigrants into the local labour market, often juggling grants from different organisations.

The International Centre

The International Centre provides a wide range of settlement services, including English language training. Because of its size and the diversity of its services, it is able to act as a "one stop" shop where immigrants are directed through a range of services – including housing. Its clientele includes many refugees. The centre has an annual operational budget of CAD 2 million (approx. € 1.4 million), which relies on seven different funders, six of which provide contracts of not more than one year at a time. The financial stability of the agency is therefore an ongoing concern, which has significant impact on the planning and organisational capacity of the agency.

The International Centre has a volunteer-run programme which focuses on helping immigrants adjust to life in Winnipeg. The courses available include basic computer skills, driver's education, English conversation classes and programmes for children. Job placement services are also available. The centre provides immigrants with assistance in preparing CVs and coaching in interview techniques, and acts as a referral agency to the various training programmes potentially available for its clients. There is also a mentoring programme which is designed to match immigrant professionals with established professionals in order to help the immigrant with licensing and career re-entry. Some 35 matches have been achieved, about half of which have been amongst engineers. The centre reports that many of these matches have helped those mentored to find work in their field. This programme is in its early stages, and finding appropriate volunteer mentors remains a challenge.

The centre also runs a workplace entry programme targeted towards young immigrants (18-30 years) with limited language abilities (Canadian language benchmark 3-4) and limited work experience in Canada. The course is five weeks full time, during which participants are paid, and aims to provide participants with a better understanding of employer's expectations and the workplace culture in Canada. A direct placement officer (DPO) works with the class during the course and assists the participants with their job search. Once a job placement is found the DPO will continue to liaise with the client and the employer to support them through any difficulties and mediate misunderstandings, thereby improving the sustainability of employment outcomes and job retention. The DPO also supports the clients through difficulties with child care, transportation, and illness. The total number of clients registered in 2005-6 were 66 and of these 44 gained employment and 22 did not complete (due to moving, returning to school or being referred to another programme).

Employment Projects of Winnipeg (EPW)

This is a job placement agency which is distinctive in that it also provides on-site training in computer skills. Staff indicate that they deal with clients who were struggling to cope with the difficulties of providing for their families at the same as trying to negotiate the hurdles encountered in finding work in their field of expertise. These immigrants often needed social support, and EPW makes an effort to provide this support by creating a receptive setting which strives to meet social as well as job search needs. The agency was also beginning to establish support and activities for youth to aid in their integration.

The involvement of other local stakeholders

Aside from local community based projects, the province has also used the Manitoba Immigrant Integration Programme, described above, to support innovative initiatives by other stakeholder in the region, including employers. Two initiatives that include employer partners in the design and delivery of the initiative are a Manitoba based credit union training project, and an Early Childhood Educator (ECE) Qualifications Recognition Project. Both of these projects have used a competency modelling technique to support the integration of immigrants into their workplaces, mapping the skills that are needed in a particular employment position and then devising ways of training and/or crediting people with prior knowledge in these skills in order to sidestep more generalised, and hence lengthier, training courses.

Early Childhood Educator (ECE) Qualifications Recognition Project

The Early Childhood Educator (ECE) Qualifications Recognition Project, for example, was set up by a representative of the Manitoba provincial Family Services and Housing unit, in order to overcome a local skills shortage of early childcare professionals. Whilst a number of local newcomers expressed an interest in working in this area, they were experiencing difficulties having their previous qualifications in this field recognised, and being forced to go through long periods of re-training in order to qualify for the profession.

The programme seeks to deal with the issue by providing competency-based routes into early childcare professional accreditation. One of these routes involves a 14 week project working with immigrants with international education that is early childhood education focused to meet the qualification requirements for the Manitoba Child Care Programme's trained level of classification. This process includes a work-based assessment and mentoring based on a competency assessment framework. Each trainee works in a placement in a childcare centre and has their skills assessed as they work. During this time they are employed as a registered childcare assistant. Assessors use previously designed standards and a learning outcome framework adapted for the project. The framework was originally designed in consultation with local colleges, professional associations and other stakeholders. The project also works with the Manitoba Academic Credential Assessment Service provided through the province's labour and immigration department to assess previous qualifications held by trainees. As of May 2006, 22 people had successfully completed the programme.

In principal, this type of programme appears to be well structured to meet the needs of immigrants wishing to take up the childcare profession. It gives some credit for education courses taken overseas and it provides the immigrant with an income while simultaneously learning and performing childcare tasks. The competency based assessment and mentoring process facilitates the recognition of qualifications. Whether this case study is transferable to other professional fields is uncertain. Canadian professional bodies do incorporate elements of competency testing in their accreditation processes. However, they usually require completion of the equivalent of the academic courses which Canadian candidates complete before conducting their competency tests. In the case of the early childcare field, the professional association does not control the accreditation process. This appears to have facilitated a more flexible approach.

Cambrian Credit Union

Another innovative programme was developed in 2004 by a group of local credit unions seeking to recruit immigrants in order to more effectively serve their diverse clientele. Credit unions are providing services to the growing ethnic communities of Winnipeg, and were dealing with high staff turnover rates amongst their customer service staff, particularly in their position of "member services representative". The credit unions therefore decided to pool resources and develop an in-house training project, with the support of the provincial government, to help local immigrants gain the skills to take on this post.

There appears to have been a strong demand from immigrants to take up the programme. Some 80 have applied to each round of the programme with about 40 being selected. Immigrants with the basic competency skills – literacy and numeracy – are sought. Those meeting the skill requirements are given a five week orientation and training course during which time they do not receive any payment. Those successfully completing this course are given three month workplacement trial periods, with ongoing training and support, at entry level pay rates (CAD 10 per hour). If they are able to complete the required tasks, they are appointed to the credit union staff, with the great majority (78%) being appointed to permanent positions. The credit union industry is perhaps particularly well suited to this type of initiative, having both a community based approach, and strong pre-existing networks between its institutions. The province of Manitoba also played an important role in galvanizing the initiative, supporting the employers by providing a trainer, and the initial investment in the competency profiling. The project is unusual in that it was not directed at professional immigrants. There are large numbers of clerical workers among the immigrants entering under the refugee and family reunion programmes, as well as accompanying family members of skilled immigrants, to which such a project may be particularly appropriate.

Analysis

Policy and programme effectiveness

A number of persisting barriers to the effective labour market integration of immigrants in Canada have been identified during the course of the study, including credential recognition, the requirement of Canadian work experience, and communication skills. While this is not an exhaustive list, they are the main elements that are identified by both immigrants and employers. The key question to be addressed here, therefore, is whether the local initiatives that are being implemented are actually addressing these barriers and improving the labour market situation of local immigrants.

The question of credential recognition in Canada operates on two levels. First, for professions and trades that are regulated or licensed, it involves a complex web of stakeholders including the occupational regulatory body, post secondary institutions, and employers. In Canada, the regulation of professions and trades falls under provincial jurisdiction, so that effective policy and programme responses on this issue need to be provincial in nature. Many of the bridging programmes that have been developed are responsive to these realities, and include the various stakeholders in the development and implementation of the programme. Such projects are also provincially resourced. The benefit of bridging courses is that they allow immigrants to quickly up-skill and enter the labour market, a factor that is crucial in a context where local stakeholders state that labour market experience which is over two years old is considered out of date by employers.[6] The shortfall in bridging programmes however, is that to be effective they need to be occupation specific, and are therefore limited in scope and size. They also tend to be expensive and face significant challenges in terms of their sustainability.

The second level of credential recognition impacts those occupations that are not regulated or licensed, and where the issue of recognition falls to the employer alone. Here is where the barrier of Canadian experience becomes an issue. Many employers use the requirement of Canadian experience as a proxy when they are faced with credentials that they do not recognise or are not familiar with. Where employers have had direct experience with an applicant, through an internship or mentoring relationship, the results are highly successful as employers gain confidence in an immigrant's skills. A number of the local initiatives examined, such as the PRIIME government on-the-job immersion programme and TRIEC in Toronto, recognise this and use both public and private sector funding to provide access to paid work experience. These projects have relatively high success rates, however, the cost of implementing these projects and the need for employer participation again makes them necessarily small in scale. The need to attract employers also means that the eligibility criteria are set high, and candidates may be considered as those with the greatest chance of finding employment, which may lead to "creaming" effects.

Addressing employer capacity to recognise previously acquired competences and skills is a much larger issue. While there are tools available to support employers in this, including credential assessment services, the issue requires a systematic approach to working with employers, which is not currently being undertaken. The employer based initiatives undertaken by the credit unions and the Early Childhood Educator (ECE) Qualifications Recognition Project in Winnipeg illustrate the proactive approaches which can be taken by employers themselves on credential recognition, and the useful role that can be played by regional government in providing "seed-funding" grants to support such innovation. However, competency assessment mechanisms ultimately need to be developed in a more systematic way and effectively disseminated so as to avoid companies and other organisations "reinventing the wheel".

While interventions such as occupation specific bridging programmes, and employment experience initiatives seem to get to the heart of the problem of immigrant integration into the Canadian labour force, much of the focus of federally funded service interventions at the local level is on initial settlement needs, or broad based generic labour market access programmes that do not address the particularities of the immigrant experience. In part this is related to resourcing issues, and the fact that local service providers are able to provide more basic and more short-term support mechanisms to a larger number of immigrants at a lower cost. This type of support does not necessarily provide longer term labour market integration at a level commensurate with their previous qualifications and skills. In addition, as many of these short-term programmes are funded and evaluated on performance based management systems, this runs the risk of clients being encouraged toward the "any job" outcome, which may in itself result in underemployment.

Communication skills are repeatedly cited by employers in Canada as one of the key barriers they face when employing immigrants. In addition, the shift to non-English speaking source countries (as it relates outside of Québec) and the requirement of high levels of education create challenges in terms of appropriate labour market placement. That is, more highly skilled positions in the labour market will generally require high levels of language competence because of concomitant management responsibilities. While the federal government does place great emphasis on language training support, this is not generally provided to a level that is sufficient for labour market requirements. Some provinces, like Manitoba, are providing higher levels of language training, and a new programme stream developed by Citizenship and Immigration Canada, Enhanced Language Training, may be an opportunity to expand access to higher level communication skills that will be relevant for the labour market. As well, within many of the bridging programmes developed, occupation-specific language training is included as a core element, and takes the participant to the level required for professional competence.

Much of the attention of federal and provincial policy and programme development has been focused on highly skilled immigrants. This is in line with the priorities of the federal government in the selection process. However, a large percentage of immigrants still arrive under the family class or as refugees,[7] and experience their settlement and labour market entry differently than skilled immigrants. The broader range of supports provided through the Immigrant Settlement Adjustment Programme (ISAP) and Language Instruction for Newcomers to Canada (LINC), both funded by Citizenship and Immigration Canada, address some of the immediate needs of this group. However, refugee claimants are not eligible for either of these programmes.

In addition, much support is targeted towards recent immigrants, whereas longer term immigrants may still experience barriers to the labour market, particularly when they have been locked into situations of underemployment. The COSTI project in Toronto, for example, reported that they were in some cases assisting people who were still experiencing problems integrating after 15 years in Canada, mainly by using charitable contributions.

Further, in the context of rising pockets of deprivation in cities such as Toronto and Winnipeg, it is evident that local initiatives are being faced with wider sets of problems which can indirectly affect the labour market integration of immigrants and their offspring such as poor housing, geographical isolation and issues surrounding educational participation and performance. Projects which are physically based in such communities, such as the Humber College's Rexdale Employment Resource Centre outside of Toronto, are important mechanisms for identifying these issues and supporting immigrants in tackling them, although such centres would benefit from flexible funding mechanisms to address the variety of different issues which residents of such areas inevitably face.

Impact of governance framework

A key challenge in the Canadian context is the complicated roles and relationships that exist between the federal and provincial governments in the development of policy and programmes to support labour market integration of immigrants. Federal-provincial agreements have been signed to delineate particular roles and responsibilities and to address the issue of shared responsibility and ensure coordination. However, despite the fact that it is at the local level that emerging issues associated with the local settlement of immigrants are most clearly felt, city level authorities are not yet effectively included in the higher level planning and policy activities. In addition to challenges of vertical coordination between the different levels of government, a further problem is the division of the issue of immigration integration itself into two discrete policy areas of immigrant settlement and labour market access. As such, the coordination is also a challenge horizontally at both federal and provincial levels of government.

In Québec, the recent establishment of regional action plans and the development of regional conferences involving mayors and municipalities as part of the strategy "Shared values, common interests" is a clear step towards developing a multi-level governance approach to this issue. In addition, the inter-service agreements which have been developed between the different ministries working in this field can only help in local coordination. The establishment of an intergovernmental relations committee within TRIEC in Toronto can also be seen to be a direct response to this issue. The committee has brought together local representatives from four federal departments (Citizenship and Immigration Canada, Service Canada, Canadian Heritage, Industry Canada), three provincial ministries (Citizenship and Immigration, Training, Colleges and Universities, and Economic Development and Trade) and three municipal/regional governments. The objective of the committee is to create new mechanisms for intergovernmental cooperation, including information sharing, joint analysis of local service delivery, and ultimately, joint planning and priority setting. An important outcome of this committee after two years is a mapping document that identifies the local gaps in service and a series of recommendations for policy change.

The role of NGOs in service delivery

While policy development, planning and priority setting happens at both the federal and provincial levels, services for immigrants are delivered through NGOs and other service providers at the local level. At this level there is also an apparent lack of communication and coordination, which reduces the ability of service delivery organisations to avoid gaps and duplication, share good practice and ensure that complementary services are well linked. In Ontario and Manitoba, Service Canada bases its initial assessment centres within NGOs, and this assists in encouraging local NGOs to refer immigrants to other local providers once their training and support needs have been assessed. In Québec, only certain services are provided by NGOs, through partnership agreements. However it is often the most established NGOs that fall within such referral networks and other providers can become more isolated.

NGOs and other local service providers apply, and in some cases compete, for funding from federal and provincial governments, to provide settlement and employment services. As such, the provision of services is very much defined within the federal and provincial governments' policy framework. In addition, many of these contracts are short term (one year), or renewable annually, creating administrative burdens for organisations that often lack the capacity to maintain the level of reporting or proposal development required. Some NGOs receive additional financing from donors (including charitable foundations), thus supporting more flexibility in their range of service provision. However, reliance on a patchwork of grants creates stress and makes planning and development difficult for an organisation.

The capacity of larger organisations like COSTI, or the co-location of smaller agencies, makes it possible to take a holistic approach to the needs of individual immigrant clients. Staff are expected to pay attention to a wide range of client needs and where appropriate to refer the client to the relevant services located within the agency. These services include advice on housing, referral to various social services, including health and education. This arrangement has many advantages for immigrants in that it saves them from searching around for services from diverse providers. However, this capacity is a function of the organisation's scale and is not a consequence of any deliberate policy by federal or provincial governments. Indeed, the competitive structure of the arrangements whereby NGOs bid to provide immigrant services means that there is no guarantee that any particular organisation will reach COSTI's size or be able to maintain its service range over time.

The fact that NGOs deliver a raft of different services to immigrants in addition to providing support with accessing the local labour market can create the risk that those advising immigrants are not fully focused on current labour market realities or in communication with a sufficiently large or diverse group of employers. A number of the local initiatives reviewed have overcome this through developing a strong networking approach. The PROMIS agency in Montréal for example capitalises on its location in the community to involve a large number of small to medium sized enterprises (SMEs) in providing placements for PRIIME, although SMEs are traditionally a "hard to reach" group in the provision of work experience opportunities. The JEM initiative has also built on an existing business community to develop a large database of employers, keeping up with their needs through the organisation of sector based roundtables. In Toronto, the TRIEC initiative has provided a useful mechanism for linking employers and NGOs through a partnership approach. While migrants principally access TRIEC programmes through a network of community based NGOs, these programmes are designed and marketed through a city wide public-private partnership, resulting in participation by significant national and international high profile companies, who can then act as a role model for others. Such a public-private partnership approach could be usefully transferred to other cities in Canada.

Conclusions and issues for consideration

The economic and demographic imperatives that make immigration a priority for Canada, mean that there is genuine interest and political will on the part of all stakeholders to create a system that produces more successful outcomes for the benefit of immigrants, and for Canadian society. Below are a series of issues for consideration based on the above scan and analysis of the Canadian context.

Programme alignment with changing profile of immigrants

The Canadian government has an extensive network of local services in place, but these largely relate to immediate settlement supports and basic language needs (though Québec offers additional services). The changing profile of immigrants in the last two decades has not been met with a related change in services. There is a need to actively address the fact that both skilled and unskilled immigrants may need more appropriate and effective supports to integrate into the Canadian labour market.

Specifically in the case of skilled immigrants, there is a need to expand the current programme of language training to meet the demands of the labour market for skilled professionals. The current provision of training only to a basic skills level in most provinces may be sufficient for unskilled employment; however, this is not adequate for those immigrants who are arriving under the skilled category. Given that the objective of the skilled immigrant selection system is to attract immigrants with skills that will benefit the economy, it follows that the appropriate supports to ensure their entry into the labour market are in place.

Much of the employment programming that is available is focused on how to find a job; that is, labour market information, curriculum vitae preparation, and interviewing skills. However, the initiatives that have demonstrated successful outcomes are those that link individuals directly with employers, through mentoring relationships, internships, or actual placement. There are less of these programmes available and they are not available to the scale required. There is a need therefore to expand access to these kinds of initiatives. As well, in order to ensure that employers will participate, they should be included in the development and delivery of such programmes so that they are designed to meet the needs of both immigrants and employers.

In addition, flexible funding needs to be provided to local initiatives to help immigrants overcome the wider set of factors which can operate as barriers to employment for both high and low skilled immigrants, particularly those people who have become concentrated in the emerging pockets of poverty which exist within cities. Issues such as poor accessibility, a lack of suitable housing, and poor educational outcomes of children can all have detrimental impacts on long term labour market integration.

Multi-stakeholder coordination and collaboration

The issue of immigrant labour market integration in Canada is one that is inherently multi-stakeholder. Given the regional nature of Canada, and the varying contexts from city to city, it is important to develop solutions that respond to the particularities of the local context and the local stakeholders. However, there are no dedicated government resources, federal or provincial (except in Québec), to support this kind of local collaboration. Partnerships such as TRIEC in Toronto represent an innovative way of stimulating and maintaining such collaboration at the local level. A government programme that supports local coordination would be a useful strategy to engage more effectively local stakeholders and identify local solutions.

Another aspect of local coordination is the inclusion of cities in immigration policy. Even though much of the local integration work falls to city governments and their agencies, cities have limited input into the design of policy and programmes, and in decisions about resources. To bring this experience and expertise into the process, there needs to be a place for cities in the development of immigration policy. This role could be included through federal-provincial-municipal agreements that allow for joint planning and allocation decisions by all levels of government, and coordination at a local level to meet local needs.

Throughout the Canadian example, there is also a repeated problem of horizontal coordination, although each of the provinces is working on this issue. There is an explicit need for a national framework, which can address the unique situation of each province, to resolve the silo effect of discrete and separate policy directions for immigration and labour market entry. Such a framework would inform federal-provincial agreements and/or interdepartmental agreements that deal with these issues and ensure integrated planning and implementation. It would also facilitate inter-provincial migration for workers.

Service providing organisations

A unique feature of the Canadian approach is the reliance on community-based, non-profit organisations (NGOs) to deliver immigrant services. Their focus has been initial settlement services, particularly language services and employment support, as well as other relevant services including health, education and housing. The community-based model of service delivery provides most services free of charge. They often aim to create a sense of community for their clients and are prepared to advocate on their behalf.

The larger organisations, or co-located organisations, are often best equipped to deal with recently arrived immigrants because they are able to provide a one-stop shop where immigrants can be guided through the maze of services available, many of which could be provided "in-house". However, much of the funding received by the agencies derives from short-term service contracts (one to three years) with federal or provincial government ministries. A policy of ensuring that at least a few comprehensive service providers were available to immigrants in each major urban centre, combined with guarantees from federal and provincial ministries of core funding to these providers, would be helpful for both immigrants and service providers.

In order to ensure that such organisations are able to provide good quality advice to immigrants and link them directly into jobs it will be crucial that employers participate as fully as possible in local initiatives. Federal and provincial policy makers should take advantage of the growing business case for employing migrants, in the context of demographic change, to develop projects which encourage employer participation, and give a positive profile to those who have developed good practice in this area. The TRIEC Hire Immigrants project represents a good model for such action.

As NGOs are in many cases the front line of service delivery to immigrants in Canada it is important that their experiences are communicated directly to those government officials who are responsible for both allocating federal funding and designing immigration programmes. Their experiences of both service gaps (such as funding for childcare provision for immigrants with dependents whilst training) and the current barriers which immigrants are experiencing to the labour market, are crucial information which can be used to evolve federal and provincial programmes so that they keep up with the changing nature of immigrants and their labour market challenge.

Pre-arrival and selection

It is important that immigrants have access to information and meaningful credential assessment and accreditation pre-immigration. Such information could better facilitate labour market entry upon arrival in Canada. While there are federal and provincial websites on this topic, it would, in particular, be beneficial if greater efforts were made to inform immigrants coming to Canada under the skills programme that they may need to be adaptable and change profession on arrival. This could help manage the expectations of new immigrants, and eliminate some of the frustration which skilled migrants currently experience when they are unable to continue their chosen career on arrival in Canada.

In the longer term, a better articulation between the immigrant selection systems developed at the national and provincial levels in Canada, and the skills in demand within particular local areas and provinces may lead to more successful labour market outcomes. The Canada-Québec Accord provides the province with a strong role in determining immigration selection, and the ability to search for certain skills amongst new migrants, particular the ability to speak French. The provincial nominee programmes which have been developed elsewhere in Canada, for example in Manitoba, also allow for skills selection, although it is evident that monitoring changing regional skills demands can prove a challenge and other competing factors, such as loyalty to a particular province, can take priority.

The future

To conclude, Canada has much to gain from a continued immigration programme that addresses its objectives of growth and nation building, but there is a need for a sharp and focused national vision of how to achieve this. There is an ongoing challenge to develop the right mix of policies and programmes to realize this vision, and many challenges in negotiating and coordinating roles and responsibilities. Both leadership and partnership are essential in building an effective system that supports the newly arrived immigrant, so that both Canada and it's immigrants can enjoy the benefits.

Notes

1. The Canadian provinces have a considerable amount of responsibility relative to the federal government, including jurisdiction over many public goods such as healthcare, education, welfare, and intra-provincial transportation. The provinces receive transfer payments from the federal government as well as exacting their own taxes. The Canadian provinces significantly increased their responsibilities between the 1950s and the 1970s and now represent just under 40% of the federation's taxing and spending power, making Canada one of the most decentralised countries of the OECD. See OECD (2002).

2. In 2004, unemployment in Canada, at 7.3%, stood just above the OECD average of 6.9%, while the share of individuals who had been unemployed for more than one year, at 9.5%, remained among the lowest in the OECD. The unemployment rate in 2005 was 6.8%. See OECD (2006).

3. See Galabuzi (2001).

4. Under the terms of the Canada-Québec Labour Market Agreement, Québec is responsible for determining the labour market priorities for the province: designing, implementing and evaluating active employment measures; providing a labour exchange service; determining the service needs of employment insurance users; providing referral to appropriate services and employment counselling; helping people establish plans for acquisition of the occupational skills they need and guiding them in a successful job search; producing Québec labour market information; and participating in the improvement of the pan-Canadian labour market information system.

5. The employment rate for newcomers in Manitoba and Saskatchewan stood at 65% after they had been in the country for six months. After they had been in Canada for one year, their employment rate increased to 73% and this rate generally remained the same after two years (74%). The combined employment rate of newcomers in these two provinces was higher at all three benchmark periods than in any other individual province or region.

6. This factor was reported by a number of stakeholders across the case study regions, with employers in the TRIEC partnership in particular stressing that the aim should be to get immigrants into the labour market as soon as possible after arrival at a level commensurate with their skills.

7. In 2004 the breakdown of the migration inflow was as follows: 25.2% work, 57.9% family, 16.8% humanitarian, 0.1% others (source OECD, 2005).

Bibliography

Association of Universities and Colleges of Canada (2002), "Trends in Higher Education", Ontario.

Bruce, D. (2001), "Help Wanted: Results of CFIB Surveys on the Shortage of Qualified Labour", Canadian Federation of Independent Business, Ottawa.

Bourgeois, A. and A. Debus (2006), "Help Wanted: Long-term Vacancies a Major Small Business Challenge", Canadian Federation of Independent Business, Ottawa.

Canadian Labour and Business Centre (2005), "Handbook: Immigration and Skills Shortages", Ottawa.

Citizenship and Immigration Canada (1994), "Into the 21st Century: A strategy for Immigration and Citizenship", Ottawa.

Citizenship and Immigration Canada (2003), "The Monitor", Ottawa.

Citizenship and Immigration Canada (2004), "Report on Plans and Priorities 2004-2005", Ottawa.

Citizenship and Immigration Canada (2006), "Facts and Figures", Ottawa.

Feist, M.G. (2003), "Success Skills Centre", *Government of Canada Immigration Committee Hearings*, Winnipeg, Manitoba, 12 Feb.

Galabuzi, G.E. (2001), *Canada's Creeping Economic Apartheid: the Economic Segregation and Social Marginalisation of Racialised Groups*. Centre for Social Justice (CSJ) Foundation, Toronto.

Government of Québec (2004), *Shared Valued, Common Interests, Action Plan 2004-2007*, Québec.

International Centre (2005), *Annual Report 2004-2005*, Winnipeg.

Manitoba Labour and Immigration (2005), *Manitoba Immigration Facts, 2004 Statistical Report*. Winnipeg.

Ministry of Immigration and Cultural Communities (2005), "Integration of Immigrants in the Labour Market", Briefing report prepared for the OECD-LEED study visit.

OECD (2002), *Territorial Reviews Canada*, OECD, Paris.

OECD (2006a), *International Migration Outlook*, OECD, Paris.

OECD (2006b), *Employment Outlook, Boosting Jobs and Incomes*, OECD, Paris.

Public Policy Forum (2004), *Bringing Employers into the Immigration Debate: Survey and Conference*, Ottawa.

Reitz, J.G. (2003), "Educational Expansion and the employment Success of Immigrants in the United State and Canada, 1970-1990", in Jeffrey G. Reitz (ed.), *Host Societies and the Reception of Immigrants*, Centre for Comparative Immigration Studies, University of California, San Diego.

Statistics Canada (2001), "Immigrants in the Canadian Labour Force, A Provincial and Occupational Overview", *Census 2001*, Ottawa.

Statistics Canada (2003a), *Earnings of Canadians*, Ottawa.

Statistics Canada (2003b), *Longitudinal Survey of Immigrants to Canada: Progress and Challenges of New Immigrants in the Workforce*, Ottawa.

Statistics Canada (2003c), *Education in Canada: Raising the Standard*, Ottawa.

Statistics Canada (2005), *Longitudinal Survey of Immigrants to Canada – A Portrait of Early Settlement Experiences*, Ottawa.

Statistics Canada (2006), *Longitudinal Survey of Immigrants to Canada: A Regional Perspective of the Labour Market Experiences*, Ottawa.

Sweetman, A. (2005), "Immigration as a Labour Market Strategy – European and North American Perspectives".

United Way of Greater Toronto and the Canadian Council on Social Development (2004), *The Geography of Neighbourhood Poverty: 1981-2001*, United Way of Greater Toronto, Toronto.

Chapter 3

Innovating in the Supply of Services to Meet the Needs of Immigrants in Italy

by
Jonathan Chaloff

Local authorities play an important role in supporting integration in Italy, particularly in the provision of emergency management and access to affordable housing. Local NGOs, often connected to the Catholic Church, also play a key role, partly through supporting the development of social networks which are crucial in a country where much employment is advertised informally. At the regional level, the European Social Fund has provided an important means of supporting access to training, and chambers of commerce have been active in supporting immigrant entrepreneurship and developing innovative bilateral training schemes with regions in sending countries. While such local and regional initiatives have had success in helping people into jobs, their ability to support longer term integration in Italy is more doubtful, partly due to a lack of emphasis on long term career planning and development.

3. INNOVATING IN THE SUPPLY OF SERVICES TO MEET THE NEEDS OF IMMIGRANTS IN ITALY

Introduction

The nature of immigrant integration differs from country to country, depending on the migration history of each country, the characteristics of newcomers, existing programmes to assist immigrants and the host countries' general social and economic conditions. Immigration policy is decided at the national level, but its effects are felt at the local (regional, provincial and municipal) level. This means that specific policies targeted towards the social and labour integration of immigrants are often left to – and developed by – local level authorities. Varying roles are also attributed to the activities of third-sector organisations and trade unions, often with large differences in the approaches and services involved.

This chapter examines the efficacy of the local implementation of policies to improve the integration of immigrants into the labour market in Italy. It explores the initiatives taken in three Italian local contexts in order to understand how local political actors formulate their policies concerning the inclusion of immigrants in the labour market and the wider social fabric, and provide insights into policy successes and failures. The main issues determining the employment situation of immigrants in Italy, ranging from the upgrading of skills, recognition of qualifications, matching of supply and demand, and social integration are also identified and discussed.

The autonomous province of Trento, the municipality of Milan, and the region of Piemonte were selected as a starting point for this study, due to: i) their different levels of decentralisation and local governance (perceptible in the different degrees of power held at each level); and ii) because of the different characteristics and parameters of their local labour markets. The three case study areas each have very different institutional, cultural and economic identities. Trento is an autonomous province with dynamic small businesses and an important seasonal economy in tourism and agriculture; Piemonte is a region containing a large city, Turin, undergoing significant industrial restructuring, and with a long history of internal and international immigration. Milan is the heart of the Italian industrial and service economy.

The three areas also differ widely in terms of their administrative identity. The autonomous province of Trento is a net recipient of public money, with a powerful hold over the local economy; Piemonte is a regional authority responsible for providing guidelines and directing funds; and Milan is saddled with complex social issues but does not have responsibility for labour policy, which is held by the province. Milan is also often in competition with outlying municipalities in the same province to attract resources and provide services for employers.

The objectives of authorities in each area in relation to the local integration of immigrants are similar:

- To respond to demands from business for appropriate labour (each area has low unemployment and makes use of immigrant labour).
- To improve employability. Labour force participation is low, especially in relation to regular employment. Pension data consistently show that many labour migrants are not regularly employed, but work in the informal economy. This is particularly true for women and important local sectors such as domestic work and services.
- To maintain social cohesion. Large scale immigration is a social issue because of the precariety and risks faced by many migrants. Similarly, it is a political issue to which the local population is well attuned and local administrations feel that they must be seen to be governing the phenomenon rather than reacting to emergencies.

General migration trends: economic conditions and legislation

In order to understand the context for local initiatives supporting immigrant integration – and the limits in which they must operate – it is important to be aware of the Italian national policy environment and the current economic situation in Italy. The section that follows identifies the main features of the Italian labour market, the role of immigrant workers within this labour market and the nature of Italian immigration and integration policies, including the quota system for workers, permit types and conditions of stay.

Since the mid 1990s, the reform of the Italian labour market has been directed towards liberalising employment contracts and offering fiscal incentives for job creation. This has translated into strong employment growth (employment grew on average by 0.1 between 1991 and 2001, having accelerated in 2002 and 2003 to rates of 1.5% and 1.0 respectively). This evolution has been however accompanied by a decelerating productivity.[1]

Although product market competition intensified in the 1990s, increased globalisation has moderately eroded Italy's external competitiveness during recent years as reflected by the decrease in the market shares of the export sector. However, according to the OECD (2003), there is considerable scope for improvement if Italy's competitive strengths are used well. Strengths which can be cited include the following: *a)* a very high rate of entrepreneurship; *b)* clusters of small firms profiting from economies of scale and achieving high quality; c) high private savings rate indicating an availability of home capital for domestic investment; and d) a relatively high labour productivity level.

Concerning recent labour market evolution, while the employment to population ratio and the labour force participation rate have continuously increased in the last decade to reach levels of 56.2% and 61.6% respectively in 2003, they still remain below the EU and OECD averages.[2] On the other hand, the unemployment rate has considerably decreased, having fallen from 11.5% in 1999 to 8.8% in 2003, considerably narrowing the gap with the EU-15. However, large differences persist between the north and the south of Italy in terms of productivity levels and employment and unemployment rates. This explains why foreign labour tends to concentrate in the north of Italy as there are more opportunities, particular as the internal movement of the national population from south to north, has decreased.[3]

A considerable share of Italian employment is within the informal economy. According to the OECD (2004), the share of informal economic activity represents 16 % of the Italian GDP. In fact, the informal economy has risen in the past few years according to ISTAT figures on the share of irregular workers (from 13.4% in 1992 to 15.1% in 2000). In the literature, a range of causes are quoted, including institutional rigidities in the formal sector, such as heavy taxes and working hour restrictions (Reyneri, 1998, OECD 2003). The sectors most affected by the informal economy are agriculture, retail trade, hotels and restaurants, road transport and domestic services.[4]

To reduce the diffusion of the informal economy, government incentives were offered in 2001 to firms and workers. Participation in this programme was lower than expected forcing the government to constantly adapt and postpone the deadline for firms to declare their informal activity and restructuring plans (OECD, 2003). A positive sign has nevertheless been observed in the increase in workers' registration within social security institutions. The 2002 amnesty to regularise undocumented migrants has clearly contributed to this evolution, as well as other labour market measures included in the 2002 "Pact for Italy" (i.e. tax incentive for permanent hirings and public loans for new self employment).[5] On the other hand, the industrial base of Italy, which is characterised by a high concentration of SMEs in the northern and central regions, operating in sectors of light industry (shoes, furniture, textiles, etc.), construction, agriculture, and services (tourism, etc.) has attracted a foreign workforce in a context of labour supply shortages. The labour offered in these sectors has been characterised as low-skilled, with low levels of job security, not always attractive to the national labour force.

Migrants in the Italian labour market

Until 1973 Italy was a major emigration country, sending millions of workers abroad, many permanently. In the 1970s and 80s, this migratory pattern changed and Italy started to receive workers from abroad and by 1997 the net flow of remittances had reversed. Between 1986 and 2004, the legally resident foreign population rose from under 300 000 to an estimated 2.6 million (Caritas 2004), accounting for 4.5% of the total population. Immigration to Italy is quite heterogeneous: the leading countries of origin are Romania, Albania and Morocco, each comprising just over 10% of the total. Other important foreign populations include Ukraine, China, Philippines and Poland. Most of these immigrants are young people (aged between 20 and 40 years) who are in Italy for economic reasons.

Table 3.2 shows the different role played by migrant labour in different Italian regions. Unemployment varies widely among regions from 23.4% in Calabria to 2.4% in Trentino; internal migration has declined to the point where it is no longer considered a solution for closing this gap. Foreign-born workers make up 16.5% of all job starts nationally, ranging from 2.9% in isolated Sardegna to 39.1% in Trentino. While the Italian Labour Force Survey does not distinguish between foreign or foreign-born and Italian workers,

Table 3.1. **Foreign residents in Italy holding a residence permit, 1985-2003**

	Total residence permits (at 1 January)	*Of which*, non-EU
1985	263 731	133 431
1986	289 068	151 714
1987	380 425	227 734
1988	422 678	258 464
1989	319 291	226 369
1990	550 457	422 489
1991	692 630	571 621
1992	648 935	548 531
1993	589 457	485 426
1994	649 102	540 993
1995	677 791	563 158
1996	729 159	606 974
1997	986 020	857 897
1998	1 022 896	887 689
1999	1 090 820	948 692
2000	1 340 655	1 194 792
2001	1 379 749	1 233 584
2002	1 448 392	1 308 335
2003	1 503 286	1 352 420
2004	2 193 999	2 040 530

Source: Istat (2004); Dossier Caritas (2004). Permits considered here exclude minors.

immigrant workers make up an important part of the labour market, far out of proportion to the 4.5% of the population they now represent. In particular, areas of Italy with lower unemployment make significant use of immigrants to meet labour demand.

Table 3.2. **Regional unemployment and migrant labour**

Region	Average regional unemployment, 2003 (in %)[a]	Jobs starts by non-EU workers, 2003 (% of total)[b]	Foreign permit holders, 2003[c]	Increase in permit holders, 2003	Expected hires of non-EU workers, 2004[d]	Quota for entry of foreign workers, 2004[c]
Abruzzo	5.4	16.3	32 873	11 661	6 163	930
Basilicata	16.1	7.2	5 782	2 307	1 286	400
Calabria	23.4	5.6	33 485	16 010	3 747	565
Campania	20.2	5.6	111 596	53 558	11 727	630
Emilia-Romagna	3.1	22.3	271 756	69 969	20 989	2 430
Friuli-Venezia	3.9	25.3	62 052	13 028	6 394	1 230
Lazio	8.7	11.6	330 695	92 109	14 848	1 820
Liguria	6	16.4	57 834	22 474	5 423	670
Lombardia	3.6	21.6	502 610	155 842	36 928	2 800
Marche	3.8	20.2	64 989	17 899	6 640	1 120
Molise	12.3	7.9	3 635	1 240	754	350
Piemonte	4.8	18.4	167 615	59 665	15 888	1 330
Puglia	13.8	4.9	43 163	11 995	9 294	955
Sardegna	16.9	2.9	14 893	3 188	3 824	407
Sicilia	20.1	6.3	65 194	15 488	8 121	915
Toscana	4.7	20.1	175 026	63 893	11 857	1 200
Trentino-Alto Adige	2.4	39.1	43 366	5 274	5 741	1 000
Umbria	5.2	23.3	43 845	13 917	3 612	555
Valle d'Aosta	4.1	15.4	3 792	922	632	73
Veneto	3.4	23.8	213 798	60 274	12 141	2 620
Total Italy	8.7	16.5	2 193 999	690 713	195 009	22 000

Source: a) Istat (2004); b) Inail (2004), adjusted for missing data; c) Data are for 31/12/2003, Dossier Caritas (2004); d) Excelsior Unioncamere (2004); e) These data exclude seasonal workers, Ministry of Labour (2004).

The legally resident foreign population rose by 28.2% in 2003, almost entirely because of workers regularised under the 2002 Law. While about half were domestic workers, half claimed contract employment. In addition, employers predicted hiring up to 195 000 additional foreign workers in 2004, indicating further demand. Most of these expected hires were in the northern part of the country (half in just four industrial regions: Lombardia, Veneto, Piemonte and Emilia-Romagna). At this time, the government placed sharp limits on importing workers, establishing quotas of just 22 000 contract workers. Almost 90% of the supposed "immigrant labour" needs, therefore, would have to be met by immigrants already in the country. This makes matching supply and demand essential in order to meet the needs of employers.

Labour supply shortages have been felt in specific sectors, mostly those demanding low-skilled workers. In addition, there has more recently been a supply shortage for some specialised workers, especially in the construction sector, but also in industry, tourism and services. The Excelsior Information System, created for *Unioncamere* in agreement with the Ministry of Labour, annually analyses expected Italian labour market demand by enterprises.[6] Of the 2004 estimates, 52% were in the industrial sector.

Immigrant workers frequently take jobs that the native population is unwilling to take. These occupations have been described by Ambrosini (2004) as the "five-p jobs": *pesanti, precari, pericolosi, poco pagati, penalizzati socialmente* (heavy, precarious, dangerous, poorly paid, socially penalised), or the "three-D jobs" (dirty, dangerous, and demanding). Immigrant women are typically employed in the informal economy as housekeepers or private carers for elderly people. This role is not reflected in the Excelsior system, since the employers are individuals rather than businesses.

Table 3.3 shows the employment sectors which most demand immigrant workers and their expected training needs. About half of immigrant employees are sought with no prior experience, and therefore for the least qualified jobs in the field. Nonetheless, most are expected to require training. This is especially true in some specialised industrial sectors and in health care. This has major implications for the national vocational training system, as will be discussed below.

The number of non-EU-born entrepreneurs in Italy has risen sharply. On 31 March 2005, there were 181 773 such entrepreneurs registered at chambers of commerce, from 67 440 five years earlier, while the number of Italian-owned businesses held steady at 3.3 million. Women represent less than 10% of the total number of non-EU entrepreneurs. These enterprises are concentrated in the sectors of commerce (42.3% of total), construction (26.8%), and manufacturing (11.7%). The most active nationalities are Moroccans (17.4%), followed by Chinese (11%), Swiss (8.6%), Albanians (7.8%), Romanians (6.6%) and Senegalese (6.5%) and are mainly located in the regions of Lombardia (33 018), Tuscany (18 544), Emilia Romagna (17 735), Veneto (16 839), and Lazio (16 114). In all five regions non-EU entrepreneurs represented more than 6% of all entrepreneurs.[7]

Particular sectors, both of employment and of self-employment, are often identified with particular immigrant groups (Campani, 1993). For instance, commerce mainly attracts immigrants from Morocco, Senegal and China. Domestic services employ women from Philippines, Poland and South America. This occupational distribution is accompanied by the regional distribution of migration chains, which involves the concentration of certain nationalities in specific regions within the country (Triandafyllidou and Veikou, 2001).

Table 3.3. **New hires and expected demand of immigrants, including training needs, 2003-2004**

Employment sector	Foreign-born hires, 2003[a]	Expected demand for immigrant labour, 2004	Percentage of all hires, 2004	Percentage requiring training	Percentage having no prior experience
Hotels and restaurants	70 544	1 859	33.5	53.3	54.2
Construction industry	65 065	35 490	34.1	51.8	31.6
Transport and postal services	29 425	1 433	33.1	55.4	43.1
Metal industry	24 017	12 632	35.9	72.7	48.8
Retail trade	18 855	14 334	22.4	80.9	59.8
Wholesale trade	16 381	5 959	18.5	65.4	56.4
Food industry	14 436	5 341	28.8	76.7	57.7
Textile industry	1 399	6 235	28.3	68.1	46.9
Health care	8 870	10 948	43.2	83.2	29.8
Mechanical industry	897	6 751	24.1	78.4	42.9
Rubber industry	5 502	2 746	36.3	85.3	73.3
Wood/Furniture industry	4 962	5 213	32.3	68.3	44.4
Electrical industry	4 879	3 885	25.6	82.5	57.2
Auto repair	4 669	4 505	22.2	73.6	42.4
Paper industry	2 765	1 694	22.6	80.7	56.5
Banking/Financial services	2 606	1 624	8.4	74.4	62.7
Mining	796	539	23.5	63.8	44.2
Electricity/Gas/Water industry	268	341	11.5	72.1	51.1
Other	139 422	..	..	..	..
Unspecified	337 155	..	..	..	..
Total	771 813	..	..	..	..

Source: Excelsior Unioncamere – Ministry of Labour, reported in Documento programmematico 2004-2006. a) INAIL/DNA, Caritas 2004.

Italian migration policy and legislation

The first attempt to create modern immigration legislation was made in 1986 (Law 943/1986), which regulated the entry of immigrants seeking employment, and regularised immigrants who could prove such employment. The sharp rise in migration in the late 1980s and the breakdown of the old European order led to the passing of another, broader law in 1990 (Law 39/1990, known as the "*Martelli law*"), with special provisions regarding immigration including the annual planning of migratory flows, and certain norms regarding the rights and obligations of foreigners in Italy, their stay and work conditions, and other matters regarding family reunion and social integration. Asylum – which had not yet seriously affected Italy – was also addressed.

Immigration became a significant issue in the 1990s, leading to Law 40/1998 (the so-called *Turco-Napolitano* law or *Testo Unico*), issued by the centre-left government. This created a three-pillar immigration policy that has since been upheld by the centre-right coalition based on: *a)* fighting illegal migration; *b)* regulating legal migration; and *c)* integrating resident foreigners. The first pillar concentrated on bilateral agreements and criminal penalties, the second on a quota system, and the third on a national immigration fund distributed to regions. The government was required to publish three-year planning documents for immigration. Entry to Italy was allowed within the national quotas and with either a job offer, or "sponsorship" by a legal Italian resident.

In 2002, the 1998 immigration law was revised. Law 189/2002 (known as the *Bossi-Fini* Law) imposes further restrictions on entry and tightens the conditions for stay: integration measures are left intact. The main elements of the current immigration law are shown in Box 3.1.

A number of actors are involved in policy-making concerning immigration. The principal ministries are the Ministry of the Interior (*Ministero dell'Interno*), which includes the local police (dealing with residence permit issuing), and the prefectures (dealing with local security issues and the regularisation of immigration flows) and the Ministry of Labour and Social Policy, which regulates issues concerning the labour market. Within the Ministry of Labour, the Non-EU Immigrants' Service (*Servizio Extracomunitari*) is responsible for determining the annual quotas, monitoring the regularisation of immigrants, bilateral agreements, etc. Other stakeholders include local authorities, a national conference, and NGOs and social parties (Chaloff, 2004).

It is important to specify the meaning of "integration" in Italian immigration policy. Italy as a whole is not formally a "migration" country, like Canada or Australia, nor is it declaredly "multicultural", as Holland and Sweden have announced in recent years. Its migration policy is based on limiting migration into the country to meet specific labour demand. At the same time, immigrant workers have certain rights: to eventual family reunification, to gradual reassurance regarding the possibility of staying in the country and parity of access to public services. The Italian citizenship law is separate from the 1998 immigration framework law and is highly restrictive in both letter and practice, with 90% of applications for naturalisation being rejected. Nonetheless, the Law 40/1998 rests on three pillars, of which one is "integration". The broad assumption underlying the legislation is that labour market integration – employment – is a necessary and sufficient condition to guarantee social integration, when coupled with parity of right of access to public services. The "integration" pillar is supported by an annual fund of about € 40 million filtered through the regions to local authorities and civil society.

The main reference point for immigrants, besides the provincial police station responsible for documents, is the "immigrant service" or "foreigners'

> **Box 3.1. Italian Migration Law 40/1988 as modified by law 189/2002**
>
> **The Quota system**
>
> The number of authorisations for entry for work purposes is established annually after hearing the Committee for the Coordination and Monitoring* and the relevant Parliamentary commissions.
>
> **Entry conditions**
>
> Non-EU immigrants can enter Italy only with a "residence contract" (*contratto di soggiorno*) – i.e. a contract of dependent employment with an employer (a firm or a family), according to availability within the quota system.
>
> A needs test for foreign workers was added in 2002, requiring the employment office to publish the job opening; if there is no answer after 20 days, the prefecture authorises the entry of a new non-EU worker.
>
> The employer has to guarantee the availability of housing for the worker, complying with the minimum standards laid down by the law for public housing, and also payment of travel expenses for the workers to return home.
>
> A "sponsor" system was created by the 1998 law but eliminated by the 2002 Law.
>
> Entry for self-employment is subject to the self-employment quotas.
>
> **Residence permit limits**
>
> The residence permit varies depending on the type of work :
>
> - A total of nine months for seasonal work. Starting in 2002, foreigners coming to Italy for at least two consecutive years may be granted a multi-annual permit for up to three years for seasonal work, or, within the quota, a normal work permit.
> - No more than one year for dependent temporary workers and no more than two years for non-temporary workers, self-employed work, or family reunification.
> - Renewals are subject to the same time limits (the 1998 Law allowed for renewals of twice the length).
>
> Non-EU workers who lose their job have a maximum of six months to find a new job, after which they face expulsion. The 1998 time limit was for the duration of the permit and not less than 12 months.
>
> Applicants for a first or renewal residence permit must be fingerprinted (introduced in 2002).
>
> Anyone with a residence permit that allows indefinite renewal (i.e., work or family), and who earns enough to provide for himself/herself (and family) might request a 10-year automatically renewable residence card after six years in Italy (compared to 5 years under the 1998 Law).
>
> * The committee consists of four ministers and a regional or autonomous provincial council chairman.

office" created in almost all municipalities with a significant immigrant presence. While provinces tend to assign responsibility to their department for social services, municipalities have generally constituted a specific office for dealing with integration issues.

The management of foreign labour flows in Italy essentially centres on the quota system. It is intended that there should be a three-year programme spelling out the guidelines for quotas over the period, but the decree authorising the following year's entry quotas (*flussi di ingresso*) is meant to be passed by 30 November annually. In lieu of the decree, the previous year's quota is reapplied. The quota system has been plagued by delays. Annual decrees are frequently issued past the deadline, which causes postponements in the submission of applications and in the regularisation process.[8] Law 189/2002 specifies that, if appropriate, further decrees may be issued during the year. This creates problems for seasonal workers in agriculture, where all requests have to be collected and all permits issued before the beginning of the harvesting season. Authorisations must be issued before July, in order to be sent to Italian embassies or consulates which in turn have to issue visas to the workers before August. Delays and backlogs at consulates are such that some applicants and employers talk of bribery occurring during this stage.

Legal entry for work was set at 58 000 persons in 1998 and 1999, increasing to 83 000 in 2000 and to 89 400 in 2001. During the period 2002-2004, the annual decree set quotas for the entry of 79 500 immigrant workers annually, of whom 50 000 were for seasonal work only. Students and other foreigners with non-work permits can convert their permits for work within certain limits of the quota. (Triandafyllidou and Veikou, 2001). Family reunification in Italy is exempt from the quotas.[9] Those with a family permit are allowed, but not required, to work.

Regularisations

The quotas have always fallen short of national estimates of demand for foreign labour (as estimated by the Excelsior system) and applications to provincial labour offices almost always far exceed the available supply (Zanfrini, 2003). Many workers, in fact, arrive undocumented and work unregistered, hoping either to establish a relationship with an employer willing to undertake the complicated bureaucratic procedure necessary for legal entry, or to support their application during one of the periodic regularisations. The quotas, in this sense, have been identified as unproductive (Lemaître, 2003).

Italy's position in the centre of the Mediterranean, extensive coastline and important tourism and pilgrimage industry makes it a relatively accessible country for Europe-bound immigrants. The existence of a considerable informal economy, the rapid growth of the domestic and personal services sector and the predominance of small businesses provide work for undocumented migrants. Proof of this can be found in the periodic regularisations (five times in sixteen years: 1986, 1990, 1996, 1998 and 2002), allowing the cumulative regularisation of more than 2 million migrants, although many were repeat regularisations of the same individual who had fallen back into irregular status after failing to meet criteria for permit renewal.

The latest regularisation in September 2002 was aimed at two types of irregular immigrant workers: domestic workers and home-helpers; and workers involved in other kinds of low skilled employment. Previously documented foreigners whose residence permits had expired were also able to regularise their situation. Applicants had to prove that they had been hired before June 10, 2002, and had never received a deportation order. By the end of 2003, 689 604 regularisation applications were registered. The impact of this regularisation was to increase the legally resident population of foreigners by about 50% in most areas.

Refugees and asylum-seekers

Italy, alone in the EU, does not have a framework asylum law. Currently, political asylum is regulated by Article 1 of Law 39/1990 and by a few articles of the immigration Law 189/2002. Law 39/1990 abrogated the Italian clause to the Geneva Convention which limited refugee status exclusively to persons from authoritarian countries in Europe. The Dublin Convention of 1990 (ratified in 1992 and in effect since 1997) introduced a second norm by which asylum seekers can be sent back to the Dublin signatory country where a prior application had been made.

Asylum seekers have traditionally been only a small component of total migration flows in Italy (around 10 000 applications annually), and delays in the asylum procedure, coupled with a lack of housing and social support, have meant that many asylum seekers fail to appear at their hearing and are presumed to have moved elsewhere. Under the Dublin Convention, many are sent back to await a new hearing. Only a third of those present for their hearing receive refugee status or a recommendation of temporary stay for humanitarian reasons.[10] Recent asylum seekers have been Turkish and Iraqi Kurds, and people from countries such as Afghanistan and Iran, with the latest flows from sub-Saharan Africa.

The average wait for an asylum hearing is 12-15 months, during which applicants have no right to work. Public support is available only for the first 45 days, after which applicants are without any support, although medical care is guaranteed. The system of protection is a national shelter and support network, co-financed by the Ministry of Interior and participating municipalities, which covers only a fraction of demand. There were 6 226 recognised refugees in Italy at the end of 2003. When recognised, refugees receive a 2 year renewable residence permit allowing them to work and have access to public assistance and then, after 5 years, they can apply for citizenship. Refugees are also exempt from the reciprocity clause governing self-employment.

Local initiatives: responding to integration problems

The following section, analyses a selection of initiatives to integrate immigrants and their families in Italy, particularly in the north of the country (Trento, Turin and Milan). In each case, the main problem faced is presented, followed by a review of relevant local initiatives and policy responses. The main mechanisms used to tackle the problem at the local level are identified, their impact is assessed and comparisons are made with similar initiatives elsewhere in Italy.

Emergency management

It should be clear from the above presentation of trends that there is a significant presence of immigrant workers in Italy who have been in the country for a short while, who are largely without resources and often lack a residence permit or a formal job contract. For local authorities, this can translate into an "emergency" situation, with visible homelessness and other signs of social exclusion. In some cases, daily encounters between the aging native population and disadvantaged newcomers can result in a perception of cultural conflict or crime; sometimes the perception of rising crime is confirmed by statistics.

Local authorities feel that they must demonstrate to citizens their ability to govern the situation or risk losing credibility and elections. While this may take the form of repressive measures, the role that migrant workers play in the local economy often means that social services and initial solutions to the problems of reception must be found. Local authorities generally have a limited number of beds available for emergency situations; further, such beds are often for disadvantaged categories of person such as drug addicts or the mentally ill, and are not suited for healthy working foreigners.

In Italy, the non-profit third sector has been at the forefront of providing emergency reception facilities, and local authorities throughout the country have learned to rely heavily on shelters and services provided by associations. The most important associations and facilities have strong links to the Catholic Church. This is in part because of the mission of the Church and in part because of the resources on which these organisations can rely:

substantial volunteer staff; clerical personnel with experience in providing basic reception services; old convents and other church property well-adapted for reception and located in city centres. Box 3.2 provides an example from Turin.

In Milan, most initial reception facilities for immigrants are also run by volunteer associations, Caritas, and the parish churches (*Farsi Prossimo* is the most important one). Funding and coordination is provided by the foreigners office of the municipality. At its peak in 1992 the system of primary reception centres offered 1 450 beds. In 1995, a temporary round table on immigrants' housing problems reconstructed and reorganised the two main first reception centres, improving the quality of the services provided and reducing the number of beds to 390. These reception centres are considered counterproductive in terms of integration and social acceptance. The six-month maximum stay is difficult to respect because of the lack of alternatives and the difficulty in finding rented accommodation.

In coordinating and managing emergency issues for the must vulnerable migrant workers, local authorities are forced to react to the large scale irregular migration created by the demand for labour, the informal economy and shortfalls in the quota system. This places public authorities in a difficult position, as they feel that they cannot take repressive measures for economic reasons (employers would protest) and political reasons (round-ups of undocumented immigrants do not usually appeal to voters). At the same time, they cannot be directly responsible for providing shelter to undocumented migrants.

Quota facilitation

A comparison between the annual quotas and the estimate of new foreign labour by enterprises, as noted above, reveals that the quotas are not enough to meet local labour needs. This means that the smooth functioning of the complicated quota procedure is even more important.

In some parts of the country, substantial seasonal labour quotas are offered. This is the case in the Trentino-Alto Adige region, where the bulk of the seasonal labour quota is assigned to the two autonomous provinces (Trento and Bolzano). The labour market in the province of Trento relies heavily on the use of seasonal workers in the sectors of agriculture and tourism. The employers' associations in Trento, as elsewhere, have long complained that the low quotas this province received were insufficient to meet labour demand. Now that the quotas have risen to meet demand, the main concern is the amount of paperwork involved in the process. In most parts of Italy, in fact, the procedure for requesting and admitting foreign workers is seen as too complicated and cumbersome.

> **Box 3.2. A non-profit reception centre and dormitory in Turin: Sermig**
>
> Sermig is a religious association that has renovated an old weapons factory owned by the region, converting it into an open house for those seeking assistance (such as single mothers, immigrants and those in need of care, a home or a job). From its roots as a base for missionary activity in developing countries, Sermig has, since 1988, offered first aid and counselling to newly arrived immigrants while they are looking for a job, in connection with the other associations (*e.g.* Caritas) offering a similar service in the city. They offer a dormitory and meals to both Italians and immigrants (80 beds for men and 40 for women). Immigrants can stay a maximum of one month if unemployed, but some of them often go to other associations and then come back after a period. Because the structure is private, it can accept homeless people regardless of their immigration status. In that sense, it serves as a vital safety valve compared to the city-run shelters, which can only accept foreigners with documents.
>
> The dormitory hours are compatible with the work done by migrants in the local economy: men must vacate the facility in the early morning in two shifts, corresponding to the starting time for day labourers working in building trades in the province of Turin; women must enter earlier and leave later, corresponding to their work as nannies and domestic workers in the city. Sermig also provides medical care through a free day clinic (nurses, specialists in different fields, and dental care), which is mainly used by immigrants.
>
> Sermig also provides longer term housing to women who are benefiting from Article 18, the anti-trafficking clause in the 1998 Law. Victims of abuse and exploitation and their children receive housing, support and counselling and mediation with local social services. The service is separately funded under Article 18. They have also created a vocational school for artisan restoration in 1995 in collaboration with APRA (Piemonte Art Restorers Association) and in partnership with several public and private institutions. This project is funded by the region of Piemonte, the province and the municipality of Turin, and the European Union through the European Social Fund. In 2004, the school provided annual vocational training for around 100 youth in traditional and endangered restoration trades and offered them employment opportunities in that field. Few immigrants, however, were involved in these courses.

To facilitate this task, Trento relies on a series of intermediaries and on a provincial institution. In 80% of the cases in Trento province, employers make a nominative request for a specific worker to their employers' association, who then contact the provincial labour office. The mediation of the employer's association is particularly useful for small farmers, who need only a few workers for a short period.

After an authorisation to enter has been issued in Italy, the next obstacle is the long queue of visa applicants at embassies and consulates. In 2003, the provincial labour office of Trento took the unusual step of sending its own staff to open an office one floor above the Italian consulate in Poland, to monitor and streamline the administrative procedures necessary for obtaining a seasonal work visa. This effectively sped up the visa procedure. In 2004 they obtained authorisation from the Ministry of Foreign Affairs to have a temporary desk in two consulates in Romania in order to monitor visas issuance for 3 000 seasonal workers.

Because foreigners are required to apply to the local police station for their residence permit within eight days, Trento saw long queues forming in the centre of the city. These queues had a political and economic cost: long lines in front of the police station raised public concern over the management of immigration inflows, and employers suffered from lost production time due to the forced absence of the worker. Such problems became even more pressing and urgent during harvest time. In 2001, the province opened a special service, CINFORMI, which has since become the main actor in issuing permits and supporting the overall integration of immigrants in the Trento province. It is a good example of public-private partnership between the province and different associations on how to deal with the quota devoted to the region, by simplifying the administrative process concerning the issue and renewal of stay permits, and introducing other integration issues (see Box 3.3).[11]

Trento is by no means the only province to suffer from issues surrounding access to permits, and more than half of Italian provinces had developed some sort of partnership for accelerating permit renewal by 2004. However, CINFORMI goes far beyond the usual services of such partnerships. There are several noteworthy factors behind CINFORMI's success. Firstly, services are provided within the same structure by different cooperatives through competitive tenders, while avoiding large differences in salaries. This has limited the tensions which exist elsewhere within such public-private organisations. Secondly, the structure has been able to identify and meet additional demands from users, offering counselling and public awareness services. Thirdly, CINFORMI sees its role as facilitating access to existing services rather than supplying a specially targeted version of the same service to an exclusively immigrant population. It is in this spirit that the centre does not offer, for example, support for immigrant entrepreneurs, but rather orients foreigners towards mainstream services.

> Box 3.3. **The province of Trento Information Centre for Immigration: CINFORMI**
>
> The CINFORMI office was created in 2001, by the province of Trento to facilitate the issue and renewal of permits for immigrants. One of its main characteristics is its integrated approach to immigration issues in co-operation with the different entities involved in the region. Its main activities are oriented towards four purposes: *a)* supporting the functioning of the admission and permit system; *b)* counselling and orientation; *c)* a call-centre; and *d)* media, information and awareness building. It also serves many other migration-related functions, including research and project proposals, but the heart of its activity lies in its role as a one-stop shop for entry and permit procedures.
>
> The reservation-system has been arranged with the prefecture to provide migrant workers with their appropriate permits. The goal of CINFORMI is to create an on-line network with the prefecture and the provincial labour office to process the same information through the creation of a common data bank in order to avoid duplications, simplify and render the whole process more efficient. The provincial labour office (*Servizio Lavoro*) provides CINFORMI with a data file of all seasonal workers authorised to enter into the province of Trento (except workers in agriculture).* CINFORMI simplified the procedure for seasonal foreign workers by issuing one receipt proving that a foreigner has applied for the residence permit.
>
> The residence permits are not issued for seasonal workers who stay less than 4 months. This is because the police station of Trento must first send applicants' fingerprints to the central archive of the foreigners office in Rome, a procedure which takes several months and is not feasible for short-term workers. While the provincial labour office, responding to repeated requests from the police station, did fingerprint short term seasonal workers in 2002, this procedure was suspended in 2003 and 2004.
>
> CINFORMI also processes residence permit applications for highly-skilled workers such as university lecturers and business representatives who are involved in collaborative work. For all other categories of applicants, CINFORMI provides information on documents that the police station requires, and checks to ensure documentation is complete. Because of the size and difficulty of moving around the province, this service is also available in local branches, helping to avoid lost working time in preparing paperwork. CINFORMI periodically electronically updates the police station on completed applications, and maintains an on-line connection allowing the police station to check all applications received. The whole system is based on a strong relationship of trust.
>
> * Seasonal workers for short term work (i.e. less than 4 months) in agriculture obtain their residence permit through another system. Authorisation to enter is issued by the police station, which transmits the receipt to the employers' associations, who provide it to appropriate employers. Employers then provide foreign workers with this receipt when they come to the province of Trento.

The other areas examined during the case study revealed different approaches to the issue of facilitating the quota system. For example, the region of Piemonte took part, along with four other regions (Veneto, Emilia

Romagna, Toscana and Campania) in a study of regional experiences with the quota system conducted by Italia Lavoro[12] (Italia Lavoro, 2004). The quota approved by the central government was always much lower than that requested by Piemonte enterprises, and not sufficient to meet the needs of the labour market. In some cases only 30% of the quota requested was approved. In 2004, the provincial department of labour for Turin received more than 3 000 applications for 379 available slots; in Milan it received more than 2 500 applications for 700 available slots.

Furthermore, in relation to the quota system, Italia Lavoro found no reliable model or standardised procedure for the estimation of labour market needs and sustainable flows. The current estimates were considered approximate and inaccurate: provincial labour departments telephone the employers' associations asking the number of immigrant workers they need. They then communicate this information to the regional council, and through that to the Ministry. This makes it difficult to estimate labour market needs in some sectors (*i.e.* housekeepers and carers).

In fact, in Piemonte and in Milan, the quota system was seen as largely irrelevant in planning integration measures. These areas, with large populations of settled immigrants, do not look to the quotas to meet their labour needs. Like most regions or provinces, they take the quota as given because they do not feel that they can influence the central government, and devote little effort to streamlining or supporting the system. The only exception is the Piemonte province of Cuneo, which has been able to make a case for a relatively high entry quota for seasonal agricultural workers.

The ability of the province of Trento to successfully govern entry under the quota system was fundamental in making the system work for the province. Starting in 2003 the province of Trento, almost alone in Italy, managed to influence the central government and to obtain the requested seasonal quota. The province convinced the central government of its efficient match of supply and demand of foreign labour. It could be supposed that the central government would not have assigned these high quotas if Trento had not demonstrated its ability to manage the flows and to prevent the workers from staying in Italy at the end of their contracts.

Management of the authorisation system at a local level has led, at least in the case of Trento, to the development of advanced public services that, while initially created with the scope of facilitating an administrative procedure, have evolved into a point of reference and management of a wide range of integration issues. The need to develop local solutions to bureaucratic hurdles can, in the best of cases, bring public administrations into contact with immigrants and lead to a greater understanding of their needs, whether job-related or not. At the same time, this kind of parallel quota and permit management service is a means by which the central government – which arguably should bear the burden within the police – shifts administrative costs onto local authorities. It is therefore a case of good practice compensating for a failure elsewhere in the system.

Regularisation

Regularisation – also known as amnesty – has been the primary means by which Italy has granted permits to foreign workers. Amnesties have taken place on average every four years and created an enormous administrative workload and demand for information. This has led to the involvement of both local authorities and the third sector, with a consequent reinforcement of the role of the latter in ensuring that national policy is implemented and that immigrants actually benefit from the regularisation.

To a greater extent than previously, the 2002 regularisation served as a stimulus to many associations to provide support to applicants. Applications were to be submitted at post offices, where there was no assistance. The short application period (60 days) and the need to prepare documentation and pension payments meant that many foreigners turned to associations for support in filling out forms and providing evidence. In some cases, associations defended workers in cases where their employers refused to regularise them, or when employers insisted – illegally – that the workers themselves pay prior pension contributions.

Trade unions were in the forefront of this assistance. In Milan, the CGIL alone handled 30 000 applications. Equally important was the ACLI-Colf, the Catholic Worker's Association for domestic workers, which set up branches around the metropolitan area to help domestic workers with their procedures. This contact reinforced the role of these associations as representatives of immigrant workers, especially in a situation where institutions were unable to develop a coordinated response.

Trade unions were not alone in their involvement. In the region of Lombardia, the industrial employers' association, *Assolombarda*, sent its own personnel to provide assistance in the prefecture of Milan for the regularisation of contract employees. In Trento, where the regularisation had more limited effects (the foreign population rose by 16% rather than by 50 or 60% as in Lombardia or Piemonte), CINFORMI, the existing public agency of the province, was able to support the regularisation.

Language provision

Although Italian is said to be the fourth most-studied foreign language in the world, most immigrant workers arrive in Italy with few or no Italian language skills. This sharply restricts professional opportunities and social integration. Poor Italian language skills were highlighted by employers as one of the major obstacles to providing vocational training for example. Since most training opportunities are available in Italian only, and most employers expect their immigrant workers to receive some training, a necessary precondition is knowledge of the Italian language.

During the 1990s, as the immigrant population in Italy grew, a wide variety of language courses came to be offered by local authorities and by the third sector. These courses varied considerably in terms of length, quality, and curriculum, and issued certificates which were not universally recognised. Some were offered at no charge by volunteer organisations; in other cases, municipalities tendered out these courses to the third sector. At the time, adult education was offered in some public schools, but played a very limited role in meeting the Italian language needs of new immigrants.

In 1997 the Ministry of Public Instruction (now Ministry of Instruction, University and Research) carried out a major reform of the adult education system (Ministry Order 455/97), reorganising the adult education sector to meet the needs of three main user groups: those lacking school certificates (elementary and middle school); those needing Italian language skills; and those interested in other courses. This last category includes professional skills such as photography and computer skills, but the public school system cannot and does not compete with the professional training certification system, run by the Ministry of Labour.

The Permanent Local Centre for Adult Education (CTP – *Centro territorial permanente per l'educazione in età adulta*) was also created, with the assignment of elementary and middle school teachers to adult education. The system expanded rapidly to include around 600 schools by 2001. In 2001/2002, 76 819 foreign students took classes at a CTP, including 42 855 students in language integration courses, 11 298 in introductory basic language skills classes and 22 666 in middle school certificate classes. The latter are important for immigrants because they are usually a prerequisite for enrolment in publicly funded vocational training courses.

The autonomous province of Trento is not part of the national education system and therefore does not follow the same procedures; it does, however, use its provincial education agency in a similar way, through five different schools scattered around the province. In addition to the language and school certificates offered by the national CTP system, Trento also offers assistance in certifying prior instruction and provides secondary school certification.

For the purposes of this case study, it is important to note the rapid integration of the CTP into the local integration policy in each of the areas examined. In some cases, such as in the municipality of Turin, the local school was already the site for language training, and becoming a CTP simply granted the local authority more resources. Local authorities ceased to sponsor separate language classes for immigrants and started to work with the CTPs in the area to coordinate language, literacy and middle school certification for all. Their involvement sometimes took the form of providing additional staff from the budget of the local authority to support the Ministry-paid schoolteachers. The courses offered by the third sector – which filled an important role during the disorganisation of the 1990's – were slowly eliminated through better coordination and competition from the official educational structures. For those without documents, who are not officially allowed to enrol in CTPs, alternative education is still mainly provided by volunteer organisations such as Caritas.

Reliance on a national public system has solved the problems of a lack of certification and the uncoordinated and often duplicatory supply of language courses. When compared to the vocational training arena, where coordination and duplication remains a problem, language training can be considered largely resolved by the CTP system.

Vocational training

As discussed above, Italian employers express concerns about the level of qualification of immigrants, particularly in specialised and highly skilled labour sectors. Vocational training is considered to be very important in order to increase the quality of jobs performed by immigrants.

There are two main kinds of vocational training initiatives for foreigners: training in the country of origin and training in Italy within the existing professional training system. The former training is touted as a keystone in both current admission policy and in regional development programmes. The latter generally involves courses organised at the regional and local level, primarily with funding through the European Social Fund.

As regards training abroad, Law 189/2002 (art. 23) encourages training programmes in countries of origin, which may be aimed towards providing specific skills, in order to: *a)* match demands from Italian firms for particular sectors and job positions; *b)* favour recruitment in Italian firms operating in the countries of origin; *c)* foster economic and independent entrepreneurial initiatives in the country of origin. Foreigners trained under these programmes have priority of access under the quota system.

Such training courses already existed previously. For example, the Ministry of Labour signed an agreement with the Association of Italian Construction Companies (ANCE) in 2001 for the training of construction workers in Poland and Tunisia, who would then be able to enter Italy.[13] Because of the small size of most employers and the time frame of demand, courses are difficult to organise. Since 2002, the Ministry of Foreign Affairs has provided support for training courses in Albania, Tunisia and Morocco (Chaloff and Piperno, 2004).

Such courses are increasingly popular, especially within the context of regional development initiatives. An example of a recent successful programme for vocational training between Italy and the country of origin can be found in Trento (see Box 3.4).

> Box 3.4. **Training foreign workers in their country of origin: A Trento initiative**
>
> Concerning training and upgrading skills, some initiatives have recently been launched to train immigrants in the country of origin (mainly in Romania and Tunisia), in order to meet demand from Trentino firms. In order to meet demand for qualified seasonal workers in the tourism industry, the Association of Commerce and Tourism (*Unione del Commercio e del Turismo*) in 2004 started a bilateral project with the Romanian professional school for Hotel and Catering "Unione Forma School" in Bucharest.
>
> The project is intended to address long-term tourism sector labour needs. This project, the first of this type in Italy, is organised within the initiative "Cooperation Romania-Italy, Summer 2004", jointly run by the province of Trento, the Association of Commerce and Tourism, and Trentino Federation of Co-operatives. The course was divided in different phases. In the first phase, 81 students were selected for Italian language training in Bucharest. Those with good results came to Italy in June 2004 for another two weeks of language training. During the third phase, students had three months of professional training in different tourist businesses in the province of Trento, followed by additional professional training in their country of origin. At the end of 2004, tourist enterprises involved in this project (about 50) offered a seasonal work contract to successful students. A similar project is planned for Hungary and Bulgaria.
>
> The advantages to employers are clear: the demand for trained Italian-language staff in the tourism sector is very high. Training costs are lower in Romania than in Trento. Trainees, on the other hand, are able to benefit from being given priority in the seasonal labour quota and a relationship with the trade association that sponsors their visa application.

A number of examples of this kind of initiative also emerged in other Italian regions. For example, the region of Lombardia promotes training programmes in countries of origin, aimed at providing specific skills to meet regional needs. Different courses have been organised in Tunisia and Slovakia during the last year (18 Tunisians and 14 Slovaks in a training course for specialised construction workers for example) and the CVs of the participants have been catalogued on a special on-line database (*Passaporto Lavoro*) allowing employers in Lombardia to examine and call candidates if needed. A course for tourism operators was also organised in Moldavia and the CVs of these operators were catalogued in an on-line register. One defect of this system is that most employers seek workers they already know, while the courses are offered to those who would receive priority among the few non-nominative requests.

Further, because of the small number of participants, this kind of training does not play a major role in meeting local labour market demand. In fact, such vocational training abroad is only a tiny – and perhaps only politically significant – aspect of the overall training policy. This can be seen in the Piemonte initiatives. *Italia Lavoro Piemonte*, for example, offered a micro-project to assist five young immigrants from Morocco into employment in artisanship enterprises in the city of Turin, with a five-month apprenticeship in Turin and additional training in Marrakech.

In recent years, labour market measures which include targeted vocational and language training for non-EU workers have largely been implemented through the European Social Fund (Objective 3[14] and the Employment Initiative), to facilitate integration into work. In each of the case study areas, ESF-funded training was an important element of local integration policy. In Trento, for example, about two-thirds of funds for immigrants are for training.

In Trento, courses are aimed specifically at immigrants in the field of caring and cultural mediaton. Access to these courses requires a valid residence permit, previous work experience in the field, a high school certificate and good knowledge of the Italian language. These requisites are in practice often difficult to meet. Employers' associations, in collaboration with the province, also offer a number of professional training courses in a variety of specialisations, especially in industry and manufacturing, and setting up new businesses. Nonetheless, few employers – especially small businesses – are willing to sacrifice working time to upgrade the skills of their current employees.

The region of Piemonte provides an example of the organisation of training policy on a much larger scale. The region spends far more on training foreigners with ESF monies than it spends on social integration initiatives with its special integration fund from Law 286/98. The emphasis of the region is on improving the quality of employment, including that of immigrants. Within the three-year regional policy programmes (2001-2003), a number of initiatives have been set up with the aim to increase the employment chances of non-EU immigrants in securing jobs that are offered by public and private entities in the region. This effort was coordinated by the region and funded primarily by the ESF, within its 2000-2006 programme (€ 1 000 million). The region of Piemonte has tried to establish strong links between vocational training, orientation and job placement initiatives, in collaboration and synergy with the region's vocational training and employment department, and social policies department.

Normally, ESF courses do not specifically target immigrants. For example, in the 41 professional courses set up by the region of Piemonte in the 2003/2004 academic year, in which 38 712 people participated, fewer than 700 were in courses created specifically for immigrants. Yet almost 10% of overall participants were non-EU immigrants (3 628 participants), demonstrating the mainstreaming of immigrants into the vocational training system. Some important distinctions did, however, emerge: immigrants were twice as likely to take ongoing ("permanent") training courses (150-200 hours) than the more intensive vocational training for the unemployed (400-600 hours). The latter, in fact, do not allow residence permit renewal for unemployed immigrants.

Specific training programmes sometimes address the incompatibility between duration of training and residence permit requirements. The province of Turin, within the three-year project (2001-2003) financed by the region of Piemonte, promoted a number of immigrant-specific actions, involving 180 employed and 360 unemployed immigrants. The programme was implemented through the organisation of vocational training and apprenticeships in local enterprises, allowing permit renewal during training.

The training courses in which immigrants participate show a sharp gender bias. Men are usually directed towards courses for welders, metalworkers, industrial machine operators, waiters, whereas women are directed towards courses relating to care-giving and auxiliary social assistance. The Department for Vocational Training and Employment based their programming of courses on a preliminary analysis of labour market demand, in order to avoid misplaced investments in training that would prove incapable of meeting the needs of labour market.

Immigrants with a higher level of education are frequently oriented towards courses on cultural mediation. Until 2001, cultural mediation training was not homogeneous (length of the courses, programmes, and criteria of selection of the participants), but since then, the region has made an effort to better define and standardise these courses. Even so, most of the cultural mediators could not find full-time, or even part-time, employment after finishing the course.

The region of Lombardia, like that of Piemonte, allocates financial resources to the provinces, which further allocate these resources to municipalities and local organisations. The region of Lombardia budgeted

€ 95 million for Professional Formation and Employment 2000-06, and part of this funding has been directed to immigrants.

A number of critical points regarding vocational training and immigrants emerged in the case studies. First, the European Social Fund plays a vital role in the system, and the changes in this fund after 2006 will have a major impact on training opportunities. In addition, regions play an important role in establishing guidelines for training priorities. Most of the investments are made in courses that are not specifically designed for immigrants.

Asylum seekers and refugees in the labour market

In sharp contrast to other European countries, asylum seekers and refugees make up only a small fraction of the foreign population (about 1.5%). In Piemonte, and the province of Milan and Trento they were about 650, 1 000 and 220 respectively at the start of 2003. Nonetheless, compared to other categories they are more vulnerable and have more rights. Asylum seekers arrive in Italy with no prior support network and receive only nominal assistance unless admitted to the system of protection, for which there is a waiting list; even within the system of protection, they receive little more than shelter and orientation during the year-long wait for their asylum hearing. They are therefore largely the responsibility of local authorities, who must arrange for their shelter and other needs. Refugees, on the other hand, have the right to stay in the country but have no special assistance.

Local authorities are under pressure to keep asylum seekers off the streets and out of trouble during their lengthy waiting period and to assist refugees in settling. Asylum seekers are generally prohibited from participating in ESF and other publicly funded vocational training courses because they cannot demonstrate their employment status (some regions have however begun to specifically allow access to these courses for asylum seekers). One solution which has been piloted is the training apprenticeship (*tirocinio formativo*), a flexible form of vocational training introduced in 1998 (Law 196/97) and which is not considered legally to represent employment.

The training apprenticeship is a contract between three parties: the promoter, the enterprise where the apprenticeship will take place and the apprentice him or herself. The promoter can be one of a number of different kinds of authorised public and private educational and professional institute. The contract specifies the tutor assigned, the content of the training and the insurance and liability issues involved. The promoter informs local institutions of the apprenticeship and monitors the training to ensure that it is not tantamount to formal contract work. The duration can be up to 12 months. For asylum seekers, this is particularly convenient, since their residence permit is for a duration of three months and is renewable, allowing them to participate in a series of 3-month apprenticeships. The apprenticeship is unpaid, but can include travel and meal costs and a reimbursement for time (not considered the same as wages). This allows businesses to actually pay asylum seekers, which would otherwise be impossible.

The training apprenticeship for asylum seekers was first experimented in Ravenna, Agrigento and Ragusa, and later transferred on a larger scale to an ESF EQUAL project dealing with asylum seeker and refugee integration, Integ.r.a (see Box 3.5).

Local authorities play a key role in these initiatives, providing guarantees for asylum seekers and refugees and reassuring enterprises that these trainees are supported by local institutions. Key factors for success were a good relationship with employers or their associations, careful vetting of the apprentices and continuous tutoring. The advantage for local authorities was clear in keeping the asylum seekers busy during their long waiting period and in providing them with a head start in finding a job in the event of approval of their asylum application. The same mechanism of training apprenticeships could be used with other categories of immigrants.

Matching supply and demand

Institutional responsibility for matching supply and demand in the labour market rests with the provinces, primarily through the Employment Services. Historically, the key element of these services was the unemployment office, now renamed "employment centre" and assigned an active role in promoting employment and orienting job seekers. These centres play an important role in monitoring formal employment but are largely excluded from matching supply and demand in a context where most contacts are informal. A recent study by the IOM (2005) showed how these centres are still struggling to meet their new role. Immigrants make up a significant number of their users but few benefit from the full range of resources offered.

For example, in Milan, the employment centres provide information via internet for immigrants and employers, available in seven languages on regulations, work contracts, etc. These centres are also able to orient users towards the principal organisations present in the province of Milan, active in promoting initiatives aimed at facilitating immigrants' integration. Yet these employment centres are little used by businesses (about 10%) and even less by foreign immigrants (about 2%) in matching supply and demand.

Provincial employment services are also challenged by the plethora of vocational training opportunities available, many sponsored through the ESF and run by different authorities. For municipalities attempting to address this

> **Box 3.5. Training apprenticeships for asylum seekers and refugees**
>
> Integ.r.a is a project funded by EQUAL through the Italian Ministry of Labour and involves 7 municipalities in developing innovative practices for socio-economic integration of asylum seekers and refugees. In fact, under Italian law, the training apprenticeship does not represent a form of work and is not governed by the same strict rules and criteria that regulate traditional forms of vocational training. Since they are clearly governed by a legal framework that does not exclude asylum seekers, training apprenticeships appear to be the best tool to facilitate a first legal approach to the labour market for asylum seekers.
>
> Training apprenticeships were used by six Integ.r.a. partner municipalities (Bergamo, Forlì, Genova, Ancona, Rome and Bitonto) for 120 asylum seekers and refugees and, notwithstanding some differences, had the following common features:
>
> - Asylum seekers were included in training apprenticeships a few months after their entry in Italy, after acquiring some basic Italian literacy.
>
> - Participation in training apprenticeships was preceded by orientation guidance with a specific focus on the features and the dynamics of the Italian labour market, on the rights and obligations of employees, on security at work, giving a full overview of the territorial institutions dealing with labour issues. Furthermore, before his/her inclusion in the apprenticeship, the asylum seeker normally undertook a skills audit in order to be helped to identify his/her prior knowledge, aptitude and skills. This process helps develop appropriate work inclusion routes for the beneficiaries. Skills acquired through the apprenticeship can be used even in case of repatriation.
>
> - The selection of firms took into account promising economic sectors for later employment and privileged those firms with particular experience and awareness of asylum seekers and refugees. In most cases apprentices went to firms where their previous knowledge could be used. Apprenticeship had to be monitored, which required rigorous objectives and constant checks, including exclusion of firms which didn't comply with conditions. The main problem in the apprenticeship was insufficient language skills among asylum seekers.
>
> The advantage for employers lies in the availability of trainees whose insurance and other costs are covered by an outside institution and who receive supplementary training at no cost to the employer. Participating businesses were found in areas where labour demand is so great that many were tempted to employ irregular workers; the apprenticeship provides them with a legal alternative. Trainees, on the other hand, have the opportunity to develop a closer relationship with potential employers and to engage in useful activity during the lengthy application period.
>
> The instrument proved extremely effective. Among those asylum seekers who completed the apprenticeship and were granted refugee status, almost all were hired on an indefinite contract.

issue, resources are even more limited and the legislation denies them a formal role in the employment system. Even so, the fact that municipalities are in contact with resident immigrants through other services means that they can play an active role within the matching process. The challenge for administrations of all levels is to create a relationship with other institutions and stakeholders.

The overlapping and conflicting roles and objectives of institutions and stakeholders is particularly evident in the city of Milan, where the municipality, the province and the region are governed by different coalitions and the coordination of stakeholders involved is extremely complex. The problem of limited coordination and contested leadership was addressed in the evolution of a comprehensive Pact for Employment involving 18 different stakeholders. The municipality, which is normally excluded from an active role in employment services, thus became the coordinator for a wide range of initiatives; the Pact also became a vehicle for attracting and managing ESF resources (see Box 3.6).

It should be noted that the Pact did not bundle all employment services in Milan into a single structure. For example, the municipality of Milan's foreigners office is contracted to run a job information counter, with the following objectives: *i)* promoting the empowerment of immigrant workers by considering the characteristics of the local labour market; *ii)* developing labour and entrepreneurship services; *iii)* helping and supporting employers. Funded through the European Commission's Equal Programme, the counter's activity covers all work related issues, including skills upgrading opportunities and recognition of educational achievements.

There are also some employment sectors, such as domestic work, where public-private partnership services have been able to formalise the matching of supply and demand, providing guarantees for employers and better contractual conditions for employees.

The region of Lombardia also continues to promote its own projects in the area of orientation. The regional Employment Agency (*Agenzia per l'impiego della Lombardia*) promoted the project "Research-initiative aimed at analysing characteristics of immigrants registered as unemployed, and experimentation of measures for their integration into the labour market". This project started in May 2003 and has been running for 18 months, in collaboration with a temporary consortia.[15] The measures have been directed towards professional orientation and training of immigrants, inclusion in the labour market, and support for the creation of new artisan's enterprises.

The first phase of the project used employment centres in their traditional role of registering both job seekers and job offers. Pre-selection interviews used skills assessments. Certification of professional skills was

> ## Box 3.6. **The Pact for Employment in the City of Milan**
>
> In 1998 the municipality of Milan signed agreements with trade unions for local development and better matching of supply and demand. In 1999 this was extended to employer's associations and became the "Employment pact for the city of Milan" (*Patto per il lavoro nella città di Milan*). The objective is to encourage the insertion in the labour market of disadvantaged segments of the labour force – immigrants, long-term unemployed workers, unemployed people aged over 40, and socially disadvantaged young people. The innovative projects to be developed in the framework of this Pact required the creation of a structure to confirm and monitor activity; this was created in 2000 with the "Patto Milan Lavoro", with the province of Milan, the region of Lombardia, 4 trade unions and 11 employers' associations.
>
> This employment pact envisaged the creation of a one-stop shop (counter) for employment, coordination of vocational training and a wide variety of employment contracts, to meet both the needs of employers for skilled labour and the rights of workers to job protection.
>
> A number of development objectives were included in the framework of this agreement, including the use of abandoned areas and the channelling of funds towards training for priority human resource needs. The significant urban redevelopment project underway, for example, requires advanced construction trade skills that employers were struggling to find.
>
> The *Milan Lavoro Counter* is contracted out to the province of Milan. By mid-2004 it had provided orientation service to 3 266 people, created a data base of 9 500 CVs, and a data base on the most frequently offered jobs in the province (1 175 contracts have been signed so far, including 329 immigrants, 103 men and 226 women). It also runs a training service, in cooperation with both public and private vocational training centres (91 vocational trainings had been run since 2000, attended by 1 377 people). An agreement with the Cariplo Foundation provided scholarships to all participants in these courses (for about € 470 each).

performed by various centres of vocational training, which validated the level of immigrant's professional skills. These centres also provided individual counselling on the procedure for recognition of professional qualifications, and on appropriate vocational training courses. Thus, they deal with specific problems encountered by individual immigrants in relation to their inclusion in the labour market. Finally, they provide professional orientation for the groups of immigrants, by organising information meetings on vocational training and employment opportunities. 200 immigrants with a high level of education (secondary school and university) have been involved in the project in the province of Milan.

Other initiatives for matching supply and demand are offered by non governmental organisations and associations. One of the most important employment sectors – and one which draws little interest from traditional stakeholders – is the vast informal domestic work sector. An attempt to bring some legality and protection into this sector – which is based on a family-to-individual employment relationship – was launched by ACLI in Milan (see Box 3.7).

The other case study areas, Trento and Piemonte, showed more seamless coordination between institutions in less complex and fragmented contexts. Nonetheless, the challenges involved in intervening to match supply and demand and increase the quality of employment remain the same, especially in a system where formal employment services play a marginal role. Existing structures for integrating immigrants into society have a natural tendency to try to increase their orientation services into employment, even when this is the specific responsibility of the provincial employment services; the dominance of ESF projects also makes coordination both complicated and essential.

Promoting entrepreneurship

Entrepreneurship among migrants is a vital economic force in most countries. Italy can be a difficult entrepreneurial environment, yet immigrants often aim to start businesses. Recent growth in the number of entrepreneurs in Italy is entirely due to immigrants. This explains a great deal of the enthusiasm from local stakeholders such as chambers of commerce, whose native Italian enrolment has been shrinking, and crafts associations such as the CNA or Confartigianato. These bodies play a key role in supporting entrepreneurial activity by immigrants.

The problems faced by immigrant entrepreneurs are similar throughout the country: unfamiliarity with the culture and economy of Italy, little access to information, poor credit, limited business language skills, difficulty in obtaining recognition of professional skills, and lack of involvement in the social context of professional associations. These are the areas where institutions work to support immigrant entrepreneurs. On the other hand, there are a number of strengths which immigrants bring to entrepreneurship: an "entrepreneurial" culture, a willingness to take risks and a strong "ethnic" network on which to rely.

In Milan, the chamber of commerce is active in supporting immigrant entrepreneurs through its agency Formaper. Through ESF projects and its own institutional activity, it has worked to address the special requirements of self-employed immigrants (75% of the foreign-born owned firms in Milan are individuals; 6.5% of immigrants in 2003 were self-employed). The chamber of

> **Box 3.7. ACLI and its attempt to match supply and demand in domestic work in Milan**
>
> A noteworthy initiative was promoted in the Milan region by Acli (Associazioni Cristiane Lavoratori Italiani – a Christian association of Italian workers) during the 2002 regularisation. An information centre (*Sportello Immigrati*) was opened to provide immigrants and their employers with free information. Advice was given on how to fill in the regularisation declaration and how to calculate back taxes to be paid for regularisation. Acli, like the other major civil society actors, opened offices for this service throughout the whole province. Now that the regularisation process is over, the main office dedicated to this purpose is still working on immigrant work related issues.
>
> In this sense, Acli-Colf[1] has also recently launched a project in Milan called "*I Lari*"" in cooperation with *Obiettivo Lavoro*,[2] consisting in an office for matching job offers and seekers in the field of caring and house keeping. The aim is to offer families a better way to organise their search for help, while providing job opportunities to job seekers. It plans to provide vocational training and skills upgrading in household services and domestic care, in order to address the cultural and linguistic problems involved in working with Italian families. Interestingly, the approach is twofold in that it aims to support and assist the needs and rights of both Italian families and immigrant workers.
>
> The Acli-Colf initiative, which is only in its initial phase, is noteworthy for its attempt to assimilate domestic work in the broader temporary labour market. One of the characteristics of household work is the high degree of tax evasion and undocumented labour involved. The exclusive agreement between *Obiettivo Lavoro* and Acli-Colf aims to draw families into the legal labour market, guaranteeing quality labour in return for the higher costs of virtuous behaviour in declaring domestic workers.
>
> 1. During the 1990s, Acli lobbied hard for the recognition of domestic workers in Italy as a professional category requiring a standard national contract. This was achieved in 2001, and since then their interest has focused on immigrant integration in the local labour market.
> 2. The largest Italian private human resource company supplying temporary workers.

commerce has promoted mentoring by other immigrants of the same community, in order to draw the "ethnic" network into an institutional framework. It has also attempted to mediate with banks to facilitate access to credit, one of the most serious obstacles to growth. Notwithstanding these efforts, the high birth rate of immigrant businesses is accompanied by a high mortality rate; even with a good business plan, it is still hard to start a business in Italy.

Self-employment is also widespread in the region of Piemonte and there are various programmes for assisting immigrants wishing to start entrepreneurial activities. In 2003, the chamber of commerce of Turin published a guide in the nine principal foreign languages spoken in the region, providing information on laws and authorisations, and on services available (sanitary, educational, etc.), which would be useful for immigrants wishing to start a business. Long-term support to businesses is also provided. The chamber plans to open a front-office with cultural mediators better able to communicate with immigrant entrepreneurs.

More intensive projects are run by the local branches of the main trade associations of artisans and craftsmen. In Turin, for example, a project "*Dedalo*" has been run since 2000 by the National Artisan Confederation (CNA), in collaboration with *Alma Terra* (see Box 3.9) and *Confesercenti Torino*, with financial support from the province of Turin and the region of Piemonte. Their entrepreneurial development programmes focus on developing business plans, providing training and technical assistance on contract compliance, regulation, and procedures on obtaining financial credits from banks. Cultural mediators from different countries were also employed. Between September 2000 and March 2003, CNA supported 80 non-EU immigrant enterprises. The project provides information not only to immigrants who want to start a business, but also to those who already have a functioning enterprise. Current plans are to organise a series of short courses on entrepreneurial culture and to survey the availability of local institutions to provide immigrant enterprises with micro-credit.

In Trento, self-employment has not historically been of major interest to immigrants; nonetheless, the importance of SMEs in the provincial economy and the recourse to subcontracting have recently increased the role of immigrant entrepreneurs, even if as subcontractors, immigrants do not compete with existing businesses but rather improve the chain of local production. In 2001, a pilot research-action was launched by the local Association of Craftsmen and Small Enterprises to better understand the current situation of immigrants' entrepreneurship in the province (see Box 3.8).

Similar initiatives exist elsewhere in Italy. The CNA, among others, has aggressively recruited immigrant entrepreneurs for a number of years. In Bologna, for example, the CNA opened a special office for immigrant entrepreneurs, open two days a week and providing a wide range of consulting, orientation and mediation services for the more than 500 immigrant entrepreneurs. The service supports the development of business plans and runs training courses for entrepreneurs. Here, too, bureaucratic obstacles and the reluctance of banks to provide credit remain the main difficulties.

> Box 3.8. **Trento research action for immigrant entrepreneurs**
>
> The Association of Craftsmen and Small Enterprises of the province of Trento used ESF funds for a research action on "Craft and Immigration", a 3-year project ending in 2004. The project began with an analysis of crafts and small enterprises in the province and interviews with different key players. Entrepreneurship was only one of three areas of interest; the other theme areas included native employers and their new immigrant employees. As far as immigrant entrepreneurship is concerned, the association was able to promote the project because immigrants had chosen to work in high-risk and subsidiary sectors where they did not compete with native enterprises. In fact, many, in transportation and construction, move into gaps created when their former employers abandon low-margin high-risk segments of the supply and production chain.
>
> Training for entrepreneurs concentrated on the market and credit system (subcontracting, pricing and credit); labour legislation (different contracts); and job safety rules and regulations. Training involved some units for both immigrant employees and entrepreneurs (Italian language for the workplace), some specifically for entrepreneurs and some for all groups including Italian employers (workplace safety).
>
> The number of participants was quite low compared to the staff involved (teacher, coordinator and mediators), but the results were positive and useful as a pilot for future initiatives to improve workplace culture and respect for safety norms, as well as improving the position of immigrant workers in the labour market.

Entrepreneurial activity by immigrants has been recognised as an essential aspect of growth by those organisations which represent the sector. Other institutions, such as banks, have been less quick to adjust to change. Nonetheless, the increase in training activity demonstrates that an awareness of the importance of immigrant entrepreneurship has influenced local labour market planning strategies.

Improving women's employment: the role of social capital

At the end of 2003 there were about a half million immigrants working legally in the domestic sector, almost all of them women. This sector, which includes housekeepers, cleaning women, nannies and carers for the elderly, is the dominant sector for employment for immigrant women in Italy. Wages tend to be low (around the minimum wage of € 5.90/hour, with 24-36 hours a week of paid work) and chances for promotion are extremely limited. Yet the educational level gained by the women in their home country was often quite high (one study found that half of Filipina and one-quarter of Polish and Peruvian nannies held university degrees).

Once employed in the domestic sector, it is extremely difficult for women to change job category. There is a continuous demand within the domestic sector that allows for some improvement in contractual conditions, but there has been little effort to change the nature of the work done by immigrant women. In each of the areas examined in the course of this case study, the concentration of women in the domestic labour market was taken for granted by institutions as a necessary response to demand; at the same time, vocational training courses involved more men than women.

One important obstacle faced by immigrants to changing their job categories is a lack of social capital – relations of trust and reciprocity with native Italians who can serve as gatekeepers to better employment or opportunities. In fact, most studies involving employers – whether by ISFOL, the chambers of commerce or other research groups or institutions – have found that the majority of employers seek employees not through temporary work agencies or public employment centres but through informal channels. In the province of Turin, a 2003 study found that 57% of businesses hired new employees through contacts with friends and family; 14% were acquaintances of current employees (Ricerche e Progetti, 2003). This penalises newcomers to the labour market and especially migrants, who are less likely to have an extended social network.

The grassroots cultural and social initiative examined in Turin – the Alma Mater permanent centre – was seen to have the unintentional effect of establishing close relationships between women leading to better employment outcomes (sees Box 3.9). Alma Mater provides a strong example of the empowerment of female immigrants and of permanent labour market insertion through training. Alma Mater's projects provide vocational training and qualifications for women wishing to escape from low skilled-low paid jobs. They have involved close working with banks and other businesses who are the intended employers of the trained women. Such relationships were difficult to achieve and relied on years of work by the association in acquiring social capital and credibility. The intensive work required necessarily limits the types of courses offered and the numbers of migrant women who can benefit.

Alma Mater also serves as a meeting place for foreign and Italian women, providing social activities and common cultural and social projects. Women working together in this context establish friendship bonds. These ties have often led to upward movement in the labour market. Nonetheless, the women of Alma Mater do not consider this to be a noteworthy outcome of their activity, since it is not within the framework of a single project and is neither extendable nor fundable.

> **Box 3.9. Alma Mater: intercultural centre promoting quality employment for women in Turin**
>
> Alma Mater is a strong example of the empowerment of women immigrants and of permanent labour market insertion through training. In 1993, Alma Terra created an intercultural centre, "Alma Mater", for both immigrant and Italian women, with the support of the municipal council, the regional commission for equal opportunity, and trade union organisations. Other partners have ranged from banks, firms, to chambers of commerce, depending on the project. The centre has also applied for EU grants for specific projects. The objective of the centre is to improve the social status of immigrant women living in Turin and encourage them to exercise their individual skills. Activities include:
>
> **Professional re-qualification courses and language courses**: a number of courses in cultural mediation have been realised in recent years in co-operation with other institutions. The centre also organises Italian language courses, differentiated according to prior educational level (in 2003, 180 immigrant women participated in these courses).
>
> **Integration into the labour market**: the centre organises sessions for immigrant women on useful mechanisms and tools for entering the Italian labour market. It also offers legal advice and provides educational and job search assistance. In 2002, the centre, together with the Turin municipality and the trade unions, supported and monitored a project to integrate immigrants women into the banking sector, a high-status sector compared to domestic work. Professional training on banking was organised, and at the end of the course 12 non-EU women were employed by different Italian banks with long term contracts as bank-clerks. This project was followed by others: a training course for IT specialists with the aim to integrate an additional 30 immigrant women as managers in trade cooperatives and firms. A baby-sitting service (for pre-school children) is offered by the centre to support working immigrant women while they train and search for a job.

Housing

Housing plays an important role in the integration of immigrants in local labour markets in Italy because of the general housing crisis. Home ownership is close to 80% among Italians and social housing accounts for less than 5% of the market. Mortgage conditions are not favourable. This means that the migrant labour force – both Italian and foreign – is forced into an overcrowded rental market; furthermore, many Italian homeowners prefer not to place their vacant homes onto the rental market because of concern about lengthy eviction procedures and fiscal issues.

An additional problem for foreign workers is discrimination. Discrimination in the job market is closely linked to segregation and discrimination in housing. Housing is in fact an important source of exclusion for all immigrants in Italy; flat listings often openly specify that the flat will not be let to foreigners. In some cases, the reason for discrimination is formulated in economic terms (fear of tenant not paying rent regularly, damages to the house, etc.). Discrimination is exacerbated by the speculative local real estate market, the low number of flats available, high rents (the average monthly rent is € 300-350 to let bedsits or single rooms) (Quassoli *et al*, 2001). High rents often lead to the overcrowding of tenants. Some landlords take advantage of the difficulties faced by immigrants in finding accommodation and offer accommodation that is not considered to be fit for the local Italian population at prices far above the market rate.

In many areas of the industrial north, housing costs are the main obstacle to local labour market development and internal migration. Employers have recognised this and become involved in seeking solutions. In addition, Law 189/2002 requires employers to provide their immigrant workers, with accommodation meeting the minimum standards of public residential housing. Although the law allows foreigners who hold residence card, or a residence permit valid for at least two years and a job, access to public housing on the same terms as Italian nationals, public housing is far too limited to meet the needs of the foreign population. The fact that immigrants, with larger families and smaller incomes, often have priority in the assigning of vacant public housing units has given rise to some resentment. Different regions have tried to defuse this by tightening the eligibility conditions (Piemonte requires long-term employment contracts) or placing a ceiling on access for immigrants (Trento has a quota).

Solutions can mainly be found in the private and public-private partnership arena. A number of agencies have been created in Italy in the past decade, providing a model for such partnerships. One of the best-known examples is Casa Amica (see Box 3.10). These agencies attempt to acquire property in order to rent or sell it to individuals who otherwise lack the income or credit guarantees to rent or purchase a home.

Another model successfully created by a public-private partnership is the rental agency of Forlì. In this case, local authorities worked with employers to acquire – or rent – property for workers. The agency manages about 25 flats, of which three-quarters are for immigrant or temporary Italian workers. Rent is deducted directly from the workers' pay checks. The agency is financially self-sufficient and uses the surplus from its shared housing units to subsidise the apartments it rents to immigrant families.

> ## Box 3.10. **Casa Amica:**
> ## A non-profit association for housing access
>
> Casa Amica was created in 1993 by a consortium of 16 public and private bodies, led by the province of Bergamo and comprising trade unions and associations. Its objective was to improve access to adequate housing by Italians in need and immigrants. Four banks supported the initiative. The number of associates reached 76 by 2003.
>
> The Association conducts research on the local housing situation and creates projects to meet housing needs. The main project has run since 2000 – when it received seed money from the Cariplo Foundation – and involves the construction of temporary housing facilities and the creation of a non-profit housing agency. Casa Amica is involved in the purchase and renovation of buildings for rental to single-parent families. It is also involved in a project with a network of small towns to build a 27-unit building for rental to immigrants and Italians in need.
>
> Casa Amica manages 132 apartments in the province of Bergamo. It offers four different rental contracts: rent; mortgage guaranteed by Casa Amica; lodging cost for shared units; and rental with the option to purchase. More than 1 000 people have lived in Casa Amica properties.
>
> Casa Amica is not just a rental agency. It mediates with homeowners to place units on the market and monitors and supports its tenants, mediating between immigrants and their neighbours to reduce conflict.

Other initiatives were also identified in the case studies areas. Trento provides credit to firms and co-operatives to help them in the field of building, renovation, and purchase of housing for foreign workers. The province has financed firms for a 5-year period to reduce the rents set by firms to accommodate foreign workers. About 80 flats were allocated to immigrant workers in 2003 with the help of this measure.

Since October 2002 the province of Trento has allowed firms to build dormitories on their property, annexed to industrial spaces (*foresteria*). The law defines the number of beds that each *foresteria* can have. For example, a firm with 60 workers can construct a *foresteria* with a maximum of 12 beds. Workers – including foreign workers – can live in the dormitory for one year, and can then renew for another year. Since 2003, three such dormitories have been built. These structures are not meant to be permanent housing as they restrict housing to a single employee and prevent family reunification. This urban planning rule is not a social solution but a zoning reform. In Italy, residential and industrial areas are normally zoned in different areas, so the decision to allow the dormitories to be built represents a marked departure from normally rigid zoning principles. The regulation contains no social considerations, such as safeguards for the number of workers per bed or the availability of consumer services in industrial areas.

The province also offers rent and mortgage subsidies to help private actors in the field of building, renovation, and housing purchase. The mechanism used is that of the deed of future sale: a cooperative purchases the apartment, restructures it and decides its final cost. An immigrant interested in purchasing, if able to meet the payments, pays the initial down payment to reduce the mortgage repayments. In 2002, of all applications for mortgage subsidies, 41% were by immigrants.

The municipality of Trento has also intiated a project run by a non-profit organisation called *Patto Casa,* to help certain disadvantaged groups, in particular immigrants, to find housing, based on existing Italian models. *Patto Casa* will mediate between owners and disadvantaged families, including immigrants, who are not able to provide guarantees. The association will hold the lease and sublet to the renter, at lower market rates than those currently available to foreigners. Moreover, it will provide comprehensive consultancy on housing problems ranging from legal advice to the search for rental accommodation or home purchases, stipulation of mortgages, conventions with banks, public notaries and other professionals in the sector. This kind of intermediation and guarantee has been unsuccessful elsewhere in Italy (Perugia and Firenze, for example) because of persistent reluctance of homeowners to rent to foreigners.

Patto Casa also aims to purchase and reconstruct apartments to be assigned to disadvantaged families, including those of immigrants, as well as to underwrite mortgages for immigrants with mortgages. In the event of default or departure, the cooperative will find a new owner under the same terms of condition as the previous one.

In Piemonte, Cicsene (Italian Centre of Collaboration for Construction Development of Emergent Nations; *Centro Italiano di Collaborazione per lo Sviluppo Edilizio delle Nazioni Emergenti*) has tried to imitate and transfer a successful French initiative to build autonomous housing complexes. In 1995, Cicsene was the main promoter of the Diogene Project, financially supported by the EU, the region Piemonte and the municipality of Turin. It consisted of a deposit fund for associations who rent apartments and sublet them to immigrant families, guaranteeing rent to landlords. The deposit money covers the payment of a maximum of three months rent in arrears, plus any legal expenses and damage caused by the lodgers. Only 40 rental contracts are currently running under these special conditions.

Charitable and religious institutions also offer dwellings or rent accommodation for immigrants. One of the first reception centres was Sermig in Turin (see Box 3.2). Thanks to the close collaboration with voluntary associations and charities, immigrants in Turin have access to 240 beds made available by the Catholic associations, 160 flats and 16 pre-fabricated constructions provided by lay voluntary associations, and 10 more apartments from Caritas. There are also co-operatives and housing associations that mostly act as guarantors.

In Milan much of the effort has been devoted to providing emergency shelter, although the municipality loaned 500 apartments to an association which renovated them with funding from the region Lombardia and assigned them to disadvantaged families; 15% were assigned to immigrants. There are no large social real estate agencies that provide access to the private rental market by offering mediation services and guarantees to landlords. Some co-operatives and associations focus on renovation of flats to be rented to immigrants. The co-operative Dar currently has 130 apartments, rented at affordable prices to immigrants.

The diminishing supply of social housing and low turnover rates mean that solutions to the housing problem must be found in the private sector. Employers are interested in finding solutions, but even with the involvement of local authorities and banks, most initiatives are limited in the number of units involved. Where employers are a driving force in locating housing for their workers, the role of local authorities is especially important in safeguarding the employee from abuse of this dependent relationship.

Conclusions and issues for consideration

The case studies of Trento, Turin and Milan reveal very different local initiatives for integrating immigrants into the labour market, notwithstanding the fact that immigration policy is developed at the national level. The primary role of municipal services in integration has been demonstrated; due in part to the broader devolution in public services underway in Italy and in part to the recognition that integration is best handled at the local level.

Local authorities give considerable importance to their institutional role in supporting and guiding the integration of immigrants. This is evident in the creation of special services for foreigners, the research and analyses funded by these authorities and the wide range of projects in which administrations are involved. However, this has sometimes led to the development of a system which is driven by institutional priorities rather than by the immigrants themselves. Local governance institutions are considerably influenced by political (public opinion) and economic (social partners) stakeholders in their perception of the needs of the immigrant population.

The close cooperation between employers and local authorities is a strong factor in each of the local integration policies examined. Local economic actors can bring leverage to bear on vocational training and housing policy, linking such policies to immediate local needs. Local authorities and institutions, on the other hand, are able to plan for a longer period. Entrepreneurial associations were among the first to see their future in the provision of services to the immigrant population and to invest accordingly.

For this reason, the tradition of collaboration or coordination with other stakeholders has determined the ability of each local authority to take leadership in the governance of integration, especially in the labour market. While the role of different forms of local government – autonomous province, municipality and region – has conditioned the options available, factors such as funding, competition and cooperation with other administrative functions, political homogeneity and conflict, relations with civil society and distribution of responsibility have all affected the variety of initiatives and interventions launched.

Given the wide variety of initiatives, then, can such initiatives have a major effect on integration of immigrants in the local labour market? If integration is defined as *participation* in the labour market, then all three areas show a high degree of success. Participation of immigrants in the labour market meets demand – mostly at the lowest level of the professional scale, concentrated in unskilled work. Further, in all three regions, short term employment contracts predominate. Given the new legal framework for residence permits and their renewal, immigrants have little bargaining power. In this sense, initiatives to improve the match between supply and demand – especially in the low-skilled labour market where there are few barriers to entry for foreigners – can maintain labour force participation and prevent expulsion.

If integration is considered as quality employment with the same conditions for immigrant workers as for Italians, then success stories are rarer. Immigrants, like Italians, mostly manage to find jobs through their social networks of personal acquaintances and contacts. This obviates much of the effect that could be achieved by official services for employment access or the bureaucratic matching of supply and demand. It also highlights the importance and the value of initiatives that increase the horizontal and vertical social relations of migrants, since this capital can be transformed into an improved position in the labour market (*i.e.* social centres, training apprenticeships). Such initiatives are frequently small-scale, with employment outcomes which can be difficult to evaluate in the short term, yet which have a major effect on individuals, especially women in domestic employment.

Employment services are still struggling to adapt to such an individualised approach. The same problem also appears in relation to vocational training. Vocational training seems to be more institutionally-driven than demand-driven; even when courses are well-matched to the labour market, there appears to be little individual analysis and recognition of the educational attainments and needs of immigrants.

Self-employment has emerged as a desirable objective for immigrants in the labour market, seen positively by both Italians and immigrants themselves. The most effective initiatives seemed to be those driven by market mechanisms (*i.e.* by the need of chambers of commerce or trade associations to govern and recruit foreigners to replace an ageing and ever less entrepreneurial Italian population). The main obstacles lie in the complex bureaucracy involved and in poor access to credit; this is also where most investment is being made.

The Italian system for governance of local integration policy for immigrants is conditioned by a number of institutional factors which limit the possibility of change: *a)* the dominance of the ESF in vocational training and the important role assigned to regions and to national priorities; *b)* the project-based cooperation that results from the tendering system for integration funds; *c)* the fact that municipal services coordinate shelter and social orientation for immigrants. The system reflects the fragmentation of Italian social actors, the extensive civil society in Italy and the dominance of the social partners in determining the direction of local economic policy. Local authorities, in the end, have difficulty assuming control, given the myriad of stakeholders and subcontracted and external service providers involved.

This governance model has however a number of advantages for the integration of immigrants, including flexibility and a potential capacity for rapid evolution. The system has generated many different solutions for integration that no single actor can address alone. On the other hand, the model places the burden on local authorities to coordinate actions and rationalise limited resources for the greatest effect. This chapter has listed a number of good practices, but what makes these practices transferable is the institutional framework of cooperation in which they were created, more than any specific statute or content. It is here that the challenge lies.

Notes

1. For further information see OECD (2003) and OECD (2004).
2. According to OECD (2004), in 2003, the employment to population rate of the EU-15 reached 64.8% and the total OECD average 65%, whereas the labour force participation rate was of 70.3% and 69.8% respectively.
3. The quarterly Labour Force Survey does not provide data on unemployment by nationality or country of birth, so no reliable figures on the unemployment of foreigners exist.

4. According to the OECD (2003), whereas in the south the phenomena of the underground economy is characterised more by a high presence of unregistered firms, in the north it is characterised by hiring undeclared workers in registered firms.

5. In July 2002, the government and the social partners agreed "the Pact for Italy" whose objectives are the following: *a)* build up a modern and efficient labour market; *b)* reduce the underground economy; *c)* reinforce education and training; *d)* reduce fiscal pressure especially on low-income families, and, e) apply a supply-side approach to the regional policies in the Mezzogiorno (OECD, 2003).

6. Italian Union of Chambers of Commerce, Industry, Crafts and Agriculture. For further information see http://excelsior.unioncamere.net.

7. Source: Unioncamere (*www.unioncamere.it*).

8. For example, in 2002, the annual decree was approved only in mid-October and permitted the entry of 20 500 people. That year, only 10 000 visas were issued under the quota system. Moreover, *ad hoc* decrees were introduced to allow the entrance of seasonal workers (33 000 in February, 6 400 in March, 6 600 in May, 10 000 in July, and a further 3 000 self-employed workers in March).

9. Foreigners who have held a permit for dependent or self-employment work, study or religious reasons for at least one year, or a residence card (art. 29) can apply for reunification with: *a)* spouse; *b)* dependent children; *c)* dependent parents. Parents over age sixty-five are allowed to enter under family reunion only if they can prove that no other child can provide for them in their native country; siblings and other relatives are not entitled to legal entry.

10. According to OECD (2005), the rejection rate remains very high (around 90%), but many of those rejected succeed in acquiring a humanitarian permit that is issued at the discretion of the local police foreigner's office.

11. For further information see: *www.immigrazione.provincia.tn.it/cinformi*.

12. Italia Lavoro is an agency of the Ministry of Labour and Social Welfare created in 1997, with the aim of developing active employment policies with a particular focus on vulnerable groups in Italian areas with a high unemployment rate.

13. See Ministry of Labour Circulars 84, 91 and 98/2001.

14. This EU Objective aimed towards the integration or reintegration into the labour market of the long-term unemployed or those at risk of long-term unemployment; strengthening of initial training and integration of young people into the labour market; and integration or reintegration into the labour market of people at risk from social exclusion.

15. Ernst and Young Financial Business Advisors, Ernst and Young Business School, and *Centro Informazione e Educazione allo Sviluppo (CIES)*.

Bibliography

Ambrosini, M. and F. Berti (2004), *Immigrazione e lavoro*, Franco Angeli, Milan.

Ambrosini, M. (2003), "Work", IRES report.

Campani, G. (1993), "I reticoli sociali delle donne immigrate in Italia", in Università degli Studi di Roma La Sapienza (ed.), *Immigrazione in Europa, solidarietà e conflitto*, Dipartimento di Sociologia, CEDISS, Roma.

Caritas (2004), "Immigrazione: Dossier Statistico 2004".

Chaloff, J. (2004), "From Labour Emigration to Labour Recruitment: The Case of Italy in Migration for Employment – Bilateral Agreements at a Crossroads", OECD, Paris.

Chaloff, J and F. Piperno, (2004), "Italy" in Niessen, J. Y. Schibel and R. Magoni (eds.), *International Migration and Relation with Third Countries: EU and US Approaches*, Migration Policy Group.

International Organisation of Migration (2005), "Al servizio degli immigrati: Modalità di intervento e professionalità presenti all' interno dei Centri per l'impiego", Rome.

Italia Lavoro (2004), "Ricerca Azione: Analisi delle esperienze regionali relative ai nuovi ingressi per quota per motivi di lavoro di immigrati. Ipotesi per la sperimentazione di un modello di gestione", Rome

Lemaître, G. (2003), "La regolazione dei flussi migratori internazionali", CNEL, Documenti 29, Atti del Seminario di Studio "*Regolazione dei flussi migratori: tra programmemazione e precarietà degli interventi*", 3.12.2003.

OECD (2003), *Economic Survey: Italy*, OECD Publication, Paris.

OECD (2004), *Employment Outlook*, OECD Publication, Paris.

OECD (2005), *Trends in International Migration*, Sopemi 2004, OECD Publication, Paris.

Provincia Autonoma di Trento (2003), "L'immigrazione in Trentino. Rapporto annuale 2003", CINFORMI, Assessorato alle Politiche Sociali. Servizio per le Politiche Sociale.

Quassoli, F., Bohnish, Gabas, Gasa And Jansen (2001), "Housing Policies, Problems and Coping Strategies in Bologna, Frankfurt, Barcelona and Groningen", in *Social Exclusion as a Multidimensional Process: Sub-cultural and Formally Assisted Strategies of Coping with and Avoiding Social Exclusion*; European commission, Brussels.

Reyneri, E. (1998), "The Role of the Underground Economy in Irregular Migration to Italy: Cause or Effect?" in *Journal of Ethnic and Migration Studies*, 25, 2.

Ricerche e Progetti (2003), "Ricerca di mercato e analisi dei Servizi per il Lavoro rivolti alle imprese esistenti nella Provincia di Torino", in *Notizie R&P – Ricerche e Progetti* 10, 2.

Triandafyllidou, A. And M. Veikou, (2001), "Immigration Policy and its Implementation in Italy: The State of the Art in Migration Pathways" in A. Triandafyllidou (ed.) *A Historic, Demographic and Policy Review of Four Countries of the European Union*, European Commission, Brussels.

Zanfrini, L. (2003), "Employment Needs of Firms and Planning of Flows", IRES report.

Zanfrini, L. (2004), "Il lavoro degli immigrati a Milan", Research presented during the OECD study visit in Milan, 24 June 2004.

ISBN 92-64-02895-1
From Immigration to Integration
Local Solutions to a Global Challenge
© OECD 2006

Chapter 4

Routes into Employment for Refugees: A Review of Local Approaches in London

by
Anne E. Green

> London is one of the world's global cities and is the engine of the UK migration system. A wide variety of initiatives exist to support the integration of immigrants into the labour market, including those targeted towards refugees. At the local level, refugees are often helped by immigrant associations and community organisations that are felt to offer a supportive environment for new arrivals. In partnership with the public sector, such organisations have developed innovative education and training initiatives including projects to support the recognition of qualifications gained overseas. However the piecemeal development of such support over a number of years has led to a relatively fragmented system, which is reliant on relatively short term and unpredictable funding. In this context partnerships and networks play a crucial role in supporting both coordination and sustainability in support to refugees in the city.

Introduction

London is one of the world's global cities and is distinctive in the United Kingdom (UK) context by virtue of its sheer size, population diversity and economic structure. It is the engine of the UK migration system, with a net inflow of young people and those building their careers and a net outflow of people at later stages in the life course. It is also a key hub in the global economy and international migration system, such that Inner London has the most diverse population in Europe. London is the key destination in the UK for both international and internal migrants, and has been described as an "escalator region": providing unparalleled opportunities in the UK context for accessing a wide range of specialised employment, and for gaining upward social mobility (Fielding, 1992). London has also historically received a significant number of refugees. Between 2000 and 2002 at least half of all immigration to London came through the asylum route and London has the largest concentration of refugees and asylum seekers in the UK (GLA, 2004). As a group, refugees suffer particular problems in accessing the labour market. While the Department for Work and Pensions (DWP) does not publish official statistics on refugee unemployment, estimates suggest that refugees have an unemployment rate of 36% – more than six times the national average (DWP, 2003). In evidence presented to the Work and Pensions Select Committee on the DWP's services to ethnic minorities, the Refugee Council quoted previous research suggesting refugee unemployment rates of between 60% and 90% (Refugee Council, 2003).

This chapter examines the efficacy of the local implementation of initiatives to improve the integration of refugees in the labour market (and social life more generally) in London, exploring a selection of initiatives in order to look at how the political, economic and ethnic actors of local administrations formulate their policies in this field, and to provide insights into policy successes and failures. It should be noted that these insights are based on information gained in case study visits and interviews, and any other available evidence. In many instances, a lack of robust statistics on outputs, and more especially outcomes, limits the specificity of the assessments made.

It is important to note that people seeking asylum are only allowed to work in the UK after they have been granted refugee status. The situation regarding the labour market participation of asylum seekers changed in July 2002, with the withdrawal of their concession to work in the UK, except in a voluntary capacity. Hence, although many local initiatives offer support to asylum seekers in addition to refugees, help with labour market integration for this group has to be given with a longer-term perspective in mind, rather than promoting direct access to the labour market.

The scale of immigration to London and the numbers of people from different backgrounds involved, means that there is scope for greater specialisation in provision than in other parts of the UK and in other towns and cities: what is feasible in London due to clustering of the refugee population may not be feasible elsewhere. Nevertheless, issues determining refugees' employment situation – ranging from recognition of qualifications, the need for retraining, matching of supply with demand, etc., are of more general relevance.

The legislative and policy framework for integration

In order fully to understand the context for local initiatives being implemented in London, it is important to be aware of the legislative and policy framework for migration and the integration of immigrants in the UK. In recent years the national migration policy framework has been subject to rapid change, with important new strategies on migration, refugees and asylum seekers announced in February/March 2005 and subsequently confirmed in the proposed programme of legislation for the parliamentary session 2005/6. Trends in migration generally, and also in asylum claims, set the context for policy developments, and are described in more detail below.

Migration trends

Migration is a complex issue, and despite improvements in data provision,[1] some types of migration are difficult to measure (Salt and Clarke, 2005). According to the 3rd quarter of 2005 Labour Force Survey (LFS), 4.8 million people in the UK (just over 8% of the UK population) and 2 million people in London (28% of London's population) were born outside the UK. At UK level, 36% of these residents were born in Asia, 26% elsewhere in Europe and 21% in Africa. According to the LFS, 44% of recent inflows of working age immigrants who entered the UK between 2000 and 2004 settled in London. In contrast, only 9.4% of UK born individuals of working age live in London (Centre for Research and Analysis of Migration, 2005).[2] Turning to data on citizenship, the overall picture of migration in the UK in recent years is one of rising overall net gains, with net losses of British nationals and net gains of foreign nationals, with underlying fluctuations in the nationality composition of the flows. In the 3rd quarter of 2004 (before EU enlargement), there were nearly 2.86 million foreign nationals living in the UK (4.9% of the population). 43% of them European, followed by 25% from Asia and 17% from Africa (Salt and Clarke, 2005).[3]

Migrants enter the UK by a number of different routes. Given the focus on refugees, the main emphasis here is on the asylum route. Until the 1990s, the UK received relatively few asylum claims and a high proportion of those seeking asylum were awarded refugee status. In the 1990s this began to change as a result of several factors. The collapse of communism in Central and Eastern Europe, coupled with the outbreak of war in Yugoslavia, led to an exodus of people, including many asylum seekers, to the UK (as to other parts of western Europe). Failed states, such as Somalia and Afghanistan, emerged. The UK received large numbers of asylum seekers from both countries. Other factors in the rise of asylum seeking included reductions in the price of international air travel, the development of highly organised trafficking networks linked to organised crime, and also a greater awareness in developing countries (*e.g.* through satellite television) of the relative prosperity in countries such as the UK. Key features in the relative attractiveness of the UK as a destination (*vis-à-vis* other EU countries) were a relatively strong economy offering a ready supply of work, the global reach of the English language and the perception of the UK as a tolerant society.

As the number of asylum seekers increased, especially from the late 1990s, delays in the processing of asylum claims in the UK rose. This meant that applicants without genuine protection needs were often able to remain in the country for several years and establish roots making it difficult to return them to their home countries. All these circumstances combined to make the asylum route into the UK attractive for prospective economic migrants. The result of this upsurge in the number of asylum seekers was that in the years 2000 to 2002 the UK had consistently the highest number (in absolute terms) of asylum applicants of any EU country. However, partly as a result of a series of legislative and other reforms, but also reflecting global trends, by 2004 the number of asylum applicants had fallen to 40 000 (including dependants) – this was 60% lower than the equivalent figure for 2002 (approximately 100 000).

In relation to debates on immigration and integration in the UK it is salient to note at the outset that data on international migration are limited: problems include under-enumeration and the fact that integration is not covered effectively in secondary data sources. In secondary data analyses in the UK on migration, "country of birth" and "ethnic group" are amongst the categories most frequently used.[4] Most official and research data do not signify current nationality and do not differentiate between recent arrivals and second or third generation residents/citizens.[5] This both reflects and helps explain the fact that in the UK the term "ethnic minorities"[6] is closely related to "immigration", which itself is closely related to "racial groups" or "black". In the popular understanding (and probably outside the largest cities, in particular), "immigrant" can mean people who are not white, most specifically, persons whose recent origins are in the Caribbean, Asia or Africa. In this way, in popular parlance "immigrant" can include people who have been born in Britain (Wrench and Modood, 2000).

London is the largest city in the UK with a population of around 7.5 million, and a resident workforce of around 3.4 million. It is demographically and economically dynamic, characterised by an outflow of international migrants and a more significant inflow. This net international migration inflow, combined with population increase through natural change, has led to faster population growth in London than in the rest of the UK. Migrants are highly concentrated, and increasingly so, in London. Inner London has over five times more foreigners than it would have were they evenly distributed across the UK (Salt, 2005).

A special Guardian supplement in January 2005 entitled "London: the world in one city" suggested that London could reasonably lay claim to being the most diverse city on earth.[7] In 2005 over 2 million Londoners (around 30% of the total population) were born outside the UK.[8] Of these 7% were born in Ireland, 12% in other EU15 countries, 6% in other EU25 countries, 6% elsewhere in Europe, 12% in the Americas and Caribbean, 26% in Africa, 17% in the Indian sub-continent, 11% in the remainder of Asia and 3% in Australasia and elsewhere. 29% of London's population is from ethnic minority groups: a proportion around five times greater than the UK average. Over 80% of London's labour force growth in the medium-term is projected to come from people with a BME (i.e. black and minority ethnic) background.

London's migrant population (defined as those born outside the UK) has a different profile from the migrant population living in the rest of the UK. London's migrants are more likely to be from developing countries and more likely to be from ethnic and religious minority groups than those living outside London. They are also more likely to be recent arrivals or foreign nationals than migrants living in the rest of the UK. London's migrant population has a quite different age structure from that of the UK-born Londoners: it is heavily skewed towards the working age group, with a low proportion of children (6%) relative to the UK born population (26%), so reflecting typical migration patterns were those who migrate tend to do so before they have had children. The number of refugees in London and in the UK cannot be estimated with any confidence, but it is likely that refugees in London make up a majority of all those in the UK. Settlement of refugees in large numbers has happened in London over a longer period than in any other UK region. Moreover, the range of nationalities, ethnic and linguistic groups making up the refugee population is greater in London than anywhere else in the UK (GLA, 2004).

Migration policy

The UK government strongly embraces the principle of managed migration, coupled with tough measures to tackle abuse of the asylum system (outlined below) and illegal immigration, while at the same time working to build tolerance and enthusiasm for legal migration. The policy of opening up the "managed migration" route makes explicit recognition of the potential role for migration to address labour market deficiencies. This underlies the strategy of liberalising economic migration through formal means that recognises that migrants make a positive net contribution to the economy, especially in key professions and some unskilled occupations.

In 2005, there were several managed migration routes of special relevance from a labour market perspective for those from outside the EU. These include: i) work permits (i.e. a permit for a person a do a specific job at a specific location[9]) – the main mechanism for managing non-EU labour immigration into the UK;[10] ii) the Highly Skilled Migrant Programme (involving a system of points) to facilitate entry into the UK to meet labour market needs – especially in the case of finance, business management, ICT and medical occupations; and iii) the Seasonal Agricultural Workers' Scheme (SAWS) (which mainly focuses on younger workers and forms an important underpinning for some local economies in rural areas) and the Sector Based Scheme (SBS) (covering sectors where there was perceived to be a high demand for workers – initially hospitality and food processing).[11] Others enter the UK as students, as working holiday makers, or through family formation and reunion, and some of these will be active in the labour market. However, while acknowledging the significance of work permits and other routes of entry under managed migration policy for labour migration, since the focus here is on refugees, it is appropriate to consider the development of the asylum system in greater detail.

In relation to the development of the asylum system, the UK was one of the original signatories to the 1951 Geneva Convention relating to the Status of Refugees. Under the UK asylum system, each individual claim for asylum is considered on its individual merits by trained caseworkers. If an individual is found to have a well founded fear of persecution under the Convention, (s)he will be granted refugee status. If (s)he does not fall within a Convention ground, it will also be considered whether (s)he should be granted temporary leave to remain in the UK for 3 years on human rights grounds. All asylum seekers have the right to an appeal against a negative decision on their claim and they will only be removed from the UK if this does not breach obligations under the European Convention on Human Rights. While asylum claims are being processed, claimants are allowed to claim support from the National

Asylum Support Service (NASS),[12] who provide services such as accommodation (where necessary) and financial support.

As the numbers of asylum seekers rose in the 1990s, and especially in the period from 2000 to 2002, many of those seeking asylum in the UK were found not to have protection needs. However the record in removing failed asylum seekers was so poor that public confidence in the integrity of the asylum system declined.

The government responded by taking a number of measures to deter unfounded asylum applications. Legislation in 2002 introduced a system of appeals from abroad for clearly unfounded asylum claims made by nationals from a designated list of safe countries of origin. In 2004 a new criminal offence for asylum seekers and illegal immigrants arriving in the UK without documents who can offer no reasonable excuse was introduced; this contributed to a 50% decline in the number of undocumented asylum seekers arriving at UK ports of entry between the final quarter of 2003 and the final quarter of 2004. Steps were taken to simplify the UK's asylum appeals system, which was one of the most complex in Europe, so reducing delays in the system.

Non-legislative reforms have included introduction of a target to decide at least 80% of claims within two months, so speeding up the asylum process. There has been a tightening up of policy on subsidiary protection with country policies that had given nationals of certain countries (such as Iraq and Somalia) exceptional leave to remain. Restrictions were introduced in 2004 on the access to free legal aid for asylum seekers, so reducing multiple opportunities for appeal and delay. A series of measures were taken to tighten border controls. Co-operation with European partners has also been a crucial element in driving down asylum intake in the UK, with the closure of the Sangatte Red Cross centre, which had become a magnet for prospective illegal immigrants and asylum seekers trying to reach the UK through the Channel Tunnel being a high profile example of reform. Further changes to the asylum process designed to meet the Prime Minister's "tipping point target" of ensuring that by the end of 2005 the number of failed asylum seekers removed from the UK is greater than the number of claimants awarded refugee status and subsidiary protection, include a "New Asylum Model" of end to end case management (with the same team dealing with an individual claim from initial decision through to the final outcome), coupled with an initiative to improve the quality of initial decisions and the training given to asylum caseworkers.

The rise in the number of asylum seekers in the late 1990s placed acute pressure on services in London, Kent and other parts of south-eastern England. From April 2000 asylum seekers who qualify for NASS support and who need both subsistence and accommodation, are offered accommodation outside London and the South East. Under this "dispersal regime" asylum seekers have no choice as to where they are accommodated, unless they are able to support themselves (for example, through family or friends). Originally, NASS planned to allocate dispersal accommodation according to applicants' cultural and social needs in "cluster areas" in large cities where there was an existing multi-ethnic population and a supporting infrastructure of voluntary and community groups, but in practice allocations have been driven primarily by housing availability. In September 2003 there were nearly 52 000 asylum seekers, including dependants, supported in NASS accommodation across the UK, with the largest concentrations in the northern regions of England, the West Midlands and Scotland.[13] At this time there were around a further 34 000 asylum seekers in receipt of subsistence-only support, of whom nearly three-quarters were located in London. Hence, London retains the largest single concentration of asylum seekers. While the dispersal policy has placed pressure on resources in destination areas, little evidence has been forthcoming about the impact of the dispersal policy on the sustainability of London-based projects.

From the purpose of this research a crucial reform was the withdrawal of the employment concession, whereby asylum seekers who had not had an initial decision within 6 months had a right to work, in July 2002. This was done because it was considered that access to the labour market was acting as a "pull" factor encouraging economic migrants to claim asylum in the UK. It also reflected Ministers' intention to make a clear distinction between asylum seekers and economic migrants, and in so doing give greater public confidence in effective immigration controls, rather than to blur the two categories.[14] All asylum seekers are permitted to do voluntary work in the UK and it is government policy to support labour market integration of successful asylum applicants.

The shape and direction of UK migration and asylum policy is likely to change further in the near future. In February 2005 the government announced a 5-Year Strategy on asylum and immigration endorsing its managed migration policy (Home Office, 2005a). Key measures in the strategy relating to migration and the labour market include: i) a transparent points system for those entering the UK to work or study; ii) financial bonds for specific categories where there has been evidence of abuse, to guarantee that migrants return home; iii) only skilled workers are to be allowed to settle long-term in the UK and there will be tests on English language (oral and written) and knowledge of the UK for everyone who wants to stay permanently; and iv) fixed penalty fines for employers for each illegal worker they employ. The points system referred to in i) is designed to sweep away the complexity of the current system. Instead, it is proposed that there will be four tiers: tier 1 – the highly skilled (can enter the UK with no job offer); tier 2 – those with qualifications above National Vocational Qualification (NVQ) level 2; tier 3 – low skilled migration (to be phased out); and tier 4 – specialist categories (including footballers and journalists). It is intended that points system associated with these tiers will be adjusted in response to skill shortages and changes in the labour market by an independent skills advisory body (to be set up by the government in association with the Skills for Business Network[15]).

In relation to asylum, the Strategy reaffirmed the government's commitment to the Geneva Convention. However, it also proposed that refugees should no longer be granted immediate settlement in the UK, but should instead be granted five years' temporary leave. If the situation in their countries of origin had improved sufficiently, they would be expected to return there. Only if this were not the case, would they be eligible for settlement. Hence, these proposed changes would make for longer periods of uncertainty for immigrants (and also employers).

Labour market policy framework in relation to integration

UK labour market policy since 1997 has had a strong supply-side bias. Labour market participation has been regarded as *the* key route out of social exclusion. A multiplicity of initiatives has been introduced to enhance labour market participation and employability. The New Deals (for young people, those aged 25 years and over, those aged 50 years and over, lone parents, the disabled, partners, and various other groups) focusing on the longer-term unemployed and excluded groups form the centre-piece of welfare-to-work initiatives.[16] A key feature of the New Deal initiatives is the use of Personal Advisers to provide one-to-one guidance for New Deal clients. In the spirit of enhanced flexibility to meet individual needs, in 2004 the DWP set out how Jobcentre Plus support might evolve to provide more tailored individual help, by building flexibility into the development of programmes, so enabling enhanced response to specific local needs. In order to better "make work pay" a National Minimum Wage has been introduced, as have a series of "in-work benefits". However, it is salient to note that since London is a high cost area (particularly in relation to housing), and the tax and benefit system is defined nationally (albeit with some regional adjustments to take account of differential housing costs), concern has been expressed that higher costs of housing, council tax, childcare and transport costs mean that the tax and benefit system has a different impact on work incentives in London than elsewhere in the UK (Strategy Unit, 2004). In relation to skills there has long been concern about the "long tail" of poorly qualified workers in the UK labour market and in 2003 a National Skills Strategy was set out to enhance access to training for those with no/ low qualifications (DfES, 2003).

Turning specifically to migrants, a range of levels of support to enter to the labour market is available to immigrants and refugees, while asylum seekers lie outside the system of labour market support following the withdrawal of any right to work in July 2002. In relation to access to benefits: i) refugees have full access to all social security benefits, so long as they meet normal conditions of eligibility; ii) a person who has indefinite leave to remain has access to income related benefits on the same basis as a UK national; and iii) migrants workers who are third country nationals are subject to immigration control and are not entitled to income related benefits, although they may qualify for contributory benefits after making necessary National Insurance contributions.

In the case of refugees not currently in employment, the strategy for labour market integration rests on encouraging more refugees to use Jobcentre Plus (currently only around half of refugees use Jobcentre Plus services), and by building stronger partnerships involving the voluntary and community sectors – including Ethnic Minority Outreach Work involving intermediaries, and delivering services that meet the needs of refugee customers. Access to Jobcentre Plus programmes and support is being enhanced and a Refugee Operational Framework established in 2005.

It is salient to note here a number of key features concerning Jobcentre Plus that are of relevance to the nature and type of support refugees are likely to receive. First, the activities of Jobcentre Plus are focused on those who are claiming unemployment and inactive benefits. Secondly, and following on from this, Jobcentre Plus activities are focused mainly on those with poorer qualifications, and a disproportionately large number of vacancies handled by Jobcentre Plus are associated with lower-skilled occupations.[17] Thirdly, Jobcentre Plus is a target driven organisation: the emphasis is on getting those hardest to help into jobs – and individuals from certain sub-groups (*e.g.* ethnic minority groups,[18] lone parents, etc.) and in certain deprived areas (defined on a postcode basis) are associated with higher points scores. This means that Jobcentre Plus services are geared towards those who are entitled to claim benefits and who have lower skills levels, as opposed to highly qualified migrants who are not claiming benefits.

In addition to those developments outlined above, the *Refugee Employment Strategy* (DWP, 2005) and *National Strategy for Refugee Integration* (Home Office, 2005b)[19] highlighted plans: i) to replace automatic payments of income support to all refugees with a loan system targeted at helping integration; and ii) for a mentoring scheme to give new refugees intensive one-to-one support with a dedicated "SUNRISE" (Strategic Update of National Refugee Integration Services) caseworker to help them find work, update specialist skills and work towards longer-term integration objectives (as set out in Personal Integration Plans).

The developments outlined above represent a cross-government strategy, requiring co-ordination across government and a wide range of support agencies, designed to ensure that refugees are able to make "a full and positive contribution to society". It is recognised that integration is a complex process, and that its achievement can be measured in many different ways. Eight indicators have been selected covering three themes: achieving full potential, contributing to communities and accessing services. The eight indicators relate to: *i)* employment; *ii)* English language attainment; *iii)* volunteering; *iv)* contact with community organisations; *v)* housing standards; *vi)* take-up of British citizenship; *vii)* reporting of racial, cultural or religious harassment and *viii)* access to education. However, because the strategic policy framework focuses primarily on integration through employment, integration can only begin in the fullest sense when an asylum seeker becomes a refugee. Some local initiatives are concerned about this, expressing the view that from the individual perspective the ideal is for integration to begin "on day one", and that a denial of the opportunity to work (except in a voluntary capacity) may militate against their longer-term integration. There is a tension here between the aims of case workers in local refugee and community groups dealing with specific individual cases (often irrespective of their legal status) on the one hand,[20] and national government policy to ensure that the concept of asylum is not corroded on the other.

In summary, in the context of an unprecedented rise in the number of refugees and asylum seekers since the early 1990s, with a peak in the early years of the 21st century, the policy environment has been volatile. The main parameters of government policy in relation to refugees and asylum seekers over the last decade have been identified (Zetter and Pearl, 2005) as: *i)* deterrence of unfounded asylum claims; *ii)* accelerated and strict status determination procedures; *iii)* containment of public expenditure on refugees and asylum seekers; *iv)* co-ordination and centralisation of policy and implementation; *v)* dispersal of asylum seekers from housing pressure areas in London and the South East; *vi)* development of a "managed migration" programme for economic migrants in relation to labour market needs and skill shortages; and *vii)* development of policies for integration of refugees and asylum seekers with leave to remain.

The London governance context

The governance framework in London provides an important context for the local implementation of migration policy in the UK.[21] The paradox of London is "weak government, strong economic growth".[22] In part, "weak government" stems from London's relatively fragmented and unsettled system of governance, characterised by a tension between a neighbourhood and metropolitan system. Key reforms occurred in 1965, 1986 and 2000.

In 1986 the Greater London Council was abolished, depriving London of a key tier of governance at a London-wide level. A London-wide tier was reintroduced in 2000 with the election of London's first Mayor (subsequently re-elected in 2004) and 25 elected members in a Greater London Assembly.[23] The key units of local government remained 32 very powerful boroughs (plus the City of London), with responsibilities including education (at school level), housing, social services and local planning. In addition to the boroughs at local level and the Greater London Assembly and Mayor at a London-wide level, policy at the UK government level is also of relevance to the local integration of refugees and other immigrants in London. The Home Office is responsible for regulating immigration and for working with individuals and communities to build a safe, just and tolerant society. The DWP is responsible for the welfare reform agenda, while Jobcentre Plus delivers help and advice on jobs and training for people who can work and financial help for those who cannot. The Department for Education and Skills (DfES) is concerned with the education and skills agenda, while the Department of Health and five strategic health authorities across London have responsibility for health.

The London Development Agency (LDA) is a GLA body with responsibilities to: i) promote business efficiency, investment and competitiveness in London; ii) promote employment in London; and iii) enhance the development and application of skills relevant to employment in London. However, the LDA is not a mainstream funder of learning and skills. Rather funding rests with the five local Learning and Skills Councils (LSCs) in London (responsible for planning and funding vocational education and training), the Higher Education Funding Council for England, Jobcentre Plus, the Government Office for London, Business Link (providing advice for people running or thinking of starting their own businesses) 26 separate Sector Skills Councils, and the local authorities (i.e. boroughs). The LDA endeavours to influence these other organisations through partnership working, and to pilot, gap fund and test ideas. Alongside the organisations listed above are a range of civic organisations and professional bodies with whom the LDA works. Indeed, the London Skills Commission, led by the LDA and the London LSC group, works on behalf of businesses and individuals in London to plan and deliver joint employment and skills programmes which meet local and regional needs. The Commission is a strategic alliance of key London organisations from the public, private and voluntary sectors that have joined together to develop a more dynamic and equitable labour market. Under the guidance of the London Skills Commission, the Framework for Regional Employment and Skills Action (FRESA) sets out how London's key funding and planning organisations will work together to ensure London can maintain and improve on its position as the leading European global city. The FRESA is both a programme of action which identifies the steps to achieving a healthy labour market, and an agreement to work together to better meet real needs and deliver co-ordinated action in the future.[24]

Overall, in London, as across the UK as a whole, there is a patchwork of national, regional and local actors responsible for different aspects of migrant integration – including central government departments and agencies, regional agencies, local government and NGOs. Alongside these, refugee and community organisations (RCOs) and the voluntary sector also play an important role. This makes for a complex picture – particularly in relation to funding of activities, when often several sources of funding are likely to be of relevance to a particular initiative or project.

As of mid 2006, London's Mayor is – by agreement with the Home Office – taking responsibility for leading work on refugee integration in London. He is supported in this role by a new Board for Refugee Integration in London (BRIL). The Board brings together key London decision-makers from statutory, community and voluntary sectors, including the Home Office, Metropolitan Police Authority, Jobcentre Plus, the London Housing Federation, the London National Health Service, London Children and Young People's Forum, London Voluntary Service Council and the Refugee Council, as well as two refugee members who are delegates from the Mayor's Refugee Advisory Panel.[25] BRIL's first task is to develop a citywide strategy, for publication in late 2007. The strategy will consider how the different agencies and communities can work together and will focus on five key areas: employment training and enterprise; housing; health; community safety; children and young people (including education).

Migrants and refugees in the UK and London labour markets

A further important context for local initiatives supporting the integration of refugees in London is the labour market itself. Recent UK economic performance has been characterised by the OECD as "relatively strong", with a GDP growth rate of 3.1% in 2004 and unemployment at 4.7%. This economic growth, coupled with a flexible labour market, is a key factor underlying the continuation of the resurgence of economic migration into the UK.

London is distinctive in a UK context in displaying strong economic growth alongside low levels of employment. Output per capita in London is 46% higher than in the UK. Yet the employment rate, at around 70%, is comparable to that in the north east (the poorest region in England). Despite the similarity in employment rates, in London the key issue is not necessarily one of demand maximisation (as it is in the north east). Rather in the case of London there are strong links between jobs in London and residents in surrounding regions. The result is that economic growth in London has not delivered social inclusion for all the residents of London (especially Inner London), since levels of non-employment remain high relative to other parts of the UK. This suggests that immigrants with lack of English and poor skills are likely to face particular difficulty in labour market integration in Inner London *vis-à-vis* some other parts of the UK.

London is economically, socially and spatially divided. The fact that there are disproportionate numbers of people at both ends of the income distribution, underlines the high levels of inequality in the London labour market. In turn, this makes for high levels of deprivation, with 38% of children in London (55% in Inner London) living in income poverty.

A key challenge for London is to link economic growth in London to the residents of London (whether born in the UK or elsewhere and from whatever ethnic group). This means overcoming barriers to participation, and equipping residents with the skills necessary to compete successfully for jobs. Here it is salient to note that London also has a distinctive employment structure relative to the UK: it has a greater than national average share of employment in service industries – most notably in ICT, business services and creative industries, while occupationally, higher level non-manual occupations (including managers and professionals) are over-represented relative to the UK average. Despite this "professionalisation" of the employment structure, there is also continuing demand for labour in jobs requiring low skills levels. The polarisation in the London labour market means that it is difficult for people in lower level jobs to rise up the organisational ladder. Moreover, the National Minimum Wage is worth relatively less in London than in the rest of the UK (due to higher living costs in London than elsewhere), so low wage employment is not necessarily as attractive in London as it might be in other parts of the UK relative to the "certainty" of income from benefits.

Experience of migrants and refugees in the labour market

Currently, migrants experience mixed success in the labour market, and are found disproportionately at both ends of the skills continuum: *i.e.* in professional occupations and in unskilled occupations. This is particularly so in London *vis-à-vis* other parts of the UK, since the capital attracts both very highly qualified immigrants and also many less skilled, newly arrived immigrants who may be far from "job ready". Where migrants find themselves on the skills continuum is correlated with a number of factors. These include: i) method of entry to the UK – with those entering by legal means tending to experience greatest success in the labour market; ii) level of education – with those who have highest levels of education, and qualifications that are recognised as transferable to the UK, tending to enjoy greatest success in labour market terms; iii) English language fluency – a crucial determinant of labour market success: language proficiency is likely to reduce the gap between the UK-born and migrants considerably; iv) years since in-migration – generally labour market outcomes improve with length of stay in the UK and v) acculturation (Home Office, 2002). Other factors are also likely to be important, but may be difficult to quantify.

Given the features and factors outlined above, it is not possible, or indeed helpful, to think of a generic experience for migrant workers in general or for refugees more specifically. Drawing on anecdotes, SERTUC (the Southern and Eastern Region Trades Union Congress) identifies contrasting positions of migrant workers in the London labour market.[26] First, there are those migrant workers coming to London with good English language skills and good technical skills – for whom there is a high degree of horizontal labour market mobility and a reasonable degree of upward mobility, as a result of London having a dynamic labour market, a history of diversity and some skills shortages. Secondly, migrant workers who have poor English skills and/or no technical or academic qualifications (or at least none that are recognised and readily transferable) find the London labour market a much more hostile place: "it is commonplace for a migrant worker to become trapped in a low skill, low wage occupation, such as office cleaning, food processing, washing-up in restaurants. For such workers, there might be considerable horizontal mobility, in that they can move from one restaurant to another." Many migrant workers do not have full access to the labour market and "become dependent on intermediaries, friends, family, and gangmasters" to access work. Whilst this potentially offers a degree of support, it can often lock migrants into a negative situation. There are a high number of low-paid jobs in London and migrant workers do endure poor employment practices and infringements of employment rights, particularly within the informal economy.[27] Sweat-shops still exist in London, for example in the rag trade in north and east London. There is considerable evidence of exploitation of women in the "sex industry". There are considerable opportunities to work in the retail industry but the pay levels are often very poor, the hours long or insecure and opportunities for advancement limited.

Arguably, some London services – especially at the bottom end of the labour market – depend on the cheap labour that the informal economy provides. Research focusing on employment of illegal migrant workers in the restaurant and clothing sectors found that in the former sector employment of undocumented workers was a response to labour shortages while in the latter cost was the principal motive for employment of illegal workers (with widespread evasion of the National Minimum Wage) (Ram, Edwards and Jones, 2002). At national level government strategies to combat illegal working include an on-line Employers' Toolkit, designed to improve employers' understanding of their legal obligations and the benefits of using legal migrant labour, heavy fines for infringements of employment regulations in respect of migrants and much better information about documentation they should be seeking from migrants. The Trades Union Congress (TUC) have also emphasised the exploitative conditions underlying illegal employment (Anderson and Rogaly, 2005). Overall, an unknown number of migrants work illegally.[28] Figures on migrant numbers from the new EU member states (known as the A8) have been called into question by the failure of many to register as required, although an early official assessment points to a reduction in illegal working amongst A8 nationals (Portes and French, 2005). Moreover, many migrants entitled to work freely in the UK switch in and out of (il)legality, as do employers, such that calls have been made to shift the balance from "sticks" towards "carrots" in order to encourage transition into the formal economy (Copisarow and Barbour, 2004). Hence, problems and confusion over definitions confound attempts to estimate the extent of illegal working.[29] In November 2003, the Secretary of State for Work and Pensions admitted that there were 1.8 million surplus National Insurance (NI) numbers in circulation – but it is unknown how many of these relate to the indigenous population working in the informal economy, and how many relate to migrant workers. What is clear is that, setting the law and its enforcement to one side, labour shortages in a large and relatively strong economy such as London provide an environment conducive to the creation of opportunities for illegal working. Most methods for calculating the size of the informal economy in the UK suggest that it is growing faster than the formal economy (Small Business Council, 2004). One journalist summed up the situation as follows: "… the numbers are fraught with difficulty. However, it appears safe to conclude from the evidence that the scale of illegal working is very substantial, larger than previously acknowledged, and a major factor in Britain's economic competitiveness" (Lawrence, 2005).

Research on the experience of refugees has highlighted relatively low levels of labour market participation and evidence for "occupational downgrading" amongst those in employment – suggesting that their skills are not being used to their full potential, especially in the case of those with involvement in professional jobs prior to migration (see for example, Dumper, 2002). Information collected on job search also points to occupational downgrading (Bloch, 2002). Moreover, the diversity of employment on offer to refugees is frequently much more limited than the work that they had previously been able to carry out before coming to Britain.

The GLA has undertaken extensive analysis of labour market outcomes by country of birth and ethnic group in London using Labour Force Survey and 2001 Census of Population data; refugees are not identified, but nevertheless this source is of value in providing contextual insights into the diversity of experience of different population sub-groups in the labour market (Spence, 2005). Key features of economic position by country of birth are outlined in Table 4.1 This shows that 61% of the migrant population were in employment in 2002/03 compared with 74% of UK born Londoners. While those born outside the UK make up 35% of persons of working age in London, they comprise 42% of the unemployed and 45% of the economically inactive.

Table 4.1. **Economic position by country of birth, Greater London, 2002/03**

	Country of birth			% total			Migrants as % of all persons
	All countries	Born in UK	Born outside UK	All	Born in UK	Born outside UK	
All persons working age	4 719 000	3 084 000	1 634 000	100	100	100	*34.6*
Economically active	3 534 000	2 428 000	1 106 000	74.9	78.7	67.7	*31.3*
In employment	3 285 000	2 284 000	1 001 000	69.6	74.1	61.2	*30.5*
In employment (exc. full-time students)	3 149 000	2 191 000	957 000	73.9	78.4	65.4	*30.4*
Unemployed	250 000	144 000	106 000	5.3	4.7	6.5	*42.3*
Economically inactive	1 184 000	656 000	528 000	25.1	21.3	32.3	*44.6*
Sick or disabled	261 000	152 000	109 000	5.5	4.9	6.7	*41.7*
Looking after home/family	405 000	202 000	203 000	8.6	6.5	12.4	*50.1*
Student	320 000	193 000	126 000	6.8	6.3	7.7	*39.6*
Other reason	199 000	109 000	90 000	4.2	3.5	5.5	*45.2*

Source: Annual local area Labour Force Survey 2002/03; from Spence (2005).

More detailed disaggregation of employment rates of working age residents by country of birth (see Figure 4.1[30]) shows that while those born in high income countries outside the UK have an employment rate of 75%, the employment rate for those from developing countries is only 61.4%, compared with a London average of 73.9%. Data from the 2001 Census allowing a finer level of disaggregation by country (see Figure 4.2) reveals that while employment rates for those from Australia and South Africa exceed 83%, for those from Somalia the employment rate is a mere 16.4%. In sectoral terms, those born outside the UK are disproportionately concentrated in hotels and restaurants. In occupational terms, those born outside the UK are disproportionately concentrated in elementary occupations, process, plant and machine operative occupations and personal service occupations. This broad aggregate picture, however, masks considerable diversity and polarity in labour market outcomes. Within the developing country category, some groups (*e.g.* people from Somalia) face a very high degree of exclusion from the labour market. Triangulating with data sources on the origins of asylum applicants and refugees, it is likely that groups such as Somalians comprise a high proportion of refugees.

Figure 4.1. **Employment rates (working age) of Greater London residents by country of birth, 2002/03**

Country of birth	Employment rate (%)
Born in UK	78.4
Outside UK	65.4
High income countries	75.0
Developing countries	61.4
East Europe and Central Asia	52.7
South Asia	54.9
Sub-Saharan Africa	68.0
Middle East and North Africa	55.9
Latin America and Caribbean	65.4
East Asia, Pacific and other	71.3

London average 73.9%

Employment rates (%), excluding full-time students

Source: Annual local area Labour Force Survey, 2002/03.

Figure 4.2. **Employment rates for London's larger migrant populations, 2001**

Country	Employment rate (%)
Australia	85.5
South Africa	83.9
Germany	79.8
France and Monaco	78.8
Kenya	75.9
USA	75.6
Italy	75.4
Hong Kong	73.8
Ghana	72.2
Nigeria	71.8
Sri Lanka	67.8
Ireland	65.5
India	64.9
Jamaica	62.3
Cyprus	54.2
Pakistan	48.4
Bangladesh	36.8
Turkey	35.9
Somalia	16.4

Employment rate (%), excluding full-time students, age 16-64

Source: 2001 Census, Commissioned Tables C0116 and C0116a.

Barriers to labour market integration for refugees

The problems that migrants face in entering and moving within the UK labour market are many and varied, reflecting the fact that they are a diverse group. Refugees in particular, experience certain barriers (such as legal issues and access to work permits while still claiming asylum) which can make access to the labour market more difficult. However they also share many barriers with other immigrant groups, including technical issues (for example, recognition of qualifications), access to social welfare benefits, a lack of understanding of the labour market, a lack of knowledge of job search processes, a lack of appropriate work experience and discrimination. Arguably most fundamentally, many migrants face problems with basic English and a lack of more advanced language skills: it is salient to note that lack of language emerges repeatedly in research studies (Bloch, 2002) as a barrier to participation in training and employment, and to mobility within the labour market. Yet employment is crucial to the psychological well-being of refugees, and lack of employment is highly correlated with exclusion.

With regard to barriers to employment, a distinction may be made between: i) things that refugees and other migrants can change – through gaining knowledge, enhancing skills and changing attitudes; and ii) factors outside their control. In the first category, newly arrived immigrants may face a lack of knowledge of the range of employment opportunities available, equal opportunities and employment legislation in relation to job hunting and in the workplace, the level of competition for jobs, workplace practices, procedures, jargon, how to describe "home" qualifications, transferability of skills, and how to access training in the UK. Specifically in relation to the practicalities of job search, issues faced by migrants may include lack of familiarity with the language of job hunting and of knowledge of how vacancies occur and how they are publicised, of the UK style of CV and application forms, internet applications, interview techniques (including telephone interviews) and self advocacy (in some instances there may be cross-cultural difficulties with notions of self interest or self promotion). Attitudinal and emotional issues acting as barriers to labour market integration for some migrants include disorientation (which may be as a result of anxiety, stress or trauma in the case of refugees[31]), loss of identity and sense of self-esteem, low motivation – due to long periods out of work and training, loss of employment-related networks, feeling discriminated against, and feeling unwanted and outcast, which in turn may contribute to further lack of confidence. In the face of such issues, use of successfully established migrants as role models for more newly arrived migrants may prove positive in boosting confidence, providing advice and sharing experiences.

In the second category of "factors outside their control", refugees and other migrants may face access difficulties – for example, English language support may not be outreached into the community or available at the level needed, or if a required training course is available costs of childcare, travel, training fees, etc, may be prohibitive, so precluding access. Migrants may face prejudice/ discrimination from employers who may be reluctant to hire migrants or who refuse to recognise their qualifications and skills. Refugees, in particular, may be at the mercy of poor communication links between RCOs,

Jobcentre Plus and employers. In relation to this latter point, and in the light of developments outlined in the Refugee Employment Strategy and National Strategy for Refugee Integration, it is salient to note that research with refugees across Europe (Jonker, 2004) has emphasised that in contrast to support from the voluntary sector, in general, interviewees felt that they did not receive any or little useful support from public sector organisations in their attempts to enter the labour market. The interviewees attributed this to lack of knowledge of refugees' specific needs, the value of their diplomas, their focus on the low income sector and their strict rules and regulations that are not designed for refugees. One interviewee in the UK described his experience with the local job centre as follows: "Job Centres are funny places, because they do not ask what your skills are, but simply look at the available jobs that are often low level and badly paid".

Barriers to full labour market integration are faced not only by those outside the labour market, but also by those who are in employment. For example, professionals engaged in low grade jobs may suffer poor motivation, as well as some redundancy in skills which are no longer practised. Likewise, some migrants may work long hours in poorly paid jobs (the so-called "strawberry fields syndrome"), such that financial hardship and/or a lack of time, opportunity, energy or inclination to engage in further training with a view to moving upwards within the labour market.

Research with employers (IES, 2004) has reiterated the importance placed on English language training relevant to employment and on work experience. Yet, with regard to work experience, while highlighting the likely value of voluntary work and workplacements for refugees, research with refugees (Jonker, 2004) indicates that many feel that their prior qualifications and work experience are underestimated by employers. This suggests that there is a need for awareness raising amongst employers, as do concerns expressed by employers about documentation clarifying that permission to work has been granted. However, in the context of the proposed legislative changes extending the period of uncertainty regarding permission to stay in the UK, it is salient to note the claim of a Rwandan office manager that: "Asylum seekers with permission to work[32] can only find low paid (cleaning) jobs. Proper jobs are not available because employers think you will be sent home" (Jonker, 2004). Research with employers (IES, 2004) has also highlighted the impact of negative media reporting on the perceptions of employers, while research with refugees indicates that many blame politicians and the media for creating a negative image of migrants, and refugees in particular. The issues raised here highlight some of the difficulties of achieving the balance between building tolerance and enthusiasm for legal migration, while implementing a tough stance on illegal immigration.

Local initiatives: responding to integration problems of refugees

The analysis of local initiatives below follows a thematic approach, focusing on the main types of instrument used to support labour market integration in London, including access to education and training, English language support, recognition of qualifications, acculturation to the UK labour market, accessing employment and mentoring, encouraging entrepreneurship, general support to build social and community capital, and signposting/onward referral.

It is important to recognize, however, that many of the specific initiatives to target the barriers experienced by refugees in London are developed and managed through an integrated partnership approach – as exemplified by the suite of projects which have been developed under the auspices of the Renewal partnership between RCOs and the statutory sector in West London (see Box 4.1).

Renewal stresses that an integrated, partnership approach is crucial for tackling refugee integration, as it involves tackling a series of long-term problems that are interlinked and cannot be dealt with in isolation. The partnership considers that it is vital that social integration factors are viewed alongside economic integration and are addressed in genuine partnership with refugees. In addition, Renewal provides a degree of continuity for RCOs within a field dominated by short-term funding programmes, and a degree of capacity building support, which can be time intensive and require assistance over a number of years. In the long term, Renewal feels that the mainstreaming of RCOs will be the key to sustaining effective refugee employment services.

Access to education and training

Access to education and training is fundamental to the integration of refugees, and, in particular, to their adaptation to the UK labour market. It is generally acknowledged that the UK has a relatively flexible and open training system, offering opportunities for lifelong learning after the end of compulsory education. This should act to the advantage of refugees. Yet flexibility and openness can mean that it is difficult to gain a full understanding of how the system works, and to select appropriate courses.

The Refugee Education Training and Advisory Service (RETAS) provides a range of guides and services to refugees in the UK. One example of general information provision is a "Handbook on Education for Refugees in the UK", providing an overview and introduction to the education system, and including sources for further information. Specifically, it covers the following issues: i) overview of the British Educational System – schools, post 16, higher education; ii) refugees and education – definitions, what educational advice

> ### Box 4.1. **Renewal**
>
> Renewal is a 7-year programme with 5 staff running until 2007, with Ealing Primary Care Trust as the Accountable Body.
>
> *Funding*: SRB6 grant of £6 million (approx € 8.9 million) via the LDA, with a further £10 million (approx € 14.8 million) estimated leverage.
>
> *Geographical coverage*: West London – defined as the boroughs of Brent, Ealing, Hammersmith and Fulham, Harrow, Hillingdon and Hounslow, with a combined population of 1.38 million people, of whom it is estimated that 60 000-69 000 are refugees and asylum seekers (i.e. 4.7% of the population).
>
> *Partners*: borough Refugee Forums and WESTREP (a forum of forums in West London), local authorities, NHS Primary Care Trusts, Connexions London West, London West LSC and the Association of London Government
>
> *Aims*: to
>
> - Support refugees in West London.
> - Overcome barriers to accessing services in health, employment and training, youth.
> - Build capacity of RCOs.
> - Create a step change in the way public services respond to the needs of refugees.
>
> *Activities*:
>
> - Project funding – small, medium and large scales.
> - Capacity building activity.
> - Facilitation/brokering of partnerships.
> - Research and mapping exercises.
> - Advocacy at sub-regional level and beyond.

and guidance involves; *iii)* refugee children and education; *iv)* post-16 provision – outline of different types of provision; *v)* English language provision – types of courses, qualifications; *vi)* undergraduate courses – types of degrees, entry requirements, application procedures, funding; *vi)* postgraduate study.

RETAS services are designed to help refugees in the UK who are over 16 years of age to access education, training and employment (including self-employment). Education advice services provided by the RETAS Advice Team in 2003 spanned both individuals and service providers. Activities included one-to-one advice and guidance, group sessions for refugees and asylum seekers at RCO premises and local colleges,[33] training sessions for service providers, and financial assistance for clients.[34] It is estimated that over 2,000 refugees and asylum seekers are helped each year.

On a smaller scale, and at a more local level, many RCOs aim to facilitate access to training for their members. An example of a specific project is the Hillingdon Somali Women's Group ICT Training Project. This project commenced in January 2002, in partnership with Uxbridge College, at a local community centre. The centre is in close proximity to an estate where many refugees live and many project participants are refugees. The project objectives are provision of ICT training and a range of other (mainly entry level) training opportunities including English language skills, study support and job preparation for local refugee women, with a view to assisting them with progression into employment. Uxbridge College outreach and provide tutorage at the community centre. Drop-in advice is also available. In this way the women can learn in an environment which is comfortable to them whilst also obtaining professional help. A second example is the Tower Foundation in south-east London which is running a training course for local residents (many of whom are also refugees) leading to a NVQ (National Vocational Qualification) Level 2 qualification in Health and Social Care (which should enable access to employment as a Care Assistant). Both of these projects exemplify provision of training in a local and familiar setting, for residents who may well be unwilling or unable to access the mainstream – at least in the first instance.

While some local projects are concerned mainly with training in order to gain the qualifications that are necessary to gain entry into particular occupations, others place greater priority on acquiring specific skills likely to be of use in gaining employment (although this is rarely their sole objective). An example is provided by the Women's Textiles and Dressmaking Project, run by the Arab Group in Hounslow and the Suburbs. The Arab Group supports the Arab community with a number of different projects in the fields of education, employment, social welfare, cultural activities and sport. The Textiles and Dressmaking Project was financed by a grant from Renewal and ran for nine hours per week over three sessions from April 2002 to March 2005. Project objectives were to enhance education and learning skills of Arab women in the area (some of whom are refugees), to teach dressmaking skills as a process to empowerment and to up-skill clients to increase their opportunities for employment. 42 candidates were trained at the project, of whom 18 gained a formal vocational qualification in fashion and dressmaking. Eight jobs were created for project participants in linen and upholstery factories, two women opened their own tailoring businesses and eight women were employed in a clothing factory. Key outcomes of the project are empowerment of local refugee women and their families (largely as a result of increased confidence) and reduction of hidden unemployment.

> ### Box 4.2. **RAAD Large Scale Employment and Training Project**
>
> Commencing in September 2002, the aim of this West London-based project was to:
>
> 1. Assist refugee and asylum seekers to access information on training, job searching and self-employment initiatives.
> 2. Work with employers in order to increase their awareness of existing skills and potential amongst refugees and asylum seekers.
> 3. Forge partnerships with institutions providing training for refugees.
>
> Project *activities* encompassed:
>
> - IT training with ESOL support.
> - Provision of information, advice and guidance to refugees on training and self-employment.
> - One-to-one job search sessions.
> - CV preparation.
> - Training in interview techniques.
> - Confidence building and coaching sessions.
> - Support with accreditation of prior learning.
> - A volunteers' training programme.
> - Mentoring of RCOs to develop kite mark standards in advice and guidance.
>
> The *holistic approach* – offering support for individuals, organisations and businesses – involving the attempt to increase demand for refugee employment, as well as making individuals more job ready, has been identified as a crucial factor in the success of the project.
>
> *Outputs* – To date, 111 jobs have been created in a variety of fields (including medicine, industry, the voluntary sector, customer services and the retail sector) and 329 qualifications have been obtained (including ESOL, IT and fork lift truck driving).
>
> The *outcomes* of the project are wide ranging, spanning social inclusion, parents becoming role models for their children, confidence building and helping refugee professionals become integrated into the labour market.

From an evaluation perspective, it is salient to note that this project had clearly identified objectives, outputs and (especially) outcomes. Reflecting on the experience of the project, it was noted that lack of crèche proved a difficulty in recruiting to the project – and that there would have been scope for including this in the grant application. While in general it is clear that "tailor made" courses including confidence building activity and workplacements tend to be successful, this particular project found that it took time and effort to persuade employers to take on project participants for work experience, (especially in the case of those participants who wore hejab).

Training and support for migrants and refugees is often delivered within a broader set of activities and support. Exemplifying this broader approach, the RAAD Large Scale Employment and Training project (supported by Renewal) has delivered a raft of different forms of support including training designed to enhance employment prospects. Types of support offered include skills development, help with job search, and work with employers to in an attempt to open up employment opportunities for project participants (see Box 4.2).

English language support

Across London there is a wide range of ESOL (English for Speakers of Other Languages) provision.[35] Despite the fact that expenditure on ESOL and the volume of provision has risen significantly over the last few years, and the fact that around 50% of national provision is in London (KPMG, 2005), a report on London by the Strategy Unit in 2004 suggested that the volume of demand for ESOL in London far outstripped supply. Whilst ESOL provision is still somewhat patchy, there have been some concerted efforts by the Regional Skills Partnership in coordinating a more strategic approach to the delivery of services and funding. A key issue is how and whether provision matches the needs of learners and the demands of the economy[36] – in terms of level (introductory, intermediate, specialist), content (specifically in relation to fulfilling workplace needs) and availability (geographically and temporally). With increasing emphasis from government, the trades unions and employers on the English language,[37] and with the Home Office confirming in 2004 that in order to gain citizenship individuals would have to be able to demonstrate achievement of English language at Entry Level 3 or higher, several initiatives have reported greater enrolment in English language classes.

Confidence and fluency in English is accepted as essential to social integration and moreover opens up access to a wider range of potential jobs in a service-oriented labour market. In this respect, command of English in a business related context is highlighted as important. However, the specialist language required by a mechanic in a garage is likely to be different from that needed in a hospital. Hence, there is a need for courses to be targeted to the needs of users, and for ESOL courses to be tailored to sectoral and occupational needs. So, for example, refugee professionals often require higher level language programmes. The experience of the Renewal initiative shows that such courses, in combination with adaptation programmes and workplacements as part of a specialist package works well. In order to tailor English language learning to user needs, English Language On-line is being piloted in South London. Likewise, with an emphasis on English in specific workplace contexts, Bilingual

Vocational courses which focus on vocabulary migrants are likely to need have been established in Croydon. In general, evidence gleaned during the case study visit suggests that while migrants' English language capability (varying with the job in question) and the precise level and nature of English language proficiency demanded by employers is heterogeneous, in general, the emphasis should be on ensuring individuals have sufficient language ability to function in a specific workplace environment as quickly as possible, rather than to ensure maximum language competence if this delays entry to the labour market.

Although not targeted specifically at refugees, the Centre for Filipinos (CF) – a registered charity formed to provide services for Filipino nationals and their families living in London and the UK, operating in two centres in the London boroughs of Camden and Hammersmith and Fulham – also provides an example of the role of the development of ESOL classes to serve the needs of migrants who have been unable to access mainstream education because they lack confidence and have very little free time owing to working long hours. In response, the CF provides a Sunday School, offering ESOL classes for Filipino migrant workers and their families, as well as IT courses, information, advice and guidance services and confidence building workshops. With ESF/LDA funding, from 2005 the English classes are to be combined with computer classes, so focusing more on English in a work-oriented context.

Recognition of qualifications

Recognition of qualifications (and training) is essential to ensure that migrants and refugees are getting the support, information and advice they need to fully integrate into the UK employment market. Such recognition can show the extent to which migrants have qualifications (and skills) relevant to shortage sectors.

The National Academic Recognition Information Centre for the UK (UK NARIC) is a private organisation contracted by the DfES to provide official guidance on the UK level of overseas qualifications.[38] It is funded partly by the DfES and partly by corporate membership. UK NARIC holds a global qualifications database which is used as a guide for benchmarking qualifications from all over the world. This database provides a means of determining the UK academic level of overseas qualifications.

UK NARIC services form an essential component of other projects, involving broader labour integration aims than recognition of qualifications per se. The Migrants and Refugees Qualifications project is one such example. This is a pan-London project, involving the five London LSCs, and the LDA, in conjunction with UK NARIC. Other partners include the Government Office for London, Jobcentre Plus, City and Guilds, the London Open College Network, the National Institute of Adult Continuing Education and Kingston Racial Equality Council. This project aimed to identify the transferable skills and qualifications of migrant workers (including refugees) with a right to work in the UK and supports them to fulfil their potential in the employment market. The outputs specified for the project over its lifetime were 1 000 migrants accessing NARIC services. Interestingly, the project also had an economic orientation, in that it was targeted towards skills shortage sectors, such as construction, engineering and teaching. Migrants proceed through the project in four sequential stages. The first stage is concerned with "identification" of eligible clients (often through Information Advice and Guidance Partnerships), onward referral to UK NARIC and support to complete a Migrant Skills Questionnaire.[39] In the second "qualification comparability" stage, NARIC completes qualification comparability documentation and informs the client accordingly. The third stage is "skills analysis", in which each client receives from NARIC a document that "maps" the additional training/learning needed to be qualified and competent to UK industry standards. The fourth stage embraces "local guidance, support and active brokerage", involving one-to-one counselling and guidance, production of a personal development plan, brokerage of additional skills (basic ESOL, vocational, academic, etc.), and arranging work experience. DfES recognises that in order to evaluate the impact of the project and gain an insight into outcomes, it would have been useful to track project participants through the various stages of the project and into subsequent education/training/employment.

It might be that an individual is already competent to work in the desired sector, or that there is a need to retrain, to upskill or take English language training. Analyses from the project show that many migrants have qualifications relevant to UK shortage sectors. However, confining discussion to "qualifications" tends to discount the "skills" (not necessarily captured by "qualifications") that migrants have. Yet qualifications are easier to compare and to map than are skills, and the importance placed by many employers on "soft" skills and relevant work experience alongside qualifications remains an important issue facing migrants to the UK, suggesting that except in sectors/occupations facing very severe shortages, qualifications alone may not be enough to enable a migrant to access employment at a level commensurate with his/her skills.

Acculturation to UK society and the labour market

The RETAS Refugee Arrival Project notes that refugees are mainly aged 32-45 years. Most have work experience, and while (re)training may be necessary it is often not sufficient for gaining entry to employment. Rather what is needed is knowledge of civil rights, an understanding of the UK labour market, how it operates and the recruitment process, and employment support. While there appears to be a trend towards greater recognition of the need for, and provision of, employment support, initiatives addressing broader issues of acculturation to UK society and the labour market appear less well developed to date.

The types of help needed by refugees to navigate and acculture to the UK labour market include job search skills (not many refugees know how to apply for jobs in the UK), help in compiling a CV (which may be an alien concept for some people) and advice on interview behaviour. To address some of these issues, the RETAS Employment Service offers a series of 2-week job search and orientation courses were run throughout the year, including an overview of the UK job market, individual careers assessment and preparing a CV. In order to gain understanding of cross-cultural issues, refugees may need unpaid work experience. However, RETAS had had difficulty in getting unpaid work experience with the private sector; it is easier to go to NGOs and the voluntary sector. A possible strategy could be to go from the voluntary sector to the private sector, but some jobs are not available in the voluntary sector, so this is not a viable option in all cases. Refugees (and other migrants) may also need help with "business English", which is not necessarily covered by ESOL courses.

Another example of a project that does attempt to provide an element of acculturation to the UK labour market, alongside other education, training and work experience is the Bridge to Work Project, part of the Continuing Education and Training Service (CETS) in Croydon, receiving funding from the Single Regeneration Budget (SRB).[40] Forty-five people from professional backgrounds abroad access the Bridge programme each year, of whom approximately 30% are refugees and asylum seekers. The aims of Bridge to Work are to get students into work in their chosen profession, establish the equivalence of their qualifications, build confidence, improve interpersonal and language skills, introduce students to UK work culture and explore cultural issues, provide a workplacement, fund further training and/or requalification, develop IT skills, provide careers information advice and guidance, and to provide assistance in all aspects of job search. Approximately 30% of participants have a workplacement. While no statistics were made available for workplacements for different sub-groups participating in the project or for directly comparable programmes, it is recognised that the proportion of participants with workplacements is lower than would be desirable, and the project's Work Experience Co-ordinator is endeavouring to widen the project's profile amongst employers and other organisations in order to secure more workplacements.[41] In general, one or two students gain employment during their course, with others often finding employment some time after leaving the project (having taken extra training and/or gaining more work experience).

Accessing employment

At a strategic level the Employability Forum, an independent umbrella organisation[42] which promotes the skills and experience of refugees in the UK, has engaged with policy makers and employers on key issues affecting refugee employment. Through the co-ordination of an Employer Network and Policy Group, they have promoted change to policy and practices to ensure that refugees have equal access to employment in the UK. They have lobbied for refugees to receive clear permission to work documentation, to be provided with NI numbers, and greater access to bank accounts. This work has been carried out in parallel with meetings of refugee agencies and other voluntary organisations in order to ensure that key messages are carried from people working directly with refugees to a wider audience of employers, policy makers and professional organisations.

In terms of more specific employment support for migrants and refugees, initiatives tend to be best developed for professionals (as exemplified by the Bridge to Work project). It might be expected that refugees would find it easier to get into unregulated professions (such as engineering), than into regulated professions (such as medicine), but this is not necessarily the case. The advantage of an unregulated profession is that it is not absolutely necessary for a migrant to go through a lengthy and costly requalification process; rather it is possible to look for work straight away. However, the disadvantage of an unregulated profession is that the path to employment is not necessarily clear, and depending on the migrant's previous experience, can be complex and unpredictable.

In the case of engineering, RETAS established an Action for the Capital's Refugee Engineers Project in response to the high unemployment rate amongst skilled refugee engineers in London co-existing alongside skill shortages in engineering. The aim is to provide training, job search skills and resources to help qualified engineers find suitable jobs. An Employment Resource Handbook for Refugee Engineers was published in December 2004 (Rogic and Feldman, 2004). The handbook aims to serve as a concise guide to refugee engineers who are looking for work in the sector, by providing essential information to make refugee engineers aware of the job hunting culture in the UK and providing an overview of the profession and sector. The first issue covered is refugees' entitlement to employment – encompassing permission to work for people with refugees' status, including details of proof of permission to work, permission to work for asylum seekers,[43] NI numbers, etc. The handbook also contains sections on the UK education system and engineering qualifications – including details of engineering qualifications, entry requirements for engineering courses, recognition of overseas qualifications; the engineering profession in the UK – covering engineering as an unregulated profession, different engineering titles, seeking registration with a professional institution, etc.; and the UK engineering sector – with information on skill shortages, engineering categories, and an overview of London's economy. Practical information on finding a job includes preparing to look for a job (including where to look for jobs); work experience (possible routes include temporary jobs; courses with workplacements; volunteering); questions on your skills, personal qualities and knowledge; understanding job requirements; and how to apply for jobs (different types of CV, CV writing; and details of job interviews – with sample questions). A number of case studies are provided and the appendices present details of engineering institutions, Internet resources for engineers, newspapers and magazines with job adverts for engineers, refugee assisting organisations, etc.

Turning to a regulated profession, according to a conservative Refugee Council figure there are nearly 1 000 refugee medical doctors in Britain unable to work because of qualification difficulties, despite substantial experience in their native countries. The British Medical Association estimates that the National Health Service (NHS) was in 2003 short of 20 000 doctors and consultants. In an effort to provide the necessary support for doctors to enter employment, RETAS has established a Re-qualification of Doctors scheme. This involves Education Action's Employment Team providing initial advice on medical re-qualification and employment opportunities in the NHS. This is followed by a mentoring stage where a UK doctor coaches a refugee doctor. It is evident that employment support is a necessary adjunct to recognition of qualifications.

Drawing on the experience of the initiatives outlined above, a new "orientation course" – PRESTO (Professional Refugees into Employment through Support, Training and On-Line Learning) is being developed by Education Action International and other partners. Funded by EU EQUAL, the project is concerned with the testing and dissemination of innovative training and employment packages to support refugee professionals and provide empowerment models in particular for refugees in the health, education and engineering sectors and for vulnerable groups such as women.

More generally, some RCOs attempt to provide employment support for their members. For example, the Iranian Association, a registered charity set up in 1984 to assist the refugee community in settlement and integration into British society, applied for funding from Renewal for an Advice, Guidance and Outreach Employment Project. Working with partners including West Thames College and Jobcentre Plus, Renewal funds quality marked advice and guidance, training in CV writing, interview techniques and mentoring, to supplement several existing IT, ESOL and numeracy courses.

As highlighted above in the examples of the Women's Textiles and Dressmaking Project, and the Bridge to Work Project, engaging with employers and finding opportunities for workplacements often proves difficult. Likewise, the Centre for Filipinos is making increased efforts to develop links with employers. After initial success with ethnic businesses in a small number of niche sectors, links are being developed with an Internet provider in an attempt to advertise the skills of trainees and draw in a wider range of employers to provide employment support and workplacements.

Mentoring

Mentoring is a key element of several of the initiatives outlined above. Mentoring is a process by which one person assists another to grow and learn in a safe and sympathetic relationship. To enhance success, training is needed for both mentors and mentees. For example, the Refugee Council has trained and matched 90 volunteer mentors with refugees seeking employment. Mentors and mentees have had both face-to-face sessions and have kept in touch by email.

A number of mentoring schemes tailored to the needs of refugees have been offered by agencies (such as Education Action International, RETAS and RWA) with expertise in employment, education, and integration issues of refugees to the UK. Mentee health professionals report that mentoring has proved particularly successful for them, with mentors facilitating their access to, and initial progress within the NHS. The goals of mentoring sessions in the Mentoring Programme for Refugee Doctors are to provide refugee doctors with advice on the UK Health System, medical career paths, professional registration, recruitment processes, specialist training, employment opportunities; to facilitate access of refugee doctors to clinical attachments, employment opportunities and further training; to support refugee doctors in search for appropriate employment. More general mentoring assistance is provided in the Mentoring for Employment scheme, which is targeted at unemployed refugees and asylum seekers with permission to work who are currently on benefits and seeking employment. Other mentoring schemes – including those for Refugee Women and Refugee Children – are not focused so exclusively on employment, but rather are concerned with easing the transition to UK society, and so may have implications for enhancing labour market integration in due course.

Encouraging and supporting entrepreneurship

Traditionally migrant businesses have been concentrated in their own communities, and have focused on ethnic markets. Research on BME owned businesses in London (LDA, 2005) (not distinguishing between different generations) shows that there has been a shift away from ethnic and niche markets into more mainstream and international growth sectors over the last decade, such that there is a trend towards greater complexity and diversity of firms established by people from ethnic minority backgrounds, although many remain relatively concentrated by locality and sector. In 2004 there were 66 000 BME owned businesses in London, accounting for 20% of London's businesses, employing over 560 000 people.[44] They generated an estimated £90 billion of sales revenue (approx. € 133 billion) – accounting for 11% of all businesses in London. However, BME businesses are at the lower end of the size scale: 53% of BME-owned businesses employ less than five staff, and there is a tendency to start up in "low barrier to entry" and saturated markets. These findings are reinforced by research by the London Development Agency (2004) based on interviews with 172 refugees, highlighting the concentration of refugee businesses in transport (minicab), catering and restaurants, low value retail, ethnic niche services/products, internet cafes and small scale construction (LDA, 2004).

The LDA has strong a interest in encouraging and supporting entrepreneurship, reflecting its mission of helping to sustain and increase wealth and prosperity, while at the same time proactively tackling economic disadvantage, and fulfilling a strategic and leadership role to promote business efficiency, investment and competitiveness. LDA-funded business support and investment programmes include City Growth Strategies, Access to Finance initiative, Regional Venture Capital Fund, Young Enterprise, LDA2, inward investment and business retention programmes and LDA-funded Business Link. Other LDA funded programmes have a specific BME focus (and will include refugees from BME groups), including a Procurement Development Programme – aimed at assisting and equipping SMEs to tender successfully for public sector contracts.

Within the context of BME enterprises generally performing well in the UK, specific difficulties faced by migrant entrepreneurs include lack of knowledge of UK business culture and regulations, and of existing business support services. RETAS runs Business Start-Up courses specifically focusing on issues and information related to the small business environment in the UK. Access to finance can also pose particular difficulties for migrant/refugee entrepreneurs.

Support to build social and community capital

As hinted in previous subsections, many RCOs are active not only in English language and education/training/employment support, but also in building social and community capital. The West London Refugee Employment and Training Initiative (RETI), a voluntary organisation based in Hounslow working with asylum seekers and refugees in West London, with a mission to reduce high levels of unemployment amongst refugee communities, provides not only employment, training and advice on small business start-ups, but also advice on housing and welfare benefits, and on drugs issues. Partners include schools, Jobcentre Plus and Hounslow Economic Development Unit. What beneficiaries value is the "localness" and "informality" of RETI. Renewal argues that RCOs should be placed at the heart of any refugee employment and training programme because of common language, cultural setting, shared experiences and the support offered by community networks.

The Global Grants Programme (see Box 4.3), funded by the ESF, the five London LSCs, the Association of London government and the LDA, provides funding support in the form of small project grants to small non-governmental, voluntary and community organisations.[45] By positive interventions, projects are aimed at tackling barriers to unemployment and moving people the first step(s) towards the labour market, thus creating greater equality of opportunity for the individuals assisted, and supporting wider social inclusion. As well as more conventional skills training and development and employment advice, eligible actions for "moving people towards employment" include confidence building, motivational activities, gaining skills through practical tasks (often involving less need for English language skills in the first instance) and building social capital. The focus on "engagement" (sometimes through arts, music and drama), means that overall, there is a strong emphasis on "soft" outcomes – such as confidence building and motivation – as measured by "distance travelled". The rationale for the deliberate focus on small community groups at grass-roots level is that these are the organisations most able to reach excluded groups, and provide a comfortable and secure environment in the first instance for those who are most excluded, so providing a necessary bridge into mainstream provision.

Signposting

The success (or otherwise) of the initiatives outlined in previous sub-sections rests not only on the extent to which they achieve their goals, but also on whether they can successfully "signpost" migrants and refugees to: i) more relevant and further support provided by other organisations (whether other NGOs or the mainstream), and ii) assistance in other spheres relevant to integration – such as health, housing, etc. This is an issue of particular importance in the London context, given the dynamism of the city and the proliferation of organisations concerned with labour market integration for migrants and refugees.

In theory, the fact that many organisations are competing for a limited pot of money available from the same or similar funding sources could lead either to an enhancement of energy being placed on "signposting" (since one project/organisation is unable to provide the full package of support required), or to a neglect of "signposting" activity (given that resources are inevitably

Box 4.3. **Global Grants: eligibility criteria, outputs and exemplar projects**

The key characteristics of the Global Grants project include:

Eligibility of organisations to receive grants: Small non-governmental organisations with no more than 2 full-time equivalent staff and have an income of no more than £60 000 (approx. € 88 600) for the last complete financial year.

Maximum grant size: £10 000 (approx. € 14 800)

Grant application process: Emphasis on simplicity: there is a short application form and a simple assessment. Filling in the forms is part of the capacity building process.

Number of organisations receiving grants: 299 in the 2002-03 programme and more than 300 grants in the 2003-04 programme.

Beneficiaries: Priority is given to projects for/involving people with disabilities, lone parents, people belonging to ethnic minorities experiencing most disadvantage in the labour market, refugees and asylum seekers, ex-offenders, and people living in the most deprived areas. In the period from March 2002 to November 2003 90% of beneficiaries were from BME groups. Almost 60% of beneficiaries are refugees.

Outputs: 2 205 for projects in the 2002-03 programme – made up of 272 individuals in full-time employment, 209 in part-time employment, 334 in other employment (not categorised), 111 self-employed, 334 in voluntary work (seen as a valuable step towards employment), 945 further education and training.

Exemplar projects:

- *Society for the Advancement of Black Arts*: aims to promote cultural diversity and development through the arts – 15 young people took part in a 6-month programme of public relations, media and events management training.
- *50+ Elderly Asian Club*: a voluntary/community organisation providing employment training programmes, running workshops and offering counselling to black and minority elderly people in the local area.
- *African Empowerment Group*: Five women training with a view to setting up a community enterprise in painting and decorating.
- *Latin American Integration Community Centre*: reducing the isolation of mothers and enhancing employability through ESOL classes.
- *Cameroon Asylum Seekers Association*: website design skills for self-employment and freelance work.
- *Shree Kutch Satsang Swaminarayan Community Centre*: set up a pilot programme within the community centre in Woolwich to equip individuals with security installation skills – this is an example of a project which helped unemployed people move towards a job while at the same time producing a community benefit.

concentrated on immediate delivery issues or efforts to secure further funding to ensure continuation of activity).

The PRESTO project currently in development (mentioned above) provides a rare example of a planned activity where the emphasis is deliberately on collaboration, as opposed to competition. The project is based on many of the key voluntary agencies in the field developing a partnership approach where previously there has often been competition. In order to do this a referral strategy is being developed, drawing up progression routes offering options involving services delivered by all partners; (the PRESTO partners are Education Action International [RETAS], the Islington Training Network, the British Refugee Council, London Metropolitan University, the Refugee Women's Association, the London Advice Service Alliance, Careconnect Learning, the Employability Forum, Refugees and Asylum Seekers Initiative for Skills Employability Ltd, Eventsforce Solutions Ltd, Islington Enterprise Agency and Manor Garden Welfare Trust). Collaborative work is also planned to facilitate progression for refugees into employment by linking with professional institutions, employers and training institutions, and extending links with the NHS, engineering institutions and the DfES.

Overall policy effectiveness and coherence at the local level

There is a multiplicity of local projects/initiatives in London to support refugees. In general, local initiatives in London have grown up *organically* in a *piecemeal* manner. Over time, this has led to a (arguably overly) *complex* system. In turn, this reflects the complexity of the London economy, and more especially the complexity, dynamism and flux in governance structures (i.e. "institutional clutter"). The result is that it is difficult for anyone (including those concerned with strategy formulation and delivery, let alone newcomers trying to identify pathways and navigate their way around the system) to gain a clear view of the overall scope of policies and initiatives designed to aid integration into the labour market and society more generally.

Those in the private sector (especially small and medium-sized employers) are faced with a complex public sector and legislative framework. Work with employers suggests that is necessary for the public sector to organise itself to display clarity, consistency and long-term commitment in engaging with employers. Relatively frequent attempts to rationalise and so simplify existing structures may be counterproductive (at least in the short term) in spawning confusion. Uncertainty may be further enhanced by planned legislative changes regarding granting refugees temporary, rather than permanent, leave to remain in the first instance.

In order to tackle this complexity a number of meso level sub-regional partnerships have emerged which provide some degree of co-ordination. One example is provided by the Renewal partnership in West London. It has adopted a strategic, structured approach towards engaging RCOs and the statutory sector via the borough Refugee Forums. Renewal's Mid Term Evaluation in 2004 highlighted its successful track record of project delivery (encompassing strengthening capacity of Refugee Forums, provision of small grants, development of opportunities for volunteers, school-community liaison, work with young people, etc.), combined with an ability to broker a multi-sectoral partnership. It has facilitated opportunities for networking amongst RCOs. Over this period it has earned the respect and trust of the refugee communities as well as the statutory and voluntary sector: it is perceived as an "honest broker". The evaluation noted that more attention needed to be given to developing stronger joint working links with other stakeholders.

While Renewal is a strategic entity at the sub-regional level, at the pan-London level, LORECA (London Refugee Economic Action) (see Box 4.4) has been established in 2004 by the LDA as the lead body on employment, enterprise and training for refugee and asylum seekers in London. It may be conceptualised as facilitating the development of a strategic co-ordinated approach, taking an overarching position above sub-regional entities, such as Renewal:

LORECA → Renewal → Refugee Forums → RCOs → Refugees

The vision is for a lead body that can draw together the work done by a large number of RCOs and NGOs working with refugees and asylum seekers, as well as the local and national government bodies involved. The aim is for LORECA to establish itself as the key body in London that can speak authoritatively with government, employer bodies, funding organisations, training providers and professional bodies about the needs of refugees and asylum seekers. The guiding principle of LORECA is "strategy not delivery": the work of the LORECA is to be focused at a strategic level with an emphasis upon co-ordinating information and service provision; it will not become involved in service delivery to individual refugees and asylum seekers.

The needs of migrants integrating into the labour market are many and varied. A trend is discernible towards a more client-centred (i.e. individualised) approach in which advice and services are geared to individual needs, in turn implying enhanced flexibility. Comments from providers and beneficiaries suggest that the localness and informality of many of the small projects which operate in London are valued at the first stage of engagement and integration for those who are most excluded.[46] At this first stage, the emphasis is often on "soft outcomes". However, evaluation of such projects is often poorly developed and only formative in nature, and some questions must remain over the quality of some provision.

> **Box 4.4. LORECA strategic goals and activities**
>
> The strategic goals and activities of LORECA are:
>
> - To improve the understanding of the needs of refugees and asylum seekers in relation to employment, training and enterprise issues – through acting as a clearing house for needs assessment and research, and for commissioning new research to fill gaps in knowledge and understanding.
>
> - To strategically plan and co-ordinate the activities of those from the statutory, voluntary and community sectors working on employment, training and enterprise issues for refugees and asylum seekers – by commissioning research to map service provision, establishing working groups to tackle key issues (*e.g.* ESOL), advise on the implementation of the LDA's strategy for the development and delivery of employment, training and enterprise activities, etc.
>
> - To improve the quantity and quality of employment, training and enterprise services for refugees and asylum seekers in the capital – by developing and establishing a tracking system for monitoring the outcomes of education, employment and training services for refugees in London; by commissioning audits of projects and services to ensure quantity and assure quality; by funding demonstration projects on a time-limited basis to fill identified needs in service; etc.
>
> - To work with employers and employers' associations to better understand their needs and promote the contribution that refugees and asylum seekers may make to addressing these needs – by undertaking promotional activities to share information with employers and employers' organisations on the range of skills available from London's refugee communities; and by ensuring that guidance on the employment of refugees is readily available to SMEs (through Business Links, etc.).
>
> - To identify strategic policy or legislative changes that would support the achievement of these goals and advocate through appropriate fora for these changes – by producing reports highlighting issues with strategic policy or legislative implications; and participating in relevant fora at London-wide, national and European levels.

In both social and economic terms, and specifically with regard to getting individuals into employment, it is becoming increasingly important to develop a longer-term focus on helping individuals into sustainable employment commensurate with their skills, rather than into any job. However, the success of such an approach rests firmly on collaboration rather than competition, on commonality in target structures of different organisations, and on clear and effective signposting between organisations/services. Some of the more recent projects and initiatives – including the establishment of LORECA – point the way forward in this regard.

Conclusions and issues for consideration

Drawing on this research, it is clear that a number of key challenges exist for stakeholders in London seeking to enhance the labour market integration of refugees.

Enhancing labour market integration: getting employers involved

The large and dynamic "London labour market" is made up of a complex mosaic of both segmented and overlapping sectoral and occupational labour markets which vary in their spatial extent: some extend well beyond the confines of the administrative boundary of London, whereas others are much more localised, covering only part of London. Individuals tend to confine their job search to only certain of these labour markets.

As is the case with the UK labour market more generally, the London labour market is open and flexible by EU standards. There are large numbers of employment opportunities in which an individual can work on a full-time basis without having fluent English – in both formal and informal sectors. While no estimates of the size of the informal sector have been forthcoming, several interviewees made reference to a "large informal employment sector", with wage rates in some sub-strata – dependent on migrant labour – being characterised as "very low". Concerns were expressed that "many" migrants worked in the informal economy, and may remain "locked into" poor jobs through cultural and family connections. The role of private sector recruitment agencies and temporary work agencies in contributing to this segmentation remains poorly understood.

Despite relatively high levels of non-employment by UK standards, the London labour market is characterised by skills shortages and gaps – particularly in some sectors and occupations (including engineering, construction, teaching and the health service). Hence in theory, even if not always in practice, there are numerous employment opportunities for highly skilled refugees (and other immigrants). While the contribution of immigrant doctors and nurses to the NHS is well-recognised, there remain many refugees with equivalent qualifications and skills who are working in low-skilled and low-paid jobs. Hence, the challenge of labour market integration of refugees is not only to facilitate entry into the labour market and so raise employment rates (i.e. a concern with the *quantity* of employment), but also to better deploy and utilise the skills of refugees (i.e. a concern with employment *quality*) – for the benefit of the individuals concerned, but also for the London economy. Giving refugees time and help to decide on employment options rather than rushing them into an unsuitable job increases the likelihood of them staying in the job.[47] The trade unions (amongst others) recognise that the quality of the experience of employment in London is important for migrants, and that there is a need to broaden London's offer on employment rights, and are lobbying accordingly to improve the situation.

Although many suffer skills shortages and skills gaps, private sector employers tend to be conspicuous by their absence from local initiatives concerned with labour market integration of refugees (and other immigrants). RCOs reported difficulties in finding workplacements outside the voluntary sector. Those employers who do work with migrants/refugees are often unwilling to come forward to publicise their work in the prevailing political climate surrounding immigration, since they feel that potential adverse publicity that might follow "putting their heads above the parapet" could be damaging to their businesses. In turn this leads to a lack of "good practice" examples for others to follow. Yet there is a need to look beyond corporate social responsibility to publicise the business case for employers to recruit immigrants and refugees – especially beyond stereotype BME-owned businesses with products/markets associated with minority ethnic groups (*e.g.* Indian food, a sector which is particularly successful in the UK). There is a need for organisations to work with employers to remove the stigma attached to hiring and employing refugees.

Local stakeholders reported that the sheer complexity and bureaucracy of the system means that it is relatively easy for employers to be in breach of employment regulations inadvertently. Employment regulation and bureaucracy, in combination with a hostile political climate, serve to "stack up the risk" for employers to recruit recent immigrants. Instability of institutional frameworks stimulates uncertainty, such that – at least in the short-term – streamlining of the immigration system and employment regulations, adds to overall complexity. Hence, a lack of employer involvement is in some ways understandable, yet this very lack of involvement means that employers may be absent from setting the agenda. One possible way forward may be to develop a strategy of "enhanced targeting" of employers, perhaps involving particular sectors (in partnership with the Sector Skills Councils) and forging relationships with particular colleges and projects.

Emphasising and tackling acculturation

While proficiency in the English language has long been regarded as of key importance, and the need for general language training to support acculturation is endorsed, there was increasing recognition amongst local stakeholders of the need to target language training more effectively to different stages of refugee integration. Although general language training is key to supporting acculturation at the first stages of integration, training in business English and work-related English geared to specific sectors is crucial to ensuring that refugees are ultimately "job ready". This is especially so given the value that employers place on "soft skills"[48] and "work-based skills".[49] There was some evidence in London of moves towards combining English language training with other elements of vocational training.

There is a need to encourage understanding amongst refugees about how London, and UK society in general, works. If immigrants and refugees are acculturated in a more systematic manner, it will help to facilitate their acquisition of the "soft skills" that employers want and need. At the national level, the pilots developed by the Home Office for the incorporation of language training into citizenship classes represent an important step in this direction. In addition, in London, training courses often include an explanation of the workings of the UK labour market, CV writing and presentation at interview. Mentoring can also be effective in introducing migrants to the work culture in particular professions/sectors. However, there are gaps remaining in catering for highly qualified migrants, in particular, in their attempts to find out about cultural norms and how UK society operates. The paucity of means available to this, and other groups, to acculturate themselves, hinders the acquisition of the "soft skills" that would facilitate their labour market integration.

RCOs stressed the value of outreach projects. A key issue in the importance of outreach projects is engaging refugees, in the first instance, in an environment where they feel comfortable. However, in order to advance acculturation and integration, and to combat any possibility of ghettoisation, there is a need to encourage refugees to extend their horizons and move beyond the "comfort zone" of their immediate local area and community to mix more widely and encounter new challenges. This is analogous to supplementing "bonding" social capital with "bridging" social capital, so as to achieve a more healthy balance between the two. For example, having taken a NVQ 2 level qualification in a community group setting, there could be greater emphasis placed on encouragement to take a follow up NVQ 3 qualification at a local college or with an alternative mainstream provider.

Establishing a coherent policy framework

A number of the local stakeholders raised concerns that the restriction placed on the employment of asylum seekers in 2002 sent conflicting signals to employers and the broader public in relation to the positive contribution made by migrants to the UK economy and meeting labour market shortages. The UK government's rationale for this measure, which includes reducing the "blurring" between the economic migration and asylum route and channelling economic migrants through a new points system, needs to be communicated more effectively to the local level. The national policy of keeping waiting time for asylum decisions to a minimum it also crucial for the longer term integration of refugees, as local stakeholders expressed concerns that skills not used during this time are at risk of becoming redundant. Lack of participation in the labour market for asylum seekers was seen as a source of declining motivation and a loss of self esteem, and the fuelling of public perceptions about this group being a "burden on society".

Both the UK government and the Mayor of London promote a pro-diversity message, in which immigration and diversity is hailed as an "opportunity". Moreover, London aligns itself with global cities outside the UK in undertaking useful work relating to refugees, migration and diversity (European Refugee Fund, 2004). While London has the largest concentration of refugees and economic migrants in the UK, other regions have also adopted strongly pro-migration stances, as exemplified by the "Fresh Talent" Initiative in Scotland (Scottish Executive, 2004)[50] which sets out to attract incomers in the face of projected population decline.

However, good news does not sell newspapers, and the tendency is for positive messages not to get reported. Sections of the national media – particularly the populist tabloids, often use emotive language to promote mainly anti-migration messages. Public discourse as a whole in the UK often fuses and confuses: *i)* the established ethnic minority population, *ii)* asylum seekers, *iii)* refugees and *iv)* the role played by migrants in the labour market/economy. In this context there is a need for all levels of government to work towards ensuring that messages sent out to employers/the general public are more consistent and grounded. There is scope for the LDA and its partners to develop a better evidence base as to the contribution made by migrants in general to the economy. An ongoing project commissioned by the LDA International Team on the "Competitive Benefits of Diversity", in which London's experience in relation to diversity and innovation, trade, quality of life, enterprise, markets for new products and other topics is being contrasted with New York, Amsterdam and Berlin, should go some way towards filling this gap. A view was expressed, and endorsed by local stakeholders, that there could also be scope, to place greater emphasis on combining "tradition" with "diversity" within London. Thus, in the London context: "tradition" gives the city the confidence to be open and adaptable, while diversity spawns creativity and thereby greater openness.

Publications such as the glossy "West London People: An introduction to communities and faiths" produced by West London Partnerships on Community Cohesion, which introduces West London as a home to many people by incorporating profiles of different residents and their reflections on West London and their origin society (if applicable), providing an introduction to different faiths, and presenting a series of myths and facts about refugees and asylum seekers, provide a powerful example of how diversity can be celebrated while at the same time helping to raise awareness about, and increase sensitivity towards, immigrants and refugees (West London Partnerships on Community Cohesion, 2005). In turn, this potentially has positive spillovers: once awareness has been heightened and attitudes begin to change, the stigma employers attach to hiring and employing and refugees and other migrants may begin to disappear, and it may become easier to engage employers.

Instability in frameworks

One key recurring theme in the case study visit was "instability" – in relation to London governance, the broader institutional framework and in funding regimes. This in turn raises questions concerned with efficient and effective use of limited resources, such as: i) To what extent does this instability mean that energy is expended on securing continuity of funding and on continual innovation rather than delivery of services?; and ii) To what extent does the context of instability lead to a proliferation of meso-level organisations to co-ordinate the activities of smaller groups and provide an interface with key agencies – so making for a greater multiplicity/complexity of organisational structures?

With regard to funding, much of the work undertaken with refugees is funding driven. Many RCOs are competing for similar sources (e.g. from the European Social Fund, from a fragmented public sector, from lottery sources, etc) of limited and unstable funding. There is a clear need to identify and harvest new sources of funding if organisations are to expand their scope of operations. While there is not the same tradition in the UK, as, for example, in the USA, of working with philanthropies, there is scope for placing greater emphasis on mobilising philanthropies as a source of funding. Likewise, there is scope for greater effort to be made to encourage large private sector employers and employers' organisations to get involved with funding training and work-related acculturation initiatives,[51] especially since they stand to benefit from the contribution of migrants/refugees. However, the very instability in frameworks militates against the clarity, consistency and commitment that the private sector wants to see before committing resources.

Instability in institutional frameworks and in funding regimes helps to breed "short-termism", which may be characterised by an undue emphasis on "quick wins" when it is sustainable outcomes that are of crucial importance in the medium- and long-term. Chasing funding, and what several interviewees described as an "over-emphasis" on the drive to be "innovative", can have consequences for the quality of projects. The short-term nature of project funding can engender an emphasis on outputs rather than on outcomes, when it is the latter that should be used to measure the true degree of integration of migrants/refugees into the labour market. In some (perhaps many) instances there is scope for monitoring systems to be better developed, and to ensure greater clarity in translating outputs into outcomes. Only when evaluation is more consistently embedded in projects from the outset will the empirical evidence base enabling a robust evaluation of "what works" be available, so enabling a more grounded assessment of where and how to direct limited resources.

Multiplicity of projects and the need for strategic co-ordination

Another recurring theme in the case study visit was "complexity" – in part stemming from the "instability" highlighted above. Many interviewees considered that London could boast "strength in depth" in terms of numbers of community organisations and other organisations concerned with formulation and delivery of refugee/migrant integration projects; indeed, labour market integration initiatives for refugees and other immigrants are predominantly organised on a project-basis, not on a structural basis. Yet many of the same people highlighted a lack of co-ordination in the face of the ensuing complexity. This set of circumstances raises a number of key questions: i) To what extent are projects duplicating each other? ii) To what extent is "good practice" captured? iii) In the context of limited resources, does such a multiplicity of projects represent value for money? iv) To what extent are some groups (especially those who do not fall within the Jobcentre Plus target groups) falling into the interstices between organisations?

The Mayor's new Board for Refugee Integration in London is a promising new step towards greater strategic coordination on this issue. By bringing together key London decision-makers representing the statutory, community and voluntary sectors to develop a citywide strategy covering five different policy areas, the new Board should enable a more holistic and inclusive policy approach, while also ensuring that policy decisions are made which are relevant to the particular London context.

On a more practical level, some of the smaller community groups valued the assistance of sub-regional organisation (for example, Renewal in West London). Although still in its infancy, the emergence of LORECA at a pan-London level could prove to have a positive impact on the integration of immigrants and refugees into the London labour market. As an umbrella organisation, LORECA will have the opportunity to play an advocacy role with the government (including the new Board) and the private sector. Additionally, it is likely that LORECA will, over time, acquire the institutional leverage to unofficially regulate the actions of organisations assisting immigrants and refugees. LORECA is well-positioned to take a proactive role in establishing a robust evidence base and in ensuring the development of associated monitoring systems by setting minimum data collection requirements in order to answer questions such as: i) what interventions are most cost-effective; ii) on what activities should resources be concentrated?; iii) do persons involved in voluntary work find paid work more quickly than those who do not?; and iv) what delivery mechanisms work best for different sub-groups? Whether or not LORECA takes on this role, it is important that such an evidence base is established in order to capture, and to ensure the survival of, successful strategies, and to enable dissemination of good practice.

LORECA has adopted a policy of prioritising refugees. It can be argued that some prioritisation is necessary at the outset, but it could be useful to have a network operating within London which focuses on the labour market integration of all recent immigrants. Moreover, in the light of a recent downturn in the number of asylum seekers and refugees to London, such a broader orientation might be prudent. Moreover, all "newcomers" to London (from elsewhere within the UK as well as from outside) are likely to benefit from information on how to access the labour market, accommodation, health provision and other services in the city.

Notes

1. Encompassing surveys (such as the Labour Force Survey [LFS] and the International Passenger Survey [IPS]) and administrative records (on numbers granted settlement or citizenship).
2. For further details on immigrant communities see also Kyambi (2005).
3. See also IPPR (2004).
4. Reflecting their availability in key sources including the LFS and Census of Population.
5. Although using the LFS it is possible to distinguish between these groups to some extent.
6. In the UK "ethnic minorities" tend to be dealt with as a separate category from "immigrants", but the "ethnic minorities" category tends not to be disaggregated to distinguish those born in the UK and those born outside the UK.
7. London attracts population from all over the world and over 300 languages are spoken in the city.
8. While London has easily the largest proportion of foreign-born population of any part of the UK, for comparison it is salient to note that the population of New York is 42% foreign-born, that of Toronto 49% and that of Los Angeles 61%.
9. The Work Permit system is employer-led. Work Permit holders have to have appropriate qualifications for employment and have a guaranteed job on entry to the UK. Their labour market integration needs are therefore likely to be less than those of migrants arriving by other routes.
10. The number of work permits issued rose from just under 33 000 in 1995 to 139 000 in 2004. Of the 139 000 work permits issued in 2004, around two-thirds represented "new" foreign workers; (the rest were already working in the UK).

In 2003, 85 300 people work permits and first permissions (i.e. permits issued for the first time on behalf of foreigners already in the UK) were represent the largest single category out of a total of 238 600 workers in the UK. For further details see Salt and Clarke (2005).

11. For further details see Clarke and Salt (2003) and Ippr (2004). It should be noted that quotas for the SAWS and SBS were cut from 2004/2005 following the accession of 10 further states to the EU. Many workers under these schemes came from countries that joined the EU in May 2004.

12. NASS was established by the Home Office under the terms of the Immigration and Asylum Act 1999 and has been operating since April 2000.

13. Although asylum seekers do not have the right to work, it is salient to note that many of the local areas with available housing to which asylum seekers were dispersed are characterised by higher than average levels of deprivation and non-employment in the UK context.

14. This change also helps to make a clearer distinction between asylum seekers and refugees.

15. The implication is that Sector Skills Councils will play a key role.

16. Some information on the performance of ethnic minorities New Deal programmes is available, but no distinction is made between those who were born in the UK and those born elsewhere. Data for 2002 reported in Volume II of a report prepared by the House of Commons Work and Pensions Committee (2005) shows that ethnic minorities are over-represented in each of the New Deal programmes, comprising 20% of participants on the New Deal for Young People, 14% of participants on New Deal 25plus and 11% on the New Deal for Lone Parents. Over the calendar year 2002 job entry rates for ethnic minorities relative to white people were 74% for the New Deal for Young People, 86% for the New Deal 25plus and 83% for the New Deal for Lone Parents. Analysis suggests that the apparent gap in equality of outcomes may be attributable to factors not associated directly with ethnicity. From a London perspective, it is salient to note that on New Deal 25plus: "Even though parity in outcomes is achieved within London, the fact that London accounts for nearly 60% of all ethnic minority leavers on New Deal 25plus, when combined with London's overall performance, has a significant effect on the national parity score".

17. There is no statutory obligation on employers to notify vacancies to Jobcentre Plus.

18. DWP has a Public Service Agreement (PSA) target to increase the employment rate of ethnic minority groups and significantly reduce the difference between their rate and the overall employment rate. In an attempt to increase the employment rate for ethnic minority groups an Ethnic Minority Employment Strategy has been devised by DWP. This is built around three strands: i) building employability; ii) connecting people to work; and iii) promoting equal opportunities in the workplace; with Jobcentre Plus playing a key role in delivery. [For further details of on the labour market experience of ethnic minority groups see Strategy Unit (2003)].

19. Building on work already underway, the National Refugee Integration Forum was established by the Home Office in 2001 to implement, monitor and develop the government's "Full and Equal Citizens" Strategy, which assists the integration into the UK of those granted leave to remain.

20. It is salient to note that the views expressed by some interviewees from local initiatives may reflect experience in the past of longer elapsed times in dealing with asylum claims.
21. In his response to *Integration Matters* the Mayor of London (2004) contends that regional strategy is "the key to success" in refugee integration. Moreover, with respect to labour market integration, it is salient to note that the National Skills Strategy highlighted that there is a strong regional dimension to skills issues, and that responses at regional and local levels would be required to deal with these.
22. Highlighted by Professor Tony Travers.
23. A situation which may be characterised as one of "a powerful individual in a weak upper tier".
24. The establishment of Regional Skills Partnerships (RSPs) in the English Regions in December 2003, following the publication of the 2003 National Skills Strategy, re-emphasises this partnership approach.
25. The Mayor's Refugee Advisory Panel brings together 50 London refugees – a cross-section of the city's diverse refugee population – to guide the Mayor and Board in their work.
26. Brief prepared by the SERTUC, 24th February 2005. This brief draws in part upon Goldsmiths College research for a preliminary report "Towards a Refugee Employment Strategy".
27. It is probable that failed asylum seekers are especially likely to get caught up in this type of work.
28. Research has been undertaken on methodologies for calculating the size of the illegal population in the UK (irrespective of whether they are working or not) – see Pinkerton, McLaughlan and Salt (2004). At the end of June 2005 the Home Office published a central estimate of 430,000 (within a range from 310 000 to 570,000) – see Woodbridge (2005). It is not known what proportion of this unauthorised migrant population is in work.
29. In the UK there has been no appetite, to date, to offer general amnesties to illegal workers.
30. For more detailed information see Spence (2005).
31. Some refugees may have experienced torture or trauma before moving to the UK, which may lead to psychological problems that increase the time taken to integrate into the labour market.
32. It is likely that the instance referred to here predates the removal of permission to work for asylum seekers.
33. Topics covered in such sessions included financing refugee education, the British educational system, professional requalification for overseas qualified doctors, teachers and nurses, young refugees and access to education and training.
34. Grant programmes in 2003 included an Initial Study Grant – assisting 63 women and 10 disabled clients with the cost of their fees, travel and childcare to attend courses; and a LADDER Study Grant – offering financial assistance to 160 young asylum seekers towards their travel expenses to college, and towards books and equipment.

35. The majority of ESOL provision is funded by the LSC. However, Jobcentre Plus also funds a number of initiatives combining language with generic work skills and involving close collaboration with employers.

36. Across the UK temporal variations in migration flows means that there may be difficulties in ensuring ESOL provision.

37. As reflected by a joint statement by the Home Office, the TUC and the Confederation of British Industry (CBI) to support managed migration in the interests of the UK economy and support the English language and other skills development needs of migrants.

38. NARIC is a network of national centres in member states of the European Union, the EEA and associated countries in Central Eastern Europe and Cyprus. Each centre provides advice and information on the academic recognition of diplomas and periods of study abroad.

39. The Migrant Skills Questionnaire covers personal details, employment history (last two jobs, either paid or unpaid, before coming to the UK; occupation you wish to practise in the UK; years of work experience), qualifications (country of award; type of qualification, list of course modules; structure of training [theory *versus* practice]; course duration; usual entry level); English language proficiency (understanding/speaking/reading/writing); examinations in English; basis on which English has been used (*e.g.* beginner, social, professional, mother tongue); and any additional information.

40. SRB provided resources to support regeneration initiatives in England carried out by local regeneration partnerships. Its priority is to enhance the quality of life of local people in areas of need by reducing the gap between deprived and other areas, and between different groups.

41. The project is competing for workplacements with other projects, and, in some instances, with students on further and/or higher education courses.

42. The Employability Forum is funded by the City Parochial Foundation. The Forum comprises employers, government departments and agencies, voluntary and refugee organisations.

43. The concession that allowed asylum seekers to work, if they had lived in the UK for 6 months or more and had not reached a decision on their claim, was withdrawn in July 2002. Asylum seekers do not need to have permission to work in order to undertake voluntary work.

44. Some of these businesses will be owned by refugees, but the number of such businesses is not distinguished.

45. Note that Global Grants is not dealing exclusively with refugees and other migrants.

46. This finding is endorsed in a review encompassing all workless people and communities – see Ritchie, Casebourne and Rick (2005).

47. This same point applies, albeit perhaps with less force, to the UK-born unemployed in the context of a labour market policy framework espousing a "work first" orientation. Pressures to place individuals into work as quickly as possible may sometimes prevent some advisers from supporting immigrants into higher level jobs, through recognising other qualifications and skills, and encouraging them to build on previous qualifications gained overseas.

48. "Soft skills" are particular key or core skills which employers look for to complement the technical skills and experience of their staff. They typically comprise: team work; communication skills; problem solving ability; leadership skills; planning and customer service skills.

49. As emphasised in IER and IFF Research (2004).

50. Also see *http://scotlandistheplace.com*.

51. A further benefit of involving private sector resources is likely to be that "good" projects/ initiatives will be identified and reinforced, since such money will be directed in a sustained fashion only at the "best".

Bibliography

Anderson B. and Rogaly B. (2005), *Forced Labour and Migration to the UK*, TUC, London.

Bloch A. (2002) "Refugees' Opportunities and Barriers in Employment and Training", *DWP Research Report* 179, DWP, London.

Centre for Research and Analysis of Migration (2005), "Basic Facts on Immigration to the United Kingdom", *CReAM Fact Sheet* 1, Centre for Research and Analysis of Migration, University College London.

Clarke J. and Salt J. (2003), "Work Permits and Foreign Labour in the UK: A Statistical Review", *Labour Market Trends*, November 2003, 563-74.

Copisarow R. and Barbour A. (2004), *Self-employed People in the Informal Economy – Evidence, Implications and Policy Recommendations*, Street (UK) and Community Links, Birmingham and London.

Department for Education and Skills (DfES) (2003), *Skills Strategy White Paper: 21st Century Skills*, DfES, London.

Dumper H. (2002), *Missed Opportunities: A Skills Audit of Refugee Women in London from the Teaching, Nursing and Medical Professions*, Mayor of London in association with the Refugee Women's Association, London.

Department for Work and Pensions (DWP) (2004), *Building on New Deal: Local solutions meeting individual needs*, DWP, Sheffield.

DWP (2003), *Working to Rebuild Lives: A Preliminary Report towards a Refugee Employment Strategy*, DWP, Sheffield.

DWP (2005), *Working to Rebuild Lives: A Refugee Employment Strategy*, DWP, Sheffield.

European Monitoring Centre on Racism and Xenophobia (EUMC) (2005), *Majorities' Attitudes Towards Minorities: Key Findings from the Eurobarometer and the European Social Survey*, EUMC, Vienna.

European Refugee Fund (2004), *Europe Land of Asylum: Reception and Social Inclusion of Asylum Seekers and Refugees in three European Capital Cities*, Rome.

Fielding A.J. (1992), "Migration and Social Mobility: South East England as an Escalator Region", *Regional Studies* 26, 1-15.

Greater London Authority (2004), *Response by the Mayor of London to Home Office Consultation – Integration Matters: a National Strategy for Refugee Integration*, GLA, London.

Home Office (2002), *Migrants in the UK: their Characteristics and Labour Market Outcomes and Impacts*, RDS Occasional Paper 82.

Home Office (2005), *Controlling Our Borders: Making Migration Work for Britain*, Home Office, London.

Home Office (2005), *A National Strategy for Refugee Integration*, Home Office, London.

House of Commons Work and Pensions Committee (2005), *Department for Work and Pensions: Delivery of Services to Ethnic Minority Clients*, HMSO, London.

IER and IFF Research (2004), *National Employers Skills Survey 2003: Key Findings*, Learning and Skills Council, Coventry.

IES (2004), *Employing Refugees – Some Organisations' Experience*, IES, Brighton.

IPPR (2004), *Labour Migration to the UK: an ippr FactFile*, IPPR, London.

Jonker B. (2004), *Resource Project Refugees' Contribution to Europe – Overall Summary*, Education Action International RETAS.

KPMG (2005), "KPMG Review of English for Speakers of Other Languages (ESOL)". Report for the Department for Education and Skills Skills for Life Strategy Unit and the Learning and Skills Council.

Kyambi S. (2005), *Beyond Black and White: Mapping New Immigrant Communities*, IPPR, London.

Lawrence F. (2005), "How Many Work Illegally in UK? It's Not Easy to Find Out", *The Guardian*, 11 January 2005.

London Development Agency (2005), *Redefining London's BME-owned Businesses*, LDA, London.

Mayor of London (2004), *Ready for Business: The contribution of black businesses to London's economy*, GLA, London.

London Development Agency (2004), "Refugees and the London Economy: Maximising the Economic Potential and Impact of London's Refugee Communities", Draft Research Report prepared for the LDA by Michael Bell Associates.

OECD (2004), *Trends in International Migration*. OECD, Paris.

Pinkerton C., McLaughlan G. and Salt J. (2004), "Sizing the Illegally Resident Population in the UK", *Home Office Online Report* 58/04.

Portes J. and French S. (2005), "The Impact of Free Movement of Workers from Central and Eastern Europe on the UK Labour Market: Early Evidence", *DWP Working Paper* 18.

Ram M., Edwards P. and Jones T. (2002), *Employers and Illegal Migrant Workers in the Clothing and Restaurant Sectors*, mimeo.

Refugee Council (2003), *The Refugee Council's Evidence to the Work and Pensions Select Committee on the Department for Work and Pension's Services to Ethnic Minorities*, Refugee Council, London.

Ritchie H., Casebourne J. and Rick J. (2005), "Understanding Workless People and Communities: a Literature Review", *DWP Research Report* 255. Corporate Document Services, Leeds.

Rogic J. and Feldman P. (2004), *Employment Resource Handbook for Refugee Engineers*, Education Action International, London.

Salt J. (2005), "Types of Migration in Europe", Paper for the European Population Conference 2005, Strasbourg.

Salt J. and Clarke J. (2005), "Migration matters", *Prospect* 110, 46-51.

Scottish Executive (2004), *New Scots: Attracting Fresh Talent to Meet the Challenge of Growth*, The Stationery Office, Edinburgh.

Small Business Council (2004), *Small Businesses in the Informal Economy: Making the transition to the formal economy*, Small Business Council, London.

Spence L. (2005), *Country of Birth and Labour Market Outcomes in London*, GLA, London.

Strategy Unit (2003), *Ethnic Minorities in the Labour Market*, Strategy Unit, Cabinet Office, London.

Strategy Unit (2004), *London Project Report*, Strategy Unit, Cabinet Office, London.

West London Partnerships on Community Cohesion (2005), *West London People: An Introduction to Communities and Faiths*, London Borough of Ealing, London.

Woodbridge J. (2005), "Sizing the unauthorised (illegal) migrant population in the United Kingdom in 2001", *Home Office Online Report 29/05*.

Wrench J. and Modood T. (2000), "The Effectiveness of Employment Equality Policies in Relation to Immigrants and Ethnic Minorities in the UK", Report commissioned by the ILO, Geneva.

Zetter R. with Pearl M. (2005), *Still Surviving and Now Settling: Refugees, Asylum Seekers and a Renewed Role for Housing Associations*, Oxford Brookes University, Oxford.

Chapter 5

Local Responses to a New Issue: Integrating Immigrants in Spain

by
Mary P. Corcoran

Spain is increasingly becoming "the immigration country of Europe" with high rates of immigration being accompanied by a new national integration strategy and a comprehensive regularisation programme. Partnerships between NGOs, local authorities and the public employment service have generated effective local integration mechanisms in Madrid, Barcelona and Lleida, accompanied by the development of a more inclusive idea of citizenship in certain local areas, leading to the mainstreaming of services for immigrants. In Lleida the potential for employers associations to improve the employment conditions of temporary agricultural workers is also demonstrated. Despite this new found dynamism, many local initiatives experience problems in helping migrants into a labour market which increasingly offers temporary and insecure work without strong chances of career progression.

This chapter examines the role of local initiatives to support the integration of immigrants in Spain, a country which has recently been experiencing high rates of immigration. It examines a number of case studies from province of Barcelona, the province of Lleida and the region of Madrid in order to develop an insight into the mechanisms that are in existence to provide for the economic, social and civic integration of immigrants, and the ways in which such initiatives are linked to wider governance structures and economic and employment development policies. The selection of these case study areas has allowed for a wide range of themes to be explored including: the efficacy of different levels of governance, the experiences of immigrants in different kinds of labour markets, urban-rural differences in terms of both the demands for, and needs of services provided to immigrants, employment, training, social provision and citizenship issues.

The Spanish labour market and migration context

Main characteristics of the labour market

The recent *OECD Economic Survey of Spain* has described Spain's economic performance as remarkable over the last ten years. The standard of living differential with the euro area average has reduced from 20% to less than 13% between 1995 and 2003. Fiscal consolidation, the fall in interest rates due to the introduction of the single currency, structural reforms pursued since the mid-1990s and a surge in immigration have created a virtuous circle of rising economic activity sustained by strong job creation (OECD, 2005a)

The positive economic outlook in Spain disguises some ongoing labour market issues, however. The structural characteristics of the labour market have traditionally included low levels of participation and relatively high levels of unemployment, especially among women and young people (see Table 5.1). The overall unemployment rate, while declining, is still relatively high at 9.2% in 2005 (OECD, 2006). Participation rates are improving, and between 1993 and 2003, women's employment grew from 31.5% to 46.8%, the second highest rise (after Ireland) across the OECD countries (OECD, 2005b). However, since the 1990s Spain has suffered from high rates of temporary employment, and high levels of job rotation. Temporary contracts now account for a third of all employees, as compared with an average for all OECD countries of 13% (OECD, 2005c).

Table 5.1. **Employment and unemployment rates, 2000-2004**

	2001	2002	2003	2004
Employment population ratio				
Total (15-64 years)	58.8	59.5	60.7	62.0
Male (15-64 years)	73.8	73.9	74.5	74.9
Female (15-64 years)	43.8	44.9	46.8	49.0
Youth (15-24 years)	37.1	36.6	36.8	38.4
Unemployment rate				
Total (15-64 years)	10.5	11.4	11.4	11.0
Male (15-64 years)	19.8	18.6	17.4	17.3
Female (15-64 years)	15.3	16.4	16.0	15.1
Youth (15-24 years)	20.8	22.2	22.7	22.0

Source: OECD Employment Outlook 2005.

The productive structure in Spain is dominated by small businesses in which labour-intensive activities remain important, the competitive advantage of which has been based traditionally on lower labour costs than in other EU countries. As in several other European countries, there is also a significant underground, irregular or informal economy. Indeed, the informal labour market is a chronic problem across a range of sectors. Schneider and Klinglmair (2004) estimate that the average size of the shadow economy (expressed as a percentage of GDP) in the years 2002-2003 in Spain was 22.3%.

Principal characteristics of migrants in Spain

Spain is rapidly becoming "the" immigration country of Europe. The foreign population in Spain has been increasing at a much faster rate than is the case in other European Union member states. As of March 2005 the number of foreigners resident in Spain stood at 2 054 453, an increase of close to 200% on the figure of 719 600 in 1999.

The large scale economic restructuring which has accompanied recent economic growth in Spain has been a pull factor for immigrants, leading to the simultaneous emergence of high earning professional enclaves in metropolitan centres (that require a range of support services) and informal economic enclaves, which rely on cheap, flexible labour (Sassen, 1990). Spain's strategic location as a bridge between Europe and Africa has also contributed to its being a particularly attractive country for immigrants in recent years (Sole and Parella, 2003), while former colonial links continue to support immigration from Latin America at a higher rate than in other European countries. Aparicio and Tornos point out that "historic and cultural links with former colonies and protectorates have played an important role in the choice of Spain as a country of destination" (Aparicio and Tornos, 2003).

Table 5.2. **Immigrants with valid residency cards or permits by continent**

	31-03-2005	31-12-2004	31-12-2003
Total foreigners	2 054 453	1 977 291	1 647 011
Total immigrants[1]	1 531 086	1 478 416	1 232 694
Total non-EU Europe	177 836	168 900	145 833
Africa	511 961	498 507	432 662
Latin America	676 220	649 122	514 485
North America	17 021	16 964	16 163
Asia	146 503	142 762	1 21 455
Oceania	1 211	1 112	1 018
Not indicated	1 072	1 049	1 028

1. Foreigners requiring work permits (i.e. non-EU).
Source: Permanent Monitoring centre for Immigration, Secretariat of State for Immigration and Emigration, Ministry of Labour and Social Affairs, 2005.

Table 5.2 contains data on the number of foreigners and immigrants in Spain on 31 March, 2005, by continent of origin. It is clear that Spain draws immigrants from all over the world although principally from Latin America and Africa. Moroccans constitute the largest single group of immigrants in Spain (396 668) followed by Ecuadorians (229 050), Colombians (145 656), Romanians (88 940), Chinese (73 936) and Peruvians (73 145). In total 676 220 immigrants were from Latin America in March 2005, roughly one third of the overall foreigner population.

Migrants by gender

Women make up nearly 50% of immigrants, although this proportion differs across different ethnic groups. Table 5.3 contains data on foreigners and immigrants in 31 March 2005 by gender and age group. The highest percentage of women comes from Latin America, constituting 54.6% of the total residents from that geographical region. Africans, especially North Africans, have a lower proportion of women immigrants at 34.6% of all immigrants from that continent. However, the countries providing the most female immigrants in absolute terms are Morocco, followed by Ecuador, Colombia, and Peru. The countries with more women than men residing in Spain are: Thailand, with 81.2% women immigrants; Guatemala, 77.1%; Kenya, 73.7% and Brazil, with 70.5% respectively, although these account for only a very small proportion of the total number of immigrants. With respect to the ages of immigrants most are of working age. 80. 9% of total immigrants are between 16 and 64 years of age. There are 280 756 individuals under the age of 16, which constitutes 13.6% of the total immigrant population, indicating a relatively low dependency rate. Individuals over the age of 64 represent 5.4% of the immigrant population, up from just 1.8% in 2003.

Table 5.3. **Immigrants with valid residency cards or permits by continent, gender and age group, 31-03-2005**

Continent	Total	% Women	Age group	
			Aged 0 to 15 years	Aged 16 to 64 years
Total foreigners	2 054 453	46.00	280 756	1 662 003
Total immigrants[1]	1 531 086	N/a	247 735	1 255 708
Total non-EU Europe	177 863	45.21	22 548	154 050
Africa	511 196	34.59	110 521	394 505
Latin America	676 220	54.58	90 253	572 654
North America	17 021	48.79	1 157	12 746
Asia	146 503	42.14	22 979	120 097
Oceania	1 211	44.63	71	1 004
Not indicated	1 072	31.28	206	652

1. Foreigners requiring work permits (i.e. non-EU).
Source: Permanent Monitoring centre for Immigration, Secretariat of State for Immigration and Emigration, Ministry of Labour and Social Affairs, 2005.

Distribution of migrants within Spain

The foreign population in Spain is unevenly distributed across the country. Indeed, fully three quarters of those considered as economic immigrants to Spain are concentrated in just five of the seventeen autonomous communities: Catalonia (22.93%); Madrid (20.64%); Andalusia (11.70%); Valencia (11.56%) and the Canary Islands (6.40%) (see Table 5.4).

There are high concentrations of immigrants in certain neighbourhoods in both Barcelona and Madrid- in the range of 25% to 32%. This is partly because newcomers often come to join other family members, already established in these urban centres. Latin American and Chinese ethnic groups are most likely to use these family/social networks, at least in the first instance, for accessing jobs and housing.

It is also the case that immigrants choose to reside in regions with higher employment rates and where they can enjoy greater employment opportunities, including informal work arrangements. African and Latin American immigrants appear more responsive than their Spanish counterparts to higher employment rates as well as to a higher likelihood of informal and self-employment (Amuedo-Dorantes and de la Rica, 2005). There are low rates of mobility among the active population in general in Spain, and major regional differences in terms of key labour market indicators. Analysis of data from the Spanish Labour Force survey indicates that immigrant flows appear to contribute to a narrowing of regional unemployment rate disparities, and thus such flows may be seen as having a positive impact in terms of socio-economic cohesion (Amuedo-Dorantes and de la Rica, 2005).

Table 5.4. **Number of immigrants with residence authorization in autonomous communities and provinces, 31-03-2005**

Autonomous community or province	Total immigrants with residency permits	% of immigrant population
Andalusia	240 475	11.70
Aragon	57 865	2.81
Asturias	17 422	0.84
Baleares	95 565	4.65
Canary Islands	131 566	6.40
Cantabria	14 540	0.70
Castilla-La Mancha	54 455	2.65
Castilla y Leon	59 824	2.91
Catalonia	470 991	22.93
Valencian Com.	237 679	11.56
Extremadura	19 643	0.95
Galicia	45 224	2.20
Madrid	424 045	20.64
Murcia	94 216	3.12
Navarra	25 783	1.25
Basque Country	39 309	1.91
La Rioja	16 226	0.78
Ceuta	2 430	0.11
Melilla	4 052	0.19
Not indicated	3 143	0.15
Total	2 054 453	100.00

Source: Permanent Monitoring centre for Immigration, Secretariat of state for Immigration and Emigration, Ministry of Labour and Social Affairs, 2005.

However, Aparicio and Tornos point out that the migratory population is currently becoming more heterogeneous and more diffuse in Spain. There has been a recent shift not only in the composition of the immigrant population but also in the pattern of settlement: "although still concentrated for the most part in a few autonomous communities and in large urban areas, immigrants now tend to be found in significant numbers in more and more parts of the country" (Aparicio and Tornos, 2003).

Socio-economic characteristics of migrants in Spain

In general, immigrants have higher labour participation rates than Spaniards (76.9% as compared with 66.7 in 2003) (OECD, 2005a). However, the unemployment rate is higher than that for the native population (14.8 as opposed to 11.0%) and the rate among foreign women is particularly high (18.2% in 2003).

Immigrants are more likely to work within particular sectors of the economy, most notably construction, agriculture, hospitality and domestic service. The percentage of workers concentrated in domestic services is particularly high: in 2002-3 around 16.4% of foreign workers in Spain were employed in "services to households" – the highest of the OECD countries reviewed (OECD, 2005b). The immigrant labour force is segmented by gender, with men mainly employed in agriculture and construction whereas women are in the domestic sector and in the hotel and catering sector (CES, 2004). Within these sectors immigrants are at a greater risk of being employed in the jobs that are least attractive to Spanish people, *i.e.* jobs that are dirty, noisy, dangerous and sometimes carried out in hazardous surroundings.[1] Further, foreigners are more likely to be employed in temporary jobs: the differential between native Spanish and foreigners in terms of the likelihood of holding a temporary job is particularly high in Spain, Portugal and Finland, all countries with high overall proportions of temporary employment (OECD, 2005b).

The level of educational attainment of immigrants is similar to the Spanish norm, and even higher among the nationals from some countries, with the exception of nationals from Africa. Indeed, Sole and Parella indicate that foreign workers are, in general over qualified for the jobs they secure in Spain. This is especially a problem effecting non EU immigrants, and women (Sole and Parella, 2003).

Illegal immigration

The relatively large informal labour market in Spain has traditionally attracted a significant number of illegal immigrants. There is a lack of data on the actual number of undocumented immigrants in Spain, who may be in the country for short periods (for example, in the agricultural and construction sectors, both in the South East and in the urban areas of Madrid and Barcelona). Neither is there data on the trajectories of legal permit holders who may over time move out of the formal economy and into the informal economy or *vice versa*.

However, the Public employment service, INEM, suggests that it may be possible to approximate the number of clandestine immigrants by finding the difference between the number of registered immigrants and the valid residency permits on a given date. Following this formula, the number of immigrants registered at Spanish town halls on 1 January 2004 was 2 442 211 individuals, while the number of valid residency permits 31 December 2003 for foreigners from nations outside of the European Economic Zone was 1 240 812.[2] Therefore, subtracting the number of valid residency permits from the number of registered residents results in an approximate figure for clandestine individuals of 1 201 399. Given the possibility of errors in the figures from the municipal register (*Padrón*) due especially to duplications or delays in removing those who no longer reside in a Spanish town and who may have moved away from Spain, and based on declarations from the President of the National Statistics Institute, 150 000 individuals may be subtracted from this figure. This leaves an admittedly tentative estimate of one million clandestine immigrants. A large number of these will have availed of the amnesty programme in operation between February and May 2005.

Attitudes to immigration

The recent rise in recent immigration, the fact that more migrants are coming from outside Europe, and the concentration of immigrants in a small number of geographic locations have all contributed to a higher visibility, and hence, to rising public concerns about the potential impact of immigration in Spain.

Such concerns have been manifested periodically in racist and xenophobic incidents. For example, in February 2000 a group of residents attacked undocumented Moroccan immigrants in El Ejido, Almería. An estimated 10 000 of the 45 000 residents of El Ejido were foreign workers, many living in slum conditions (OECD, 2004). The incident revealed the clandestine market for undocumented immigrant workers, and the exploitation and poor working conditions to which workers were subject. In August 2000, Molotov cocktails were thrown at an immigrant hostel in Lorca, Murcia. Several hundred undocumented workers, mostly Ecudorians are employed in agricultural labour in the area (Zapata-Barrero, 2003). A report published by the European Monitoring centre on Racism and Xenophobia (EUMC) concluded that racial and xenophobic violence continues to increase in Spain, almost in tandem with the increase in immigration (EUMC, 2004).

National public opinion data also indicates a rise in concerns about the "immigration problem" in recent years. Zapata-Barrero argues that generally speaking, public attitudes have been slow to catch up with social change (with the notable exception of employers) (Zapata-Barrero, 2003). In 2002, 43.4% of respondents in a national survey stated that the Spanish population was quite tolerant toward foreigners, while 10.1% stated that it was not at all tolerant. Representatives of immigrant groups and service providers also express concern about prejudicial attitudes and discriminatory treatment of immigrants, particular of women in precarious employment. Research by Sole and Parella (2003) has found that non EU-immigrants in Spain, in particular, suffer from negative discrimination compared to native workers, in terms of both access to jobs and to working conditions, independent of their educational levels, qualifications or prior work experience (Sole and Parella, 2003).

It must be stressed that negative attitudes have only emerged relatively recently, perhaps because the changing migration patterns bring increased competition with indigenous workers, (Sole and Parella, 2003) and because the issue has been amplified by the Spanish media which has conveyed emotive images and stories about the immigration issue to the Spanish population (Zapata-Barrero, 2003). It must also be acknowledged that the new Spanish government that took office in 2004 has attempted to shift the terms of debate on immigration from one based on fear to one based on acceptance and mutual respect.

Governance context

Changes to National Immigration policy

The change in Spain (as in Italy, Portugal and Ireland) from beinga country characterised by high levels of emigration to a country of immigration, has been market by a shift in policy approach, particularly following the change of government in Spain in 2004. The current period is marked "by a process of definition of an institutional framework to manage the issue of immigration" (Zapata-Barrero, 2003) and it may be said that the overall regulatory environment is in a state of flux. Since 2004, there has, in particular, been a marked re-orientation of immigration away from restriction and prevention and toward regularisation and the integration of the migrant population. This reflects a greater openness at national policy level to the possibility that net immigration may represent more of a benefit than a cost to the host society.

One of the most significant institutional changes has been the relocation of Immigration Affairs from the Ministry of the Interior to the Ministry of Labour and Social Affairs, in addition to the creation of a Secretary of State for Immigration and Emigration, and a new Directorate-General within the Ministry for the Integration of Immigrants. According to government officials, this creates a direct link between immigration and integration into the labour market. Previously, the issue was framed largely in terms of policing, with clampdowns by the authorities invariably resulting in migrant workers or rejected asylum seekers moving underground, i.e. into the informal economic sectors. The new emphasis is on filling employment gaps in the Spanish economy, in addition to supporting the social integration of disadvantaged groups. At the same time, the government is fighting against the "shadow economies" that attract and absorb illegal immigrants, or that induce regular immigrants into an illegal situation.

A key component of this approach has been the large scale regularisation programme for immigrant workers in the informal labour market that ended in May 2005. In May 2005, the number of applications made for regularisation was 690 679 (slightly below the government estimate of 800 000 illegal immigrants, partly because the regularisation only applies to those in employment). Of those, 73% (504 786) had been processed by July 2005. Shortly after the closure of the period for registration in May 2005, the government announced that 500 000 inspections would be conducted to eradicate irregular labour up until December 2005. The government have planned for the enrolment of up to 1 700 inspection officers from the Department of Labour, and an increase in the order of 11% in resources available to the inspectorate. Fines will be imposed on employers who persist in hiring undocumented workers. The onus will be on the employer to prove compliance, and the immigrant worker will be protected if he or she has been hired illegally. The regularisation process also requires that immigrants are registered with the Spanish social security system. This has occurred in 97% of the cases in which a residence or work permit has been granted and ensures that immigrants pay taxes and contribute to the social and welfare system.[3]

The regularisation process was strongly decentralised to the municipalities and to the local town halls throughout Spain, and there has been a clear mobilisation in support of this change in immigrant policy throughout all levels of Spanish society. Mayors, council officers, civil servants at national and regional levels, trade unionists and members of NGOs have all been animatedly in favour of the regularisation programme. However the ultimate success of the programme will depend on a number of factors, not least the fact that illegal immigrants regularised under this process will receive a residence permit for one year. There is a risk that some immigrants will become illegal again after that period, if they are unable to maintain their employment.

Apart from the regularisation of undocumented immigrants, a number of policy initiatives have been put in place linking national, regional and local levels in the task of integrating migrants not only into the labour force, but also into Spanish society.

A new policy for integrating immigrants in the labour market

A new Strategic Plan for Citizens and Integration (2006-09) has been developed by the Secretary of State for Immigration and Emigration through the Directorate-general for the Integration of Immigrants focusing on twelve different areas of intervention (refugees, education, employment, housing, social services, health, infants and youths, equal opportunities, women, participation, sensitivity and co-development). There is a commitment to develop working guidelines for integration, a key element of which is easing the transition to employment through a range of interventions. To prepare the plan, the Spanish government undertook wide consultation through a co-operative framework involving the regions, municipalities, academics and organisations responsible for immigrant welfare. The plan includes the provision of guidelines on the reinforcement of public services, such as the provision of housing, and the training of professionals in inter-cultural skills. The emphasis is on mainstreaming rather than the provision of special services.

The plan has been accompanied by a new Cooperation Framework for the "management of the support fund for refugees and the integration of immigrants, as well as for their educational reinforcement". It was created in 2005 through the national budget, as a tool to establish a cooperation model between the general administration of the state, the autonomous communities and local councils, with the purpose of promoting and strengthening public policies in these fields and, consequently, reinforcing social cohesion. In 2005 a budget of € 120 million was approved, followed by a budget of € 180 million in 2006, of which 50% was directed to refugees and integration, and the other 50% for educational reinforcement. In 2006, Catalonia received approximately € 40.9 million (22.45%) and Andalusia approximately € 20.5 million (11.27%).

As part of the plan and framework there is a new discretion accorded to the local and regional levels in taking forward integration projects. In 2005, 50% of the overall funding allocation to the autonomous communities was required to go to projects that had been devised and delivered locally, while in 2006 the percentage is 40%. The political will behind this initiative and the availability of funds from central government provides local service providers with the opportunity to conduct pilot projects and test experimental programmes. In other words, it is likely to expand the culture of innovation already visible at the frontline of service provision. Experimental programmes that have been found to work can be successfully mainstreamed or delivered on a wider more systematic basis.

A key priority of the new integration strategy is to identify skill demands, and to speed up the process of bringing appropriate workers to meet these demands into the country. One mechanism for doing this is to streamline the process whereby employers can establish that there is no Spanish person available to do a particular job and therefore recruit directly from abroad. In particular, INEM (the public employment service) has developed a new initiative involving the development of a catalogue of unfilled vacancies (*Catálogo de Ocupaciones de Difícil Cobertura*). Using the new register, which is updated quarterly, employers can now directly recruit immigrants for these vacancies, without having to advertise in the first instance for Spanish applicants (the previous legal procedure). While labour legislation is the responsibility of the state, the management of employment occurs at the level of the autonomous regions and so the types of job placed on the register vary from place to place. The regional branches of INEM, who oversee the register, take responsibility for establishing in advance whether or not a particular job may be legitimately filled by an immigrant, updating this decision on a quarterly basis. The catalogue of unfilled vacancies to date shows a concentration of low-level occupations, which is perhaps not surprising given the segmentation of the Spanish labour force and the fact that Spanish people are increasingly reluctant to accept low paid low skilled positions.

Legal context

The latest reform to Organic Law 4/2000 on the rights and liberties of foreigners in Spain and their social integration,[4] introduced substantial changes to the regulation of immigration, constituting the first opportunity to produce, legislatively, a change in the direction of migratory policy. The new regulations include important new changes related to requirements and circumstances for granting authorisation to foreigners to reside and work in Spain. The objective of the reforms is twofold. On the one hand, to speed up authorisations based on job vacancies that employers are unable to fill with resident workers (through the development of the catalogue of jobs that area difficult to fill), and, on the other hand, to increase control in granting these authorisations. The regularisations have been developed following consultation with a newly created body: the Tripartite Labour Commission for Immigration (*Comisión Laboral Tripartita de Inmigración*), made up of the most representative national-level social partners and the State Secretariat for Immigration and Emigration. This body will provide a permanent channel for achieving social consensus over immigration policies.

Admitting new immigrants to Spain is based primarily on the need to fill jobs and, except under extraordinary circumstances, immigrants who want to work must obtain a visa in their country of origin allowing them to work or seek employment. Under the Organic Law residence permits and work permits in Spain are independent of each other and all immigrants in Spain must apply in the first instance for a residence permit. There are thee types of residence permit:

1. For stays of less than 90 days there are traditional tourist residence permits.

2. Temporary residence permits, for more than 90 days and less than five years are granted to people who can support themselves and their families, or who have a work permit, or who have been living in Spain for five years. Residence permits may also be granted for humanitarian reasons. Residence permits are not normally granted to foreigners who have a criminal record.

3. Foreigners who have had temporary permits for a minimum of five consecutive years are entitled to a permanent residence permit.

In order to engage in labour market or any professional activity, foreigners over the age of sixteen years, must also obtain an administrative authorisation to work. Generally speaking, a work permit constitutes an authorisation to work in Spain given to foreigners over sixteen years of age. The duration of a work permit must be less than five years. Work permits are renewable and become permanent after five years of residence in the country. The following specific conditions must be met before a work permit may be granted:

- There must be a documented shortfall of labour need.
- That labour need cannot be fulfilled by INEM.

Foreign students now also have the possibility to apply for permits to become employed or self employed if they have studied for three years study in the country, allowing highly qualified immigrants trained within Spanish institutions to access the Spanish labour market.

A resident foreigner has a right to family re-unification under the terms of Organic Law 8/2000, and the 2004 regulations have sought to accelerate such re-unification procedures. Foreigners may exercise their right to family re-unification if they have resided legally in Spain for one year and have authorisation for at least one further year. They must show proof of adequate housing and sufficient resources for subsistence. A spouse may obtain his/her own individual residence permit if s/he finds employment or can provide proof of having lived with the spouse for at least two years. Children may obtain individual residence permits when they reach adulthood or when they obtain authorisation to work.

The family members of a foreign resident enjoy all the rights that the Law grants to foreign residents. This means that all foreigners under eighteen years have a right to education under the same conditions as Spanish nationals. Resident foreigners have the same rights as Spanish nationals to non-compulsory education, and all foreign residents have access to the social security system, which includes unemployment benefits. Registration in the social security system is now a pre-requisite for the validity of residence and labour permits. All foreigners have a right to emergency medical services, and independent of their legal status, have the same rights to medical care as Spanish nationals as long as they are registered in their municipality. While basic social services are granted to all immigrants, social benefits within the social security system and access to housing benefit are granted to foreign residents only and not to undocumented immigrants. Finally, in the case of work requiring special qualifications, foreign workers and foreign self-employed persons must have their qualifications recognised by the Spanish Ministry of Education and Science.

The government has recently introduced a new target of one month to process new claims for permits, and three months for reissuing. Furthermore, increased numbers of administrative staff have been assigned to speed up the permit-granting process. The establishment of the new "catalogue of unfilled vacancies" will also speed up the process of allocating work and residence permits for those whose skills are in demand.

Equality policy and the involvement of immigrant associations

The regulatory environment is undergoing a further change brought about by the introduction of equal opportunity legislation in 2003 in line with the EU Directive in this area. Recent legislation[5] provides scope for ensuring that the principle of equal treatment and non-discrimination due to racial or ethnic origins is real and effective. Workers now have the right not to be discriminated against on the grounds of racial origin, ethnicity, sexual orientation, etc., and they have a legal right to protection against bullying in the workplace. The law has also allowed for the setting up of a quasi-state body, the "Council for the Promotion of Equal Opportunities and the Non Discrimination of Persons due to their Racial or Ethnic origin" along the lines of the successful Commission for Racial Equality which has operated in the United Kingdom for several decades. The council reports to the Ministry of Labour and Social Affairs and focuses on the areas of education, employment, health, social benefits and services, housing, affiliation and participation in trade unions and business organisations, working conditions, professional development and vocational and continuing training. Its primary responsibilities include providing assistance to victims of discrimination when lodging their complaints, carrying out studies and publishing reports and promoting measures that contribute to eliminating this discrimination. There are some concerns that the close connection of the council to central government may mean that it is not perceived to have full independence or autonomy to undertake its tasks. However the aim is to ensure that the council acts with as much independence as possible. A major public awareness campaign is to be undertaken to promote the new organisation nationally and provide it with an independent identity.

A further aspect of the new policy framework for integration in Spain is the increasing importance being given to immigrant associations. Immigrant associations are particularly underdeveloped in Spain, perhaps because civil society itself has historically been weak.[6] However, the Spanish government is committed to increasing support for immigrant associations as part of a new strategy aimed at capacity building on the part of such groups and organisations. The Ministry for Labour and Social Affairs has recently signed conventions with seventeen immigrant associations and it is hoped that these Associations will become more active within the new Forum for the social Integration of Immigrants (see Box 5.1), originally established in 1995 but reconstituted in 2006 with a broader composition of membership and with new consultative responsibilities. In addition to immigrants associations, the Forum also includes administrators and other organisations that provide resources and services to immigrants. The Forum has been mandated to make recommendations on all subjects dealing with immigrants and must now be consulted with regards to any norm or general plan of action by the state that affects their integration. One of the measures to be submitted to the Forum is the new Strategic Plan for Citizens and Integration 2006-2009.[7]

In sum, there is considerable evidence of a shift toward a more integrated planning and joined-up thinking approach at the national level in Spain – particularly, between ministries dealing with migration, justice and employment issues. Furthermore, there is recognition that a cross-sectoral approach to immigration and integration involving all the main policy actors at state, regional and local level is the way forward for Spanish migration policy.

Decentralisation in the Spanish context

The new national approach to integration must, however, be seen in the context of the decentralised governance arrangements operational in Spain. Since 1979, Spain has undergone an intense period of regionalisation, and is now one of the most decentralised of the OECD countries. Responsibility for many domestic policy areas has been devolved to the 17 autonomous communities, of which Madrid and Catalonia are two examples, and two autonomous cities of Ceuta and Melilla. The autonomous communities account for about one third of public expenditure and employ more than twice as many civil servants as the central government (Mosley, 2004). They have exclusive responsibility for issues such as: government structure, territorial organisation, promotion of regional development, regional planning, urban policies agriculture, tourism, social assistance, health, education and culture.

In other areas, including labour market and employment policy, the autonomous communities share powers with the national government. In this case, the state defines policies and establishes enabling legislation, while the autonomous communities have responsibility for implementing this legislation. The public employment service has in particular been decentralised. The Employment Act of 2003 established that the national employment system now comprises both INEM (which is a public agency under the jurisdiction of the Ministry of Labour and Social Affairs) and the public employment services of each of the autonomous regions. Although the regional employment services have a degree of flexibility and can adapt labour market policy to their own regional needs, they are still required to spend funds for specified purposes and in accordance with state regulations, and have limited powers to shift funds between the budget lines.

While immigration policy itself remains under centralised control, decentralisation has lead to variations in the local and regional capacity to act

> **Box 5.1. The Forum for Social Integration of Immigrants**
>
> According to the provisions of Article 70 of Organic Law 4/2000 (amended by Royal Decree 3/2006 dated the 16 January), the Forum for Social Integration of Immigrants is the consulting, informing and advising entity for the national government, and when appropriate, for the autonomous regional and local governments in matters of immigration. Among the forum's functions are:
>
> - Draft proposals and recommendations that promote the integration of immigrants and refugees into Spanish society.
> - Receive information on programs and activities carried out by the national, regional and local governments in matters related to the social integration of immigrants.
> - Collect and channel proposals formulated by social organisations that are active in the realm of immigration.
> - Prepare an annual report.
> - Draft reports on the proposals, plans and programmes that may affect immigrants social integration as required by national governmental bodies.
>
> The membership of the Forum for the social Integration of Immigrants is composed of the following: president, two vice presidents designated as members, a secretary and 30 voting members. The members are:
>
> - Ten members representing the relevant government agencies.
> - Ten members representing the immigrants and refugees, through their legally constituted associations.
> - Ten members representing the social support organisations, to include the most representative labour unions and employers' organisations, that have an interest in the issue of immigration.
>
> Source: Ministry for Employment and Social Affairs, Secretariat of State for Immigration and Emigration

because of variance in access to resources, and because national initiatives have to be adapted to be delivered within regional policy frameworks. Aparicio and Tornos point out that the availability of regional discretion has led to variation in the support available for the integration of immigrants, with the autonomous regions of Catalonia, Andalusia and Madrid placing greater emphasis on this policy area than elsewhere, as this is where most immigrants settle (Aparicio and Tornos, 2000). Outside of these regions, resources are scarcer. According to Zapata-Barrero, "In Spain, efforts aimed at the integration of immigrants are coordinated in large measure by municipal and regional bodies. Many of these institutions however lack the necessary financing and infrastructure, which makes policy implementation difficult" (Zapata-Barrero, 2003). Therefore, even where there is a consistent national framework or a template of good practice in existence, how it is implemented (if at all) is currently dependent on local resources and conditions.

Local initiatives: responding to integration challenges

The remainder of this chapter will outline and assess local responses, initiatives and programmes designed to address barriers to the labour market integration of immigrants in the three case study regions of Madrid, Barcelona and Lleida in Spain, focusing on the roles of the principal stakeholders at the regional and local levels, before exploring the main types of instrument used.

The involvement of key stakeholders at the regional and local levels

The meso-level regions: the autonomous communities and provinces

The regional administrations in Barcelona and Madrid have been particularly active in creating strategic approaches to integration. Taking advantage of the flexibility granted to them in the decentralised system, these regions have developed effective cross sector support mechanisms for local level actors, setting out broad strategies for integration, sharing best practice and coordinating programme delivery. The kind of cross-sectoral, strategic thinking contained within the new national plan for integration is also reflected at this level.

The region of Madrid (CAM), for example, is in the process of drawing up a new plan for the integration of the Madrid community (2005-08). They aim to consult as widely as possible, and to be as inclusive as possible. All the key social players are involved in the consultations including experts in immigration from Madrid universities who form a technical support team, representatives from all programmes oriented toward immigrants, and representatives from different ministries. The plan is anchored in the community, and the aim is to bring theory and practice together through using a partnership approach. The creation of awareness in the different departments of the CAM is also an important part of the planning process. Local immigrant integration is pursued through specialist programmes aimed at immigrants, ethnic minorities, Eastern European women and women suffering from domestic violence. The budget for this work in 2004 was € 7.27 m, and a strong element of reflexivity is built into the approach through feedback initiatives.

The *Diputació de Barcelona* (the provincial government) is also committed to supporting immigrant integration as part of a wide policy to generate economic development and promote social inclusion in the region, partly through the support of local territorial employment pacts and productivity networks. The *Diputació* has adopted a particularly useful role in supporting the sharing of good practice between local areas, and acting as an information resource to municipalities. The provincial government is made up of elected representatives from 311 municipalities, to whom they give technical, economic and legal support. Approximately 200 of these municipalities are currently carrying out some work with immigrant groups, although the most activities are occurring in municipalities where there is a concentration of immigrants, such as Mataro and Santa Coloma de Gramenet. The *Diputació* supports the mainstreaming of good practice projects that they have identified within these municipalities, and encourages other municipalities to adapt successful programmes to their own localities.

The *Diputació* has also been effective in using national and European funds to support the establishment and sharing of good practice in the province. One programme supported by INEM (see Box 5.2) has aimed to insert difficult to place groups into the labour market (including immigrants) and has been delivered in 14 different municipalities. Part of the rationale behind the project was the development of a programme that had the potential to act as a model of good practice for other local entities within the province. Between 2002 and 2004, each municipality took advantage of a common training methodology, but adapted this to the client group whose needs they wished to prioritise. Service providers took a highly reflexive approach to the assessment and evaluation of the service provision using it as an opportunity to reflect on ways in which the programme methodology could be improved.

A second project funded by the European Union EQUAL programme under the title ELIONOR, focused on producing methodological guides to help municipalities to improve the productivity of women, immigrants and young unemployed people in the province (see Box 5.3). The provincial government in this instance developed a partnership with a number of territorial employment pacts, a business association and the University of Barcelona, whilst also leading a trans-European network of partners from other localities and regions (*Diputació de Barcelona*, 2003). The main aim of the project was to give the target groups the tools to access the local labour market. Training and skills development was given less emphasis because it was recognised that a number of the inactive participants in the programme, particularly women, were already relatively well qualified – other factors where therefore thought to be important in restricting labour market access, such as knowledge of local labour markets, and the particular skills demands of local employers.

The Barcelona province has also been particularly effective in supporting the delivery of multi-agency approaches at the local level. Building on the European Territorial Employment Pact initiative and the successful experience of a pact established in the Vallés Occidental in the mid-1990s, the *Diputació* have focused on creating sustainable territorial models of economic

> **Box 5.2. Experimental programme to facilitate the social and labour inclusion of non EU immigrants**
>
> The employment and economic development division of the *Diputació de Barcelona* has developed a labour insertion programme directed at groups with special difficulties in accessing the labour force. The total budget of € 753 940 was funded primarily by INEM (82%) with the *Diputació* contributing (18%). Four experimental programmes were developed focusing on improving labour participation of women, labour insertion programme for people over 45 years, program of transition from school to work for early school leavers and a programme of welfare and insertion of immigrants. The programmes ran during 2002 and 2003 in a number of different municipalities. In total 2 344 were contacted, 717 were interviewed, 206 ended the program and 106 were successful in accessing the labour market.
>
> The programme of welfare and insertion of immigrants targeted those between the ages of 25 and 45 years. Much emphasis in this programme was placed on practical, activist and participatory skills, and building networks between the immigrants and companies/relevant professionals. This programme showed the highest rate of insertion at 33%. The number of people contacted was 479, the number interviewed 184, the number of participants 111, 58 ended the programme and 36 were successful in accessing the labour market.
>
> The strong points of the programme as determined in the evaluation:
>
> - The strength of the coordination mechanisms particularly between local entities, the *Diputació de Barcelona* and the Employment offices.
> - The relatively high level of labour market insertion given the particular difficulties of the target groups.
> - High degree of collaboration between the municipal administration and the local enterprise network. (collaborating partners included Association of Construction of Catalonia, Federation of Construction and Woodwork of CCOO (trade union), Managers Association of Cronella, and Chocolat's Museum).
>
> Weaker points:
>
> - A high number of immigrants are excluded from projects of this kind because of their irregular status.
> - Timing of project is crucial as programmes that run during holiday times, for example, are a disincentive to participation.

development and have secured 20 new territorial agreements or employment pacts through which a wide range of social actors agree to promote employment through participation, consultation, networking, improving quality of service, evaluation and innovation. These have proved to be a useful mechanism for encouraging people to work together across administrative and sectoral boundaries on immigrant integration. In addition, the pacts have been able to work on issues which are not covered by mainstream programmes such as support for undocumented immigrant workers.

> **Box 5.3. The Elionor project**
>
> This European EQUAL project, led by the *Diputació* de Barcelona, involves a number of transnational partners across Europe. The project was conceived to help the inactive population (women, youth and immigrants) into employment and, in particular, to support persons without serious qualification problems in these groups. The work undertaken comprised a preliminary study of factors leading to inactivity in each locality and the production of material and methodologies for subsequent action. The project aims to provide the target groups with information on the labour market, how it functions and the jobs most frequently offered – in other words, to bring the job market and the inactive population (those who have never worked) closer together, and to provide the inactive with the technological skills required to enter employment.
>
> Source: Diputació de Barcelona (2003).

Local authorities

Local authorities have the power to act relatively autonomously in Spain, and two municipalities studied in the province of Barcelona (Mataro and Santa Coloma de Gramenet) each showed considerable latitude in terms of developing strategic initiatives and making choices about service delivery for immigrants. As local authorities do not have specific competency for employment issues, the focus was mainly on wider social cohesion issues, tackling poverty and providing emergency provision where necessary. However support in accessing employment was also provided in both these municipalities as one important aspect to supporting such wider social cohesion.

The two local authorities are both guided by a broad strategy to create a shared notion of citizenship and cohesion in their community (see Box 5.4). In the municipality of Mataro for example, it was felt that it is not enough to have strategies for the integration of immigrants, without also devising strategies for working with the indigenous community to counteract negative perception of immigrants. This has involved the development of programmes for sensitising the indigenous community to ethnic diversity and a new citizenship plan which focuses on the mainstreaming of services, stating that all local programmes must welcome new arrivals. The citizenship plan was developed under the auspices of a special council made up of 35 representatives of municipal groups, citizen groups, and immigrant associations.

To achieve the objectives of the new plan, the town council in Mataro has proposed fourteen action programmes aimed at the integration of newly arrived immigrants, coexistence, and respect for the diversity and quality of life of citizens. These action programmes include the provision of information on vocational guidance (facilitating access to information and services); mediation (facilitating communication and reciprocal knowledge, ensuring understanding between newly arrived people and public services); an accommodation programme; and a programme for aiding job integration (with professional training and integration of those with particular difficulties). The programmes provide personalised and/or group assistance depending on what is deemed appropriate.

The aim of the job placement support programme, for example, is to guarantee vocational training and inclusion in the labour market for groups with difficulties and advise and qualify individuals who wish to join the labour market under good quality employment conditions. The programme is conducted with the participation of the IMPEM (*Institut Municipal de Promoció Econòmica de Mataró*). 21.4% of the users of the IMPEM service in 2004 were immigrants. In keeping with the general support for mainstreaming, the programme does not provide specific services to immigrants, but encourages them to use the municipal employment promotion services through personalised and group counselling. The municipality takes a cross sector approach and collaborates with other economic actors in the delivery of professional training.

The strategy in Mataro to target both the immigrant and non-immigrant population is also reflected at a practical level in the design of a local flagship project, the "Local Institute for Economic Promotion". This centre provides a range of employment insertion and training programmes to immigrants and native born unemployed people alike, and the centre also houses incubator units for start up companies. Given the range of services, not just to immigrants but also to all residents of the municipality, the centre is viewed as a facility for the community as a whole. It thus has the potential to act as a mechanism for social integration and for developing human capital in the wider community, not just among immigrants.

While following the same broad strategy, the local authority in Santa Coloma de Gramenet has taken a more targeted approach to supporting immigrants in practice. Since 2001, the town council of Santa Coloma de Gramenet has carried out an Integral Action Programme aimed at preventing

> Box 5.4. **Strategies to promote common citizenship and interculturalism, Mataro and Santa Coloma de Gramenet**
>
> **A. Mataro's New Citizenship Plan**
>
> Like many other municipalities in the Barcelona province, Mataro adopted a pact for new citizenship-*Pla Nova Ciutadania* in 2001. This pact has three key strategies:
>
> - Integration of newly arrived immigrants in accordance with democratic principles and guaranteeing the rights and duties of all citizens.
> - The normalisation of service provision, equality of opportunity and quality of life for all citizens.
> - Promotion of cultural and social change with the consent and support of all social actors and political parties.
>
> **B. Principles underpinning the city's Intercultural Coexistence Development Plan, Santa Coloma de Gramenet**
>
> Similarly the principles which underpin the development plan in Santa Colama de Gramenet include:
>
> - Recognition of the rights and duties of all citizens whether they are indigenous or immigrant.
> - Work against social, economic and political exclusion (for example try to move beyond ethnic barriers by getting employers to look beyond the colour of a job applicant's skin).
> - Promote equal opportunities.
> - Right to participate in associations and vote in municipal elections.
> - Need for a reception site to provide legal advice for immigrants advising them of their rights and obligations.
> - Promotion of co-responsibility with all elements of society.

social exclusion of newly arrived immigrants, working on actions that promote equal opportunities. The programme was developed by the local Department of Social Services and Economic Promotion, in collaboration with the Department of Labour of the regional government of Catalonia. Responsibility for taking forward the principle actions of the programme has been delegated to a local development company, Grameimpuls S.A, which is responsible for managing local economic and employment promotion policies. The company directs its activities at members of the local population that have been excluded from the standard training and occupational services, due to a lack of professional qualifications and/or lack of knowledge of their surroundings.

The local development company in Santa Coloma de Gramenet has the advantage of having access to the relatively wide range of powers normally allocated to local authorities whilst also retaining a relatively focused approach on economic development and integration issues. The company engages in many different activities, from providing training and education services and social support to migrants to carrying out neighbourhood mediation, attempting to regularise the local informal economy and influencing regional accessibility plans. The director of the centre has been able to build up a strong local profile as a representative dealing with immigrant issues, and has build up relations of trust with local employers, community organisations and government representatives. He feels that this trust is an essential element in supporting change and help immigrants out of situations of deprivation.

The local activities being taken forward by the two municipalities of Mataro and Santa Coloma de Gramenet confirm the findings of Zapata-Barrero and Gómez and Tornos that not all local authorities have the same levels of financing and infrastructure to support the integration of immigrants. The two municipalities differ considerably in terms of their socio-economic profile (see Box 5.5). Mataro enjoys a higher than average income (compared to other municipalities in Barcelona) and can generate more resources for local development. Indeed, one reason why the Local Institute

---

Box 5.5. **Socio-economic conditions in Santa Coloma de Gramenet and Mataro**

Santa Coloma de Gramenet is a municipality with more than 120 000 residents, about 25 km north of Barcelona city. It is one of the poorer suburbs of the province, with a weak economy and relative poor infrastructure. It is characterised by relative low income, low educational levels, low working skills and relatively high levels of recent immigration. In 2004, the number of immigrants stood at 16 000 which constitutes about 13.3% of the total population. Despite the many difficulties in this municipality, there has been an impressive mobilisation in the locality to address issues of labour market integration, spearheaded by a local development company, Grameimpuls S.A.

Mataro is a relatively successful municipality on the coast, 25 km North of Barcelona. 15 000 (12.5%) of the 117 000 population are immigrants. Compared to Santa Coloma de Gramenet and other municipalities in the province, Mataro has a high rate of economic activity, particularly in construction, agriculture and increasingly, tourism. The majority of immigrants in the locality come from Morocco, with the remaining groups coming from China, Gambia, Senegal and South America.

for Economic Promotion has been able to offer such a wide set of services to the local community is that it is partly funded by rates raised from local businesses. Santa Coloma de Gramenent, in contrast, has a poorer socio-economic profile and a weaker tax base, and therefore, cannot provide the same level of services. Accordingly, resources are directed specifically at those in most need, whereas in Mataro the services are more mainstreamed.

Non-governmental organisations (NGOs)

In both Mataro and Santa Coloma de Gramenet, NGOs were seen as a key resource for working with immigrant groups, in particular as they are able to work with immigrants who are excluded from mainstream services, either because they lack a work permit, or because they need more holistic support and advice.

NGOs are seen as effective in providing front line services in Spain in that they offer an integrated, client-driven approach. The region of Madrid has developed an NGO based system of local integration services for immigrants called the CASI programme (see Box 5.6). Each local authority area in the region has a CASI, which are managed by NGOs that compete for contracts in an open tendering process, and the programme has been identified as a model of good practice at the European level.

A key focus of the CASI programme is the integration of immigrants, particularly those who are in vulnerable circumstances. Each CASI client is dealt with from a holistic point of view. A team of professionals are provided locally (some drawn from the immigrant groups themselves) to provide a range of complementary supports, with clients being offered five different services within the same location, including social work, legal, labour, inter-cultural, and social/educational services. In addition the centres provide emergency accommodation.

The CASIs are often located in areas with a high concentration of immigrants. In particular rising house prices in Madrid have forced many migrants to settle in neighbourhoods on the outskirts of the city. Because they are based in local communities, the NGOs which run the CASI projects are able to offer a client based approach which is both welcoming and accessible to these local immigrants. Immigrants are offered services regardless of their legal status and in 2004, 17 000 people made use of CASI services.

An important aspect of the CASI model is that while being based on localised NGO provision, the programme also offers a mainstreamed approach. The entire region of Madrid is covered by CASI initiatives and all the local NGOs work to similar goals and methodologies, leading to a consistency in provision. There is a degree of in built flexibility in the programme, however, so that individual CASIs may take the most appropriate approach to

Box 5.6. **The CASI programme in Madrid**

The region of Madrid has devolved responsibility for front line emergency service provision to the CASI programme (*Centro de Atención Social a Inmigrantes*), a network of 19 Immigrant Assistance centres located throughout the metropolitan area. These centres are a second level support mechanism provided to complement the basic assistance provided by the general social services. They are intended to facilitate the social integration of immigrants who arrive in vulnerable circumstances and require higher than normal levels of social intervention. The objectives of the authorities in each area are broadly similar:

- To improve the employability skills of immigrants by identifying appropriate interventions and support programmes.
- To contribute to social cohesion by developing programmes and initiatives that actively affirm the presence of immigrants in the community, that codify their responsibilities and rights, and that seek to foment positive channels of communication between immigrants and the indigenous local communities in Spain.

The services offered by the CASI are in two streams:

1. Social assistance programme
    - social work support
    - socio-economic
    - psychological
    - legal
    - inter-cultural and education
2. Emergency admittance programme for people needing housing, for example.

The focus of CASI interventions is:

Individuals/families: people who turn to the CASI for specific needs that cannot be covered through the regular social services system.

Groups: use of the possibilities offered by groups and work with social networks for example: environment adaptation groups, domestic organisation, communication skills, entertainment and leisure, environmental preservation, etc.

Community: coexistence roundtables in neighbourhoods and municipalities, participation in neighbourhood associations, social services, public and private entities, cultural and social associations related to immigration, etc.

reflect specific local problems, and opportunities. In particular, each CASI receives a block grant rather than specific budget lines, which allows a freedom of expenditure.

The degree of budgetary discretion has allowed the CASIs to develop projects that are geared to the specific issues that occur in the local communities. For example, at the CASI in Fuenlabrada, Madrid, staff identified an information deficit among immigrant parents in relation to schools. Many parents did not fully understand the school system and there was no mechanism for providing information or explanations for them. So the CASI in co-operation with the parents association, the schoolteachers and social services developed a pilot project to provide information and support to parents in the April-June period in advance of the new school year, starting in September. They have also developed intercultural projects in local schools involving parents, teachers and school children.

Similarly, in the CASI located in Ciudad Lineal, Madrid a number of specialist projects were developed to deal with problems specific to that locality. The "Night Owl" project involved trained professionals visiting parks and other public places at night to identify homeless people and help to direct them to appropriate housing and social services. A second project is directed at second-generation immigrant children who form a gang culture that is transplanted from their countries of origin. They engage in territorial fights with other ethnic groups. Service providers from the CASI actively try to recruit these young people into activities such as dance programmes in order to provide an alternative to street violence.

In sum, the advantages of the CASI model include the provision of a standardised, professional service across Madrid while devolving considerable autonomy to each CASI to develop tailored programmes and initiatives based on local needs assessment. The tendering process of the programme presents some problems for NGOs however. The Madrid community stipulates that NGOs must re-tender every few years for the CASI programme which may be disruptive of programme provision, and certainly militates against longer term planning. From the viewpoint of CAM, the tendering process ensures that experienced professionals deliver effective services on the ground, however if a local contract is awarded to a new NGO there are implications for the continuity of programmes already put in place by existing service providers.

Trades unions

Trade unions representatives were seen as key partners in the citizenship strategy being taken forward in Mataro, Barcelona. The fact that the trade unions in Spain have a relatively broad membership and are not always restricted to particular employment sectors can be seen to facilitate their involvement in broader integration issues at the local level. Sole and Parella (2003) argue, however, that in general the involvement of trade unions in immigration issues has been rather ambiguous. It has been difficult for the unions to represent the interests of those who work in the secondary and hidden economy, particularly as these workers are in direct competition with workers within the formal economy. The costs involved in potentially losing the membership of the formal economy workers, outweigh the potential benefits of representing immigrants in the secondary and informal sectors.

The trade unions have, however, put their weight behind the new government initiative on reform of immigrant and employment policy and have played an important role in the evolution and implementation of policies directed at immigrants. The establishment of the Tripartite Labour Commission for Immigration Issues at national level ensures that new integration policies are discussed in a tri-partite way between government, employers and trade unions, and the creation of the employment Catalogue under the auspices of INEM, in particular, is the outcome of social dialogue in the matter of labour regulation. Spanish trade unions have taken a pro-active role in the extension of immigrant rights, and the fight against prejudice and xenophobia, and have also been relatively innovative in providing training courses for new immigrants in skilled areas such as plumbing and electronics, and continuous education programmes targeted at immigrants who arrive with degrees. They have also taken a particular interest in the domestic work area which is notoriously unregulated and have lobbied for the reform of social security so that domestic workers may have the same rights as other workers.

Employers associations

Employers associations can also play an important role in tackling rights and quality of work issues. This was illustrated in the province of Lleida. The local farmers association (*Unió de Pagesos*, member of the Spanish network of agricultural and livestock organisations, COAG) has developed a useful model for promoting good quality employment for immigrants, bringing small-scale farmers together to co-ordinate and improve working conditions for temporary migrants (of up to nine months duration), and providing a variety of different forms of accommodation, training and social support (see Box 5.7).

The success of this case is based on two factors in particular: *a)* the strong motivation, care and commitment of managers and members of the *Unió de Pagesos*, and *b)* the need for a reliable workforce (the loss of the annual harvest is at stake). The advantage of the scheme from the employer's point of view is that the employees are accessible (through accommodation on site) and anti-

> ### Box 5.7. **The Unió de Pagesos de Catalyuna**
>
> In Lleida, local administrators, entrepreneurs, the farmers association and the NGOs all work together in the management of seasonal immigration. In Bellpuig and Mollerusa in the Lleida region, the *Unió de Pagesos* works with local councils to actively manage and promote a flow of migration between countries of origin- primarily, Romania, Colombia and Morocco and the rural localities. They provide jobs, accommodation and some cultural activities for the workers during their sojourn in Spain, in addition to social support such as accompanying workers to hospital. It is required that these workers are paid the national wage rate, that they have access to housing and that at the end of the labour season the person returns to their country of origin. The work of recruitment and labour management is carried out by farmer's representatives, relieving the individual farmer of having to do this for themselves.
>
> Nufri, for example, a private fruit processing company that operates throughout Spain, has a factory near Mollerusa. A programme for the provision of better accommodation for workers has been developed here through an innovative partnership between the company and the *Unió de Pagesos*, to provide air- conditioned units close to the factory for seasonal workers. The accommodation is paid for by the company, and conforms to regional government guidelines. There is no doubt that the enlightened approach taken by the *Unió de Pagesos*, has improved the conditions of the seasonal workers, through offering them better quality housing conditions during their stay in Spain and taking responsibility for the worker's general well being.

social behaviour or absenteeism can be more easily managed. On the other hand, the migrant workers have no additional commuting costs because they live and work locally, and are at least guaranteed a minimum standard of comfort in their accommodation, which would not necessarily be the case on the open market.

By working in partnership with the local council and private companies to bring in foreign workers for designated periods of time on an annual basis, the association has taken account of the transient nature of the rural migrant population in Spain. The project has an especially temporary notion of integration, and indeed, the awareness raising and community event activities that are organised by the association seem to be more about maintaining morale and increasing the acceptance of migrants amongst the mainstream population, rather than ensuring the integration of individual migrants. One of the progressive aspects of their programme, however, is the *transactional model* that supports the creation of development projects and leadership training programmes in the immigrants' country of origin. Developing ongoing links with specific localities in sending countries has both supported a sustainable supply of workers and built a strong degree of trust, whilst also supporting local development overseas.

The *Unió de Pagesos* work in other local areas across Catalonia, and their approach has been shared with other regions. They have also come together to link shorter-term demands for migrant work to provide an ongoing work programme that allows migrants to move between different regions and stay longer in Spain. According to Ministry of Labour and Social Affairs officials in Madrid, the innovative integration model developed by the association has also been used elsewhere, although not always as successfully, partly because other regions in Spain do not have the same resource base as Catalonia (Rodríguez-Pose, 2003).

The instruments used

The previous section has focused on the main stakeholders involved in the local integration of immigrants in the case study areas we reviewed in Spain. However it is also worth focusing in more detail on the main instruments used.

Developing employability skills

The local initiatives visited in Spain used a relatively large set of tools and instruments to support greater access to the labour market for immigrant groups. For example, Grameimpuls S.A offers users the following services to immigrants, adapting their opening hours to the availability of their clients:

Within the programmes offered in the municipalities of Barcelona and Madrid, the main focus appeared to be on developing employability skills, however, rather than placing people in jobs. In the municipality of Santa Coloma de Gramenet, for example, there is a recognition that the immigrant client group is starting from a low skill base, and so the emphasis, as practitioners on the ground see it, has to be on personal development and literacy. As one practitioner commented, "The programme is not commensurate with normal employment programmes because very often you are dealing with a client base that lacks skills, knowledge and language". This is reflected in the percentage of participants achieving and maintaining employment through their labour market insertion programmes (for which data was available for 2001-3, see Table 5.5).

In the CASI in Fuenlabrada, Madrid staff operated a three-fold model to identify people at different stages of work readiness that proved very useful in directing resources toward those most in need. Each client at the CASI has a personal interview during which there is an assessment of skills. The focus is

> **Box 5.8. Training by Grameimpuls S.A to support labour market access by immigrants**
>
> Grameimpuls S.A offers users the following services to immigrants, adapting their opening hours to the availability of their clients:
>
> - Professional information and guidance.
> - Basic training in trades (construction, lamp-making, welding and clothes industry machine operators).
> - Knowledge of the Spanish and Catalonian languages.
> - Familiarity with the surroundings.
> - Knowledge of job searching techniques.
> - On-the-job training.
> - Labour exchange.
> - Referrals to other training resources for increased specialisation.

Table 5.5. **Number of participants achieving and maintaining employment**

Date	Number of participants	Number securing employment	Number still in work the following year
2001	71	37	22
2002	86	38	23
2003	83	40	23

on getting the client to decide on a career or job path so that they can become self-supporting. Staff noted that those with highest employability were people with work permits and professional skills. They found it easiest to find a job, and crucially, easier to hold onto a job. The emphasis of support to this group was therefore help in finding a job, or appropriate occupational training. Those who are deemed to have low employability skills – generally women with children who have no Spanish and who are socially isolated – receive social and personal development training, are taught how to read maps and manage public space, and are given language and literacy classes. Tailoring resources to the particular needs of each immigrant requires considerable capacity and resources on the part of the service providers.

The diversity of the immigrant population and the variations in the contexts of reception, mean than no one model of labour market integration can be deployed at the local level. Rather, strategies and initiatives have to be evolved that address the specificities of each local case. A number of the local initiatives studied recognise, for example, that certain groups in the population have particular problems accessing employment and that cultural factors have to be taken account when helping migrants to access local labour markets. It was also evident that attempts had been made to adapt labour market programmes at the local level to the particular lifestyles of migrants. For example, Santa Coloma de Gramenet run training courses all year around, and adapt the hours of operation and the services provided to the needs of the user. They felt this was necessary so that people could combine language and skills acquisition, and personal development programmes with their religious, ethnic, and familial obligations and responsibilities. Women who work in the home can access such programmes at times when their partners are available to take care of children.

In fact, several of the service providers particularly targeted female migrants in their work. Women face specific issues when they come to Spain as part of the family reunification programme. As part of the programme they do not have an automatic right to a work permit and therefore cannot access employment service support in finding work. Furthermore, some women are illiterate on arrival and have no knowledge of the locality nor of the facilities and services that might be available to them. Women's status in the host country is frequently linked to their husband's status through the family reunification clause. If they wish to become independent of their husband (because of ill treatment for example), they are often forced into the informal economy to look for a job, particularly in the domestic services sector.[8]

A number of the women being supported by the CASIs in Madrid are socially isolated and need considerable interventions before they can even be considered for employment programmes. These interventions take the form of a package that focuses on developing social and personal autonomy; language learning and identifying the immigrant's existing skills. CASIs are sometimes distracted from their main function of providing for the general integration of immigrants, however, because they are required to provide emergency housing and high levels of psychological and social support to women who are victims of domestic violence. Adequate childcare is also a factor. Forty per cent of the client base of the CASI in Fuenlabrada, Madrid is made up of pregnant women or women with young children, and it can be very difficult for such women to secure sustainable employment and balance work life with domestic commitments.

The Elionor project being taken forward by the province of Barcelona has also developed a particular approach for helping migrant women, set out in their Methodological Guide for Working with Inactive Women (*Diputacío de Barcelona*, 2004a). The guide emphasizes the importance of encouraging inactive women to develop a balance of skills which will allow them to develop and enhance their own capacities, abilities and attitudes; identify the characteristics and demands of the job market; build their employability, become more goal oriented and develop a job/career trajectory. As in the CASI project, there is a focus here on empowering women in terms of their diagnostic, relational and coping skills. Meeting the range of needs of these women is seen as a crucial prior step to labour market insertion initiatives.

A second target group being taken into consideration by the ELIONOR project is that of inactive youth. Youth participation rates are particularly low in the Spanish labour market and this is a problem that also affects migrant youth. In Santa Coloma de Gramenet, for example, local practitioners expressed concerns about unemployed young immigrants, who were not being served by their programmes, and were living on the margins of Spanish society. The methodology for helping such young people developed by the Elionor project involves taking a triangulated approach focusing on the person, the job and the insertion process in the job market (*Diputacío de Barcelona*, 2004b). Considerable attention is paid to analysing the job market, researching companies and identifying their needs, and encouraging companies to become involved in training programmes and job orientations. The service does not end when a job contract is secured but continues into the workplace. The local job services continue to act as mediators where difficulties arise on the job, and to liaise with the company with respect to new job opportunities and initiatives.

In another project, the *Diputació* has used an even more targeted approach to helping specific groups within the migrant population. When developing a project to support women and young people without residence permits they decided to further segment their target groups into "incidence groups", reflecting the different barriers which are faced by specific types of individual. Participants in the programme underwent an occupational analysis of strengths, weaknesses, potentials and barriers before identifying appropriate actions to support their labour market integration.

There continue, nevertheless, to be cultural and social barriers that militate against both women and men getting involved in training programmes. All the integration programmes examined operated some selection procedures and access to mainstream services is only open to legal immigrants. Consequently, some groups of people, often very vulnerable, are excluded from existing services and risk being further marginalised.

Engaging employers and the business sector

The focus of a number of the local initiatives on employability rather than direct labour insertion partly reflects the variety of barriers which immigrants experience to the labour market and the need for both education and training, and perhaps the level of competency of local institutions. However it also reflects a wider problem that local level initiatives find it hard to identify sustainable jobs for their clients. Officials at the *Diputació de Barcelona* point out that they have had considerable difficulty in securing sustainable jobs for migrants. As one representative of the local development company, Grameimpuls S.A commented "The problem is not getting a job; it is providing people with employability skills so they could potentially get a better job, but the market is very tight. The labour market is precarious".

Although the labour market can be partly blamed for this situation, local initiatives in fact partly contribute to the problem by providing training in particular areas, most notably, construction, culinary skills, and domestic service, which are notable for their transient and contingent nature. The IMPEM vocational training actions being taken forward by Mataro, for example, focused on relatively vulnerable positions such as that of waiters, kitchen assistants and domestic employees. In Santa Coloma de Gramenet, the primary area of labour insertion was the construction sector. In Ciudad Lineal, Madrid the kinds of jobs that clients of the CASI are most likely to obtain are as waiters, domestic cleaning and in construction. Although it may be more likely that immigrants will find local employment in these sectors, which traditionally have a high concentration of foreign employees, these sectors also have a high proportion of temporary work, which means that immigrants frequently go in and out of employment without making a great deal of progress toward more sustainable integration or developing a defined career trajectory.

One of the key challenges facing service providers in helping migrants to access jobs is motivating the business sector to become an active partner in skills development and training programmes. Labour market insertion programmes in both Santa Coloma de Gramenet and in Mataro are constrained because of the difficulties staff face in engaging employers within the business community. Despite having a relatively broad membership, the council responsible for the development of the Matero citizenship plan did not involve any local businesses, for example. Officials at the province of *Barcelona* acknowledge that taking the initiative with employers, and encouraging them to hire immigrants, is a key area that required more attention. The province has started to work to a greater extent with employers in more general sense, especially within the context of European projects. The *Diputació de Barcelona* works with one hundred and fifty technicians who act as intermediary agents between the business community and the labour market. This is an evolving strategy which has proved challenging because staff are not used to working with business, having had hitherto a primarily social orientation.

NGOs in Madrid also identified that awareness creation among employers was an important aspect of their work. Through their outreach work the NGOs are attempting to break down traditional barriers between NGOs and employers and develop a methodology for promoting corporate social responsibility. Some NGOs work with employers directly to place immigrants in work – for example, the Red Cross (Madrid) dealt with 60 000 clients in 2004 (53% of whom were female), and succeeded in inserting 28% of those in the labour market. In general, NGOs are also becoming increasingly concerned about the quality of employment on offer to immigrants and the levels of immigrant insertion into the labour market. NGOs now raise this issue more frequently with the employers with whom they were working. Representatives suggested that companies that perform well in terms of hiring and the conditions offered to immigrants should be showcased as positive examples, however there seems to be limited action in this area to date.

Heretofore, one of the problems faced by prospective employers was the time they were required to expend processing prospective employees. The market moves quickly and the municipality needs to be able to respond accordingly. Staff at the local development company in Santa Coloma de Gramenet saw the processing of paper work as an impediment to securing jobs for their clients. It is hoped that the new centralised catalogue of "jobs that are difficult to fill" (*Catálogo de Ocupaciones de Difícil Cobertura*) may help to overcome bureaucratic barriers for prospective employers.

Promoting inter-groups relations

While work is a key mechanism of integration, in a multi-cultural society, other facets of the integration process must of necessity be addressed. The literature on immigration has long highlighted the importance of social networks in facilitating the migration process.[9] It is through social networks that norms operate and are reproduced and maintained in the host country. Social networks also provide the circuits through which information, opinion, attitudes, goods and services flow. They are therefore crucial to the socialisation of new immigrants into the ethnic community. In the municipalities of Mataro and Santa Coloma de Gramenet service providers on the ground showed a high degree of awareness in relation to this form of social capital, and, as discussed above, have put in place a number of initiatives to further the social and cultural cohesion of immigrants locally. Mataro's "new citizenship plan" includes the explicit recognition that addressing the indigenous population's attitude is one face of developing positive inter-group relations and better social integration, for example.

A further focus of the local initiatives reviewed was on tackling general issues effecting urban communities that have a high percentage of immigrants. Sole and Parella argue that there are three main dimensions to the rejection of immigrants by host communities in Spain, "lack of personal safety, fear that the presence of immigrants will lead to a loss of identity and of the neighbourhood and competition for work and public resources" (Sole and Parella, 2003). Practitioners on the ground in Santa Coloma de Gramenet found that people pay more attention to noise and neighbour issues when they can be redefined as problems created by immigrants. The changing demographic composition of the local neighbourhood means that the traditional social networks of the indigenous community are receding, and new neighbours are arriving who have unfamiliar lifestyles and do not always share the same customs. The level of diversity is also on the increase, with more than 129 nationalities present in the municipality in December 2004. Some local people experience this as an "invasion", and social stigmatisation and social stereotyping are prevalent.

Part of the work of the local development company, Grameimpuls S.A is to counteract these negative stereotypes by actively encouraging the indigenous community and the immigrant community to work together, to avoid "ethnicising" local problems. Grameimpuls S.A is innovative in that it places an emphasis on its dual role in both teaching and learning from immigrants. They also demonstrate commitment to the local delivery of services and programmes, and to the deployment of local staff with insider knowledge of the immigrant communities they serve. These mediators or intermediaries work with municipalities and promote the programmes that are available. For example, Grameimpuls S.A has developed neighbourhood councils for conflict resolution. These provide a forum where people can talk about problems and how to resolve them. The main aim is to manage and resolve social conflicts before they develop into ethnic conflicts.

Grameimpuls S.A also engages in informal low-level surveillance to identify possible illegal activities or enterprises. Mediators are used to try and help businesses to legitimate themselves in the first instance. If that is not possible attempts are made to close them down. The initiative takes the view that immigrants must be seen to conform to social and legal norms in order to gain local acceptance.

According to local staff at Grameimpuls S.A, children of earlier generations of immigrants also have difficulties coping. There are few role models in the locality for this younger generation and there is a 40% school failure rate in the municipality. One strategy adapted is through the promotion of inter-culturalism in schools. By encouraging children to learn about the different languages, cultural and ethnic practices in the community they hope to confront social stereotypes and guard against the emergence of anti-social behaviour. Grameimpuls S.A actively support the creation of circuits for discussion and exchange in local schools. They also foster exchanges between sports clubs and families to increase mutual understanding and thus, provide mechanisms for integration.

In a similar vein, the CASI in Fuenlabrada, Madrid is re-directing its energies toward challenging the stereotypes and prejudices among the indigenous communities that act as barriers to integration, through, for example, inviting non-immigrant neighbourhood groups to make use of the CASI facilities such as meeting rooms. The CASI in Ciudad Lineal has a major housing problem in the locality. To address this issue and also improve inter-group relations they are working on an initiative that encourages older people living alone to sublet a room in their house to an immigrant in need of housing, in return for the latter performing some domestic services. This is a transaction that is outside market relations, based more along the lines of the Time Bank scheme that has been successfully developed in socially deprived areas in British cities.[10] The big challenge is developing trust between older people and new immigrants, so professionals have been assigned to mediate between both parties and to follow up and monitor arrangements. The focus of the CASIs on attitudes towards immigrants within wider society will be given added impetus by the stated goal of addressing prejudice which is likely to be incorporated explicitly into the new strategic plan currently being devised by the region of Madrid's Ministry of Labour and Social Affairs.

Despite the local emphasis on social cohesion and networking however, a major concern in Spain is the absence of immigrant representatives from civil society and the third sector in initiatives being developed at the local level. Elsewhere in Europe, immigrant associations often play a useful role in representing the needs of different migrant groups, ensuring that these needs are appropriately addressed in local projects and programmes, and in some cases directly delivering training and other services to their members. Officials at the region of Madrid recognise the relative weakness of immigrant associations and have launched a tender to provide subsidies to associations that qualify. These associations lack training and experience in representing their ethnic groups, and the CAM is actively considering providing such training through its cultural mediators programme.

Greater participation by immigrant groups, particularly those who are most vulnerable in the design and delivery of public services would constitute a practical example of active citizenship involvement and offer a range of possibilities including co-production, partnership, delegation and control. The increased consultative role being offered to immigrant associations at the national level, the Mataro new citizenship plan and the ethos that underlies the Grameimpuls S.A local development company, are attempts to affirm an "active" citizenship role for Spain's immigrants. It is important that this affirmative approach, which emphasises capacity building on the part of immigrants, is diffused into civil society and across all governance levels.

Conclusions and issues for consideration

In contemporary Spain, a number of key issues confront local and national government as each adapts to the reality of increased immigration, seasonal worker flows and the presence of undocumented immigrants, refugees and asylum seekers. In March 2005, the number of immigrants stood at just over 2 million. Following regularisation, this figure will have climbed to between 2.6 and 2.7 million, which constitutes between 5.5-6% of the Spanish population.

Sharing good practice between provinces and regions

The decentralised governance arrangements in Spain create a particular context for local interventions to support the integration of immigrants. In both Barcelona and Madrid, it is clear that the regional level has benefited from the flexibility available to them to develop strong strategies for integration involving a large number of stakeholders. The replication of the integrated, cross-sectoral approach being supported at the national level has produced valuable regional strategies targeted at both immigrants and the wider indigenous population. In the province of Barcelona, the networking between municipalities facilitated and supported by the provincial government has provided a particularly useful mechanism for information sharing, pilot-project testing and good practice exchange at local government level. This network model of governance could very usefully be adopted elsewhere.

At the local level, the joined up customised services for immigrants (the CASI programme, Grameimpuls S.A and the IMPEM in Barcelona) also offer useful templates for other local areas. The CASIs in particular offer a good example of a strong, local and flexible approach that has been successfully mainstreamed so that consistent services are offered throughout the Madrid region. The compactness of these local agencies, with a dedicated cross-sector team working on the ground, allows them the flexibility that is often lacking within larger, more bureaucratised institutions. Such flexibility is supported by the relative freedom which individual CASIs are allowed in expending their budgets. This type of delivery model should be supported and extended, where possible, by national and regional government.

Decentralisation has also produced differential access to resources at the local level, however, and certain policy contradictions. There has been strong shift in national policy support towards a broader approach to integration, evidenced by the new Directorate-general for the Integration of Immigrants the Support Fund for Refugees, the acceleration of procedures for family regrouping and the Integration of Immigrants and the Strategic Plan for Citizens and Integration 2006-9. However, national immigration policy is still frequently dealt with from an employment perspective, whereas the regional and local levels are more concerned with ensuring social integration and citizenship in order to create local social cohesion. The national emphasis on permit based employment integration, for example, prevents the decentralised branches of national institutions, such as the employment services, from providing integration support to immigrants without work permits. The 2004 regularisation allows city councils to grant residence permits to immigrants on the grounds of exceptional circumstances. However in many cases NGOs are left to fill in the gaps. There also appears to be some confusion about the role of local municipalities in dealing with labour market issues. Authorities such as Santa Coloma de Gramenet are increasingly becoming involved in employment issues as a principal mechanism for broader social integration, despite the fact that they do not have specific competencies in this area.

The initiatives reviewed as part of this study were from two autonomous regions (Catalonia and Madrid) which have placed particular emphasis on the integration of immigrants as they have a high concentration of these groups. However, if Aparicio and Tornos are correct and the immigrant population is becoming more diffuse in Spain (Aparicio and Tornos, 2003), it is important that other regions also take forward similar initiatives. A recent OECD study has found that the rapid decentralisation in Spain has been accompanied by policy fragmentation and a lack of communication and co-ordination between and across levels of government, resulting in a limited diffusion of best practice (Giorno and Joumard, 2005). The national government needs therefore to play an important role in supporting the circulation of good practice between regions in order to overcome this relative lack of information sharing. Even where best practice is known about, regions may not have the resources to implement similar initiatives. Improved funding for the provincial and regional governments, and the more generalised establishment of local ring-fenced budgets for immigrant labour market and integration programmes, would make it possible for the good practice identified in the case study regions to be adopted elsewhere. The targeting of a significant percentage of funding for the new integration strategy to regional and local level actors will be of considerable help in this process.

Building local capacities

It is evident that some local projects succeed because there is a key local actor in place who can build local relationships in addition to having political leverage. Such "social entrepreneurs" can be valuable in raising the profile of immigration issues and building trust with other local stakeholders, including employers. Dependency on such individuals can make local projects vulnerable in the long-term however, and can also make service provision paternalistic in character. Capacity building would be beneficial to help local projects to develop more robust mechanisms of service delivery for the longer term.

Moving from employability to longer term employment

In addition, despite the good practice which is evident in the case study regions, a number of problems remain in the approach to the labour market integration at the local level. Local initiatives often have problems getting immigrants into permanent jobs and there is a certain level of circularity with immigrants coming in and out of training programmes as they find temporary and unsustainable employment. These problems reflect a national level paradox in that the concept of integration being given priority by the new Spanish government (which implies equalisation of rights and responsibilities with the Spanish citizenry) is modelled on a traditional industrial economic model where immigrants can access relatively well paid, unionised, secure employment in traditional manufacturing and service sectors. This in turn would provide them with the wherewithal to put down roots in a community and to become socially as well as economically integrated. However, increasingly, one of the demands of the post-industrial economy is for labour power that is service oriented, flexible, mobile and relatively cheap.[11] Hence, there is a demand for an immigrant workforce that can be hired on short-term contracts. In such a scenario, a "good job" becomes more elusive and the experience of work (particularly for immigrants) becomes more transient and contingent.

There is, however, scope for local level actors in Spain to better adapt their programmes to help immigrants avoid the traps of low paid temporary employment. The current emphasis is on short term employability skills and the possibility of creating career paths or job trajectories that might lead to social mobility and greater access to more secure employment is not frequently explored, despite the fact that many immigrants who possess educational credentials are currently under-employed in unskilled jobs. The case studies revealed relatively few initiatives that specifically targeted such immigrants or that offered higher end skills training. There seems to be considerable scope to develop skills based programmes that target more highly skilled immigrants at the local level and support their onward progression in the labour market. The recognition of existing skills is also a matter of concern, and qualifications obtained in other jurisdictions are not readily acknowledged in Spain as is the case in many OECD countries. INEM should continue to work closely with the trade unions and employers associations to devise policies and programmes that will address the ethno-stratification of the workplace and improve employment conditions and training opportunities for those in the low skilled occupations which are still so essential to the Spanish economy.

At the other end of the scale, it is clear that some migrants are still excluded from local level initiatives. Barriers remain in terms of access to labour market insertion programmes (particularly where work permits are required for access) and the fact that local integration programmes operate some selection procedures means that they can be out of reach for the most vulnerable. There is a risk in the longer term that this may result in greater marginalisation for some groups of immigrants and related problems of disaffection. Local level actors need to ensure that such groups are brought into programmes as far as possible and are better addressed through mainstream provision, including providing outreach services to specific communities where necessary.

Involving wider stakeholders

There is a clear attempt by officials at the regional and local levels to involve a wide range of different stakeholders in the integration of immigrants. However it is clear that there is still some way to go in effectively engaging the business sector in integration issues in Spain (Sole and Parella, 2003). The newly constituted Council for the Promotion of Equal Opportunities and the Non Discrimination of Persons due to their Racial or Ethnic Origin should go some way toward encouraging good practice amongst businesses in the employment of immigrants and ethnic minorities, whilst also ameliorating the situation of immigrants who have been discriminated against. But the success of this council will depend on raising awareness of its existence and being seen to process cases both with sensitivity and efficacy.

It is important that the new council works in partnership with the Forum for the Social Integration of Immigrants, the trade unions and NGOs to pursue actively an anti-discrimination agenda and affirm the rights and responsibilities of Spain's immigrants. The council is at an early stage of development and needs to promote its national visibility and assure potential clients of its independence from government. It is recommended that the council adopt a multi-level communications strategy in terms of information dissemination, education on the rights and responsibilities of employers and employees, and the promotion of greater inter-cultural understanding in the workplace. Such a strategy should include actively demonstrating the economic contribution of immigrants to Spanish society, and show-piecing the success stories of immigrant entrepreneurs. This would help to counter-balance negative stereotypes in the media of the immigrant population. The council could also set up an advisory panel to actively engage employers and the business sector (both indigenous and immigrant) in promoting the rights and well being of workers.

It is also clear that much of the work done to help integrate immigrants at the local level in Spain is carried out by NGOs whose resources are limited. They rely to a great extend on volunteerism, private donation and European grants such as EQUAL in addition to funds from the central administration. NGOs in Spain provide professional services to a range of immigrant client groups, and would benefit from having a more secure funding basis. European grants in particular are less likely to be available in the future given the needs of new member states of the EU. The government could provide a lead in this area by establishing an NGO network perhaps as a sub-group of the Forum for the Social Integration of Immigrants, making funding on a multi-annual basis for inter-cultural and cross-sectoral initiatives that are oriented toward the integration of immigrants and the mainstreaming of immigrant services in Spanish society.

Tackling the informal economy

Service providers in both Barcelona and Madrid emphasize the need to keep up the pressure in tackling the informal economy. Despite the recent regularisation programme, there are fears that the existence of this economy had become tacitly accepted by the authorities, because workers in the informal sector are prepared to do jobs that no one else will do. Concerns were expressed by a representative of an immigrant group in Mataro, Barcelona, for example, that "the law is made to deflect people from pursuing their rights and to allow a blind eye for the black economy. It is easy to get benefit out of people in informal economy, they are easy to manipulate and exploit". The regularisation programme is viewed positively at the local level as an important mechanism for moving people out of the informal economy and into more formally regulated employment. However, the current scheme is only a temporary regularisation, and most service providers did not believe that this will signal an end to informal economic activity in the medium to long term. While it may become residualised, it will not disappear. It is likely therefore that service providers on the ground will continue to deal with undocumented immigrants for the foreseeable future, and that there will be an ongoing reliance on NGOs to support the undocumented migrants who do not fall under the remit of government offices and mainstream employment services.

Supporting the wider participation of immigrants in society

Local initiatives in Spain appear to be particularly aware of the wide variety of factors which contribute to social inclusion and integration for migrant groups. The citizenship plan in Mataro, the neighbourhood mediation activities of Santa Coloma and the Lleida programme of community activities for temporary workers all show an appreciation of the fact that integration in the wider sense "implies a process of mutual acceptance and adaptation of cultural features that are exchanged on the basis of equality" (Sole and Parella, 2003). Inter-cultural initiatives such as those in place in the communities of Santa Coloma de Gramenet and Mataro offer examples of local practice in this area; however local practitioners believe that inter-cultural mediations need to become an integral part of all services provided to immigrants. This means more than just language translation but also training in conflict resolution and an openness to the transformation and adaptation of programmes to the cultural values and norms of immigrants.

Despite this, it must be noted that the prospect of full integration of Spain's immigrants in terms of their capacity to enjoy the full range of rights and responsibilities available to Spanish citizens is still some way off. For example, the right to vote, even at local level, has not been seriously considered, although this right is available to non EU immigrants in other EU member states. A task force should be established under the auspices of the national government, drawing on the expertise of the new Council for Equal Treatment and the Forum for the Social Integration of Immigrants to examine mechanisms for strengthening immigrant political participation and civic engagement. As part of its remit, this task force should work cross-sectorally, and explore, for example, the impact of local initiatives such as the new citizenship plan in Mataro in devising national strategy. This task force could also feed into other governance institutions and bodies concerned more generally with political practice and associational life in Spain.

In the course of this study it also seemed apparent that the state and its agents are *providing for* immigrants, rather than immigrant groups and communities being active agents in articulating their needs and drawing down resources for themselves. This may be a consequence of a number of factors including the "newness" of mass immigration into Spain, and the low level of organisation of immigrant communities. It is possible that ethnic leaders and role models will emerge in the years ahead. In the meantime there is scope for a tailored programme aimed at the training and development of immigrant associations so that they are enabled to participate more fully in civil society and in the social partnership structures of local and national government. The NGOs could play a useful role here by devising appropriate training and development programmes, and mentoring newly formed immigrant associations.

Successful efforts to involve communities in their own governance are generally tailored to local circumstances and usually involve an empowering element. Successful involvement is predicated on sharing power and responsibility and on trust. Immigrant communities, individuals and groups can only progress in Spanish society if they can articulate their interests, and if they can develop the capacity to address them in partnership with host society agencies and institutions. Indeed, greater participation by immigrant groups in the design and delivery of public and social services would constitute a practical example of active citizenship involvement and offer a range of possibilities including co-production, partnership, delegation and control.

Notes

1. Sole and Parella (2003) point out that immigrants are clustered at the lowest level of the occupation structure. They refer to this process as the ethno-stratification of the job market. Furthermore, according to Cachon (1997) sectors with high concentration of immigrants offer the lowest employment conditions in terms of human capital, labour relations, working conditions and wage levels.
2. Figures provided by INEM April 2005.
3. The inspectorate will not have jurisdiction over domestic employment, which means that workers in this sector will remain vulnerable to exploitation.
4. Organic Law 14/2003, dated 20 November 2004.
5. Section 2 of Title II of Law 62/2003 dated 30 December.
6. Blakeley (2001), for example, suggests that civil society in Spain is characterised by low levels of associational life and a "particularistic" political culture.
7. The GRECO plan introduced by the previous government was abandoned when the socialist government came to power in 2004.
8. This point was made by a representative of an immigrant women's group in Mataro, Barcelona. The increasing employment of women in the domestic economy throughout Europe is highlighted by Cancedda (2001).
9. See for example Yucel (1987).
10. The Time Bank is a scheme which converts the hours that people spend with their community voluntarily helping each other into a type of tradable currency.
11. There is of course a parallel demand for highly skilled workers in sectors such as finance, law and technology but crucially, these highly paid workers rely on a whole host of goods and services that are generally provided by low income, immigrant groups. See Sassen (1998).

Bibliography

Amuedo-Dorantes, C. and S. de la Rica (2005), "Immigrant Responsiveness to Labour Market Conditions and its Implications on Regional Disparities: Evidence from Spain", Discussion Paper Series, Germany: IZA Institute for the Study of Labour, Bonn.

Anderson. B. (2000), "Doing the Dirty Work", Zed books, London.

Aparicio, R. and Tornos, A. (2000), "Immigration and Integration Policy: Towards an Analysis of Spanish Integration Policy for Immigrants and CIMs", EFFNATIS Working paper 32 Instituto Universitario de Estudios sobre Migraciones, Universidad Pontificia Comillas de Madrid (UPCO).

Aparicio, R. and Tornos, A. (2003), "Towards an Analysis of Spanish Integration Policy" pp. 213-251 in F. Heckman and D. Schnaper (eds.), *The integration of immigrants in European societies: national difference and trends of convergence*, Lucius and Lucius, Stuttgart.

Barou, J. (1987), "In the Aftermath of Colonization: Black African Immigrants in France" in H.C. Buechler and J. M. Buechler, *Migrants in Europe*, Greenwood Press, Westport.

Blakeley, G. (2001), "Building State and Civil Society in Spain" in Simona Piattoni et al. (eds.). *Clientelism, Interests, and Democratic Representation: The European Experience in Historical Perspective*, Cambridge University Press, Cambridge.

Bohning, W.R. (1991), "Integration and Immigration Pressures in Western Europe", International Labour Review, Vol. 130, No. 4, pp. 445-458.

Bulmer and Solomos (1998), "Introduction: Rethinking Ethnic and Racial Studies in Ethnic and Racial Studies", Vol. 21, Sept.

Cachon, L. (1997), "Notas sobre la Segmentación del Mercado de Trabajo y la Segregación Sectorial de los Inmigrantes en España", paper presented at the conference, La Inmigración en España, Madrid, 16-18 October.

Cancedda, A. (2001), "Employment in Household Services", European Foundation.

Corcoran, M.P. (1993), *Irish Illegals: Transients Between Two Societies*, Greenwood Press, Westport.

Diputació de Barcelona (2004a), "Guía metodológica para trabajar con mujeres inactivas", Methodological guide for working with inactive women.

Diputació de Barcelona (2004b), Guía metodológica para cercar a los jóvenes inactivos al Mercado laboral, Methodological Guide for Bringing Inactive Young People into the Employment Market.

Diputació de Barcelona (2003), "Good Practices and Gender Audit, Tools for Local Policy", Olympia de Gouges Project, Institut d'Edicions.

Eaton, M. (1993), "Foreign Residents and Illegal Immigrants: os Negros em Portugal", Ethnic and Racial Studies, Vol. 16, No. 3.

Economic and social council (2004), "Immigration and the Labour Market in Spain", CES: Comité Económico y social.

Ehrenreich, B. and A. Hochschild (eds.) (2004), *Global Woman: Nannies, Maids and Sex Workers in the New Economy*, Henry Holt, New York.

European Monitoring Centre on Racism and Xenophobia (EUMC) (2004), *National Analytical Study on Racist Violence and Crime, Raxen Focal Point for Spain*.

Giorno, C. and I. Joumard (2005), "Getting the Most Out of Public Sector Decentralisation in Spain", OECD Economics Department Working Papers, No. 436, OECD, Paris.

Morales Diez de Ulzurrun (2003), "Ever Less Engaged Citizens? Political Participation and Associational Membership in Spain", Working Paper Number 220, Institut de Ciencies Politiques I socials, Barcelona.

Mosley, H. (2004), "Spain: Towards an Integrated Approach to Economic and Employment Development", OECD, *New Forms of Governance for Economic Development*, OECD, Paris.

OECD (2004), *New Forms of Governance for Economic Development*, OECD, Paris.

OECD (2005a), *Economic Survey of Spain, 2005*, OECD, Paris.

OECD (2005b), *Trends in International Migration: SOPEMI 2004 Edition*, OECD, Paris.

OECD (2005c), *Factbook 2005: Economics, Environment and Social Statistics*, OECD, Paris.

OECD (2006), *OECD Employment Outlook Boosting Jobs and Incomes*, OECD, Paris.

Oso, L. (2000), "Estrategias migratorias y de movilidad social de las mujeres ecuatorianas y colombianas en situación irregular: servicio doméstico y prostitución", in Mujeres inmigrantes en la irregularidad. Pobreza, marginación laboral y prostitución, Instituto de la Mujer, Madrid, unpublished report.

Rodríguez-Pose, A. (2003), "Human Capital and Regional Disparities in the EU" paper prepared for the Joint Conference of the European Commission and European Investment Bank on Human Capital, Employment, Productivity and Growth, Brussels, 19 Sept.

Sassen, S. (1990), *The Mobility of Labour and Capital*, Cambridge University Press, New York.

Schneider, F and Klinglmair, R. (2004), "Shadow Economies Around the World: What Do We Know?" Cesifo Working Paper No. 1167.

Secretaría de Estado de Inmigración y Emigración (2003), "Statistical Yearbook of Foreigners", Madrid.

Sole, C. and S. Parella. (2003), "The Labour Market and Racial Discrimination in Spain", *Journal of Ethnic and Migration Studies*, Vol. 29, No. 1, January : pp. 121-140.

Sole, C. and E. Herrera (1991), *Los Trabajadores Extranjeros en Cataluña, Integración o racismo?* CIS, Madrid

Yucel, A.E. (1987), "Turkish Migrant Workers in the Federal Republic of Germany: A Case Study", in H.C. Buechler and J.M. Buechler, *Migrants in Europe*, Greenwood Press, Westport.

Zapata-Barrero, R. (2003), "EU and US Approaches to the Management of Immigration: Spain", Migration Policy Group, Brussels.

ISBN 92-64-02895-1
From Immigration to Integration
Local Solutions to a Global Challenge
© OECD 2006

Chapter 6

Focusing on the Young: Integration in Switzerland

by
Steve Fenton

> *The apprenticeship system is a key mechanism for labour market integration in Switzerland and is therefore considered crucial for young immigrants arriving in the country. Vocational training schools play an important role in integration in Geneva, Neuchâtel and Zurich, linking employers, migrants and the public policy system. In addition, mentoring and networking activities are a popular mechanism to support access to placements. However apprenticeships may not provide for all training needs and a not-for-profit organisation in Neuchâtel provides an alternative training model effective in meeting more short term skills shortages. Discrimination persists however, amongst local employers in Switzerland, and there are concerns that tackling training needs may not be a sufficient tool for labour market integration without the existence of a strong anti-discrimination legislation in the country.*

This chapter analyses initiatives which have been taken forward at the local level to support the integration of immigrants into the labour market in Switzerland. More specifically, it focuses on the integration of young immigrants, examining local initiatives to support the integration of this target group in Geneva, Neuchâtel and Zurich. The key theme for analysis is the role of education and training in supporting access to employment and wider social integration, focusing on direct training initiatives, and schemes to promote networking and mentoring in order to bridge the gap between young people, training institutions, and employers. In each case the role of the national, regional and local policy context in supporting the effectiveness of these initiatives is analysed.

The policy context

The concept of integration is central to this study both in its inception and throughout the process of gathering information and analysis. It has its roots both in traditions of sociological analysis and in paradigms of the politics of migration, settlement and cultural diversity in established nation-states. In the case of Switzerland it has recently become the central term of debate, and of governmental policy with regard to those whom the Swiss state designates as "foreigners". Since the late 1990s, no doubt influenced by policy discourses in the European Union, the Swiss federal government has declared an interest in exploring the concept of integration as the guiding idea in questions of the social and political incorporation of immigrants and their descendants.

A second feature of Swiss policy is indexed by their adoption of the discourse of "civil society". Although the federal government in Switzerland has been a key player in the recent initiation of debates and policies regarding integration, it sees the policy as one to be taken up by the cantons and communes, and by voluntary organisations and active citizens in such a way that the pursuit of integration finds its way into daily routines and community living. This is partly because the federal level has only recently had a policy mandate to address the position of immigrants in society, which was previously dealt with at lower levels within the highly decentralised political system. This situation introduces a distinction between integration at the level of the civic state by contrast with integration into local communities. The first, *civic integration*, is indexed by the granting of citizenship and citizenship rights to newcomers for settlement, and the second, *communal integration*, is indexed by the social incorporation of newcomer individuals and groups into the life of local communities. Of course in Switzerland, as a highly decentralised system of governance, civic integration is also the responsibility of cantons. The distinction therefore has to be made at the local level between formal legal (citizenship, nationality) forms of integration, and integration into employment and community activities.

Until recently, policies relating to refugees and asylum, and policies relating to the integration of immigrants were dealt with by two separate offices at the federal level. Refugee questions were dealt with by the Federal Office for Refugees (FOR); while immigration, emigration and integration were handled by the Federal Office of Immigration, Integration and Emigration (IMES). In 2004 these two offices were amalgamated into a single office, the Federal Office for Migration (FOM). This combines quite different functions such as policing external borders and dealing with citizenship and integration within the country and accordingly the merger has been controversial.

The Federal Office for Migration works to co-ordinate integration policies and implementation at federal, canton, and communal levels. In addition the extra-parliamentary Federal Commission for Foreigners (see Box 6.1) has been elected by Council to advise the Federal Office for Migration and to promote integration through publicity, publications, debate and support for local integration projects.

> ### Box 6.1. **Federal Commission for Foreigners**
>
> The Federal Commission for Foreigners has a key role in stimulating debate about integration in Switzerland. In 2000 a new ordinance (Ordinance VIntA) to regulate the tasks and structure of the Federal Commission for Foreigners and the latter's relations to the Federal Office for Migration was approved. The ordinance also oversees the granting of government financial assistance for the promotion of integration (the 2005 budget amounts to 14 million Francs) and since 2001 approximately 600 integration projects have been funded annually. The Commission takes the view that "integration presupposes equal rights and chances" and that while migrants must "make efforts to become integrated in Swiss society" Swiss nationals must also "be willing to practice openness and respect towards migrants".

The federal government has also addressed the question of reform and revision of laws and ordinances which currently govern immigration and foreigner policy. The 1931 Aliens Law merely establishes the principal aims of aliens policy and all specific regulation is carried forward by ordinances. A proposed new "Foreign Nationals Act" will therefore be a "regularising" piece of legislation. The distinction between admission for EU and EFTA nationals and "Third State" nationals, for example, will be embodied in the Act. The new act, debated in Parliament in 2005, and expected to come into force in 2006, will be subject to a referendum of popular opinion in September 2006. The concept of a *legal right* to permanent residence after a stay of ten years has already been rejected, but those permanently resident for five years *may* be granted a permanent residence permit if they are seen to have successfully integrated. An important general aim of the legislation is to promote integration in Switzerland, thus recognising in law that the federal state and the cantons have a role in the promotion of the integration of foreigners. The new Act will also amend Asylum regulations in a number of important ways including what is referred to as "third state regulation". This means that asylum seekers may be returned to a safe third country in which they resided before seeking to enter Switzerland.

In Switzerland, as in other countries, employment is viewed as a critical arena for "including the excluded". In a recent document produced by the Federal Commission for Foreigners it is stated that "a major part of integration occurs at the workplace; being employed also means social recognition" (Egger, 2003). Unemployment, under-employment, and absence of tradable employment skills are seen as both problems in themselves and central to the social incorporation of immigrants, especially young immigrants. Employment is regarded, by policy-makers, as having both material and moral rewards,[1] the latter in the shape of social recognition and the regulation of daily routines. It is this area of employment and social integration which, above all, the present study was mandated to examine. Other areas which could be explored in a wider vision of integration would include the political discourses which mark off a national majority, defined in ethnic, linguistic, or religious terms, from foreigners, newcomers, and ethnic or cultural minorities; incorporation into key institutional arenas such as the justice system, public employment as teachers, police, and health workers; residential integration; and inter-marriage/partners.

The legal context: Swiss citizenship and integration: the category "foreigner"

Historically Switzerland grew as an amalgam of territories which split from neighbouring states or empires, and therefore retain broad cultural distinctions. Each of the cantons of the Swiss confederation can be assigned to one of the German, French or Italian speaking blocs, with cantons which share a common language being contiguous. Nonetheless, there is a powerful sense of what it is to be Swiss in public discourse, and this is firmly linked to the concept of citizenship. 20% of the population (a total of 1 495 008 people in 2004) does not have Swiss citizenship, despite the fact that a high proportion of this group are second and third generation foreigners who are relatively well established in Switzerland. The Council of Europe has suggested that, "Only about 2% of persons of foreign origin residing in Switzerland have received citizenship despite the fact that over half of non-citizens in Switzerland have resided there for over 20 years" (Council of Europe, 1998). More than a fifth of the permanent foreigner population with an *autorisation de sejour* or *d'establissment* were born in Switzerland, with 58% of those who are born abroad have been living in Switzerland without a break for 10 or more years. Two thirds of children or adolescents classed as "foreign" (some 237 000 persons) were born in Switzerland. The Council of Europe suggest that if all the persons possessing long term (c) residence permits in Switzerland obtained citizenship, the percentage of non-citizens in Switzerland would have fallen to around 5%.

The low number of immigrants with Swiss nationality can be explained by the fact that naturalisation is difficult to obtain in Switzerland. Recent legislative proposals to make naturalisation easier were rejected by a referendum (2004) of all Swiss nationals, a referendum which was accompanied, as with subsequent campaigns, by dramatic and tendentious advertising by far right groups. The federal government is seeking to reduce the costs of naturalisation, however, currently seen as one of the major obstacles. The federal statistics for 2005 includes a section on this question, headed "Foreigners: may be born in Switzerland but not naturalized". The report goes on to say that "more than half of residents without a Swiss passport have either been living in Switzerland for more than 15 years or were born here. Measured against the 2.5% naturalization rate there is still a large integration deficit" (Swiss Federal Statistical Office, 2005).

Work permits and mobility

Based on the provisions of the Agreement on the Free Movement of Persons, the nationals of EU/EFTA States have a right to legal residence in Switzerland. They are subject to the same employment and working conditions as Swiss citizens and permanently resident foreigners. At the same time the stance towards possible entrants from non-EU/EFTA (except for refugees and asylum seekers) is much more restrictive. What are termed "third state" nationals are subject to a preference for Swiss nationals, the preferential admission of migrants from EU/EFTA states and a quota system. In practice it is very difficult for third-state nationals to gain admission and work permits in Switzerland unless they are exceptionally well qualified persons in high demand sectors with a scarce supply of specialists.

Whilst entry for EU and EFTA nationals is based the Agreement on the Free Movement of Persons, Third state nationals are subject to the requirement to obtain a residence permit. Permits issued to Third state national are as follows:

- **B** – Annual residence permits: holders of these permits are foreigners usually staying in Switzerland for a longer term, with or without employment.
- **C** – Permanent residence permits: held by foreigners to whom a permanent residence permit has been granted after a stay of five or ten years in Switzerland.
- **L** – Short term residence permits: held by staying in Switzerland for a limited period, usually less than one year.
- **G** – Border commuter permits: held by commuters having domicile in the foreign border zones employed in neighbouring Swiss zones.

Non-EU/EFTA nationals may be admitted for training courses (as "stagiaires") and trainee permits are issued by the federal state. All other permits are issued by cantons. EU and EFTA nationals who are not working in Switzerland are not exempt from the requirement of having a residence permit, although this permit will be given to them if they have sufficient resources and meet other requirements.

The characteristics of the immigrant population

The foreigner proportion of the population of Switzerland has grown steadily from the 1960s (9.3%) to 2004 (20.2%) despite a brief fall in the 1980s. The range of source countries of immigration to Switzerland has become considerably more diverse in recent years. In the decades after the war neighbouring countries (France, Germany, Austria and Italy) very much preponderated among the suppliers of migrant workers. Others came from Spain and more recently Portugal. In 2003, of 94 049 immigrants, 67 581 were from European countries, with other sizeable contributors being African countries (5 420) South America (3 957) and Asia (11 638). In addition there were in 2003 over 21 000 asylum seekers from multiple sources including the Balkans, Somalia, Angola, Iraq, Turkey and Sri Lanka. Further, the type of migrant arriving has been changing, with an increasing proportion of new migrants entering for "family re-unification". The foreigner population is unevenly distributed across the country, being greatest in the areas bordering France, Italy and Germany/Austria and lowest in the long East-West middle belt of the country. The canton of Geneva has the highest proportion with 37.8% and the lowest – Uri – has only 8.5%

Socio-economic and educational disadvantage.

During the first wave of immigration to Switzerland, following World War II, immigrant workers were typically expected to work temporarily for short periods and return to their country of origin.² In time, Switzerland relaxed legislation which made it difficult for migrants to stay (such as a ban on family reunification, and eligibility to unemployment benefit) and the next waves of migration involved more permanent migrants who, in many cases, brought their families over too. The long-term presence of immigrants and their children has raised new policy challenges in Switzerland, including the question of integration, as described above, and the educational attainment and social mobility of second and third generation immigrants. At the same time, the insecurities of the current global market place have meant that unemployment is rising in Switzerland, and patterns of employment are becoming increasingly temporary and fragmented.

Overall, the foreigner and immigrant population in Switzerland appears to experience poorer economic circumstances and lower educational outcomes than Swiss nationals. This can be measured in terms of educational achievement, pay, levels of unemployment, and representation of, for example, young people in institutions of higher education and teacher training.³ It is also clear that the degree of disadvantage is related to recentness of migration and country of origin, those emanating from neighbouring countries such as France, Germany, and Austria performing equal to or better than Swiss nationals. The recent arrivals doing less well include those from former Yugoslavia, Turkey and Portugal, with those from Italy and Spain occupying an intermediate position.⁴

Type of employment and working conditions

While there continues to be a demand for workers in both high skill and low skill areas, the low skill areas are filled disproportionately by foreigners and immigrants in Switzerland. Whilst immigrants from northern and western European countries (like Germany, Austria and France) are likely to have educational outcomes and occupations similar to or better than the Swiss nationals, more recent immigrants from Southern Europe and the Balkans are more likely to be employed in sectors associated with lower pay and status (Swiss Federal Statistical Office, 2004a). Buttet, Gfeller and Meyer (2005) highlight the proportional share of migrant employment in certain economic sectors (construction, hotels, agriculture, restaurants) in which employment is more "unstable and insecure". The comparison of Swiss nationals with non-nationals within the labour force in the sector "restaurants, catering, and personal services", for example is as follows: Swiss nationals 7%, West and North Europeans 7%, Southern Europe 20%, Balkans 19%). This, of course, is not an unusual pattern of migration⁵ whereby in-migrant workers often take up work which is unwanted or least-wanted by indigenous workers.

To be offset against this is the fact that, as in other advanced economies, the proportion of people working in agriculture and industry continues to fall, and the proportion in managerial and professional work and routine clerical and service work continues to rise. The fact that current policies are designed to attract higher skilled immigrant workers to Switzerland represents a tacit recognition of the shift in the nature of labour demand. In addition to restricting Third Country National immigrants to highly skilled specialists, Switzerland is encouraging high skill professionals from European Union and EFTA states to work in Switzerland, along with professionals from other countries, an acknowledgement that they are unable to fill high skill professional positions without accepting foreign workers, particularly for international organisations who have their base within the country.

It should in fact be noted that there are considerable differences between the labour market contexts in each of the case study areas of Geneva, Neuchâtel and Zurich. The demand for multilingual and highly skilled professional positions is particular felt in Geneva, which is the main base for international organisations within the country. Geneva also has a particularly strong service sector. In contrast Neuchâtel has a stronger manufacturing bias, while Zurich has a more mixed economy with a particularly strong financial sector.

Unemployment

Rates of unemployment in Switzerland have been and remain significantly higher for foreigners by contrast with Swiss nationals. In 2003 the unemployment rate for foreigners was recorded as 6.6% against 2.7% for Swiss nationals, and whilst they are 25% of the working population, foreigners are 42% of the unemployed at this date. Rates of unemployment, as in many developed economies, are higher for young people (15-24 years old) and in this age group too rates are higher for foreigners (7.7%) compared with Swiss nationals (3.0%). Females are also more likely than males to be unemployed.

In a study confined to French-speaking Switzerland, Buttet *et al.* (2005) equally found considerably higher rates of unemployment among foreigners (all ages) and significant differences between nationality groups. In fact unemployment rates for Oceanic groups (3.5%) and Canada and the United States (3.8%) were lower than the rate for Swiss nationals (5.8%) and the rate for those from EU and EFTA countries (7.7%) was not much higher than the Swiss. The higher rates are to be found, for example, among those from Africa (30.2%), from other (non EU/EFTA) European countries (19.7%) and former Yugoslavia (17.1%). Of the six cantons designated as French speaking, the average unemployment rate was highest in Geneva (9.6%).

The type of sectors in which migrants work also has an impact on their unemployment rates. Buttet, et al. (2005) note the importance of poorer education and qualifications among some foreigners in unemployment but also point out that in general foreigners find work in sectors which experience higher unemployment rates, and are under-represented in low unemployment sectors. For example, prior to their unemployment, a high proportion of unemployed foreigners had a job in personal services, including hotels and restaurants. Foreigners employed as teachers (and other low unemployment occupations) are far less likely to be unemployed than foreigners in general. Buttet et al. describe the disproportionate representation of foreigners in specific sectors as "a form of ostracism from the indigenous labour market with respect to certain nationalities". The immigrant status and the weak labour-market positions of immigrant workers are also linked: workers who are non-citizens have to re-apply for residence and work permits through their current employers, leaving them in a weak bargaining position.

Social mobility

While in some countries the poor labour market success of first generation immigrants is balanced by the relative success of their children (through factors such as strong educational performance),[6] social mobility between generations in Switzerland would appear to be less marked. The OECD Thematic Review of the Transition from Initial Education to Working Life (OECD 1999) found that the second generation within Switzerland was strongly influenced by the socioeconomic situation of their parents, stating that the, "level of acquisition of skills that are useful in the labour market and in everyday life (also) reflects social stratification more closely in Switzerland than is the case elsewhere. The differences in skills… by the father's educational attainment, are considerably wider than in the other countries examined". This pattern of unequal generational transmission fits with evidence of comparatively low educational mobility in Switzerland. The study *Education at a Glance* (OECD 1999) compares eleven countries with highly developed economies with respect to "the relative chance of having completed tertiary education, for individuals with parents of different educational backgrounds". In Switzerland, "a young person whose parents hold a post-secondary degree is four to five times more likely to obtain such a degree in turn, than someone whose parents did not finish upper secondary school". The report identified that the population without secondary finishing qualifications consists largely of foreigners.

Illegal residents or "clandestins"

The number of illegal residents in Switzerland is not known. All references to the size of this population (also referred to as "*sans papiers*" and "*clandestins*") are estimates. The Swiss Federal Office for Migration has estimated a population of roughly 90 000 (2004) whilst NGOs have claimed that the figure might be as high as 300 000. Illegal residents, and particularly their children, are often taught within institutions of post-compulsory education and cantons may offer education without regard to status. But as it is not possible to take up employment, it is difficult for young people in this situation to be offered in-company placements or apprenticeships. They often therefore remain in full time education or take up work illegally in low skill sectors such as tourism, hospitality, cleaning and seasonal agriculture.[7] The issue of illegal employment is gaining in political importance in Switzerland, leading to a publication on the issue by the Federal Office for Migration in 2004, which emphasized the link between illegal immigration and labour market demand.

Tackling discrimination

A number of studies have highlighted evidence of discrimination against immigrants by employers in Switzerland. In 1999, Golder and Straubhaar used earnings data to illustrate discrimination against immigrants in income, while in 2003 Fibbi et al. provided research-based evidence of discrimination in the recruitment of individuals with an immigrant background. This latter study was based on an International Labour Organisation (ILO) methodology which tested employer responses to applications from people with different ethnic backgrounds. The results of the study show that whilst there is some (minimal) discrimination against the Portuguese, there was a high degree of discrimination against applicants from Turkey and former Yugoslavia, the other two main groups represented in the study. A comparison of responses to applications by immigrants from former Yugoslavia in French-speaking and German-speaking Switzerland show a higher rate of discrimination in German-speaking Switzerland.

By comparison with other European countries, the United States and Canada, Switzerland's legislation against racial discrimination is relatively weak being based on the declaration (1995) of what is described as an 'anti-racism penal norm' in the Swiss penal code (article 261). There is no anti-discrimination legislation and a person believing that they have been discriminated against in applications for employment has little or no legal redress. The role of the Federal Commission against Racism is largely to disseminate information and to assist in the circulation of materials designed to promote equal opportunities and the condemnation of public incitements to racial hatred. The Commission is very active in public pronouncements against xenophobia, racism and right-wing extremism. In 2004, along with Swiss Muslims, the Commission condemned the appearance in the press of an advertisement purporting to show that Muslims would soon become a majority in Switzerland. The advertisement, placed by a group close to the Swiss People's Party, came just a few weeks prior to a referendum on liberalisation of naturalisation laws. Whatever its declaratory powers and capacity to lead public opinion – which is considerable, the Commission cannot function as a body to protect individuals who have been discriminated against in labour markets or in other fields such as housing.

The governance context

The governance of Switzerland is grounded in a federal system in which the "local" states, the cantons, have a considerable degree of autonomy and discretion. The general model, with regard to foreigner and integration policy, is that the federal state establishes regulations and laws which the cantons must follow whilst retaining significant discretion in how they implement them. This is true in a number of areas relevant to foreigners and integration such as the granting of residence permits, permission to change residence and occupation, the fostering of local debate and integration projects, and the implementation of naturalisation regulations. For example, cantons prepare the reports on the basis of which decisions about granting naturalisation will be made, and vary in the manner in which examinations and enquiries for naturalisation are carried out. Whilst people who have resided in Switzerland for twelve years may apply for naturalisation, cantons differ in the application of this rule. For example, in the canton of Nidwalden, "applicants must have spent all the generally required 12 years in this canton. In Geneva, two years' residence is sufficient" (Efionayi *et al.*, 2005). The federal conference reporting in 2004 on "juridical obstacles to the integration of foreigners" also highlighted variation in the timescales for the authorisation of settlement and the application of criteria to permit family reunification, pointing out that this variation has caused a degree of dissatisfaction amongst those subject to the uncertainties of the use of cantonal discretion, particularly as such discretion is sometimes perceived as "arbitrary, influenced by political considerations, and not subject to clear rules or criteria" (Swiss Federal Office for Professional Education and Technology, 2004). The discretionary power of cantons in issuing permits is also seen as constituting an obstacle to geographical and occupational mobility for immigrants because "it limits immigrants in the choice of their place of residence and in the possibilities of finding employment" (Efionayi-Mäder *et al.*, 2003).

Cantons also vary in the degree to which they pursue policies to address language and cultural difficulties among pupils in their education systems. The Conference of Canton Directors of Public Instruction (CDIP) adopt recommendations with respect to measures designed to assist pupils whose first language is not the principal canton language but they cannot guarantee that these recommendations will be pursued with equal vigour across all cantons. Similarly cantons vary in whether they permit failed asylum seekers to take part in training courses.

The federal government has recently sought to foster some consistency between integration policies in the cantons through the appointment of "integration delegates", whose job it is to form a link between key institutions at the canton level and the federal agencies, whilst also participating in national debates attended by all delegates. Although all cantons have now appointed delegates, some cantons were readier in their response than others. Some cantons, like Geneva and Neuchâtel, have adopted integration measures into cantonal law.

It should be noted that each of the cantons reviewed in this chapter has a very different geography; while Geneva is an urban canton, Neuchâtel is largely rural and Zurich is a mixed canton with both dense urban areas and rural areas.

Local initiatives to support the integration of young people into the labour market

The remainder of the chapter will outline and assess local responses, initiatives and programmes designed to address barriers to labour market integration in Switzerland looking at the following two types of initiative in turn:

- Education and training initiatives to support access to post-compulsory vocational training.
- Initiatives to support networking, mentoring and to bridge the gap between young immigrants and the employment market.

Education and training initiatives to support access to post-compulsory vocational training

The key arena for local and state interventions to support the integration of young people in Switzerland is the system of vocational schools which provide post-compulsory education to help people first enter the labour market. With federal and canton-level support vocational schools are implementing programmes designed to strengthen training for under-skilled young people and to assist in their "insertion" into the labour market. In order to provide a context for such interventions, this section will begin with a brief explanation of how the educational system works in Switzerland.

The Swiss educational system makes a broad distinction between "compulsory" and "post-compulsory" instruction. Compulsory education takes the pupil from school entry at usually four or five years old (depending on canton) to the official school leaving age at about fifteen. Post-compulsory education is pursued typically between sixteen and twenty years old and embraces three possibilities: apprenticeship, advanced technical education, and university study. The majority of young people in Switzerland proceed from compulsory schooling into vocational education based on the dual system of training and apprenticeship. They may attain a basic federal certificate after two years and an advanced federal certificate after three or four years. Some of those who have attained the advanced certificate may progress to higher vocational education and training. When a professional baccalaureate is obtained in addition to an advanced federal certificate the student may gain direct access to a University of Applied Sciences. In 2003, 10% of students took a professional baccalaureate.

The cornerstone of a large part of vocational training is the "dual system" embracing a combination of periods of vocational school instruction with work-based learning through an apprenticeship. The apprenticeship remains a central element not only of training but also of long-term entry and acceptance into a sphere of employment. As such the system has not only economic and employment value but also a certain symbolic and moral value and it is evident that the apprenticeship retains its high value in the Swiss social order. OPET describes the dual system as the "most common form of vocational education and training' and reports that in the year of the report there were 88 479 16-year olds of whom 77 823 started vocational education and training. The courses, it argues, are "tailored to professional qualifications" leading to actual jobs in areas where there is demand. This strength of the dual system has, they suggest, led to Switzerland having one of the lowest youth unemployment rates in Europe; this claim was also acknowledged in the OECD review of the transition from initial education to working life for Switzerland.[8]

The education and training system in Switzerland is delivered via federal guidance and part-funding but is largely managed by the cantons who are responsible for implementation. The federal office supplies 25% of the funding and is responsible for course recognition, quality control, and conformity with ordinances governing education and training. The cantons supervise apprenticeship schemes, and the marketing of them, run vocational and full-time education vocational schools, and provide information and careers advice. About three quarters of students/trainees in vocational training enter commercial apprenticeships (as against full-time vocational school based courses) but proportions of young people in apprenticeships are higher in German speaking areas (86%) as against French speaking areas (72%). It should be considered that the differences between French and German speaking cantons may be culturally related. In France, apprenticeship does not play the same role as in Germany. School-based transition, also of the vocational kind, is more common in the French-speaking cantons than in the rest of the country.

Although post-compulsory education (after 15 years old) is not required by the state, in practice it is becoming the norm. Students who have little or no post-compulsory education are therefore increasingly at a disadvantage in the labour market. The federal government recently led a campaign to persuade employers to create more apprenticeship openings after some concern that the number offered was falling and that the numbers of people in the relevant age-groups had peaked. This campaign had some success in 2003 in reversing the trend in falling apprenticeship places, and the most recent evidence shows that the number of apprenticeships on offer, year-on-year, has stabilised, with some small growth possibly due to increased offers in French-speaking Switzerland.[9] However vocational schools were still reporting difficulties in finding apprenticeships. Switzerland has a smaller proportion of its young people than in comparable countries entering the university sector and gaining university level qualifications. This is partly but by no means wholly offset by the numbers in non-university tertiary education (advanced technical and vocational).

Public sector initiatives

Some students enter post-compulsory education in Switzerland without having satisfactorily completed basic education and lacking basic skills. Educational leaders say this may be especially so among foreigners, and even more so among recent immigrants, and places them at considerable disadvantage in the post-compulsory system. Because of this, local schools for vocational education are being forced to devote resources (with some state funding support) to offering "catch-up" education to students entering post-compulsory education without sufficient command of such skills. One such vocational school is managed by department of public instruction (DIP) of Geneva, which is taking forward a programme known as the "Schooling of migrant pupils" covering primary education (4-12 years old), secondary education (12-15 years old) and post-compulsory education (15-19 years old).

Vocational schools in Geneva operate in one of the most multi-ethnic environments in Switzerland. Whilst in 2003 the foreigner population of Switzerland was 20.4% of the total, in Geneva it was recorded as 37.8% (160 344 persons), almost double the national proportion, and 25% higher than Bern. This can at least partly be explained by the fact that the city hosts a large number of international organisations, along with the strong international focus of the University of Geneva. As the managers of the education system in Geneva recognise, the high foreigner population makes for very considerable language diversity: the school population of Geneva covers some 150 languages. Among pupils attending classes in the canton of Geneva, more than 40% of pupils speak a language other than French (the language of the canton) in the home, whilst in areas of the city of Geneva itself this figure is 75%.

Given the diversity of languages a main task of "integration" for the DIP lies in providing training in the French language and language improvement is found at all levels of the curriculum. One of the difficulties which the vocational school faces is the fact that students in the same age-group, who might be expected to be following the same courses, are highly varied in their level of skill in French, particularly as the target group includes both longer term residents of Switzerland and recent arrivals. The diversity of needs within the classroom is made even greater by the fact that the programme also trains non-immigrant Swiss who have fallen behind during their compulsory schooling, with these young people being educated alongside people of immigrant origin.

Given the diverse educational needs of the target group, the vocational school has been forced to develop an intensive and sensitive teaching environment, including small group teaching and the allocation of students to teachers with a full awareness of "the migration problematic" and intercultural understanding. In the past, some students have arrived in cohorts, and required special classes (for example during the exodus of asylum seekers from Kosovo, who began arriving in Switzerland in 1999; some 500 young people arrived in Geneva). The Department of Public Instruction is aware that the children of illegal immigrants to Geneva are among their pupils, but are committed to providing them with education, although access to apprenticeships – which continue to form the gateway to employment in many areas of the Swiss labour market – may not be possible for this group.

In Switzerland unemployment has historically been low, but rose rather sharply in the 1990s (reaching a high of 5.2% in 1997), fell at the end of the 1990s, and has then risen again since.[10] Throughout this period unemployment rates in Geneva have tended to be higher than the national average and companies are relatively resistant both to creating new apprenticeship opportunities and to taking on anyone who does not fulfil their ideal criteria for the job. In this climate, and with the Swiss economy still facing only modest growth predictions, vocational schools face a difficult task in trying to place youngsters who have had a weak start to their educational career. It is important to note that in Geneva, there are at least three streams in the labour market: university and specialist trained managers, professionals and business people; a middle rank of apprenticeship-trained workers with varying levels of skill; and an informal labour market which operates outside the apprenticeship and training system. Young immigrants are particularly at risk of falling into the latter group, with some young people being actively encouraged to take up work in the informal sector in immigrant-operated businesses such as the "ethnic" catering trade. One further obstacle facing the DIP is that staff are conscious of prejudicial attitudes towards foreigners and recent immigrants, however tackling this issue was seen as beyond the scope of the training project.

In responding to these multi-level challenges, the vocational school is, at least in part, guided by federal government's recent concern for developing an integration policy. The head of the DIP attends national meetings with equivalent officials from other cantons, who exchange views, and make recommendations to be followed at the cantonal level. A key federal message which has been adopted by this training initiative is that integration is achieved through language learning, vocational training and integration through apprenticeship and employment. It is further understood that language learning requires small classes, specialised staff, and individual attention.

Outcome data from the Geneva programme "education for migrant pupils" were not available but it is possible to make some observations about the appropriateness of the training offered given the context, and the characteristics of the target group. As noted above, the degree of diversity with which the Geneva education system is trying to cope is greater than anywhere else in the federation and language teaching, personal counselling, and intensive small group classes absorb the major energies of the programme. While no data is available as to the numbers of migrant pupils successfully entering apprenticeships evidence suggests that staff find it very difficult to assist the "insertion" of students into apprenticeship-based careers, and the staff themselves state that they find the unemployment in the canton to be a serious obstacle. In these circumstances there is little that the staff can do but concentrate on the basic skills of the students.

The vocational school has directly addressed the question of finding placements for its students by employing a vocational school-enterprise link worker whose task is to co-ordinate with employers. The link worker organises internships based on three eight-hour days per week on half normal apprenticeship pay. However, students report that they are frequently left on their own to find placements. Again no precise data exists on the annual success rates of the scheme but approximately one quarter are lost to the system either because the vocational school loses track of them or because they leave for jobs in the informal sector for which formal training and qualifications are not required.

Post-compulsory training in Neuchâtel: the Jet programme

The canton of Neuchâtel has also developed a post compulsory training programme aimed at young migrants. Geneva and Neuchâtel cantons are both French-speaking cantons, with a western border with France. But Neuchâtel has a much smaller population (just over 165 000 in comparison with over 400 000 in Geneva) and a significantly lower proportion of foreigners – 22.9% in

2002. Whilst in Geneva almost one quarter of the canton's population have a "most-spoken" language other than French, in Neuchâtel the corresponding figure is less than 15%. Geneva's economy is, crucially, also much more service-based. In Neuchâtel (2001) 36% of jobs were in the secondary (industrial) sector, compared with only 16% in Geneva, evidence of a much stronger industrial tradition in Neuchâtel. These labour market differences may at least partly explain different success rates between post compulsory programmes in the field of vocational training, although the historical and governance context in Neuchâtel has also played an important part.

Given its industrial background, the Neuchâtel region has a long tradition of receiving immigrants in response to manpower need, and established mechanisms for welcoming such migrants and providing assistance. Cantonal laws give voting rights to established foreigners and since the 1980s there has been cantonal legislation to promote equal opportunities. As part of the new federal level integration policy, Neuchâtel has appointed an "integration delegate", that is a cantonal official whose job it is to maintain links with federal policies and agencies and to act as a focal point for the development of integration policies in Neuchâtel. In addition to supporting training programmes for young immigrants, the integration delegate, for example, has worked with local housing authorities to attempt to avoid concentrations of specific groups in certain buildings/housing areas. Courses are provided for the public sector and schools on equal opportunities and anti-discrimination policies, and during 2006 Neuchâtel has funded a large programme of 400 events to raise public awareness of integration and identity issues.

The organisation providing post-compulsory training to migrants in Neuchâtel, the Centre Professionel du Littoral Neuchâtelois, is organised to provide education and training at levels from the elementary to the advanced. Courses are provided in *pré-apprentissage* (additional preparation before entering apprenticeship stage), *école professionnelle* (vocational training in the dual system) and *école supérieure* (advanced technical and vocational training).

The part of the CPLN structure concerned with pre-apprenticeship programmes is EAM, the Vocational school of Skills and Trades. EAM delivers transitional courses for young trainees otherwise known as the JET programme ("les classes des jeunes en transit"). The JET programme is directed at students who have recently arrived from outside Switzerland. These are mostly students who do not have sufficient command of French to take on vocational training immediately, nor enter academic-style courses. The emphasis is on "integration" in language, and Swiss society and culture. Students are welcome throughout the academic year and can follow two modules known as JET 1 and JET 2.

- JET 1: learning skills and language (1 year).

● JET 2: integration into a work setting (1 year).

Even on the pre-apprenticeship courses CPLN exercises some selection, excluding those with the most abiding personal problems, as well as those with limited French language ability. Students entering the programme must live in the canton of Neuchâtel, be between 16 and 20 years old, have a minimum knowledge of French (i.e. not be absolute beginners) and take a preliminary course of two weeks duration. The students learn French, mathematics and social skills and receive close attention from staff that circulate in classes offering help. Staff monitor attendance, progress and good behaviour. Indeed a small number are expelled or excluded from the scheme each year (five have been excluded in the current year).

Local familiarity and respect

It is clear that the JET programmes (as well as CPLN generally) are well respected locally and staff are well known to local and regional employers. This places them in a good position to persuade employers to accept trainees on apprenticeship schemes in the dual system. The sense of a local familiarity is, for example, much greater here than in Geneva where (in a more cosmopolitan situation and a more quickly changing labour market) vocational schools are less in direct touch with employers. Former students return to the vocational school to take part in festivals and publicity events, and black footballers have visited the vocational school to talk about racism in Switzerland. This indicates a strong awareness of the importance of identifying positive mentors and role models for young migrants.

Staff are conscious that asylum seekers and illegal migrants face particular difficulties accessing the labour market. Some of these students do not have work permits so the vocational school cannot insert them into the dual system, but as in Geneva they do provide training and support. The vocational school also expressed a greater difficulty in finding apprenticeships for non-Europeans as opposed to Europeans.

In general, however, the school is largely successful in finding placements for its students. The JET programme has the advantage that it is more targeted than the pre-apprenticeship training course visited in Geneva, with a focus on a carefully streamed group of recent migrants, without the inclusion of other class members such as Swiss learners who have experienced problems within the mainstream education system. This means that the group have developed a reputation for being dynamic and enthusiastic, increasing the positive reception of migrants in the wider vocational school and within local companies.

As in Geneva, most placements are within the private sector. However the canton has been particularly innovative in trying to expand the public sector employment of immigrants, establishing in law that it is not necessary to have Swiss nationality to become a civil servant except in some specific services. In addition, increasing public sector employment has been included as one of the recommendations prepared by canton's integration delegate, and the cantonal working group on integration for 2006-9.

In a region with a large number of small enterprises, a large foreigner population, a tradition of accepting foreigners; plus a high degree of policy consciousness, the JET programme, with the exception of the most intractable cases, could provide a model which other regions might follow.

A business model

Whilst the vocational schools of Geneva and Neuchâtel work within the mainstream education and training system to support vocational insertion for migrants, another model has been developed in Neuchâtel which offers a more entrepreneurial approach, and is able to adapt more quickly to ongoing industrial change and short-term employer demands.

The Neuchâtel region is particularly noted for watch and clock-making. However in the 1970s the watch industry was severely affected by the "quartz revolution" and overseas competition. Between 1970 and 1980 employment in the Swiss watch industry fell from 90 000 to 47 000. Although the industry recovered, partly by manufacturing quartz watches, and the industry is now relatively healthy, it has never recovered its former position. Industry and commerce in the Neuchâtel region has had to adapt and change, and technological innovations in particular have lead to growing demand for a more specialised workforce, making training particularly important.

The Neuchâtel Centre for Professional Integration (Couvet)

Situated in a former factory in Couvet, the Centre neuchâtelois (CNIP) is now an important regional training centre, primarily providing training for adults to give them new skills and to assist in their "reinsertion" into the labour market. It describes itself as providing training in practical and artisan skills as well as theoretical and cultural subjects. The practical training includes mechanical skills, electro-technical, assembly, and watch polishing. The centre is equipped with a considerable array of machines which support hands-on practical training. The centre also provides education in French language, mathematics, information and bureaucratic know-how. Some 70% of trainees in the centre at any time are "foreigners", frequently adult workers who have been made redundant from previous enterprises, but young migrants are also supported. There is a particular focus on retraining and re-skilling people for industrial and artisanal activities.

The centre has developed using an independent "social enterprise model". They have undertaken considerable loans from the Swiss federal government in order to invest in renovating the factory, and purchasing machinery. The centre also has on-going income from the public employment service (who provide payments for each unemployed trainee) and, to a very small degree, from the marketing its own products. This independence from the formal training system allows the centre to take a significant "demand led" approach, responding to employer needs by providing short and intensive training "close to the realities of industry", in day and evening classes. The lack of core public funding is not without its problems however – the income from the employment service is inherently unstable, as the service pays *per* individual trainee, whilst they are unemployed. If, for example, a trainee manages to find a job, this source of income is lost immediately.

The centre keeps in close touch with business enterprises for exchange of know-how and the search of possible placements, whilst also maintaining contact with the economic development department of the cantonal government. The centre places strong emphasis on the certification of competences gained through the training. At the end of each training period each person receives a declaration of their chosen option, modules followed, level reached; and an evaluation dossier containing a very precise description of the modules, and the quality of work carried out. The evaluation of a trainee covers the learning of practical skills *e.g.* manual skills, as well as intellectual qualities such as the ability to concentrate, memorise materials and use abstractions. Behaviour, personal style, team work and motivation are also felt to be important to the working environment, and are therefore also tested and validated as part of the training modules. The certification of these elements provides an important point of reference for potential employers who have expressed a particular interest in the way people work, rather than just the skills employed.

A number of those who come to the centre have in fact borne injuries or poor health as a legacy of former heavy work, including back injuries. This in some cases excludes them from the training on offer. However, the centre does provide additional support to trainees with personal difficulties which may prevent them accessing employment. Within limits, for example, the centre can offer help with alcohol-related and health problems, offering counselling, encouragement and support. The centre finds it important to offer life-training in addition to skill-training or, in the institutions own terms, "*savoir-être*" in addition to "*savoir-faire*". The social and psychological support follows a systematic induction aided by interviews and aptitude testing, all designed to assess trainees and minimise absenteeism.

With some 120 worker/trainees in CNIP at any time, the indicators of success are good. Despite its insecure financial basis, the centre exudes an air of brisk realism, energy and dynamism. Of those who leave for employment, 60% are still in employment six months later. The close contact maintained by staff with local employers, puts them in a strong position to recommend trainees for employment and to follow up their progress after leaving CNIP. The success of the centre can also be attributed to key features of its training systems: the flexibility of courses lasting from a few weeks up to two years: the professional testing and assessing of trainees for both work skills and social and personal skills; the thoroughness of personnel systems; and the high staff-trainee ratio (1/3 with 40 staff to 120 trainees). The centre also provides special help for asylum seekers, and supports the recognition of qualifications gained overseas.

In some respects it is clear that CNIP is developing training as a business as well as gearing trainees for business. Thus trainees are mostly but not all "locals", some come for instruction from France, thus exploiting a market for training itself. The principal threats to CNIP may come from the need to constantly keep up with new skill demands, the effects of technological change in industry which, for example, can make machinery redundant, the burden of start-up loans, and the delicate balance of income and expenditure.

Initiatives to support networking mentoring and to bridge the gap between young immigrants and the employment market

It has been widely recognised that a key factor in the educational, employment and business success of immigrants and minority groups is access to networks and resources, and the networks that lead to resources. In countries with large established majorities, people have acquired social capital in the shape of social connections to contacts that can inform them of opportunities and make discretionary decisions in their favour. Social theorists have used the term "network society" to capture the way in which people mobilise a "network logic" in order to plot their careers, and this has been applied to "youth transitions", the central concern with respect to the integration of young immigrants into the labour market.[11]

If training-into-work transitions were the focus of the first two projects described here, and the business model characterises the third, the fourth and fifth projects are articulated around "networks" and "mentors" as models for inserting young immigrants into the world of work. As already observed, a marked strength of the two Neuchâtel projects was their ability to connect with local employers and draw upon a good reputation in the community. The fourth project Interface Enterprises, based in Geneva, has been designed to create real links between employers and young people seeking apprenticeships, whilst a fifth project – *Incluso* based in Zurich – is a mentoring scheme placing a young immigrant with an experienced volunteer who was established in a company or organisation.

Interface Enterprises

Interface Enterprises in Geneva was created in 1998 partly in response to demands from employers for an organisation which would process the high number of demands from vocational schools and other educational institutions for work experience placements in particular sectors and skill areas. This would have the effect of shielding the enterprises from individual demands. Interface Enterprises was formed by the canton of Geneva and is managed jointly by the cantonal Department of the Economy, Employment and External Affairs and the DIP. The aim was to create an organisation which would act as a bridge between businesses (who may offer work experience, apprenticeships) and educational organisations.

Interface Enterprises records offers of internships by businesses in a database which is accessible to members of staff in educational institutions who are working with trainees looking for placements. The staff then match the profile demanded by the employer or company with that offered by the trainee. In seeking out placements, of short and long duration, with businesses in the region, Interface is appealing to companies to be public partners in skill development in the working population and to act with "corporate responsibility". The project can claim some 6 000 partner companies and 14 000 potential training opportunities. A high proportion of their clients are young immigrants.

Interface performs the role of "monitoring" companies, keeping in contact and checking on the experience of trainees, and in some cases challenging discriminatory behaviour.[12] The project has also recently set up two new initiatives to provide particular support to young migrants. For example, the PASSWORK project aims to help young migrants build local social networks which will help them to access employment, through "word of mouth". In many OECD countries, a significant percentage of employment is advertised through informal connections and social networks, and immigrants do not always have access to such networks. The PASSWORK project (which was developed following an idea from a young migrant) seeks to redress this balance. A second project being developed by Interface Enterprises aims to encourage immigrant enterprises to offer placements to young migrants. While this may prove useful, it is also the case that immigrant-led enclave businesses such as niche restaurants are often self-driven – being arenas where immigrants *do* have networks.

The success of Interface Enterprises is hard to judge given that it is virtually impossible to know how many successful trainees would have found placements leading to career development without their intervention. Although the database of "opportunities" has more than 150 users it is not freely available to, say, all job/training seekers at a readily-available online site.

Also, because it is not online there are some difficulties in ensuring that partners receive regular updated versions of the database and the system itself could be made easier to use. While Interface may put a placement-seeker in contact with a company they do not have the resources to support more vulnerable and less "work ready" individuals – who may need guidance in pursuing and sustaining a placement opportunity. Also, arguably, the most marginalised recent migrants are beyond the reach of this project, and other projects like it because of being outside of the education and training system. To help such groups would require outreach workers and organic links with associations and communities (again one of the aims of the Passwork project).

Incluso – Mentoring project by the Caritas Zurich for young migrants looking for employment

A second project to support the networking of young migrants is operational in the canton of Zurich. Zurich, like Neuchâtel, has developed a more supportive policy context for integration initiatives following the introduction of the federal level integration strategy. The canton has established its own integration programme, partly funded by the Federal Commission for Foreigners, and partly by the canton. Zurich also has a cantonal appointee for integration and foreign nationals, a position which was created following a review of the history of migration in the canton, migration policy, and the local experiences of migrants. The appointee argues that integration cannot be achieved in a top-down manner. That is to say, integration must be "worked at" in all spheres of life, through voluntary organisations and the personal relations of all Swiss and all foreigners. The aim is to "embed" integration in daily life, and, in effect, to 'mainstream' Swiss institutions with integration aims and initiatives. The canton in particular supports a community development approach, targeting all members of a local population. Their reluctance to only target migrant groups stems from the fact that migrants share some of the problems experienced by other people suffering poverty and exclusion in the region. Similarly, the canton does not work through immigrant associations, or delegate "integration work" to immigrant associations, on the grounds that the public in general should take responsibility for integration. However, projects with "intercultural leaderhip" are prefered in the bidding process for the cantonal integration programme.

The canton operationalises its community development approach through a series of local "antennae" which are in fact regional offices and contact points. Such antennae help identify problems, spread positive messages, and help with the coordination of integration projects. In the spirit of supporting broader community development, one recent pilot project involved the organisation of events open to the whole community which centred on the theme of being "proud of who we are". Another pilot provided more specific help to migrants by setting up a "writing workshop" run by volunteers to help immigrants to deal with bureaucracy, complete forms, and gain access to authorities. The canton is also trying to spread positive messages about integration, and is carrying out a number of publicity projects designed in part to overcome resistance to "integration" aims. They feel the need to take into consideration the fact that some communes report being "overwhelmed" by newcomers. The canton also financially supports German as a second language classes for immigrants.

A number of local charities and NGOs provide support for immigrants in Zurich, one of which, Incluso Zurich, has developed a more targeted approach, supporting young migrant women into apprenticeships through mentoring. Since the second quarter of 2002, *Caritas*, a Catholic charitable organisation[13] has been running the project, which started by supporting women from all age groups, and now focuses in particular on younger women. The project originated in Bern under the auspices of the Bern Information centre for Foreigners, and was carried forward by CFD (*Christlicher Friedendienst* – Christian Peace Project) an NGO dedicated to the empowerment of women and the promotion of equality in access to labour markets for migrants.

As stated above, the aim of the project is to help young female migrants to gain access to apprenticeships. The project links up a professional woman who is already in an occupation with a young migrant in search of an apprenticeship so that they can work together as a "pair" or "tandem". Training is provided, and the mentor and the young migrant are encouraged to develop a personal relationship in which the mentor can talk to the young migrant about the Swiss workplace and how access to labour market opportunities is structured. It is intended that both mentor and mentee will benefit from the experience, with both learning from the other.

The *Incluso* project works directly with both employers and individuals seeking apprenticeships, maintaining contact with some six schools in Zurich, and working with 15 and 16 year olds up to 20 year olds. The project supports 60 "tandems" each year and there is a package of support for mentors including an introduction session, training and feedback. Not all mentees remain in the scheme, and there has been some concern as to the low motivation and high drop out rates of some migrants, with a number of girls marrying or returning to their home country. Incluso report that 50% of the migrant women in these tandems manage to access apprenticeships or internships.

In some cases the mentors not only develop strong relationships with the mentees but also form links with employers on their behalf. However this is restricted by the fact that the professional women chosen rarely come from the particular sector which the young migrant is interested in, and so may have limited contacts within the field. There was a strong awareness within the Incluso project that employers may be "narrow-minded" in attitudes to foreigners and the background presence of the mentor is seen as a form of spur to good civic behaviour by employers. The mentor-employer relationship is intended to act as persuasion of the employer to act with regard to integration objectives, and to avoid discrimination.

Two case studies taken forward by the Incluso project include a Bosnian young woman with an F permit (issued to asylum seekers who have not been granted asylum but cannot be returned home) who was seeking training in care work. She had a low education level and no high school degree. The mentor helped to instil self-belief in the mentee and she ultimately achieved a placement in a care home. Another young trainee, a Sri Lankan, had particular ambitions to become a technical draughtswoman. The mentor was initially sceptical about what seemed to be a high target, especially for someone with less than perfect German, however the trainee succeeded in getting an apprenticeship largely through her strong perseverance. In this case, it was more difficult to judge how crucial the mentor's help had been, although the mentee appreciated the support in building her confidence.

Lessons from local initiatives

It is clear from analysis of projects in other European countries, many of them sponsored by the European Union, that business enterprise models, network models, and mentoring schemes have a record of success in generating employment and in improving employment and employability among minorities and excluded groups. In that sense there is less to be gained here from assessing whether, for example, networking schemes "work", but whether there are, on the one hand local features of projects which affect their viability, and on the other hand, national and structural conditions which exert a particular influence on the effectiveness of local schemes in Switzerland.

Vocational school based schemes

The benefit of local vocational school-based schemes is that vocational schools are in touch with large numbers of young people and can therefore potentially reach a broad spectrum of the age groups entering post-compulsory education. Insofar as their "clients" are members of the Swiss majority, the vocational schools are well-placed to carry integration and anti-discriminatory messages to them. The vocational school at Neuchâtel was inventive and imaginative in addressing xenophobia and racism. Where their actual or potential students are foreigners and recent immigrants, they have an institutional stake in maintaining the broadest possible reach of the courses and programmes that they offer. In short they have incentives to reach out to communities who are less likely spontaneously to demand post-compulsory education.

Since vocational schools are important local institutions there is every prospect that the vocational school and its staff are known to local employers. This credibility and networking in the local community may not be a feature of all vocational schools but where it is, as in Neuchâtel, it is very important. Vocational schools are also in a good position to add other functions to their purely educational and training function; this applies particularly to, for example, special language training and counselling functions where young immigrants may require personal help. The vocational schools in both Neuchâtel and Geneva had invested in the provision of these functions.

It is also clear that the vocational schools are embracing the integration paradigm as it is advanced and debated at the federal level. Vocational school directors have a tradition of meeting professionally with colleagues in other cantons and communes and are using this as an opportunity to exchange experience and expertise in the area of integration. Vocational schools also benefit from the work of the integration delegates who are being appointed in the cantons.

However, at least three questions face the Swiss vocational school system in its response to the integration agenda. One is the possibility that apprenticeships, the heart of post-compulsory vocational training, are less suited to the work environment than they were once were. Some observers suggest, for example, that apprenticeships were better suited to the skill requirements of an industrial economy, than to an economy based on information technology and both high and low-skill services, although they add that the Swiss system needs to adapt rather than undertake radical change (OECD, 1999b). If this were to be the case, the local economy within each canton would have an important impact on the effectiveness of pre-apprenticeship schemes put in place. The percentage of young adults who enter the labour market through apprenticeships is lower in Geneva, for example, than other cantons in the confederation, perhaps due to the city's relatively high reliance on services. This may be adding an additional barrier to the labour market for migrants whose education is concentrated in the dual system.

There have also been several recent years when the number of apprenticeships on offer has itself declined in Switzerland (OECD, 1999b). Although this was partly reversed by a national campaign to induce employers to offer apprenticeships, it is clear that local vocational schools in general are having more difficulty than usual in finding apprenticeships with employers.

Another question facing the vocational schools is how much they can invest in the education of students whose prior preparation was (possibly seriously) inadequate, or who need intensive help. The dilemma is that if vocational schools direct intensive integration work towards the most intractable cases it is on the one hand costly and on the other hand uncertain of success. While some initiatives (for example the CNIP project) are carrying out intensive personal work with trainees, others are clearly screening out difficult cases.

A third question facing vocational schools in their work to promote student places for apprenticeships is what to do when employers are inclined to discriminate against immigrant and foreigner applicants for positions. A number of the local initiatives reported discriminatory attitudes towards some of their students or clients. Given the lack of a federal anti-discrimination law, the only tool open to local vocational schools is persuasion, often on an individual basis. However, because vocational schools have valued local reputations and are respected in the business community, they are well-placed to gain more consistent collaboration from entrepreneurs in such issues. Equal opportunity agreements, for example between vocational schools and employers in the implementation of apprenticeship and internship schemes, can formalise commitments to fair treatment. Vocational schools could also work with other local partners to persuade business partners to head "flagship" equal opportunity employment programmes.

To conclude, therefore, vocational schools are now particularly well-placed to carry forward the integration agenda. This not only because they are well established institutions with a large clientele, but also because they stand in a crucial intermediary position between individuals, local communities, employers, the canton, and the federal state. Their links with federal institutions and participation in national conferences enables them to closely follow the national policy agenda. At the same time, their closeness to local communities enables them to carry this agenda forward with sensitivity to local conditions. Arguably, vocational schools could become an even greater player in local integration policy, if anti-discriminatory and integration measures were to be mainstreamed into broader educational practice.

The business model

If the vocational schools demonstrate what can be achieved by institutions which are embedded in the national education and training system, the Couvet factory-based project (CNIP) demonstrates what can be achieved outside of this system through enterprise, drive and the application of business principles. Because it itself operates with a business ideology, the CNIP is particularly well placed to understand and respond to local business needs. In particular, the flexibility of the training offered, and the consistent validation of competencies of interest to local employers has helped this project to deliver a particularly well adapted service, leading to successful employment outcomes for migrants. However, the challenges facing CNIP include the fact that the financial future of the enterprise, with its dependence on loans, can not be guaranteed.

Networks and mentoring

The observation that people gain access to jobs, positions, promotion and resources through taking advantage of networks of personal and organisational contacts has become standard in sociology and social policy, and widespread in the theory of social practice. It is clear that newly arrived migrants are one group who may face the difficulty of not having networks of this kind, or at least not networks that can lead them to sought-after resources. The local initiatives in Switzerland which provide mentoring and networking support to migrants, are therefore an important step towards assisting their inclusion and integration into the labour market. Indeed, mentoring in particular has become a widely practised form of social policy delivery across many European countries and in a wide variety of contexts.

There are however critical aspects of networking and mentoring schemes which are likely to affect their success. Mentoring schemes depend by their nature on one to one relationships so that, with a finite number of mentors available, the scope of some schemes may be limited, and it can be particularly difficult to match mentees with mentors within the specific professional sphere or sector they are interested in. There is also the question of training of mentors and funding for training – on a volunteer basis mentors may be dependent on their own good sense and good will. This can mean that the support given often takes the form of personal advice and confidence building. It is important that local initiatives working in this area refer to established good practice (for example practices adopted by Europe-wide mentoring associations[14]), thereby developing their expertise and ensuring that mentees receive more professional and objective advice.

An over-reliance on mentoring schemes at the local level could also lead to problems in the Swiss environment. The underlying assumption of mentoring schemes, that the main thing which young migrants lack is "connections" and know-how, begs the question of whether "lack of connections" is the *principal* barrier to immigrant employment as against weak educational background, or possible discrimination by employers. One of the conclusions of a recent study by Fibbi *et al.* (2003) is that, given the pervasiveness of discrimination, the "marginal labour market position" of young immigrants cannot be attributed solely to characteristics of the immigrants themselves. This suggests a need to adopt measures to address discrimination and the actions/opinions of majority actors rather than simply use a "deficit model" in relation to the personal confidence and contacts of immigrant young people. Mentoring schemes may need to be taken forward within a wider holistic approach which also incorporates work with employers and the majority in society. Further, while it is undoubtedly useful to help migrants to access local "word of mouth" networks which may lead to employment, ultimately it may be useful to reduce the local importance of such networks, through encouraging employers to adopt greater transparency in their recruitment process. Informal recruitment mechanisms are now widely regarded as discriminatory in the UK and in discrimination tribunals have been taken to be an indication of unfair practices (see Price, 2003).

Finally, by focusing on networking between individuals, the local initiatives reviewed in Switzerland currently seem to be missing an opportunity to support networking at other levels within society. In many European countries, for example, immigrant associations constitute an important network – or form of social capital – on which disadvantaged individuals can draw (Tillie, 2004). These associations are regularly drawn into the planning process for implementing integration projects and initiatives, with governments recognising that programmes of regeneration require making connections with community groups in order to embed the programmes in the areas they affect.[15] The "partnership" approach also involves voluntary agreements between public sector agencies and private sector business with the full involvement of potential target groups in enhancing labour market integration (Shaw, 2002). In the United Kingdom, for example, the education sector frequently works with community groups, including immigrant and ethnic minority groups, and one of the striking successes has been the development of supplementary schools where local organisations develop supplementary education classes outside the standard school institution.[16] Such an approach reflects research into strategies for improving educational outcomes for ethnic minority youth which show that success is associated with supplementary education and mentoring systems, as well as increased liaison with minority organisations and parents (Tikly, 2002).

In the first phases of Switzerland's migration history, immigrant associations played an important role in providing support to migrants, particular in the case of the Italian immigrants associations which had strong links back to the host country. However, policy makers at the cantonal level currently appear to be slow in drawing immigrant associations into planning and practice partnerships. The National Federation of Immigrant Associations (see Box 6.2) has however become an important focus for the articulation of immigrants' perspectives at a national level, and state that they are starting to achieve better representation and participation locally within the cantons.

> Box 6.2. **The Forum for the Integration of Migrants (FIMM Suisse)**
>
> The Forum for the Integration of Migrants (FIMM Suisse) is the umbrella organisation of associations for immigrants in Switzerland. It was founded in November 2000 in Bern. The communities of more than 50 nationalities are today represented in FIMM by some 300 delegates. In forming itself, the proponents had to transcend the particular interests of specific immigrant communities in order to create a universalist ethos of immigrant representation. FIMM seeks to establish itself as a body to be routinely consulted on policies affecting immigrants, equality and the struggle against racism and xenophobia. The organisation has now adopted a Charter for Integration which covers its fundamental principles including the primacy of individual rights over communal rights. It demands equal opportunities and a universalist concept of citizenship. It has already established a place in national policy formation and seeks to establish a constructive role at the level of cantons and communes. See *www.fimm.ch*.

Conclusions and issues for consideration

A number of conclusions can be drawn from this report, at both the local, cantonal and federal levels.

The federal government is clearly articulating significant new directions in the deployment of integration policies in Switzerland, emphasising respect, openness and equal opportunities. Due to the decentralised system within Switzerland, however, the federal level cannot guarantee the consistent implementation of these policy messages across all cantons, which differ considerably in laws, regulations, practices and political climate.

Switzerland has a distinguished record in the management of vocational training and in (low) youth unemployment, which has provided a strong route into employment for young migrants and other young people in Switzerland in the past. However, as with most advanced economies, Switzerland recognises that globalisation brings new demands on skills and vocational training. The future success of programmes to support employment access will depend on an adaptive response to such labour market change. This last would include giving consideration to whether newer forms of employment, including the fast-expanding service sector, the IT sector, and new employers such as call-centres, are as well covered by apprenticeships as more "traditional" forms of employment. The lower level of apprenticeship subscription in Geneva might suggest that they are not. It is necessary to consider whether apprenticeship is always the most suitable format for labour market entry in such sectors. Other approaches which could be developed at the local level include shorter periods of work experience which give migrant trainees an introduction to the more immediate competencies they may need in the Swiss labour market.

Vocational school-based interventions to support migrants at the local level have the benefit of a familiarity with local employers, government structures and contact with a large and broad base of training-age young people. This clearly places them in a very favourable position for the implementation of integration policies. However their success may well depend on a high degree of flexibility in response to multifarious needs in the young immigrant population and a commitment to maintain and build on their relationship with the local business sector, particularly in terms of helping to tackle discrimination. In particular, vocational schools should encourage positive recruitment practices amongst local employers providing apprenticeships, showcasing those employers who operate good practice in this area.

Equal opportunities and anti-discriminatory measures should in general be regarded as a key element of integration policies. In the absence of national legislation outlawing discrimination, public bodies, communal organisations and the cantons can take on a major "demonstration role". That is to say cantons and other public agencies can, *a)* mount publicity campaigns advocating equal opportunities and advancing positive messages about foreigners, *b)* work with local employers to encourage non-discriminatory recruitment practices and showcase local good practice and *c)* initiate their own equal opportunities programmes, including programmes to recruit foreigners into public sector employment.

The public sector offers a particular opportunity for the provision of training and employment to young immigrants in Switzerland, at the federal, cantonal and local levels. Within the European Union, the Council of Europe recommends that member states "ought to offer the opportunity of competing at all times possible for posts in the public sector", although European countries obviously vary in their implementation of this measure. In Switzerland, public sector employment is mainly held by Swiss nationals or, in rare cases, to holders of permanent residence permit. However, the canton of Neuchâtel has taken the initiative to promote public sector employment for immigrants in its recent legislation and planning. There are a number of good reasons for pursuing this measure at the local level in Switzerland as a whole. The first is that public sector employment represents a significant sector in the labour market. The second is that the public sector can implement equal opportunity and integration in an arena which its own agencies control, including the development of training courses aimed at disadvantaged groups within the labour market. The third is that non-nationals are also recipients or clients of state services, and so increasing the representation of non-nationals within the public sector may increase the appropriateness of the services on offer.

The implementation of integration measures at the local level in Switzerland will also require an effective system of monitoring and reporting back. One structure which might take on this task is the national conference of integration delegates representing cantons. Delegates could be asked or required to report on progress towards the labour market integration of immigrants and foreigners along a set of key dimensions. This would require record keeping of data (by birthplace and/or nationality status) on such dimensions as unemployment rates, employment rates, wages, successful completion of educational targets at different levels (completion of compulsory education; entry into apprenticeships; entry into higher technical and university education) and employment in public sector jobs. Longitudinal surveys and data collection are particularly useful in measuring labour market integration over time, particularly as achieving full labour market integration (in terms of employment that is appropriate to a person's skills, with equivalent pay and conditions to a native-born Swiss) can often be a relatively long-term process.

Both vocational schools and cantons should also seek immigrant organisations as allies. If, for example, vocational schools face special difficulties in the training of young immigrants, associations of immigrant communities may be well placed to offer advice and information, as well as taking a role in outreach activities, such as advertising the value of post-compulsory education to some of the least advantaged among immigrant and foreigner populations. Immigrant associations and the national federated body of immigrant associations (FIMM) could also be included as representatives on local public bodies. Where integration measures are pursued at the local level (for example the mentoring scheme in Zurich) good practice would be to include the representation of immigrant association(s) on management boards which oversee and review the progress of the projects. Charities in particular play an important role in the implementation of projects and could therefore be asked to ensure that FIMM or particular immigrant associations are represented on their boards of control. The same could be said for development agencies and other agencies involved in economic development. The canton of Zurich's prioritisation of projects with intercultural management in the bidding process for their integration programme is a strong step in this direction.

The business model of intervention, as in Neuchâtel, promises the prospect of real gains in the training and re-training of immigrant workers. The Couvet project, with its business efficiency, entrepreneurship, and well-designed training modules could be a model for other programmes, particularly as regards the flexibility of the training on offer and the precision with which skills and competencies were measured. The sustainability of such approaches is clearly an issue, however.

It remains to be seen whether more targeted approaches to meet the needs of migrants should be developed at the local level in Switzerland. While the vocational school in Neuchâtel raised the positive profile of migrants due to the tight focus on highly motivated recent migrants through their JET programme, a number of policy makers showed resistance to taking on such targeted approach. A key feature of Zurich's cantonal policy on integration was, for example, the aim to embed projects and programmes in local institutions and communities, and to treat the problems experienced by migrants as "problems of exclusion" rather than necessarily "problems particularly experienced by migrants". This resonates with the federal government's call to situate the "integration project" in civil society, and to ensure that integration is as mainstreamed as possible. However, a certain amount of targeting may be necessary in Switzerland to tackle the issues experienced by recent migrants (particularly language and acculturation to the labour market) as opposed to second or third generation migrants. In much of the debate about integration no clear distinction is made between recent immigrants and those born in Switzerland, and it is sometimes difficult to distinguish between these groups in research and data sources. This also makes it less easy to develop evidence based policy to tackle the particular problems experienced by the different generations. If, as suggested above, delegates were to report nationally on the success of integration measures in education and employment, it would be useful to make a distinction between foreigners, long-standing immigrants, and recent immigrants.

Finally, mentoring is clearly a popular approach within Switzerland to labour market integration, predicated on the idea that immigrants lack certain contacts and know-how within Swiss society. Mentoring has wide support in many European countries, however it is important that such projects are closely geared to labour market structures and needs, and that parallel work is carried out to tackle discrimination and to ensure that migrants are linked up to sustainable opportunities within the labour market. In the longer term, ensuring that vacancies are advertised in the most transparent and widespread way possible locally may be the most effective mechanism for ensuring that immigrants have equal access to information on employment opportunities.

Notes

1. See for example Levitas (2005).
2. See for example Sheldon (2001).

3. For evidence of educational inequalities see OECD (1999b) and for an account of obstacles to socio-economic success see Swiss Federal Office for Professional Education and Technology (2004).

4. For educational progression see for example, Swiss Federal Statistical Office, 2004a. In secondary level 2, Swiss nationals are three times as likely as "former-Yugoslav, Turkish, Portuguese" to be in teacher training or "Écoles préparant à la maturité".

5. First outlined by Castles and Kosack (1973).

6. Note for example educational and employment performance among some immigrant groups in the second generation of immigrant populations in the UK: see Modood et al. (1997). For a summary of the social profile of the "second generation", children born of immigrants, based on the Federal Population Census of 2000, see Fibbi et al. (2000). This volume contains summary data on second generation naturalization, country of origin, place of birth, principal language, educational level, economic activity, unemployment, and socio-economic status.

7. For Swiss federal data on illegal immigrants see Swiss federal Office of Migration (2004).

8. See OECD (1999b).

9. The most up to date information can be found in the now annual "Baromètre des places d'apprentissage" based on a survey of enterprises. See Swiss Federal Office for Professional Education and Technology (2005a).

10. See Swiss Federal Statistical Office (2004b); OECD (1999b) and AMOSA (2004).

11. See Kelly and Kenway (2001).

12. In Geneva in particular the concern for young workers/trainees was not expressed as "for foreigners", the term used in much public discourse and data, or immigrants, but specifically for **recent** immigrants, asylum seekers and illegal migrants lacking residence or work permits. A substantial proportion of these latter categories, including recent asylum seekers, were from non-European country origins.

13. For more details, see *www.topbox.ch*.

14. See for example The European Mentoring and Coaching Council, launched in 1992.

15. See for example ODPM (1997).

16. See the Qualification and Curriculum Authority (QCA) and its support for "Supplementary and Mother-tongue schools", at *www.qca.org.uk/*.

Bibliography

AMOSA (Arbeitsmarktbeobachtung Ostschweiz, Aargau und Zug) (2004), "Youth Unemployment – Analysis of the Situation in 2004 and Future Measures".

BITC (Business in the Community), Partnership Academy (2004), "*Business Action on Neighbourhood Renewal: Celebrating Black and Minority Ethnic Business and Community Support for Neighbourhood Renewal*".

Buttet, Y., P. Gfeller, A. Meyer (2005), "Chômage et nationalité", Conférence romande et tessinoise des offices cantonaux de l'emploi, ORTE, Lausanne.

Castles, S. and G. Kosack (1973), *Immigrant Workers and Class Structure in Western Europe*, Oxford University Press, Oxford.

Communauté de travail pour l'intégration des étrangers et Bureau du délégué aux étrangers (2006), Rapport de législature 2001-2005 et recommandations de la CTIE pour 2006-2009, BDE, Neuchâtel.

Egger, T. (2003), "Intégration et travail" in Commission fédérale des étrangers (eds.), *Terra Cognita* 3, BASS, Bern.

Efionayi D., J.M. Niederberger and P. Wanner (2005), "Switzerland Faces Common European Challenges", *Migration Information Source*, Migration Policy Institute, Washington.

Efionayi-Mäder, D., S. Lavenex, M. Niederberger, P. Wanner and N. Wichmann (2003), "Switzerland", in J. Niessen et al. (eds.) *EU and US Approaches to the Management of Immigration*, Migration Policy Group, Brussels.

Council of Europe (1998), "Country by Country Reports: Switzerland", *European Commission Against Racism and Intolerance*, CRI (98) 27.

Fibbi R, M. Lerch, P. Wanner, E. Mey, M. Rorato and P. Voll (2000), "L'intégration des populations issues de l'immigration en Suisse: personnes naturalisées et deuxième génération", BFS, Statistik der Schweiz, Neuchâtel.

Fibbi R., B. Kaya and E. Piguet (2003) "Le passeport ou le diplôme? Études des discriminations à l'embauche des jeunes issus de la migration", *Rapport de recherche 31*, Swiss Forum for Migration and Population Studies, Neuchâtel.

Golder, S.M. and T. Straubhaar (1999), "Discrimination in the Swiss Labour Market: An Empirical Analysis", Centre for Economic Policy Research, London.

Kelly, P. and J. Kenway (2001), "Managing Youth Transitions in the Network Society", *British Journal of the Sociology of Education*, Vol. 22, No. 1, March.

Levitas, R. (2005), *The Inclusive Society: Social Exclusion and New Labour*, Macmillan, Palgrave.

Marger, M.N. (2001), "The Use of Social and Human Capital among Canadian Business Migrants", *Journal of Ethnic and Migration Studies*, Vol. 27, No. 3, July.

Modood T., R. Berthoud, J. Lakey, J. Nazroo, P. Smith, S. Virdee and S. Beishon (1997), *Ethnic Minorities in Britain: diversity and disadvantage*, Policy Studies Institute, London.

ODPM (Office of the Deputy Prime Minister of the United Kingdom) (1997), "Involving Communities in Urban and Rural Regeneration: A Guide for Practitioners", Department of the Environment, Transport and the Regions, www.odpm.gov.uk.

OECD (1999a), *Education at a Glance*, OECD, Paris.

OECD (1999b), *Thematic Review of the Transition from Initial Education to Working Life*, OECD, Paris.

Price, A. (2003), *Human Resource Management in a Business Context*, Thomson Learning Publications.

Rath, J. (ed.), (2000), *Immigrant Businesses: the Economic Political and Social Environment*, Macmillan, Basingstoke.

Shaw, G. (2002), "Ethnic Minority Employment through Partnership", The Centre for Diversity and Business.

Sheldon, G. (2001), "Foreign Labour Employment in Switzerland: Less is Not More", *Swiss Political Science Review* 7 (2).

Swiss Federal Office for Professional Education and Technology (2004), "Entraves juridiques à l'intégration des étrangers", Rapport du Groupe de travail tripartite, Bern, 12 October.

Swiss Federal Office for Professional Education and Technology (2005a), "Baromètre des places d'apprentissage", Bern.

Swiss Federal Office of Migration (2004), "Sans-papiers en Suisse: C'est le marché de l'emploi qui est déterminant non la politique d'asile", Bern.

Swiss Federal Office for Professional Education and Technology (2005b), "Vocational Education and Training in Switzerland", Bern.

Swiss Federal Statistical Office (2004a), *La population étrangère en Suisse*, Neuchâtel.

Swiss Federal Statistical Office (2004b), *Swiss Labour Force Survey*, Neuchâtel.

Swiss Federal Statistical Office (2005), *Statistical Data on Switzerland*, Neuchâtel.

Tikly, L. (2002), "Ethnic Minority Achievement Grant: Analysis of Local Education Authority Action Plans", UK Department for Education and Skills, RR371.

Tillie, J. (2004), "Social Capital of Organisations and their Members: Explaining the Political Integration of Migrants in Amsterdam", *Journal of Ethnic and Migration Studies*, Vol. 30, May.

About the Authors

Bob Birrell is Reader in Sociology and Director of the Centre for Population and Urban Research at Monash University, Australia. He is the Joint Editor of the demographic quarterly People and Place. He was a member of the expert panel which reviewed Australia's skilled migration program in 2006. He has a PHD from Princeton University.

Jonathan Chaloff is a migration policy consultant based in Rome, Italy, for the immigration research group at CeSPI, the Centre for International Policy Studies. He is the Italian correspondent for the OECD SOPEMI system and has previously worked on immigration for the Italian think tank Censis, and within the Italian refugee reception system. In addition to publishing numerous articles and papers on immigration to Italy, he is co-editor of "Scuole e Migrazioni" (Education and Migration) (Carocci 2006).

Mary P. Corcoran is a Senior Lecturer in the Department of Sociology, National University of Ireland, Maynooth. She has worked on a number of publications relating to migration and urban sociology including co-editing *Uncertain Ireland* (Institute of Public Administration, 2006) and authoring *Irish Illegals: Transients Between Two Societies* (CT: Greenwood Press, 1993). She is a graduate of the University of Dublin, Trinity College and Columbia University, New York and was appointed an independent member to the National Economic and Social Forum in Ireland in 2004.

Steve Fenton is Professor of Sociology at the Centre for the Study of Ethnicity and Citizenship, and the Institute for Public Affairs, at the University of Bristol. He has published widely in the field of ethnicity including the book, "Ethnicity" (Polity Press, 2003). More recently he has focused on young adults in the labour market, co-authoring an article on "job shifting" in the journal Work Employment and Society (June 2006). He also works as part of a Leverhulme Trust programme focusing on national identity, social class and resentment.

Francesca Froy is a Policy Analyst in Local Economic and Employment Development at OECD. Before joining LEED in 2005 she worked in the field of local development policy at the European level, where she organised a seminar in Berlin on the integration of immigrants in metropolitan cities as part of the European Commission's IDELE programme (Innovation, Dissemination and

Exchange of Good Practice in Local Employment Development). Previously she worked for a municipality in the UK developing local employment projects related to social housing. Francesca is an anthropologist from University College London.

Sylvain Giguère is Deputy Head for Local Economic and Employment Development at OECD. A Canadian economist, he joined the OECD in 1995 and initiated a policy research agenda on governance and employment, addressing the issues of decentralisation, partnership and policy co-ordination and covering subjects ranging from labour markets and skills to economic development. Sylvain co-ordinates the LEED Division's programme of work, oversees the LEED Directing Committee sessions, and heads the OECD Forum on Partnerships and Local Governance.

Anne Green is a Principal Research Fellow at the Institute for Employment Research, University of Warwick, UK where she undertakes studies commissioned by the UK Government, the UK Economic and Social Research Council, and the European Commission on the spatial aspects of economic, social and demographic change; labour market policy; social exclusion and migration, and urban, rural and regional development. She is a fellow of the Royal Geographical Society, the Royal Society of Arts and the Regional Studies Association.

Elizabeth McIsaac is currently the Director of Policy at the Maytree Foundation, a private charitable foundation in Canada. Prior to this she was the Director of Operations for the Toronto Region Immigrant Employment Council, a project of the foundation. Before joining the Maytree Foundation in 2001, Elizabeth was the Executive Director of the Association of International Physicians and Surgeons of Ontario. Elizabeth completed her Masters in Sociology of Education at the University of Toronto.

OECD PUBLICATIONS, 2, rue André-Pascal, 75775 PARIS CEDEX 16
PRINTED IN FRANCE
(84 2006 02 1 P) ISBN 92-64-02895-1 – No. 55307 2006